MOSAICS

FOCUSING ON PARAGRAPHS IN CONTEXT

MOSAICS

FOCUSING ON PARAGRAPHS IN CONTEXT

Kim Flachmann
California State University, Bakersfield

Jane Maher
Nassau Community College

Elizabeth H. Campbell
GMI Engineering & Management Institute

Nancy Johnson
University of New Orleans

D.B. Magee
Texas Christian University

Prentice Hall
Upper Saddle River, NJ 07458

Library of Congress Cataloging-in-Publication Data

Mosaics / Kim Flachmann . . . [et al.].
  p.   cm.
  Includes index.
  ISBN 0-13-272899-0
  1. English language—Paragraphs—Problems, exercises, etc.
  2. English language—Rhetoric—Problems, exercises, etc.
  I. Flachmann, Kim.
  PE1439.M67 1997
  808′.042—dc21   96-45504
                                                              CIP

Editor-in-Chief: Charlyce Jones-Owen
Acquisitions Editor: Maggie Barbieri
Editorial Assistant: Joan Polk
Development Editor: Victoria Nelson
Director of Production and Manufacturing: Barbara Kittle
Project Manager: Maureen Richardson
Manufacturing Manager: Nick Sklitsis
Prepress and Manufacturing Buyer: Mary Ann Gloriande
Creative Design Director: Leslie Osher
Interior Design: Circa 86
Cover Design: Ximena Tamvakopoulos
Illustrator: Circa 86
Marketing Manager: Rob Mejia
Copyeditor: Kathryn Graehl

This book was set in 10.5/12 Goudy by Digitype and was printed and bound by Courier
Companies, Inc. The cover was printed by Phoenix Color Corp.

Credits appear on pages 449–450,
which constitute an extension of the copyright page.

 © 1998 by Prentice-Hall, Inc.
Simon & Schuster/A Viacom Company
Upper Saddle River, NJ 07458

Printed in the United States of America
10 9 8 7 6 5 4 3 2 1

ISBN 0-13-272899-0

Prentice-Hall International (UK) Limited, London
Prentice-Hall of Australia Pty. Limited, Sydney
Prentice-Hall Canada Inc., Toronto
Prentice-Hall Hispanoamericana, S.A., Mexico
Prentice-Hall of India Private Limited, New Delhi
Prentice-Hall of Japan, Inc., Tokyo
Simon & Schuster Asia Pte. Ltd., Singapore
Editora Prentice-Hall do Brasil, Ltda., Rio de Janeiro

CONTENTS

3

OBSERVING   66

READING AND WRITING FOR A REASON

4 EXPLAINING 111

READING AND WRITING FOR A REASON

5 INVESTIGATING 149

READING AND WRITING FOR A REASON

6 RESTATING 207

READING AND WRITING FOR A REASON

9   PROBLEM SOLVING   403

READING AND WRITING FOR A REASON

Students everywhere must learn to respond to the varying intellectual demands made on them throughout the college curriculum so that they have the best possible chance of succeeding in higher education. One extremely important part of this process is being able to analyze ideas and think critically about issues in many different subject areas. **Mosaics: Focusing on Paragraphs in Context** is the second in a series of three books that teaches the basic skills so necessary to all good academic writing. By focusing on eight primary purposes for writing in each book, this series illustrates how the companion skills of reading and writing are parts of a larger process that moves back and forth through the tasks of prereading/reading, prewriting/writing, and revising/editing. In other words, the **Mosaics** series shows how these tasks are integrated at every stage of the writing process.

ASSUMPTIONS

This text is based on the following fundamental assumptions:

1. Thinking, reading, and writing are intricately related.
2. Students learn best from discovery and experimentation rather than from instruction and abstract discussion.
3. Students must be able to transfer their writing skills to all their college courses.
4. Students profit immeasurably from studying models of both professional and student writing.
5. Students perform better in college when they learn to think critically and analytically.
6. Students learn both individually and collaboratively.

HOW THIS BOOK WORKS

This book begins with a general introduction to the writing process (Chapter 1) outlining the scope and sequence of the volume. The eight chapters that follow are each divided into three carefully integrated sections:

Reading and Writing for a Reason

Tips for Revising

Tips for Editing

Reading and Writing for a Reason. Each chapter focuses on one of the eight primary purposes for writing: recalling, observing, explaining, investigating, restating, analyzing, persuading, and problem solving. The purpose is explained and then featured in a professional essay and a student essay before the readers are asked to compose an essay of their own.

- *Learning from Published Writers* focuses on a provocative professional essay with a controlled reading level in order to introduce students to a specific purpose for writing. Each essay was chosen for its high interest and moderate readability level and serves as a springboard in form and content for the rest of the chapter.

- *Learning from Your Peers* walks students through the writing process using an actual student essay. Your students witness the development of a student essay that moves through the general recursive tasks of thinking, planning, developing, organizing, drafting, revising, and editing. The revised draft is printed in each chapter with the student changes highlighted.

- *Writing Your Own Essay* asks students to compose their own essays focusing on the purpose they have just studied. Following a brief review of the highlights of the chapter and the composing process, students are given four writing topics to choose from. After they draft, revise, and edit their essays, students are then asked some specific questions that require them to pause and reflect on their own composing process before they start another chapter.

Tips for Revising and Tips for Editing. The second and third sections of each chapter, Tips for Revising and Tips for Editing, can be taught by themselves or in conjunction with the first section. The revising sections focus on effective paragraphs in the context of essays; they progress from fairly simple to more complex revision strategies. The editing sections then serve as brief but thorough reference guides to grammar and usage; they move from the most basic usage and syntactic problems to more sophisticated writing conventions. The strategies in these sections are integrated into the first part of each chapter. In addition, the Tips for Revising and Tips for Editing include instruction and focused exercises (on both the sentence and paragraph levels) that are drawn from the professional and student essays featured in the chapter. Each Tips section begins with a checklist summarizing the tasks to be covered and ends with collaborative work for individual, small group, or entire class projects.

The specific skills taught in the three main sections of this second book in the **Mosaics** series are listed here so that you can see in abbreviated form how this particular book works:

Chapter	Reading and Writing	Tips for Revising	Tips for Editing
1	Introduction		
2	Recalling	Paragraphs	Words/Phrases/Clauses

Chapter	Reading and Writing	Tips for Revising	Tips for Editing
3	Observing	Topic Sentences	Sentence Structure
4	Explaining	Focused Paragraphs	Fragments/Run-ons
5	Investigating	Paragraph Development	Agreement
6	Restating	Paragraph Organization	Verbs/Nouns/Modifiers
7	Analyzing	Unified Paragraphs	Punctuation/Mechanics
8	Persuading	Titles/Introductions	Diction/Spelling
9	Problem Solving	Supporting/Concluding Paragraphs	Successful Sentences

UNIQUE FEATURES

Several unique and exciting features separate this book from other basic writing texts:

1. It moves students systematically from personal to academic writing.
2. It gives student writing the same attention as professional writing.
3. It illustrates all aspects of the writing process.
4. It integrates reading and writing throughout the text.
5. It teaches revising and editing through the student essays in each chapter.
6. It features culturally diverse reading selections that are of high interest to students.

THE MOSAICS SERIES

All three books in the **Mosaics** series (*Focusing on Sentences in Context, Focusing on Paragraphs in Context,* and *Focusing on Essays*) introduce the writing process as a unified whole and ask students to begin writing full essays in the very first chapter. The Tips for Revising sections, however, change the emphasis of each book: The first book highlights sentence structure, the second book paragraph development, and the third the composition of essays. The books also differ in the length and level of their reading selections, the complexity of their writing assignments, the degree of difficulty of their revising and editing strategies, and the length and level of their student writing samples. Each volume moves from personal to more academic writing in various disciplines throughout the curriculum.

The books are fully integrated in two significant ways: (1) The revising and editing strategies for each chapter are integrated into the demonstration of the writing process in the first part of each chapter, and, in turn, (2) the Tips for Revising and Tips for Editing draw examples and exercises from the professional and student essays in the first section of each chapter. This constant cross-reference and repetition of ideas and skills in different contexts throughout each chapter will help students grasp the basic procedures and potential power of the entire writing process.

Ultimately, each book in the **Mosaics** series portrays writing as a way of thinking and processing information. One by one, these books encourage students to discover how the "mosaics" of their own writing process work together to form a coherent whole. By demonstrating the interrelationship among thinking, reading, and writing on progressively more difficult levels, these books promise to help prepare your students for success in college throughout the curriculum.

ACKNOWLEDGMENTS

We want to acknowledge the support, encouragement, and sound advice of several people who have helped us through the development of the **Mosaics** series. First, Prentice Hall has provided guidance and inspiration for this project through the wisdom of Maggie Barbieri, Senior Editor of Developmental English; the insights of Vicki Nelson, Development Editor; the diligence and clairvoyance of Maureen Richardson, Project Manager; the hard work and patience of Fred Courtright, Permissions Editor; and the common sense and organization of Joan Polk, Administrative Assistant for Developmental English. Also, this book would not be a reality without the insightful persistence of Phil Miller, President of the Humanities Division at Prentice Hall.

In addition, we are especially grateful to the following reviewers who have guided us through five years of the development of this book: Karen N. Standridge, Pikes Peak Community College; Bertha F. Murray, Tallahassee Community College; Lisa Berman, Miami-Dade Community College; Mary Sauer, Indiana University Purdue University Indianapolis; Victoria Sarkisian, Marist College; Nancy S. Wright, Georgia Southern University; Violet O'Valle, Tarrant County Junior College; Nancy E. Smith, Florida Community College at Jacksonville, William T. Lawlor, University of Wisconsin-Stevens Point and Julie Detloff, Bakersfield Junior College.

We want to give very special thanks to Kelly McClain, who served as head research assistant on all three books; to Rebecca Juarez, who has truly blossomed as a research assistant; to Patti Sarr, who did an exceptional job coordinating the accompanying *Instructor's Resource Manual*; and to Susanne Christensen, who supported this project in a variety of important ways.

We also want to express our gratitude to our students, from whom we have learned so much about the writing process, about teaching, and about life itself.

Finally, we owe a tremendous personal debt to the people who have lived with this project for the last five years; they are our closest companions and our best advisors: Michael, Christopher, and Laura Flachmann; Pat Maher; Russ Campbell; Joe Blandino; and Matt Kobler. To Michael Flachmann, we owe special thanks for the valuable support and feedback he has given us through the entire process of creating this series.

MOSAICS

FOCUSING ON PARAGRAPHS IN CONTEXT

The Writing Process

What student's mind—what writer's mind—has not begun to write without knowing really where it will go, only to learn at the end where it meant to start?

—VICTOR KANTOR BURG

The simple act of using the written word to communicate makes a writer. Whether we use writing to list what we need when we shop, to send a message to a friend, to fulfill an assignment in school, or to earn a living, we are all part of a community of writers.

Any piece of writing more formal than a grocery list, however, is usually the result of a sequence of activities that seems on the surface to have nothing directly to do with the act of writing itself. This sequence of activities is called **the writing process,** and learning to follow this process to write essays is what this book is all about.

GETTING STARTED

To begin with, you should be aware of the many choices involved in the writing process. Though all writers are different, some general principles apply to everyone—students and professional writers alike. Before you can begin the process of composing an essay, you need to set aside a time and place for your writing, gather supplies, and establish a routine.

A Time and Place to Write

In her famous *A Room of One's Own,* Virginia Woolf argues that all writers have a basic need for space, privacy, and time. You need to set up your own place that suits your needs as a writer, and it should be a place where you are not distracted or interrupted. You should also set aside a special time for your writing tasks and plan to do nothing else in that time period. The dog's bath will wait until tomorrow; the kitchen appliances don't have to be polished today; drawers can be cleaned and organized some other time; the dirt on the car won't turn to concrete overnight. (These are all some of the activities that writers confess they have done to put off the inevitable beginning.)

Even if you are lucky enough to have a private study area, you may find that you still need to make some adjustments. You may decide to unplug your phone during the time you spend on your composition assignments. Or you may discover that tuning your radio to an all-night jazz station helps you shut out noises from other parts of the house but doesn't distract you in the way talk shows and rock music do. (One well-known biographer owns a "white noise" machine that he cannot write without.) The first general principle for all writers is logical: *Find a place that is comfortable where distractions can be kept to a minimum.*

Writing Equipment and Supplies

Some writers use a legal pad and a pencil to get started on a writing task; some use typewriters or word processors. Some people work best at a desk in a straight chair, while others relax in a big armchair or on a bed. Ernest Hemingway and Virginia Woolf both wrote standing at a big desk, but Woolf used pen and ink for her early drafts, whereas Hemingway worked on a typewriter. The biographer with the white noise machine types on the battered portable typewriter that H. L. Mencken, a famous journalist of the 1920s, used to write his reports and essays. If you find you are most comfortable with your computer, you may want to use it even for your prewriting and early drafts. The next general principle remains the same for all writers and for all writing tasks: *Gather your supplies before you begin work.* Who knows what great idea might escape while you search for a pen that writes, scour the house for paper, or try to find a formatted disk?

Journal Keeping

The word *journal* means "a place for daily writing." The southern novelist Frances Newman kept a purple leather notebook with her at all times. (It had to be purple, and it had to be real leather.) In this little notebook she recorded ideas, snatches of conversation, dreams, and descriptions of people, places, or objects that caught her attention. According to Newman, her last novel developed entirely from a brief description she jotted down of the figure of a young man in Michelangelo's mural on the ceiling of the Sistine Chapel.

Even though most people aren't as particular as Newman about the type of notebook they write in, journal keeping is a very popular activity. For your life as a writer, you will find a personal journal to be an invaluable tool. Now, with the advent of notebook-sized computers, your journal can even be electronic. Just be sure to back up computer entries fairly often so you don't run the risk of losing everything in a power failure or through some other unforeseen problem. Also, you may need to print hard copies to take with you to class.

A good way to establish the habit of journal writing is to use your journal for answering the questions that accompany the readings in this text. You can also jot down in your journal ideas and plans for essays as they occur to you. In addition, you can do all your prewriting activities in your journal. It is much easier to keep up with a notebook than to keep track of assorted scraps of paper. You might want to buy a loose-leaf binder or a notebook divided into several sections so that different types of entries can have their own place.

Keeping a section of your journal private is also a good idea. Sometimes, when you think on paper or let your imagination loose, you don't want to share the results—yet these notes can be very important in finding a subject to write about or developing a topic.

Now that you've chosen your time and place for writing, your writing tools, and your journal, you're ready to embark on your own writing process. In the course of this journey, you'll discover your own preferences and routines as you begin to recognize yourself as a writer.

PREWRITING

Many students are surprised by the fact that a number of vital steps come during the writing process before the act of putting words down on paper. When we speak of **prewriting,** we mean those activities that help us explore a subject, generate ideas about it, settle on a specific topic, establish a purpose, and analyze the audience for an essay. Your reading assignment and journal entries are a first step in this direction. Many writers use one or more of the following activities as an early step to stimulate their thinking in their writing process. You may find that one suits your writing process better than others, or a combination of two or more may work best for you.

Thinking

Thinking is your initial stage of exploration. It's a time to let your mind run free over the material you have to work with. Here are some activities that promise to stimulate your best thoughts:

- *Rereading*　Sometimes a good way to jump-start your thinking and writing process is to reread the professional essay in each chapter, along with your notes, your underlining, and your journal entries. Together these might give you new insights into your topic.

- *Listing*　Many writers find it helpful to jot down a list of ideas about possible essay topics or ideas for expanding a chosen topic. (See p. 73 for an example.)

- *Freewriting*　Writing freely about anything that comes to your mind is the way to *freewrite*. The act of writing itself usually makes writers think of other ideas. (See pp. 17–18 for an example.)

- *Brainstorming*   Like freewriting, *brainstorming* draws on free association. You can brainstorm alone, with a friend, or, best of all, with a group. Regardless of the method, write down *all* your ideas; the act of writing itself often leads to more ideas. (See p. 119 for an example.)

- *Clustering*   *Clustering* lets you map your ideas as fast as they come into your mind. To cluster, take a sheet of blank paper and write a key word, phrase, or sentence in the center of the page, and draw a circle around it. Next, write down and circle any more ideas you have, and connect them with lines to the thoughts they came from. This exercise usually lasts two or three minutes. (See p. 121 for an example.)

- *Discussing*   Run your ideas by friends and classmates; often they'll have a perspective on your topic—or understand your problems in locating a topic—that will put you on an entirely new path.

- *Questioning*   Journalists and many other writers routinely ask questions to generate ideas on a topic. Using some type of questioning technique can help you avoid omitting important details. Most often, the questions used to generate ideas and details on a topic are the five *w*'s and one *h*: *Who, What, Why, When, Where,* and *How.*

Planning

Planning an essay involves making some important decisions about the composition you are about to create:

- What **content** (person, event, object, etc.) do you want to focus on?

    Each of your essays should *focus* on a set of related details or ideas. Although this focus will become clearer to you as you write, you should try to make some general, preliminary decisions about your content before you begin to draft an essay. Such a commitment on your part will make your essays coherent and unified; it will also help you detect any irrelevant material.

- What is your **purpose?**

    Your purpose is your *reason for writing* an essay. Purposes for essays in this text range from the personal through the practical to the persuasive. Your purpose could be to explore your own knowledge or feelings on a topic, to share information on a subject, to find ways to solve a problem, or to persuade a reader to share your views on a controversial issue.

- Who is your **audience?**

    Your audience consists of the *people for whom your message is intended.* The more you know about the people you are trying to reach with your message, the more likely you will succeed. With information about your audience, you can tailor your comments toward them so you have a good chance of convincing them to see your topic the way you do.

- What **point of view** will you take toward your subject?

 Point of view is your *perspective on a topic*. For example, are you for or against capital punishment? Did a specific event you are writing about make you happy or sad? Once you choose a stance toward your topic, you should keep that point of view for the entire paper. A single perspective will bring consistency to your essays.

When you answer these four questions, you begin to make some commitments to the direction your essay will take. To help you prepare for making these decisions in your own writing, the questions after each professional essay in this book ask you to deal with these four issues every time you read.

Developing

After you decide on a focus, purpose, audience, and point of view for your essay, you need to expand your ideas to their fullest in your work. You are now ready to develop some specific topics that will make up the bulk of your essay. You may want to go back to the questions you used during your planning stage and use them as a starting point.

Organizing

After you generate some ideas on a topic, you need to plan the best way of presenting your ideas. What should come first? What next? Would a different way of organizing your ideas achieve your purpose better?

 In the early paragraphs of an essay, you should supply your audience with the facts they will need to understand the essay's purpose, in order to create a context for what they are about to read. By providing answers to basic questions the readers might have (*Who, What, Why, When, Where,* and *How*) or explaining the facts surrounding a particular event, you enable your audience to share your viewpoint as fully as possible.

 Then, organize your material in a way that will be most interesting to your audience. What's the most striking detail or fact about your topic? You might want to start with that. What meaning or significance does the topic have for you? You might want to end with that. Remember that those aspects of your topic that interest you are what you are most likely to write about effectively.

PUTTING WORDS ON PAPER

Drafting

When you have a basic plan of organization in mind, you are ready to start writing. **Drafting,** as you may have guessed, means writing out a first draft. At this point, you have been working both by yourself and in class, thinking, planning, developing, and organizing your ideas on your essay topic. You may want to spread out your class notes, your journal, and your clusters or lists. One more good suggestion is to write out your main idea at the top of the page or computer screen to guide you in writing your essay.

Now you're ready to write a working draft of your essay in complete sentences—no more lists and circles. As you write, try to keep a steady flow of words going. Put as much as you can on paper, but don't let worries about style, grammar, or spelling distract you; you'll deal with those details in the next two steps of the writing process. For now, just keep writing.

Revising

As you may already suspect, the process of writing is not finished with your first draft. In writing, you revise your work to make it stronger and better. **Revising** means "seeing again," and that is exactly what you try to do—see your essay again from as many different angles as possible. Sometimes others help with the process; other times you will be on your own. To revise, a writer needs some distance from his or her first draft. Ideally, you should put your draft aside for at least a day before you begin revising it.

Revision is a task that focuses on improving content and organization. (Editing, the last step, focuses on correcting grammar and spelling.) Your main goal in revising is to make sure that the purpose of your essay is clear to your audience and that your main ideas are supported with enough details and examples. In addition, you should check to be sure your organization is logical. Using the checklist in the Tips for Revising section in every chapter of this book will help you establish your own revising strategies.

If you are able to obtain feedback from your classmates in the first stages of your writing process, you may decide they have some helpful ideas you want to use in your revision. You may actually want to draw up a list of revision notes before you go through your draft. Here is a sample revision checklist with references to specific chapters for more information:

Checklist for Revising

✓ Does this essay have an interesting **title** (Chapter 8)?
✓ Is the **main idea** clear (Chapter 4)?
✓ Does the writer focus on his or her **purpose** throughout the essay (Chapter 4)?
✓ Is each main idea in a separate **paragraph** (Chapter 2)?
✓ Does the writer need to **add** anything (Chapter 5)?
✓ Does the writer need to **delete** any unnecessary details (Chapter 5)?
✓ Does the writer need to **rearrange** any of the ideas (Chapter 6)?
✓ Does the essay have a satisfactory **conclusion** (Chapter 9)?

The Tips for Revising section supplies you with detailed explanations and exercises to refer to if you need more information on any of these specific revision strategies.

Editing

After you revise, the final step in the writing process is **editing.** In this stage, you read your essay slowly and carefully to make sure no errors in grammar, mechanics, or spelling have slipped into your draft. Each chapter in this book includes focused guidelines for editing in a Tips for Editing section along with detailed explanations and exercises demonstrating those guidelines. Following is a general Checklist for Editing with references to specific chapters for further information.

Checklist for Editing

✓ Has the writer written **complete sentences** throughout the essay (Chapters 3 and 4)?
✓ Do the subjects of sentences **agree** with their verbs (Chapter 5)?
✓ Has the writer used **punctuation** correctly and effectively (Chapter 7)?
✓ Has the writer observed conventional rules for **mechanics** (Chapter 7)?
✓ Has the writer used **words** correctly (Chapter 8)?
✓ Has the writer checked the **spelling** of words (Chapter 8)?

You should use the material in the Tips for Editing sections as a reference guide in the same way you use a dictionary as a resource for spelling and defining words.

HOW TO USE THIS BOOK

Often, good writing is inspired by good reading. To ensure that you experience the full potential of each of the eight writing purposes this book presents—recalling, observing, explaining, investigating, restating, analyzing, persuading, and problem solving—every chapter after this one begins with a writing sample from a published writer. To focus your reading experience, you will do prereading and postreading activities that help you understand the strategies these published writers have used to compose their essays.

Besides reading and analyzing a professional essay, you will also follow the writing process of a fellow student and watch two drafts of his or her essay take shape through the use of specific drafting, revising, and editing strategies. The steps in the process of writing any essay constantly overlap, but you will find that developing a systematic approach to writing is important to your growth as a writer. To this end, observing the activities and thoughts of someone at your level of development will help you shape your own writing process.

After you read and study each chapter's professional and student writing samples, you'll be ready to put the process together in your own essay. The questions before and after the professional selection will help you dissect each essay and understand how it works. In addition, as you follow the writing process of another student, you will absorb ideas to work with as well as options for giving those ideas shape. All these reading and writing activities will move you closer to producing an essay of your own. After reviewing what you've learned so far in the chapter, you will be ready to tackle your own writing tasks.

You can choose from a list of four assignments. One assignment allows you to design your own topic; the other three assignments provide a purpose and audience in more specific, focused writing topics. Your instructor may assign one or more of these tasks so you can demonstrate your ability to use the contents of each chapter.

As you establish your own writing process, you'll probably be aware that not everything you're doing matches up exactly with the writing process as it is outlined here or even with what the student writer does in the book. Don't be alarmed. Part of the pleasure of writing is learning to trust your own instincts and let them create a ritual for you. Like someone learning to swim, however, you will want to be able to hold on to the edge of the pool when you feel yourself sinking—and that's the kind of security the framework of the writing process is meant to provide as you make your way through its various phases: *thinking, planning, developing, organizing, drafting, revising,* and *editing.*

After you have revised and edited the first draft of your paper, you will produce a final draft to submit to your instructor. Even at this point, however, there is still more to the process. The last section in every chapter presents a list of questions that help you reflect on your writing and your own writing process so you can learn from each writing experience:

1. What was most difficult about this assignment?
2. What was easiest?
3. What did I learn about this type of writing by completing this assignment?
4. What did I learn about my own writing process from this assignment—how I prepared to write, how I wrote the first draft, how I revised, and how I edited?

Answering these questions in your journal will give you a perspective on each of your writing tasks that you will find valuable in applying to future assignments.

As you make your way through the following eight chapters, you may find yourself returning to this chapter to reread the description of the writing process. Doing this can serve as a productive prewriting strategy for the writing topics each chapter presents. As you develop your own writing process, you may also want to modify or experiment with parts of your writing ritual. Let this chapter be your guide in charting new directions for yourself; and let the professional and student writers you encounter in the following pages be your inspiration as you set out on your journey.

THE WRITING PROCESS

THINKING   Generate as many ideas on your subject as you can in as many different ways as possible: rereading, listing, freewriting, brainstorming, clustering, discussing, and questioning.

PLANNING   Begin to give your ideas shape by deciding on your approach to your topic (your content, your purpose, your audience, and your point of view). Make a list of points you want to include in your essay.

THE WRITING PROCESS (CONTINUED)

DEVELOPING   Add more details on three or four specific, focused topics the that you have chosen from your list of general points.

ORGANIZING   Organize your material in a way that will be most interesting to your audience.

DRAFTING   Write a working draft of your essay in complete sentences.

REVISING   Consulting the Tips for Revising, revise your first draft for meaning, development, and organization.

EDITING   Consulting the Tips for Editing, edit your draft for grammar and correctness.

CHAPTER TWO

Recalling
Reading and Writing for a Reason

**I try to remember times in my life, incidents in which there
was the dominating theme of cruelty, or kindness, or
generosity, or envy, or happiness, or glee. Then I select one.**
—Maya Angelou

Recalling is the act of writing about something you have done, about something that
has happened to you, or about a person, incident, or event that is important to
you—from any point in your past. When you recall, you remember a particular
event and provide enough specific details about that event so that the reader can
picture the scene from your point of view and understand as completely as possible
what it was like to go through the experience. Recalling is probably one of the most
satisfying types of writing because it gives you an opportunity to think about yourself
and the incidents that are significant in your life.

Recalling, however, is not the same as simply writing down exactly what happened, step by step. That would be a boring exercise for both the writer and the
reader. Writing an account of your morning—the way you got out of bed, ate breakfast, got dressed, and did your morning chores—would not be of great interest to a
reader (or a writer for that matter) unless something specific happened that made
your morning significant. An event is **significant** if it helps writer and reader alike
more clearly understand something that has happened. Perhaps a particular incident
taught you a lesson, helped you realize the value of someone in your life, or made
you realize that you needed to change something about yourself or your life-style.

An event can also be significant because it helps us as readers recognize or remember something similar that has happened to us or because it helps us discover
that, despite the fact that we are all different in many ways, as human beings we often share common traits. Brent Staples, the author of the memoir *Parallel Time:
Growing Up in Black and White*, describes an event that occurred in his English class
as a way of demonstrating why the instructor, a Miss Riley, was one of the best
teachers he ever had.

> [Miss Riley] had a talent for reaching us. One day while reading to us
> she came across the word "rhubarb" and was stunned to find that none

of us had ever tasted it. Her eyes flashed amazement; you could see a novel solution taking shape. Later that week she came to class with a tray of rhubarb pielets, one for each of us. As the tray went around the room, she held aloft a stalk of rhubarb and talked about its origins. We bit into the pies in unison. "Taste how it's sweet and tangy at the same time," she said. She watched intently, as though tasting the pie through our mouths.

The incident Staples chooses is significant because it enables us as readers to appreciate—as Staples and his classmates did—Miss Riley's talent and ability to reach her students through her teaching methods and dedication. At the same time, it triggers our own memories of teachers who have changed our lives.

LEARNING FROM PUBLISHED WRITERS

Following is a recollection by a professional writer about his childhood. Although the incident is a common one—two boys getting into a fight—it is significant because it helps both the writer and reader understand how seriously children can be affected if they or their actions are misunderstood. The author, Tobias Wolff, is an award-winning short-story writer who has also composed a moving account of his experiences in the Vietnam War. The following passage is taken from a book titled *This Boy's Life* (1989), a memoir of what life was like after Wolff's parents divorced and he and his mother moved west, far away from his father and his brother. In this excerpt, Wolff describes an all-too-familiar occurrence among adolescents, the tendency to insult each other and "fight it out" to defend their honor.

Before You Read

Focusing Your Attention

Before you read this recollection, take a few moments to respond to the following questions in your journal:

1. Can you recall a fight you have had with someone (a friend, a classmate, a teammate, a family member) and the way you felt after the fight was over? Was there a winner and a loser?

2. In the story you are about to read titled "The Sissy," the writer says, "All my life, I have recognized almost at a glance those who were meant to be my friends, and they have recognized me." Do you know "almost at a glance" those people who will become your friends, or does it take a long time for you to recognize and develop friendships?

Expanding Your Vocabulary

Here are some words and their meanings that are important to your understanding of the essay. You might want to review them before you begin to read.

"The name . . . **implicated** [involved] him further in sissyhood." (paragraph 1)

"He had an **arch, subtle** [mischievous, crafty] voice" (paragraph 1)

"I'd come away **smarting** [feeling pained] from all my **exchanges** [brief conversations] with him." (paragraph 1)

"I liked his **acid** [biting, clever] wit" (paragraph 2)

"The earth was **spongy** [soggy, like a sponge]" (paragraph 5)

"a faint, steady **sibilance** [hissing sound]" (paragraph 5)

"upturned, **benevolent** [good, well-wishing] faces" (paragraph 5)

"I had **provocation** [motivation to act]" (paragraph 6)

"I saw that his **commitment** [dedication] to this fight was absolute." (paragraph 11)

"Arthur rushed me, arms **flailing** [waving wildly]" (paragraph 13)

"his nostrils streaming **gouts** [blobs] of snot" (paragraph 13)

"screaming **gibberish** [nonsense sounds] in each other's ears" (paragraph 13)

"Pepper followed . . . **lunging** [moving forward suddenly]." (paragraph 19)

"There was pleasure and **scorn** [contempt] on their faces" (paragraph 26)

"I **trudged** [walked heavily or wearily] homeward." (paragraph 28)

Tobias Wolff

The Sissy*

I was standing on the road with two other boys, my news bag still   1
heavy with papers, when I saw him coming toward us with his little dog
Pepper. The three of us started making cracks about him. His name was
Arthur Gayle, and he was the uncoolest boy in the sixth grade, maybe
even the whole camp. Arthur was a sissy. His mother was said to have

*Tobias Wolff, "The Sissy." In *This Boy's Life* (pp. 107–111). New York: Atlantic Monthly Press, 1989.

turned him into a sissy by dressing him in girls' clothes when he was little. He walked like a girl, ran like a girl, and threw like a girl. Arthur was my father's name, so that seemed okay to me, but the name Gayle implicated him further in sissyhood. He was clever. He had an arch, subtle voice that he used to good effect as an instrument of his cleverness. I'd come away smarting from all my exchanges with him.

Arthur was testy with me. He seemed to want something. At times I caught him looking at me expectantly, as if I were holding out on him. And I was. All my life I have recognized almost at a glance those who were meant to be my friends, and they have recognized me. Arthur was one of these. I liked him. I liked his acid wit and the wild stories he told and his apparent indifference to what other people thought of him. But I had withheld my friendship, because I was afraid of what it would cost me.   **2**

As Arthur came toward us he set his face in a careless smirk. He must have known we were talking about him. Instead of walking past, he turned to me and said, "Didn't your momma teach you to wash your hands after you go pee?"   **3**

My hands weren't all that yellow anymore; in fact they were nearly back to normal. I'd finished shucking the nuts weeks before.   **4**

It was springtime. The earth was spongy with melted snow, and on the warmest days, if you listened for it, you could hear a faint, steady sibilance of evaporation, almost like a light rain. The trees were hazy with new growth. Bears had begun to appear on the glistening granite faces of the mountainsides above us, taking the sun and soaking up heat from the rock; at lunchtime people came out onto their steps and watched them with upturned, benevolent faces. My mother was with me again. The nuts were all husked and drying in the attic. What did I need trouble for?   **5**

I was inclined to let it go. But I didn't like being laughed at, and I didn't like comments about my hands. Arthur had made other such comments. He was bigger than me, especially around the middle, but I factored out this weight as blubber. I could take him, I felt sure. I had provocation, and I had witnesses to carry the news. It seemed like a good time to make a point.   **6**

I started things off by calling him Fatso.   **7**

Arthur continued to smile at me. "Excuse me," he said, "but has anyone ever told you that you look exactly like a pile of wet vomit?"   **8**

We went on like this, and then I called him a sissy.   **9**

The smile left his face. And at that moment it came to me that although everyone referred to Arthur as a sissy, I had never heard anyone actually use the word in front of him. And in the same moment,   **10** seeing how everything about him changed after the word was spoken, how suddenly red and awful his face became, I understood that there must be a reason for this. A crucial bit of history I should have known about, and didn't.

His first swing caught me dead on the ear. There was an explosion inside my head, then a continuous rustling sound as of someone crumpling paper. It lasted for days. When he swung again I turned away and took his fist on the back of my head. He threw punches the way he threw balls, sidearm, with a lot of wrist, but he somehow got his weight behind them before they landed. This one knocked me to my knees. He drew back his foot and kicked me in the stomach. The papers in my bag deadened the blow, but I was stunned by the fact that he had kicked me at all. I saw that his commitment to this fight was absolute.   **11**

His dog barked in my face.   **12**

When I got up Arthur rushed me, arms flailing, fists raining on my shoulders. He almost knocked me down again, but I surprised us both by landing one on his eye. He stopped and roared. The eye was already closing up, his face gone scarlet, his nostrils streaming gouts of snot. When I saw his eye I got worried. I was ready to stop, but he wasn't. He flew at me again. I closed with him and got him in a hug to keep his arms still. We staggered over the road like drunken dancers, and then he hooked my leg and tripped me, and we rolled off the shoulder and down the long muddy embankment, both of us flailing and kicking with our knees and screaming gibberish in each other's ears. He had gone insane, I could see that, and it seemed to me that my only chance was to go insane too.   **13**

Still rolling, we hit the boggy swale at the foot of the bank. He got on top of me, I got on top of him, he got back on top of me. My news bag had armored me well when I was on my feet but now it was heavy with mud and twisted around my shoulders. I couldn't get off a good swing. All I could do was hold on to Arthur and try to keep him from getting one off at me. He struggled, then abruptly collapsed on top of me. He was panting for breath. His weight pressed me into the mud. I gathered myself and bucked him off. It took everything I had. We lay next to each other, gasping strenuously. Pepper tugged at my pant leg and growled.   **14**

Arthur stirred. He got to his feet and started up the bank. I followed him, thinking it was all over, but when he got to the top he turned and said, "Take it back."   **15**

The other boys were watching me, I shook my head.   **16**

Arthur pushed me and I began sliding down the bank.   **17**

"Take it back," he yelled.   **18**

Pepper followed me in my descent, yapping and lunging. There   **19**
hadn't been a moment since the fight began when Pepper wasn't
worrying me in some way, if only to bark and bounce around me,
and finally it was this more than anything else that made me lose
heart. It wounded my spirit to have a dog against me. I *liked* dogs. I
liked dogs more than I liked people, and I expected them to like
me back.

I started up the bank again, Pepper still at my heels.   **20**

"Take it back," Arthur said.   **21**

"Okay," I said.   **22**

"Say it."   **23**

"*Okay*. I take it back."   **24**

"No. Say, 'You're not a sissy.'"   **25**

I looked up at him and the other two boys. There was pleasure and   **26**
scorn on their faces, but not on his. He wore, instead, an expression
of such earnestness that it seemed impossible to refuse him what he
asked. I said, "You're not a sissy."

He called Pepper and turned away. When I got to the top he was   **27**
walking toward home. The other two boys were excited, restless,
twitching with the blows they'd imagined striking. They wanted to
talk about the fight, but I had lost interest in it. My clothes were
caked with mud. My news bag, full of mud and ruined papers, pulled
down on me. My ear hurt.

I trudged homeward.   **28**

 ## QUESTIONS FOR CRITICAL THINKING

THINKING CRITICALLY ABOUT CONTENT

1. Why do you think Wolff recalled the presence of Pepper, Arthur's dog? What
    role does the dog play in helping you as a reader understand the significance of
    the event?

2. Why do you think Wolff cared so little about his friends' reactions after the
    fight was over?

THINKING CRITICALLY ABOUT PURPOSE

3. What do you think is Wolff's purpose in this essay? Explain your answer.

4. Wolff describes the fight between himself and Arthur Gayle in great detail.
    What did you learn about each boy's character as a result of this detailed
    account of the fight?

THINKING CRITICALLY ABOUT AUDIENCE

5. What type of audience do you think would most understand and appreciate this recollection?

6. For which character do you think the audience will have the most sympathy—the writer or Arthur Gayle? Or do you think the audience will sympathize with both characters? Explain your answer.

THINKING CRITICALLY ABOUT POINT OF VIEW

7. On the basis of the tone and content of this recollection, how do you think Wolff feels about the fight?

8. In the opening paragraph of this recollection, Tobias Wolff is the speaker describing Arthur Gayle. Rewrite the opening paragraph of this passage, making Arthur Gayle the speaker describing Tobias Wolff.

LEARNING FROM YOUR PEERS

There are many reasons for writing about our memories. They may help us remember pleasant times with friends or relatives who have died or moved far away. Remembering specific details about events in our lives will sometimes even give us a greater understanding of who we are today. They help us examine the significance of certain events in our lives; they help us recall times when we were young and innocent; and they show us that we really have grown up. To demonstrate how to compose a recalling essay, we are going to follow the writing process of a student named Robert Montagne.

Robert's Writing Assignment: Recalling

This is the topic Robert's instructor assigned:

Family traditions, vacations and trips, special celebrations, and pleasant childhood pastimes are usually pleasant topics to write about. Sometimes, however, something unexpected happens during an event. A sudden storm comes up when we are hiking in the woods, an automobile accident cuts a vacation short, or worse. Most of us have had something unexpected happen at times when we were feeling relaxed and carefree. Later, when we look back on those incidents, we see that, although they may have been unpleasant, they made us stronger people. Think of an incident that helped you become the strong person you are today. Write an essay that recalls an experience that tested your physical strength or your strength of character.

Robert goes through the process as outlined in Chapter 1: *thinking, planning, developing, organizing, drafting, revising,* and *editing.*

Thinking

Robert's class first takes about fifteen minutes to brainstorm a list of the values that are most important to them. Robert immediately says, "Honesty." He also writes down the words *concern for others* and *kindness*. Other members of Robert's class list *charity, religious faith, acceptance of others, tolerance, consideration of others' feelings, hard work, loyalty, patriotism, fairness, social justice, including others in a group, equal opportunity for all, family traditions, friendship,* and *integrity*.

The students then spend several minutes in small groups drawing clusters in an attempt to recall when they learned the importance of these values. During a discussion of their clusters, many students in Robert's group discover that these values became clearly important to them only when the values were violated. Students recalled examples such as seeing someone who was a little overweight excluded from a sports team, witnessing an unfair arrest, and feeling that a promotion or a good grade went to a person exclusively because of his or her race.

Planning

That evening, Robert spends some time writing in his journal, trying to remember when honesty became so important to him. He knows that the one way to ruin a friendship with him is to tell him a lie. He remembers his anger when he found out that a young woman he had been dating had made up excuses about why she could not go out with him anymore. He knew that she was trying to soften the breakup, but he felt that she should have plainly told him that she did not want to go out with him anymore.

He also remembers being out for dinner with his former friend Max, who told the waiter that something was wrong with his enormous steak only after he had eaten about half of it. Max complained loudly and obnoxiously until the restaurant manager was finally called over to their table. Max convinced the manager that he should not have to pay for his meal. That was the last time Robert, who believed that Max was dishonest about the quality of the food, went anywhere with Max.

Robert cannot remember any other incidents relating to honesty, so he decides to start his math homework and forget about the essay for a while.

Developing

While Robert is working on his math, his best friend, Brian, calls and asks him to put away his books and go to a movie. Robert says, "Thanks, but I have too much work tonight." He hangs up the phone, wishing he'd started working earlier. Robert takes out his journal and starts writing about Brian. Here is what he records:

> Brian used to be able to talk me into doing anything. From the time I was five years old, I would do anything that popped into Brian's head. I did not think he could do anything wrong. Boy, this makes me sound dumb, like I can't think for myself. But Brian could always talk me into taking chances

that I would never have taken on my own. He could probably have talked

me into going over Niagara Falls with him before I got wise to him.

Suddenly Robert realizes that the first time Brian's persuasiveness did any real damage was during the fishing trip that is now legendary in both their families. He feels
sure he can write about that trip.

While his journal is open in front of him, Robert makes a list of his most immediate memories from that weekend:

Brian's parents out late

fishing/lake

boat/trailer

ice/cooler

Rise and Shine

money crisis/jail

He looks over his list again and adds a few more items before going to bed:

Brian sleeps at my house

never again

food

up early

then/oh no

Organizing

After breakfast the next morning, Robert prepares a fresh cup of coffee and starts re-
working the list of events from that fateful weekend. First he reorganizes the items.
Then he draws arrows and writes numbers all over the paper to put them in order.
He knows that he will finish his first draft quickly because he has relived that weekend in his mind so many times. His list is now ordered like this:

1. Brian's parents out late

6. fishing/lake

3. boat/trailer

4. ice/cooler/food

5. Rise and Shine/Up early

8. money crisis/jail

2.   Brian sleeps at my house

9.   never again

7.   then/oh no

Drafting

Once Robert has these ideas jotted down and numbered in sequence, he uses them to write his draft, filling in the details as he goes along.

Robert's Essay: First Draft

Main Idea: I learned responsibility and honesty on a fishing trip.

When I was 15, Brian, my best friend turned 16. We decided it would be great if we went on a fishing trip. Fishing for bass is one of my favorite things to do. We planned things very carefully. We couldn't wait, however, for the weekend to arrive. We knew that our parents would not let us go alone, so we came up with a fail-proof plan.

The next Saturday night, Brian's parents--who almost never went out--were going to be out late at a party. I told my parents that I was going to sleep at Brian's house, while he told his parents that he was sleeping at my house. Telling this lie, we still felt confident that everything would go off without a hitch. Since we were best friends, we did that often, so our parents believed us. We knew that we would not be missed until my parents came home from church; we figured that would give us plenty of time to get to the lake and fish before we had to head back home.

As soon as Brian's parents left for the party on Saturday night, we hooked up the boat trailer. The trailer hitch was a gooseneck type, which is the safest kind. Then we headed for the lake. We had our rods, the cooler, and some sandwiches we made in case we didn't catch any fish. We stopped at the corner store and bought some ice and soft drinks and filled up the car with gas. Then we got in the car, turned up the music, and cruised the back roads until we got to

Brian's grandfather Herbert's fishing camp. We felt really smart and grown-up.

Early the next morning, our fishing trip began smoothly. We had gone there so many times with our dads, and now we were there all by ourselves. We felt very smart by that time. We settled back and waited for those nibbles on our lines. The first sign of trouble came almost immediately.

The conservation officer's boat started heading toward us. But it was too late to throw our poles overboard. We were scared; however, we didn't think anything really bad would happen. The conservation officer looked serious. Imagine our surprise when he told us we were under arrest and would have to go to his office and wait there until someone brought the money for our fines. Help! We wanted to just run away and hide.

Brian and I thought and thought, but we could not think of one friend who would drive 75 miles to Greenville to rescue us and pay over $200 in fines. All of our best friends suddenly seemed distant, like mere acquaintances. We decided we had no choice but to call our parents. It was the most embarrassing feeling I have ever had. When I picked up the phone, it was all I could do to remember my own phone number.

When my dad came to get us, he told us we were lucky we didn't have to go to jail. We just said, "Yessir, yessir, yessir," all the way home. We knew we were in big trouble. Brian's dad and my dad decided that to punish us, we would each have to mow the grass for 10 Saturdays in a row to earn back the money for the fines. Also, Brian was not allowed to keep a set of car keys for six months. Our adventure turned into a nightmare, but I think we both learned a big lesson in responsibility and honesty. We never lied to our parents again. And if I am with someone who suggests doing something dishonest, that is the last time I ever talk to that person. I never want to be arrested again.

Revising

Robert has finally written a first draft of his essay, but he knows he still has a lot of work to do on it. At this point, his instructor has asked the class to focus on the structure and content of their paragraphs. The instructor explains to the class that the paragraph is a good place to start their revisions because if student writers can masterfully control their writing on the paragraph level, their entire essay will be more coherent and effective.

So Robert reviews the Checklist for Recognizing Paragraphs at the beginning of the Tips for Revising section of this chapter. His instructor explains to the class that **revising** means focusing on content, not grammar—concentrating on whether the paragraphs say exactly what the writer intends. Robert reads the Tips for Revising and completes the exercises his instructor assigns. He learns that each paragraph should have a controlling idea or topic sentence, that the sentences in each paragraph should be related to that topic sentence, and that each paragraph should contain enough details to fully develop the controlling idea. Although this chapter refers to specific features of a paragraph, the students in Robert's class know that paragraphs are working parts of an essay and that essays must have their own coherence. At this point in the course, they must recognize the basic parts of a paragraph while they remain aware of the larger context of their essays.

Returning to his draft, Robert approaches his revision slowly and carefully, making sure that each paragraph is well developed before he checks its logic. He finds that his writing is hindered in some cases by paragraphs with missing parts and in other cases by ideas that are not clearly related to one another. He tries to remedy both problems in his revised draft.

COLLABORATIVE WORK

PEER GROUP ACTIVITY

After you read the portions of the Tips for Revising your instructor assigns, turn to Robert's first draft (pp. 19–20), and complete the following tasks in small groups:

A. Put brackets around the topic sentence (for a definition, see page 29) of each paragraph.

B. In each paragraph, underline any sentences that are not related to the topic sentence.

Compare the brackets and underlining your group recorded with the marks your instructor will show you. Where do your answers differ from your instructor's? What do you need to review before writing your own essay?

CLASS ACTIVITY

As an entire class, look at the underlined portions of Robert's revised draft (pp. 23–25) to see how he changed each sentence.

A.   Did you identify the **revision** problems that Robert corrected?

B.   Do you think his changes are good ones? Discuss his changes.

Editing

Now that his paragraphs are well developed, Robert needs to do some final proofreading and editing before handing in his essay. The instructor tells the students they will need a working knowledge of basic grammar terms for the rest of the course. So Robert shifts his attention from the content of his paragraphs to specific points of grammar within his paragraphs. He reads the Tips for Editing section in this chapter to learn about verbs, nouns, pronouns, adjectives, adverbs, prepositions, conjunctions, and interjections and how they work in sentences. After he finishes the exercises that are assigned, he goes over the items in the Checklist for Editing Words, Phrases, and Clauses one by one, and he revises his draft according to these guidelines.

 ## COLLABORATIVE WORK

PEER GROUP ACTIVITY

After you read the portions of the Tips for Editing your instructor assigns, turn to Robert's first draft (pp. 19–20), and complete the following tasks in small groups:

A.   Label any of these parts of speech your instructor assigns:

  1.   Five action verbs (V) (for a definition, see p. 37)

  2.   Five nouns (N) (for a definition, see p. 40)

  3.   Five pronouns (pro) (for a definition, see p. 43)

  4.   Five adjectives (adj) (for a definition, see p. 46)

  5.   Five adverbs (adv) (for a definition, see p. 49)

  6.   Five prepositions (prep) (for a definition, see p. 51)

  7.   Five conjunctions (conj) (for a definition, see p. 55)

  8.   Five interjections (interj) (for a definition, see p. 57)

B.   Put five phrases in parentheses. (For a definition, see p. 57.)

C.   Label the subjects (S) and verbs (V) of five clauses (for definitions, see p. 62). Then mark these clauses as independent or dependent (for definitions, see pp. 62–63).

Compare your labels and marks with those your instructor will show you. Where do your marks differ from your instructor's? What do you need to review before writing your own essay?

CLASS ACTIVITY

As an entire class, look at the underlined portions of Robert's revised draft (pp. 23–25) to see how he changed each sentence.

A. Did you identify the **editing** problems that Robert corrected?

B. Do you think his changes are good ones? Discuss his changes.

Robert's Revised Essay

The Great Fishing Expedition

When I was 15, Brian, my best friend, turned 16. ~~We~~ Brian and I decided it would be great if we went on a fishing trip alone, something we had never done, to prove how grown-up we were. Fishing for bass is one of my favorite things to do. We planned ~~things~~ our fishing expedition very carefully. We couldn't wait, however, for the weekend to arrive. We made detailed lists of the supplies we would need. We studied the map to choose our route to the lake and to select our favorite fishing spots. All we needed then was an escape plan.

~~We~~ Brian and I knew that our parents would not let us go on a fishing expedition alone, so we came up with a fail-proof plan. The next Saturday night, Brian's parents--who almost never went out--were going to be out late at a party. I told my parents that I was going to sleep at Brian's house, while he told his parents that he was sleeping at my house. Telling this lie, we still felt confident that everything would go off without a hitch. Since we were best friends, we did ~~that~~ this often, so our parents believed us. We knew that we would not be missed until my parents came home from church; we figured that would give us plenty of time to get to the lake and fish before we had to head back home.

As soon as Brian's parents left for the party on Saturday night, we set out on the great fishing expedition. First, we hooked up the boat trailer. ~~The trailer hitch was a gooseneck type, which is the safest kind.~~ Then we headed for the lake/, our getaway for the weekend. We had our fly rods, ~~the~~ a white styrofoam cooler, and ~~some~~ several tuna sandwiches we made in case we didn't catch any fish. We stopped at the first small corner store we saw and bought some crushed ice and four soft drinks and filled up ~~the~~ Brian's beat-up car with gas. Then we got in the car, turned up the music, and cruised the back roads until we got to Brian's grandfather's ~~Herbert's~~ fishing camp/, tucked away in the woods. We felt really smart and grown-up.

Early the next morning, our fishing trip began smoothly. We had backed the boat into the water--no problem. We got the boat started and went chugging across the bay to our spot, four cypress trees arranged in an almost perfect square. We had gone ~~there~~ to our favorite fishing spot in the Atchafalaya Basin so many times with our dads that we knew the way, and now, except for herons and egrets, we were there all by ourselves/, casting our flies, hoping to catch bream. We felt very smart by that time/, because we began to get strikes almost immediately. Brian was jerking his rod to set his hook the first time. We settled back and waited for those nibbles on our lines. The first sign of trouble came almost immediately, chugging across the water.

When I saw t~~T~~he conservation officer's boat ~~started~~ start heading toward us/, I remembered fishing licenses, a detail our dads always took care of for us. It would have broken our hearts to throw our fishing tackle overboard. But it was too late anyway. ~~to throw our poles overboard.~~ We were scared; however, we didn't think anything really bad would happen to us. The conservation officer looked serious. Imagine our surprise when he ~~told us we were under~~ arrested us and took us ~~and would have to go~~ to his office ~~and~~ to wait ~~there~~ until someone brought the money for our fines. Help! We wanted to just run away and hide.

Brian and I thought and thought, but we could not think of one friend who would drive 75 miles to Greenville to rescue us and pay over $200 in fines. All of our best friends suddenly seemed distant, like mere acquaintances. We decided we had no choice but to call our parents. It was the most embarrassing feeling I have ever had. When I picked up the phone, it was all I could do to remember my own phone number.

When my dad came to get us, he told us we were lucky we didn't have to go to jail. <u>Wow, when we saw the scowl on his face and heard his cold tone of voice, we knew we were in trouble.</u> We just said, "Yessir, yessir, yessir," all the way home. ~~We knew we were in big trouble.~~ Brian's dad and my dad decided that to punish us, we would each have to mow the grass for 10 Saturdays in a row to earn back the money for the fines. Also, Brian was not allowed to keep a set of car keys for six months.

Our adventure turned into a nightmare, but I think we both learned a big lesson in responsibility and honesty. We never lied to our parents again. And if I am with someone who suggests doing something dishonest, that is the last time I ever talk to that person. I never want to be arrested again.

WRITING YOUR OWN RECALLING ESSAY

So far, you have seen a professional writer and a fellow student at work trying to express an idea, impression, or experience from the past. As you read the published essay and then followed the writing process of another student from first to final draft, you absorbed ideas to work with and ways of giving those ideas a form of their own. These reading and writing activities have prepared you to write your own essay focusing on a recollection that is meaningful to you.

What Have You Discovered?

Before you begin your own writing task, let's review what you have learned in this chapter so far:

- Recalling is the act of writing about something you have done, about something that has happened to you, or about a person, incident, or event that is important to you.

- Specific details are important to a good recollection.

- Understanding the significance of a recollection helps your readers see how a person, incident, or event changed you in some way.

- To present your recollection effectively, you need to organize your ideas.

- To help you shape your essay, you should learn as much as possible about your readers.

- Before you write a draft, you need to decide on a point of view toward your subject.

- After you write a draft, you should revise your essay for meaning and organization.

- After you revise your essay, you should edit its grammar, usage, and sentence structure.

Your Writing Topic

Choose one of the following topics for your recalling essay:

1. In the recollection you read at the beginning of the chapter, "The Sissy," Tobias Wolff recalls in vivid and precise detail his fight with Arthur Gayle. Wolff even describes the behavior of Gayle's dog, Pepper, during the fight. Reflect on your own childhood, and recall a relationship that you had with someone (a friend, a family member, a teacher, a classmate). Describe an incident or event that caused the relationship to change, either for better or for worse.

2. We have all had experiences that began as carefree adventures and ended up as misadventures. A national magazine is asking for honest stories about experiences that turned bad unexpectedly. The magazine will pay $200 to the writer of each essay chosen for publication. You decide to write an essay for the competition. The directions are to describe an experience so your readers can understand what it was like in detail. Find ways to reveal your feelings about this experience.

3. Your high school's alumni newsletter has asked you to submit a clear, honest essay recalling an event that influenced the values you hold today. The purpose of this essay is to give current high school students some guidelines for establishing values in their own lives. Where can they look? Where did you get your most important values? What are your most important values?

4. Create your own recalling assignment (with the assistance of your instructor), and write an essay in response to it.

When you have selected one of these topics, you should begin to work through the writing process in the same way Robert did. (You may want to reread the discussion of his writing process.) This time your purpose is to write your own recalling essay. If some tasks occur out of order, that adjustment is probably part of your personal writing ritual. Follow your instincts, and let them mold your own writing process. But make sure you've worked through all the stages to your final draft.

YOUR WRITING PROCESS

THINKING   Generate as many ideas on your subject as you can in as many different ways as possible: rereading, listing, freewriting, brainstorming, clustering, discussing, and questioning.

PLANNING   Begin to give your ideas shape by deciding on your approach to your topic (your content, your purpose, your audience, and your point of view). Make a list of points you want to include in your essay.

DEVELOPING   Add more details on three or four specific, focused topics that you have chosen from your list of general points.

ORGANIZING   Organize your material in a way that will be most interesting to your audience.

DRAFTING   Write a working draft of your essay in complete sentences.

REVISING   Consulting the Tips for Revising in this chapter (pp. 28–35), revise your first draft—paying special attention to recognizing and constructing paragraphs so they say what you want them to say.

EDITING   Consulting the Tips for Editing in this chapter (pp. 36–65), edit your draft for grammar and correctness—paying special attention to your use of words, phrases, and clauses.

Turn in your revised draft to your instructor.

Some Final Thoughts

When you have completed your own essay, answer these four questions in your journal:

1.   What was most difficult about this assignment?
2.   What was easiest?
3.   What did I learn about recalling by completing this assignment?
4.   What did I learn about my own writing process from this assignment—how I prepared to write, how I wrote the first draft, how I revised, and how I edited?

Recognizing Paragraphs

Checklist for Recognizing Paragraphs

✓ Is each paragraph **indented** to show a new unit of thought?
✓ Does the essay contain three types of paragraphs: **introduction, body,** and **conclusion**?
✓ Does each body paragraph have a **controlling idea** or **topic sentence**?
✓ Is each sentence in a body paragraph related to the paragraph's **topic sentence**?
✓ Are there enough **details** in each paragraph to support the controlling idea and make it interesting?
✓ Are paragraphs with two **controlling ideas** divided into two paragraphs?

All over the world, people collect wild mushrooms—both for use at home and for profit. Because some mushrooms are safe to eat and others are not, mushroom hunters quickly learn to recognize those that are edible. You will need to develop similar observational skills in writing as you work with paragraphs—though failure to recognize a good paragraph doesn't usually result in a stomachache. To become an effective writer and reader, you will need to recognize topic sentences and supporting sentences, and you must be able to eliminate sentences that don't contribute to a paragraph's controlling idea and add others that do.

Basic Features

A **paragraph** is a unit of thought that develops a controlling idea with descriptive, explanatory, or factual details. Well-developed paragraphs have distinguishing features that make them easy to recognize. A paragraph, like a sentence, is a complete unit of thought and is usually part of a larger composition, such as an essay or a chapter in a book. Just as purpose and audience guide your sentence writing, they should guide your composition of paragraphs.

Just as a capital letter signals a complete sentence to a reader, an indentation from the margin (like the one at the beginning of this sentence) indicates the beginning of a paragraph. This indentation signals a change in topic: The new paragraph will develop another idea related to the subject of the entire essay. We as readers expect this idea to be developed in a series of related sentences.

Types of Paragraphs

All essays contain three different types of paragraphs: introductory, body, and concluding. The first paragraph is the **introduction** of an essay; the last paragraph is its **conclusion;** and the paragraphs that fall between the introduction and the conclusion are called **body paragraphs.** A short essay usually consists of one introductory paragraph, several body paragraphs, and one concluding paragraph. In the rest of this chapter, we will be dealing only with body paragraphs.

Topic Sentences

One characteristic of a successful body paragraph is that it has a **controlling idea,** a specific point it will develop in relation to the subject of the essay. Again, the body paragraphs are those that fall between the first paragraph (the introduction) and the last paragraph (the conclusion). The controlling idea of a body paragraph is usually stated in a **topic sentence.** A topic sentence, in other words, alerts your audience to the main idea of a paragraph, and the rest of the paragraph includes only sentences related to that idea. Usually the topic sentence is the first sentence of a paragraph, but experienced writers sometimes vary the placement of their topic sentences in the paragraph or merely let the supporting sentences in the paragraph suggest the main idea. Until you gain experience in composing paragraphs, however, you should begin your paragraphs with a topic sentence.

A topic sentence should not cover a broad subject; it should focus on an idea that can be explained in one paragraph. When you compose essays in response to the assignments in this book, your audience will be most likely to understand the ideas you are describing or explaining if each paragraph begins with a topic sentence that signals what that paragraph will be about.

Look at paragraph 5 of Tobias Wolff's recollection "The Sissy," which begins with the topic sentence "It was springtime."

> It was springtime. The earth was spongy with melted snow, and on the warmest days, if you listened for it, you could hear a faint, steady sibilance of evaporation, almost like a light rain. The trees were hazy with new growth. Bears had begun to appear on the glistening granite faces of the mountainsides above us, taking the sun and soaking up heat from the rock; at lunchtime people came out onto their steps and watched them with upturned, benevolent faces. My mother was with me again. The nuts were all husked and drying in the attic. What did I need trouble for?

Wolff's paragraph is made up of seven sentences. The first sentence announces the controlling idea—springtime. The six sentences that follow develop this idea with supporting details about springtime—melting snow, new plant growth, the appearance of bears—and even conditions of the boy's home life (his mother is back, his chores are done) that give him a feeling of well-being.

Robert's essay is about a fishing trip that ended badly but taught him a significant lesson. Each topic sentence in his essay, then, must focus on a single aspect of that trip. As Robert began revising his essay, he checked each paragraph to make sure it had a topic sentence. He decided that the last sentence of paragraph 1 should actually be the topic sentence for paragraph 2 because this second paragraph explains the boys' "fail-proof plan."

First Draft: The next Saturday night, Brian's parents--who almost never went out--were going to be out late at a party. I told my parents that I was going to sleep at Brian's house, while he told his parents that he was sleeping at my house. Telling this lie, we still felt confident that everything would go off without a hitch. Since we were best friends, we did that often, so our parents believed us. We knew that we would not be missed until my parents came home from church; we figured that would give us plenty of time to get to the lake and fish before we had to head back home.

Revision: ~~We~~ **Brian and I knew that our parents would not let us go on a fishing expedition alone, so we came up with a fail-proof plan.** The next Saturday night, Brian's parents-- who almost never went out--were going to be out late at a party. I told my parents that I was going to sleep at Brian's house, while he told his parents that he was sleeping at my house. Telling this lie, we still felt confident that everything would go off without a hitch. Since we were best friends, we did this ~~that~~ often, so our parents believed us. We knew that we would not be missed until my parents came home from church; we figured that would give us plenty of time to get to the lake and fish before we had to head back home.

After Robert's revision, his second paragraph now has a clear controlling idea in its first sentence.

Exercise R2-1

State the controlling idea in paragraph 11 of Tobias Wolff's essay (p. 14).

Exercise R2-2

Compose a topic sentence for paragraph 5 of the first draft of Robert's essay (p. 20).

Exercise R2-3

Put a check mark beside any of the following sentences that are focused enough to be topic sentences for body paragraphs.

1. A successful marriage requires many things.
2. A parent and a child also need to be able to talk calmly about difficulties concerning extracurricular activities.
3. Drug dealers operate openly on the street where I live.
4. Growing up in the inner city is difficult.
5. Even though my favorite chair is not stylish, it offers me many comforts that a new one would not.
6. I have several hobbies that I enjoy when I have the time.
7. Reading Martha Grisham's mystery novels can enrich a reader's vocabulary as well as provide entertainment and mind teasers.
8. Dogs make good pets for a lot of excellent reasons.
9. In addition to its other pleasures, the Internet offers an excellent way to learn about other parts of the country.
10. Home decorating is a big business in the United States today.

Exercise R2-4

Take two of the broad sentences from Exercise R2-3, and rewrite them so that they state a controlling idea that can be developed in one body paragraph.

Supporting Sentences

Paragraph length (the number of sentences a paragraph contains) is determined by the paragraph's purpose. If the controlling idea for a paragraph is simple, the paragraph may be short. If, however, the idea is more complex, the paragraph may need several more sentences of support.

In a strong paragraph, the supporting sentences provide relevant, specific details that describe or explain the controlling idea. In the previous section, we saw how the details in paragraph 5 of Tobias Wolff's essay describe the springtime, the paragraph's controlling idea (see p. 29).

When Robert checked for controlling ideas in his paragraphs, he also checked each paragraph for supporting sentences. He decided that paragraph 4 did not develop its controlling idea sufficiently. He thought about actual details that would help his readers picture and feel his experience, and he made the following additions:

First Draft: Early the next morning, our fishing trip began

smoothly. We had gone there so many times with our dads,

and now we were there all by ourselves. We felt very

smart by that time. We settled back and waited for those

nibbles on our lines. The first sign of trouble came almost immediately.

Revision: Early the next morning, our fishing trip began smoothly. **We had backed the boat into the water--no problem. We got the boat started and went chugging across the bay to our spot, four cypress trees arranged in an almost perfect square.** We had gone ~~there~~ **to our favorite fishing spot in the Atchafalaya Basin** so many times with our dads **that we knew the way,** and now, **except for herons and egrets,** we were there all by ourselves, **casting our flies, hoping to catch bream.** We felt very smart by that time/, **because we began to get strikes almost immediately. Brian was jerking his rod to set his hook the first time.** We settled back and waited for those nibbles on our lines. The first sign of trouble came almost immediately**, chugging across the water.**

Robert's revised paragraph explains the word *there* from his first draft and adds supporting details that describe the attractions of his favorite fishing spot and the reason he and Brian were feeling so smart.

In revising his essay, Robert not only checked each paragraph for supporting sentences; he also checked for irrelevant sentences. Irrelevant sentences are those that do not help to explain the controlling idea of a paragraph. Robert found that paragraph 3 lacked a clear topic sentence and also contained some information (underlined below) that did not add to the paragraph's main idea.

First Draft: As soon as Brian's parents left for the party on Saturday night, we hooked up the boat trailer. <u>The trailer hitch was a gooseneck type, which is the safest kind.</u> Then we headed for the lake. We had our rods, the cooler, and some sandwiches we made in case we didn't catch any fish. We stopped at the corner store and bought some ice and soft drinks and filled up the car with gas. Then we got in the car, turned up the music, and cruised the back roads until we got to Brian's grandfather <u>Herbert's</u> fishing camp. We felt really smart and grown-up.

Robert deleted the irrelevant sentence, revised the topic sentence, and filled out the paragraph with details about the fishing trip.

Revision:

As soon as Brian's parents left for the party on Saturday night, **we set out on the great fishing expedition. First,** we hooked up the boat trailer. ~~The trailer hitch was a gooseneck type, which is the safest kind.~~ Then we headed for the lake/, **our getaway for the weekend.** We had our **trusty fly** rods, ~~the~~ **a white styrofoam** cooler, and ~~some~~ **several tuna** sandwiches we made in case we didn't catch any fish. We stopped at the **first small** corner store **we saw** and bought some **crushed** ice and **four** soft drinks and filled up ~~the~~ **Brian's beat-up** car with gas. Then we got in the car, turned up the music, and cruised the back roads until we got to Brian's grandfather**'s** ~~Herbert's~~ fishing camp/, **tucked away in the woods.** We felt really smart and grown-up.

Now Robert's paragraph has a topic sentence that clearly states the paragraph's controlling idea—the trip to the lake. And the rest of the sentences in the paragraph develop that idea.

Besides deleting irrelevant sentences from paragraphs, sometimes a writer needs to divide a paragraph because it contains two or more controlling ideas. As Robert reviewed his essay, he decided that his last paragraph actually contained two controlling ideas: his dad's reaction to the expedition and the importance of the outcome on Robert's own life. In his revision, Robert split the paragraph and added a sentence to explain the controlling idea for his new paragraph on his father's reaction.

First Draft:

When my dad came to get us, he told us we were lucky we didn't have to go to jail. We just said, "Yessir, yessir, yessir," all the way home. We knew we were in big trouble. Brian's dad and my dad decided that to punish us, we would each have to mow the grass for 10 Saturdays in a row to earn back the money for the fines. Also, Brian was not allowed to keep a set of car keys for six months. Our adventure turned into a nightmare, but I think we both learned a big lesson in responsibility and honesty. We never lied to our parents again. And if I am with someone who suggests doing something dishonest, that is the last time I ever talk to that person. I never want to be arrested again.

Revision: When my dad came to get us, he told us we were lucky we didn't have to go to jail. **Wow, when we saw the scowl on his face and heard his cold tone of voice, we knew we were in big trouble.** We just said, "Yessir, yessir, yessir," all the way home. ~~We knew we were in big trouble.~~ Brian's dad and my dad decided that to punish us, we would each have to mow the grass for 10 Saturdays in a row to earn back the money for the fines. Also, Brian was not allowed to keep a set of car keys for six months.

Our adventure turned into a nightmare, but I think we both learned a big lesson in responsibility and honesty. We never lied to our parents again. And if I am with someone who suggests doing something dishonest, that is the last time I ever talk to that person. I never want to be arrested again.

This revision gives the essay a much more effective conclusion. In it, Robert thinks back over the whole experience and makes some closing comments in a single concluding paragraph.

Exercise R2-5

List the supporting details in Tobias Wolff's first paragraph (pp. 12–13) that describe why the narrator and his friends believe Arthur Gayle is a sissy.

Exercise R2-6

List any questions that paragraph 5 of Robert's first draft (p. 20) leaves in your mind.

Exercise R2-7

Read the paragraph below, and eliminate the sentences that are not relevant to the controlling idea of the paragraph.

Any student's first day at a new school can be both tough and exciting. The buildings are unfamiliar, and it is easy to lose your way and be late. My cousin Amy got lost in a strange mall one time and got locked in. Planning a trip to a new school before the first day of classes can eliminate the lost feeling. Not knowing anyone can be intimidating, but the prospect of new friends and activities can be attractive. My cousin Seth is a member of a lot of clubs at his school. Joining clubs and volunteering is a good way to make friends. Trying out for school sports is another way. I really don't like baseball and track, but I like volleyball. If you extend yourself, others will help you.

Exercise R2-8

The following paragraph lacks specific supporting details. Supply supporting details from your own experience.

Many people today choose to go to college. They think that college will help them get what they want. I chose to go to college for many reasons, not just money.

COLLABORATIVE WORK

After writing a draft of your own recalling essay, exchange papers with a classmate, and do the following tasks:

A.   Underline the controlling idea for each body paragraph. If the controlling idea is implied, note in the margin what you think it is.

B.   Mark with a paragraph symbol (¶) any places where you think paragraphs should be divided so that each new paragraph focuses on only one controlling idea.

C.   Put a check mark next to any paragraphs that need more supporting sentences; cross out any irrelevant sentences; and circle any sentences that should be in another paragraph.

D.   Jot down any questions you have that a paragraph does not answer.

Then return the paper to its writer, and use the information in this section to revise your draft.

Words, Phrases, and Clauses

Checklist for Editing Words, Phrases, and Clauses

✓ Are the verbs mainly **action verbs**?
✓ Do the sentences include **nouns** that name specific persons, places, or things?
✓ Do **pronouns** replace nouns that are easy to identify?
✓ Are the **adjectives** vivid and close to the words they modify?
✓ Do the **adverbs** clearly give additional information about verbs, adjectives, and other adverbs?
✓ Does each **preposition** have an object?
✓ Does each **conjunction** connect two words, phrases, or clauses?
✓ Do **interjections** express strong feelings?
✓ Do the words in **phrases**—noun, preposition, verb, and verbal phrases—**function as a unit**?
✓ Does each sentence contain at least one **independent clause**?
✓ Does each independent clause contain at least one **subject** and one **verb**?
✓ Is each **dependent clause** connected to an independent clause?

Have you ever dressed up for a special occasion—a first date, the big dance, the concert of the year—and asked a trusted friend to check out your outfit? You hope you've done a good job pulling together the right items from your closet—the shirt, vest, jeans, shoes, and accessories that make you look like a model in a magazine ad. However, if just one part of the outfit doesn't meet your friend's approval, it's back to the closet to continue your search for that complete look.

Writers also strive for completeness as they compose sentences, paragraphs, and essays that try to satisfy their readers' expectations. In this chapter, you will learn more about that basic unit of written expression, the sentence, as well as the parts that work together to make each sentence complete: words, phrases, and clauses. Not only will you learn to identify different types of words, phrases, and clauses, but you will also see how these elements work together and how they relate to each other in a variety of ways. Armed with this knowledge, you will be able to write an interesting essay that holds your readers' attention.

Words: Identifying Parts of Speech

Every sentence is made up of a variety of words that express a complete idea or thought. Good sentences are composed of words that are carefully and confidently arranged to communicate the exact message the writer wants to send. Think of words again as the separate pieces of clothing and accessories that make up your head-turning outfit. Each word, like each item of your latest look, serves a distinct purpose.

The functions of words make them fall into one of eight categories: verbs, nouns, pronouns, adjectives, adverbs, prepositions, conjunctions, and interjections. Some words, such as *is*, can function in only one way—in this case as a verb. Other words, however, can be classified in different categories and therefore serve as different **parts of speech** depending on how they are used in a sentence. The following examples illustrate the different functions of the word *burn*:

Verb

The farmers **burn** the fields after every harvest. (*Burn* is the main verb of the sentence, telling what the farmers do.)

Noun

Yolanda's **burn** healed well. (*Burn* functions as a noun, telling what healed.)

Adjective

My mom found two **burn** marks on the sofa. (*Burn* is an adjective modifying the noun *marks*.)

Recognizing the different categories or parts of speech allows you to identify a word's function. This skill will help you see how words relate to each other as you continue to write complete sentences that communicate clearly and effectively.

Verbs

The verb is the most important word in a sentence because every other word depends on it in some way. In essence, writers build sentences around verbs, just as you build an outfit around a flashy shirt or a favorite pair of jeans. The **verbs** tell what's going on in the sentence. If there's no real action, verbs describe someone's or something's state of being, expressing something about its existence, condition, or appearance. Look at these sentences from Robert's revised recalling essay:

Action:	We **had backed** the boat into the water--no problem.
Existence:	It **was** the most embarrassing feeling I have ever had.
Condition:	We **felt** really smart and grown-up.
Appearance:	The conservation officer **looked** serious.

These verbs in Robert's sentences differ in the degree of action they express. The first verb, *backed,* refers to an action while the other three do not.

Action Verbs

An **action verb** tells what something or someone does, has done, or will do. When the verb directs action toward someone or something, it is called a **transitive verb.** Look again at one of Robert's examples:

We **had backed** the boat into the water--no problem.

We is the subject or the doer of the action. The word that receives the action of the verb is *boat* (We backed *what?*). We call this word the **direct object.** (See p. 97 for more about direct objects.) Thus, a transitive verb connects the subject with its direct object, or word that receives the action.

A verb with no direct object is called an **intransitive verb,** meaning it directs no action toward something or someone. Look at this sentence from Robert's first draft:

> Early the next morning, our fishing trip **began** smoothly.

The verb *began* does not direct action toward anyone or anything. Because *began* has no object, it is intransitive. The following examples may illustrate this effect more clearly:

Intransitive:	Scott **wrote.**
	Scott **wrote** quickly.

In the first sentence, we don't know *what* Scott wrote, only that he wrote. In the second sentence, we also know *how* he wrote, but still not *what.*

Transitive:	Scott **wrote** an essay.

What did Scott write? He wrote an essay, the direct object of the verb *wrote*.

Linking Verbs

Some verbs do not express action at all. Look again at the examples expressing *existence, condition,* and *appearance* on page 37. The verbs *was, felt,* and *looked* express states of being—statements of existence, condition, and appearance—not action. *Was, felt,* and *looked* are what we call linking verbs. This is a second way verbs can be classified.

A **linking verb** connects its subject to a word that describes or renames the subject. Look closely at Robert's sentence expressing existence:

> It **was** the most embarrassing feeling I ever had.

The verb *was* connects the subject *it* to the word *feeling,* the word that tells what *it* was. Reconsider this sentence expressing appearance:

> The conservation officer **looked** serious.

The linking verb *looked* serves as a bridge, connecting the subject *officer* and the word *serious,* which describes the officer.

Most linking verbs come from *be,* the most common linking verb. Its forms include *is, are, was, were, am, be, being,* and *been.* Other common linking verbs include *appear, become, feel, grow, look, prove, remain, seem, smell, sound, stand, stay, taste,* and *turn.* However, be aware that these and other verbs can be either action or linking verbs, depending on the sentence.

> *Action:*   Robert **grows** corn on his ten-acre farm.

The verb *grows* here is a transitive action verb because it carries action to a direct object, *corn*.

> *Linking:*   Scott **grows** anxious when he doesn't hear from his girlfriend every night.

The verb *grows* here is a linking verb because it connects *Scott*, the subject, with *anxious*, a word that describes the subject.

Here is a tip for determining whether or not a word is a linking verb: Replace the original verb with either *am*, *is*, or *are*. If the sentence makes sense, you have found a linking verb.

Exercise E2-1

In the following sentences from "The Sissy" by Tobias Wolff, underline all the verbs. Then label each verb as action *or* linking. *Finally, label each action verb as* transitive *or* intransitive.

1. Arthur was testy with me.
2. I liked his acid wit and the wild stories he told and his apparent indifference to what other people thought of him.
3. Arthur had made other such comments.
4. We lay next to each other, gasping strenuously.
5. The other two boys were excited, restless, twitching with the blows they'd imagined striking.

Exercise E2-2

In the following sentences from Robert's revised recalling essay, "The Great Fishing Expedition," underline all the verbs. Then label each as action *or* linking. *Finally, label each action verb as* transitive *or* intransitive.

1. As soon as Brian's parents left for the party on Saturday night, we set out on the great fishing expedition.
2. Then we headed for the lake, our getaway for the weekend.
3. We felt really smart and grown-up.
4. The first sign of trouble came almost immediately, chugging across the water.
5. All of our best friends suddenly seemed distant, like mere acquaintances.

Exercise E2-3

Supply verbs for the blanks in the following paragraph. Label each verb as transitive, intransitive, *or* linking.

Last weekend we (1) _____ to go Christmas shopping at a

nearby outlet mall. Setting our clock for 6 a.m., we (2) _____ out of bed and got ready in a flash. We (3) _____ on the

road within an hour. Before we got out of the city limits, Nancy

(4) _____ that she had to go to the bathroom and Bobby

(5) _____ hungry. So we (6) _____ at the

first convenience store we saw. While Bobby and Nancy were inside the store, I

(7) _____ steam coming from under the hood of my car. I

(8) _____ it out and (9) _____ water leaking

from the radiator. We all (10) _____ into the car and wisely

decided to cancel our trip.

Exercise E2-4

Write original sentences using the following words as verbs. Label these verbs as transitive, intransitive, *or* linking.

1. had been going
2. chuckled
3. remained
4. become
5. whispers

Nouns

The majority of the words in the English language are nouns. People often think of **nouns** as "naming" words because nouns point out or name specific persons (*friend, Brian, dad, officer*), places (*town, lake, Greenville*), or things. "Things" could be living plants and animals (*bush, tree, cat, fish*) or nonliving objects, like the parts of your best outfit (*shirt, vest, jeans, belt, boots*) or Robert's fishing accessories (*boat, pole, bait, sandwiches*). Additionally, nouns name ideas (*freedom, democracy*), qualities (*honesty, courage*), emotions (*fear, anxiety*), and actions (*competition, negotiations*).

Singular and Plural Nouns

Singular nouns indicate one person, place, thing, or idea, while **plural nouns** indicate more than one. Almost all nouns change form when indicating changes in number, usually adding *-s* or *-es* for plurals: *boat, boats; mile, miles; match, matches; baby, babies*. Other nouns form plurals in different ways: *woman, women; child, children; life, lives; alumnus, alumni*. Chapter 6 further discusses noun forms, including the possessive form, which indicates ownership (*baby's bib, Sally's room*).

Common and Proper Nouns

Nouns can also be categorized as common or proper. Distinguishing between the two is simple. **Common nouns,** which begin with lowercase letters, name general persons, places, or things. **Proper nouns,** which begin with capital letters, name specific persons, places, or things. Look at the following examples of common nouns from Robert's recalling essay:

Common Nouns	Proper Nouns
town	Greenville
friend	Brian
officer	Herbert
lake	Atchafalaya Basin

Concrete and Abstract Nouns

Not only can nouns be classified by what they name—persons, places, things, ideas, qualities, emotions, and actions—they can also be grouped according to perception. A **concrete noun** refers to something you can see, touch, hear, feel, or taste. Most persons, places, and things are concrete: *mom, Stewart, Maria, school, park, Disney World, dog, bee, car, computer.* An **abstract noun** names something that you cannot see, touch, hear, feel, or taste. Ideas, qualities, emotions, and actions are usually abstract: *capitalism, self-confidence, sadness, co-operation.*

Collective Nouns

Certain nouns may be singular or plural, depending on the way they are used in their sentences. Consider the word *team.* If you refer to the team as one unit that works together, then *team* is singular.

The **team is** rated number four in the nation.

However, if you mean that each team member functions individually, then *team* is plural:

The **team are** undergoing their physicals this afternoon.

(See Chapter 5 for more information about collective nouns and agreement.)

Some of the most common collective nouns are *army, audience, band, chorus, class, committee, couple, crew, crowd, family, flock, gang, herd, jury, majority, orchestra, squad, team,* and *troop.*

T I P S   F O R   E D I T I N G

Other Features of Nouns

Here are two final tips for identifying nouns.

1. Look for the words *a, an,* and *the.* These articles indicate that a noun is nearby (*a* story, *a* ticket, *an* error, *an* opportunity, *the* money, *the* lesson). Just remember that this tip does not apply to proper nouns. For example, we would never say or write *a Ken* or *the Seattle.*

2. Look for common noun endings such as *-age* (*language*), *-ance* (*defiance*), *-dom* (*kingdom*), *-ence* (*experience*), *-er* (*skier*), *-ian* (*Italian*), *-ice* (*device*), *-ism* (*communism*), *-ist* (*socialist*), *-ity* (*sincerity*), *-ment* (*development*), *-ness* (*frankness*), *-ship* (*penmanship*), *-sion* (*tension*), *-tion* (*recognition*), and *-ure* (*failure*). These word endings let you know you are dealing with a noun.

Exercise E2-5

List each noun in paragraph 1 of "The Sissy" (pp. 12–13), and indicate whether it is concrete or abstract. Then classify each noun as either common or proper and singular or plural.

Exercise E2-6

In Robert's revised recalling essay on page 24, label each noun in paragraph 4 as either concrete or abstract. Then label each noun in paragraph 5 as either singular or plural. Finally, list each common noun and each proper noun in paragraph 6.

Exercise E2-7

In the following paragraph, fill in the blanks with a noun that will make each sentence complete.

My best (1) _____ is my brother Ben. He is 18, about six feet

tall with curly brown hair. He is really a neat (2) _____ . I have

to say that he is unusual and does his own thing. For example, he likes to wear

(3) _____ during the wintertime. When he goes out, people

usually point and stare. Ben just shakes his (4) _____ and keeps

on walking. The best quality about Ben is his (5) _____ . He

would do just about anything for anyone who needs (6) _____ .

Most people also says he has a good (7) _____ . In fact, hardly

anyone ever says anything bad about him. We spend a lot of time making

(8) _____ , a favorite hobby of ours. While we're working,

we'll listen to (9) _____ and talk about our

(10) _____ .

Exercise E2-8

Write five original sentences, using the following words as nouns.

1. jury
2. point
3. lateness
4. determination
5. Michael Jordan

Pronouns

Pronouns may be almost unnoticed in writing and speech, even though these words can do anything nouns can do. Without pronouns, writers and speakers would find themselves repeating nouns over and over, producing sentences that are unnatural and boring. For example, notice how awkward the following paragraph would be if pronouns were banned:

> Robert wrote the rough draft of Robert's essay last night. Then Robert asked Robert's mother to read over Robert's essay with Robert. After Robert's mother helped Robert find errors, Robert made corrections. Then Robert set aside the essay for a day before Robert took the essay out and began revising again.

When we let pronouns take over and do their jobs, we produce much more fluent paragraphs:

> Robert wrote the rough draft of **his** essay last night. Then **he** asked **his** mother to read over **his** essay with **him.** After **she** helped Robert find errors, **he** made corrections. Then **he** set aside the essay for a day before **he** took **it** out and began revising again.

The pronouns *his, he, him, she,* and *it* allow us to avoid repeating certain nouns in the paragraph. Those nouns—*Robert, mother,* and *essay*—are called the pronouns' antecedents. An **antecedent** is the word or group of words that a pronoun refers to. Usually the antecedent comes before the pronoun, appearing either in the same sentence or in a previous sentence. Some pronouns, however, do not have antecedents. In such cases, you will have to guess what the pronoun refers to.

Personal Pronouns

The pronouns in the previous examples—*his, he, him, she,* and *it*—are all **personal pronouns.** These are the most commonly used pronouns and can be classified according to person:

First person refers to the person speaking.

Second person refers to the person spoken to.

Third person, the largest category, indicates the person, place, thing, or idea spoken about.

The following chart lists the personal pronouns by person and number:

	Singular	Plural
First person	I, me, my, mine	we, us, our, ours
Second person	you, your, yours	you, your, yours
Third person	he, him, his, she her, hers, it, its	they, them, their, theirs

Personal pronouns can also be subdivided by **case,** the form of a pronoun (or a noun) that indicates how it is used in a sentence. (For more on noun cases, see Chapter 6.) **Subjective pronouns** can replace nouns that function as subjects or subject complements. **Objective pronouns** function as any type of object in a sentence—a direct object, an indirect object, an object of a preposition. **Possessive pronouns** simply indicate possession or ownership. Look at the following chart, which groups the personal pronouns by case, number, and person.

Personal Pronouns

	Subjective	Objective	Possessive
Singular			
First Person:	I	me	my, mine
Second Person:	you	you	your, yours
Third Person:	he, she, it	him, her, it	her, hers, his, its
Plural			
First Person:	we	us	our, ours
Second Person:	you	you	your, yours
Third Person:	they	them	their, theirs

Other Pronouns

Although we use personal pronouns most often, we depend upon a variety of other pronouns to replace or refer to nouns. These additional pronouns can be grouped in one of several categories, as the following charts indicate.

Pronoun Types

Reflexive/ Intensive	Demonstrative	Relative	Interrogative	Reciprocal
Singular	**Singular**	that	who	each other
myself	this	who	whom	one another
yourself	that	whom	which	
himself	**Plural**	which	whose	
herself	these	whose		
itself	those			
Plural				
ourselves				
yourselves				
themselves				

T I P S   F O R   E D I T I N G

Indefinite Pronouns

Singular	Plural	Singular or Plural
another, anybody, anyone, anything, each, either, everybody, everyone, everything, little, much, neither, nobody, no one, nothing, one, other, somebody, someone, something	both, few, many, others, several	all, any, more, most, none, some

Pronoun or Adjective?

Some pronouns may function as adjectives, depending on how they are used in a sentence. Just put the pronoun to the following test: If the pronoun is used with a noun, it becomes an adjective, and if the pronoun replaces or refers to a noun, it functions as a pronoun.

Pronoun: We pumped the car so full of gas that **some** spilled onto the concrete.
Adjective: **Some** gas spilled onto the concrete.

Exercise E2-9

List each pronoun in paragraphs 2 and 3 of Wolff's "The Sissy" (p. 13).

Exercise E2-10

List each pronoun in paragraphs 1 through 5 of Robert's first draft (pp. 19–20).

Exercise E2-11

Rewrite the following paragraph, replacing the italicized noun or nouns with pronouns.

Have you ever received an anonymous card or letter? I did. In fact, I received several cards. To this day I still don't know who sent (1) _____ (*the cards*). I remember when I got the first card. (2) _____ (*The card*) was written in a scratchy handwriting and signed "Secret Admirer." Of course, I asked my friends Amy and Beth whether (3) _____ (*Amy and Beth*) knew who had sent (4) _____ (*the card*). Amy acted clueless while Beth smirked a little, as though (5) _____ (*Beth*) knew something was up. Anyway, over the next few weeks I got about a dozen more cards, all of (6) _____ (*the cards*) from my "secret admirer." My friend Sal said that (7) _____ (*Sal*) thought it was neat. Sal said that (8) _____ (*Sal*) wished (9) _____ (*a person*) would send (10) _____ (*Sal*) some mail.

Exercise E2-12

Use the following pronouns in original sentences.

1. themselves
2. anybody
3. those
4. each other
5. few

Adjectives

Without adjectives, our language would be drab and boring. **Adjectives** modify nouns or pronouns and provide additional information that helps us write more vividly, clearly, and specifically. Notice how Robert uses adjectives to make his sentences more colorful and informative.

First Draft:	We had our rods, the cooler, and some sandwiches we made in case we didn't catch any fish.
Revision:	We had our **trusty fly** rods, ~~the~~ **a white styrofoam** cooler, and ~~some~~ **several tuna** sandwiches we made in case we didn't catch any fish.

First Draft:	We stopped at the corner store and bought some ice and
	soft drinks and filled up the car with gas.
Revision:	We stopped at the **first small** corner store we saw and
	bought some **crushed** ice and **four** soft drinks and filled
	up ~~the~~ **Brian's beat-up** car with gas.

From Robert's examples, you can see that adjectives add information about nouns (and sometimes pronouns). The type of information the adjective gives determines whether the adjective *describes* or *limits* the noun. These are the two basic categories for grouping adjectives.

Descriptive Adjectives

Descriptive adjectives do just what the term implies—they describe, giving details about the nouns and pronouns to enhance the reader's mental image. Descriptive adjectives answer a variety of questions: What color? (a *white* cooler). What size? (a *small* store). What kind? (*tuna* sandwiches). Certain endings usually indicate descriptive adjectives. These endings include *-able* (*chewable*), *-ant* (*deviant*), *-ent* (*confident*), *-ful* (*careful*), *-ic* (*athletic*), *-ive* (*supportive*), *-less* (*careless*), *-ory* (*sensory*), *-ous* (*famous*), *-some* (*worrisome*), and *-y* (*flirty*).

Limiting Adjectives

The other category of adjectives includes words that indicate specific nouns or pronouns or words that narrow a noun's or pronoun's meaning. **Limiting adjectives** answer the following questions: How many? (*four* soft drinks). How much? (*some* crushed ice). Which one? (the *first* store).

The most common limiting adjectives are the articles *a*, *an*, and *the*.

Common Limiting Adjectives	
my, your, his, her, its, our, their	Scott took **his boat** to the lake.
this, that, these, those	Brian plans to take **that** pole back to the store because it's cracked
which, whichever, whatever	We will go out anywhere you like, **whatever** place you decide.
all, another, any, each, enough, every, few, less, little, many, more, much, several, some	On their next trip, Robert and Brian hope they catch **many** fish.
what, which, whose	**Whose** shoes are these?

T I P S   F O R   E D I T I N G

The way to identify adjectives is to find words that modify nouns and pronouns. Use adjectives to make your sentences more accurate and interesting to read.

Exercise E2-13

Identify the adjectives and the words they modify in paragraph 5 of "The Sissy" (p. 13). Do not include articles.

Exercise E2-14

List each of the adjectives and the words they modify in paragraphs 4 through 7 in Robert's revised recalling essay (pp. 24–25). Do not include articles.

Exercise E2-15

Fill in the blanks with adjectives that will complete each sentence in the following paragraph.

We went to a (1) _____ play at the Little Theater on campus. It was a (2) _____ comedy written by a

(3) _____ student at our school. The

(3) _____ actor was a (4) _____ guy who kept everyone laughing with his

(5) _____ faces and (6) _____ lines.

During (7) _____ scene he came out dressed in a

(8) _____ costume. In a (9) _____ scene, he appeared onstage in a (10) _____ box. Before the play was over, I had laughed so hard that (11) _____ sides hurt. After the play, we met the actors, including the (12) _____ star of the show. He took my hand in his (13) _____ paw, kissed it, and gave me a (14) _____ smile. Then he said, "So you're the one who was laughing so hard." All I could do was give a

(15) _____ reply of "Yes."

Exercise E2-16

Write an original sentence using the following words as adjectives.

1. Chinese
2. tasty
3. upset
4. fourth
5. thrilling

Adverbs

Like adjectives, **adverbs** supply additional information in a sentence that helps a writer express more vividly actions taking place now, in the past, or in the future. Just by looking at the word *adverb*, you can guess that adverbs are usually located close to verbs. However, adverbs also modify or relate to adjectives and other adverbs, answering the following questions:

How? (We planned things *carefully*.)

Other adverbs that tell how: *fast, quickly, slowly, secretly, freely, quietly, slyly, courageously, steadily*

When? (*Yesterday* we planned things carefully).

Other adverbs that tell when: *today, tomorrow, soon, late, early, eventually, now, then*

Where? (We planned things carefully *outside*.)

Other adverbs that tell where: *here, there, inside, up, down, uphill, downhill, forward*

How often? (We *usually* planned things carefully.)

Other adverbs that tell how often: *seldom, rarely, normally, regularly, sometimes*

To what extent? (We planned things *very* carefully.)

Other adverbs that tell to what extent: *somewhat, too, hardly, barely*

Certain negative words, such as *not* and *never*, always function as adverbs. Also, when searching for adverbs, look for words ending in *-ly*: *quickly, clearly, angrily, sweetly, happily, freely*. Remember, however, that some words ending in *-ly* are adjectives: *lonely, lovely, ugly*.

Exercise E2-17

List each adverb and the word it modifies in the following sentences from "The Sissy."

1. At times I caught him looking at me expectantly, as if I were holding out on him.
2. And in the same moment, seeing how everything about him changed after the word was spoken, how suddenly red and awful his face became, I understood that there must be a reason for this.
3. When he swung again I turned away and took his fist on the back of my head.
4. My news bag had armored me well when I was on my feet but now it was heavy with mud and twisted around my shoulders.
5. He struggled, then abruptly collapsed on top of me.

Exercise E2-18

Beginning with paragraph 4, identify each of the adverbs in Robert's first draft (pp. 19–20) and the words they modify.

Exercise E2-19

Fill in the blanks in the following paragraph with adverbs that will make each sentence complete.

(1) _____ I decided to find a new job, a

(2) _____ easy task, or so I thought. I began by

(3) _____ going through the phone book and

(4) _____ listing each business that I thought would be

hiring (5) _____ . Then I started calling. After I dialed the

first number, I (6) _____ asked to speak to the personnel

manager. The woman (7) _____ asked, "What would you

like to speak to her about?" I told her I was inquiring about possible employment.

Her tone changed (8) _____ . "Well, we're

(9) _____ hiring," she said. (10) _____ , I

thanked her and hung up the phone, (11) _____ thinking that

finding a new job may be (12) _____ difficult indeed.

Exercise E2-20

Write an original sentence for each of the following words, using them as adverbs.

1. moderately
2. fast
3. sometimes
4. down
5. somewhat

Prepositions

Remember Robert and Brian's fishing expedition? As Robert writes, "The next Saturday night, Brian's parents—who almost never went out—were going to be out late *at* a party." We don't know anything else, but the party could have been . . .

across town

after a play

down the street

for his mom's boss

with their best friends

The boldfaced words in each of these examples are **prepositions,** words that serve as connectors. Prepositions show relationships or connections between the nouns or pronouns that follow them and words located elsewhere in the sentence. The group of words beginning with a preposition and ending with a noun or pronoun—the preposition's *object*—is called a **prepositional phrase.** (See p. 58 for more about prepositional phrases.) Look at these additional examples from Robert's revised essay:

Preposition: We made detailed lists **of the supplies** we would need.

Preposition: Then we headed **for the lake,** our getaway **for the weekend.**

The simplest way to recognize prepositions is to follow these two suggestions:

1. Remember that prepositions are followed by nouns or pronouns. If that is not the case, you have most likely found an adverb.

Preposition: Scott and Brian left their cooler **in the boat.**

Adverb: Won't you come **in**?

In the second example, *in* is an adverb modifying the verb *come.* If you put the question in natural order or in sentence form, you can see that *in* has no object: *You won't come in.*

2. Study the following list so you can use it as a handy reference. Note that, **compound prepositions** are composed of more than one word.

Common Prepositions			
about	beside	in front of	past
above	besides	in place of	prior to
according to	between	inside	regarding
across	beyond	in spite of	since
after	by	instead of	through
against	by means of	into	throughout
along	concerning	like	to
along with	despite	near	toward
among	down	next to	under
apart from	during	of	underneath
around	except	off	unlike
as	except for	on	until
as for	for	onto	up
at	from	on top of	upon
because of	in	out	up to
before	in addition to	out of	with
behind	in back of	outside	within
below	in case of	over	without
beneath			

Exercise E2-21

List the prepositions and their objects in paragraph 10 of Tobias Wolff's "The Sissy" (pp. 13–14).

Exercise E2-22

List the prepositions and their objects in paragraphs 3 through 7 of the first draft of Robert's recalling essay (pp. 19–20).

Exercise E2-23

Fill in the blanks with prepositions that will complete each sentence in the following paragraph.

One day as I waited (1) _____ the bus, a tall man sat down (2) _____ me (3) _____ the bench and began talking (4) _____ the weather. I agreed that it certainly had been hot (5) _____ the city. Then I looked up and saw a police officer walking (6) _____ the sidewalk (7) _____ the street. She was looking at everyone she passed, as if she were searching (9) _____ someone. Then she spied my bench partner sitting (10) _____ me and a little lady with a huge straw hat (11) _____ her gray head. When the tall man saw the police officer, he jumped up and began running (12) _____ the street as fast as he could. (13) _____ the tall man's efforts, the police officer caught him as he scampered (14) _____ the sidewalk strollers. Then my bus came, and I rode away (15) _____ the night, filling in the blanks (16) _____ the events I had witnessed.

Exercise E2-24

Write original sentences using the following prepositions.

1. instead of
2. without
3. along

4. like
5. despite

Conjunctions

Like prepositions, **conjunctions** relate words to each other, but they also connect entire groups of words. For example, the sentence you just read includes one of the most common conjunctions, *but,* which relates two different complete ideas: the complete thought that appears before the word *but* and the complete thought that appears after it. If it weren't for conjunctions, most of our writing would appear repetitious and monotonous.

The different types of conjunctions are easy to remember because they serve different connecting purposes.

Coordinating Conjunctions

The most common conjunctions are **coordinating conjunctions:** *and, but, or, nor, for, so,* and *yet.* These words join elements of equal importance or weight, whether they are single words, groups of words, or complete ideas. Look at these examples from the first draft of Robert's essay:

Words: Our adventure turned into a nightmare, but I think we both learned a big lesson in **responsibility** *and* **honesty.**

Word groups: We felt **really smart** *and* **grown-up.**

Complete ideas: **We knew that our parents would not let us go alone,** *so* **we came up with a fail-proof plan.**

Remember that coordinating conjunctions join equal sentence elements. Don't be fooled by *but* and *for,* two words that can function as either conjunctions or prepositions.

Conjunction: Paula arrived 15 minutes early, *for* she was scheduled to begin the interview at nine sharp.

Preposition: Paula arrived 15 minutes early *for* her interview.

Correlative Conjunctions

These conjunctions are easy to identify and use because they appear in pairs: *both . . . and, either . . . or, neither . . . nor, not . . . but, not only . . . but also, whether . . . or.* Like coordinating conjunctions, **correlative conjunctions** join words, groups of words, or complete ideas.

Words:	*Both* Scott *and* Brian were punished after the fishing trip.
Word groups:	I left my keys *either* in the car *or* on my desk.
Complete ideas:	*Not only* did I find my keys *but* I *also* found a $5 bill.

Subordinating Conjunctions

One type of conjunction, the **subordinating conjunction,** joins two complete thoughts by making one thought dependent upon the other. What results is a *subordinate* or *dependent clause,* a group of words that has a subject and a verb, but that, because of the subordinating conjunction, cannot stand by itself as a complete sentence. The subordinating conjunction not only makes the clause dependent but also connects the dependent clause to the independent clause that can stand by itself. (See pp. 62–63 for a detailed discussion of dependent and independent clauses.)

The following sentences from the first draft of Robert's recalling essay will help explain this notion:

> We decided it would be great **if** we went on a fishing trip.

In this sentence the subordinating conjunction *if* joins the dependent clause *if we went on a fishing trip* to the independent clause *we decided it would be great.*

> I told my parents **that** I was going to sleep at Brian's house, **while** he
>
> told his parents **that** he was sleeping at my house.

This sentence has three subordinating conjunctions: (1) *that,* which begins the dependent clause *that I was going to sleep at Brian's house;* (2) *while,* which begins the dependent clause *while he told his parents;* and (3) *that,* which begins the final subordinate clause *that he was sleeping at my house.* The independent clause, the sentence element that can stand alone, is *I told my parents.*

Common Subordinating Conjunctions			
after	because	since	until
although	before	so	when
as	even if	so that	whenever
as if	even though	than	where
as long as	how	that	wherever
as soon as	if	though	whether
as though	in order that	unless	while

Conjunctive Adverbs

Conjunctive adverbs are unusual words because they function as conjunctions but are classified as a different part of speech, adverbs. Conjunctive adverbs are also called *transition words* because they connect or join two complete ideas, thoughts that often reveal similarities, differences, contrasts, or results. Robert uses a conjunctive adverb in a sentence in paragraph 5 of his first draft:

> We were scared; **however,** we didn't think anything really bad would
>
> happen.

One easy way to recognize conjunctive adverbs is by the punctuation. Usually conjunctive adverbs are preceded by a semicolon and followed by a comma. On some occasions, the conjunctive adverb may be set off with commas.

> We couldn't wait, **however,** for the weekend to arrive.

(See p. 297 for more about punctuation with conjunctive adverbs.)

Conjunctive Adverbs and Transition Words and Expressions			
accordingly	finally	in addition	on the other hand
also	for example	indeed	otherwise
besides	furthermore	moreover	therefore
consequently	however	nevertheless	thus

Exercise E2-25

Underline all the conjunctions and conjunctive adverbs in paragraphs 1 and 2 of "The Sissy" (pp. 12–13). Then label the conjunctions as coordinating, correlative, *or* subordinating.

Exercise E2-26

In paragraphs 3–5 of Robert's revised recalling essay (p. 23), list each of the conjunctions and conjunctive adverbs and classify the conjunctions as coordinating, correlative, *or* subordinating.

Exercise E2-27

Fill in the blanks in the following paragraph with conjunctions or conjunctive adverbs that will make each sentence complete.

(1) _____ I work two jobs and go to school, I have little spare time. (2) _____ , I try very hard to find time for myself. Sometimes I have so many things to do, (3) _____ I don't know which way to turn. (4) _____ I sit down and write everything in order of what has to be done first. I try to make a schedule; (5) _____ , sometimes I get a bit off track. For example, I had an evening of relaxation planned last night. (6) _____ a friend's car broke down, (7) _____ I went to pick him up 50 miles away. (8) _____ my friend's bad luck ruined my restful evening. (9) _____ I plan something and it doesn't pan out, I've learned not to get upset. (10) _____ I get upset, I just need more time to calm down, time I usually don't have.

Exercise E2-28

Write original sentences using the following conjunctions and conjunctive adverbs.

1. nevertheless
2. how
3. neither . . . nor
4. yet
5. therefore

Interjections

Interjections are probably the easiest part of speech to identify because of the punctuation that accompanies them. Words that express strong emotions, surprise, or disappointment are often followed by exclamation points, while milder expressions of feeling are set off by commas. Look at these examples from Robert's revised recalling essay:

> **Help!** We wanted to just run away and hide.
> **Wow,** when we saw the scowl on his face and heard his cold tone of voice, we knew we were in trouble.

Other common interjections include *ah, aha, alas, damn, goodness, gracious, great, hallelujah, hell, man, oh, oops, ouch, well, whoa, wow, yeah,* and *yippee.* These words each express a different type of emotional reaction.

Exercise E2-29

Underline the interjections in the following sentences.

1. The chill winds, alas, have swept the leaves across the meadow.
2. Yeah! We got the best seats in the house!
3. My goodness! Can't you chew with your mouth closed?
4. Man, my legs are tired after running ten miles.
5. Oh, I almost forgot that I have a dentist appointment.

Exercise E2-30

Write sentences of your own, using the following words as interjections.

1. well
2. goodness
3. good gracious
4. oh
5. oops

Phrases

In our analogy about putting together a new outfit, each article of clothing is like a word. While clothing items cover and decorate certain parts of your body, each word by itself has a specific function to perform in the sentence. **Phrases** are nothing more than words grouped together to function as a unit. Phrases cannot stand alone, however, because they lack a subject, a verb, or both.

Think of phrases as elements that work together like articles of clothing. For example, a shirt, a tie, and a sport coat are a set of clothes that men coordinate. A group of complimentary clothing items for women is skirt, blouse, and shoes. Like phrases, these clothes form units that go together.

Learning about the different ways words can be grouped into phrases and how these units function will help you put together better sentences. You will be able to communicate more clearly, specifically, and vividly, and your writing will be even more readable than it already is.

Noun Phrases

Identifying and writing noun phrases are relatively simple tasks because you have to focus on only two parts of speech—nouns and adjectives. A **noun phrase** consists of a noun and any adjectives that describe it. As a unit, the phrase functions as a noun. Look at this sentence from Robert's revised essay:

> Then we got in **the car,** turned up **the music,** and cruised **the back roads** until we got to **Brian's grandfather's fishing camp,** tucked away in **the woods.**

One special type of noun phrase is the **appositive phrase.** This group of words identifies or renames another noun. The appositive phrase can come before or after the noun it renames, but the appositive phrase should always be located next to the word it refers to. Besides nouns and adjectives, appositive phrases often include other parts of speech, such as prepositions. Look at these two sentences from Robert's essay:

> When I was 15, **Brian,** *my best friend,* turned 16.
>
> Then we headed for the **lake,** *our getaway for the weekend.*

Prepositional Phrases

You were introduced to prepositional phrases earlier in this chapter during the discussion of prepositions. Remember that a preposition is the first word in a phrase that ends with a noun or pronoun. Other words, usually adjectives, may come between the preposition and the object, making up a **prepositional phrase.** The phrase itself usually functions as an adjective or an adverb, giving additional information that helps expand the sentence's meaning. On rare occasions a prepositional phrase functions as a noun. For good examples of prepositional phrases, note the following sentence from Robert's first draft:

> We had gone there so many times **with our dads,** and now we were there all **by ourselves.**

The prepositional phrases here provide necessary information that makes the sentence more interesting and informative. Review the prepositions listed on page 52, and try to incorporate a variety of prepositional phrases in your writing.

Verb Phrases

Often verbs work together, forming groups of words called **verb phrases.** These phrases form the heart of a sentence, telling what action the subject performs. Verb phrases may consist of as few as two words or as many as four. One of the words is called the *main verb* while the other words are called *auxiliary* or *helping verbs.* The helping verbs always come first in the phrase. Look at these examples from Robert's first draft:

	Helping Main
Verb Phrases:	We **couldn't wait,** however, for the weekend to arrive.

                              Helping   Helping Main

We knew that we **would** not **be missed** until my

parents came home from church. . . .

Following is a complete list of helping verbs. Note that the verbs in the first three columns—other than *be*—can function by themselves as main verbs; they do not necessarily require helpers.

Helping Verbs				
be	do	have	can	shall
am	does	has	could	should
is	did	had	may	will
are			might	would
was			must	
were				

Don't be fooled by adverbs that sometimes break up a verb phrase—negatives (such as *not* and *never*), and words that end in *-ly*. Include only verbs when you identify verb phrases.

	Helping Adv Main
Verb Phrases:	Robert **could** hardly **finish** writing his essay before the teacher made another assignment.

                    Helping Adv   Adv   Main

Robert and Brian **will** probably never **lie** to their parents again.

Sometimes questions cause words to interrupt the verb phrase. To identify the verb phrase, rewrite the question in sentence form. Then it should be easier to isolate the verb phrase.

Question:	**Will** Robert and Brian **be going** fishing soon?

	Verb Phrase
Rewritten:	Robert and Brian **will be going** fishing soon.

Question:	**Could** Robert **have been trying** all along?

	Verb Phrase
Rewritten:	Robert **could have been trying** all along.

Verbal Phrases

You might guess that verbal phrases have something to do with verbs. You're right, in the sense that **verbals** are words that *were* verbs once. However, with certain additions—either suffixes or entire words—the verb changes its function entirely, becoming either an adjective, an adverb, or a noun. Add modifiers and other words to help complete the verbal's meaning, and you have a **verbal phrase.** As you study the different types of verbals, you will see that they never function as verbs. Verbals always act like other parts of speech. They do not have subjects that go with them. By learning how to use verbal phrases, you will make your writing more appealing.

The **participial phrase** is the only verbal phrase that functions solely as an adjective. The first word of the phrase is called a *participle*, either a present participle (formed by adding *-ing* to a verb) or a past participle (formed by adding, *-d, -ed, -en,* or *-t* to a verb). The rest of the words in the participial phrase are modifiers, and the entire phrase functions as an adjective. Here are some examples from Robert's revised essay.

	Participle
Present Participle:	*Telling* **this lie,** we still felt confident that everything
	would go off without a hitch.
Past Participle:	Then we got in the car, turned up the music, and cruised
	the back roads until we got to Brian's grandfather's

Participle
fishing camp, *tucked* **away in the woods.**

Another type of verbal phrase is the **infinitive phrase.** Forming an infinitive is easy: Simply place the word *to* in front of a verb. The infinitive begins the phrase, with additional words serving as modifiers or complements that give more details. Look at this sentence from Robert's draft:

	Infinitive
Infinitive Phrase:	I told my parents that I was going *to sleep* **at Brian's**

house, while he told his parents that he was sleeping at

my house.

The infinitive phrase *to sleep at Brian's house* begins with the infinitive *to sleep*. The prepositional phrase *at Brian's house* makes up the remainder of the infinitive phrase and tells where Brian was going to sleep. The entire phrase functions as a noun, the direct object of the verb *was going*.

Infinitive

Infinitive Phrase: Robert's attempt *to deceive* his **parents** failed.

This infinitive phrase functions as an adjective describing the noun *attempt*.

Infinitive

Infinitive Phrase: Robert sat down *to revise* his essay for the second time.

This infinitive phrase functions as an adverb modifying *down*, another adverb.

Exercise E2-31

List each noun phrase and prepositional phrase in the first two paragraphs of Tobias Wolff's "The Sissy" (pp. 12–13).

Exercise E2-32

Underline the verb phrases in paragraphs 1 through 4 of Robert's revised recalling essay on pages 23–24.

Exercise E2-33

Complete the sentences in the following paragraph by making verbal phrases, using the information supplied in parentheses.

Sang want (1) _____ (infinitive using *sleep*) because he had

worked overtime yesterday afternoon. But one of his roommates was cleaning the

house, (2) _____ (present participle form of *vacuum*) and

(3) _____ (present participle form of *move*) furniture around.

Tony, Sang's roommate, wanted everything (4) _____ (infinitive

form of *look*) nice because his parents were coming for a visit. Tony didn't know

what to do about the (5) _____ (past participle form of *batter*)

couch, (6) _____ (past participle form of *tear*) to shreds by their

cat Mr. Tigs. (7) _____ (present participle form of *drag*) himself

out of bed, Sang found an old bedspread (8) _____ (infinitive form of *cover*) the couch. (9) _____ (gerund form of *fix*) up the couch was Sang's contribution to housecleaning before he went back to bed, (10) _____ (present participle form of *dream*) of more peaceful days.

Exercise E2-34

Write original sentences using the following phrases.

1.   remembered her first day of school
2.   is sending out invitations for the party
3.   has sunk in the river
4.   will attend college and receive a degree
5.   was energized by food and sleep

Clauses

Like phrases, **clauses** are groups of words. Phrases are distinguished from clauses by the words that make up each group. As you learned earlier in this chapter, phrases are composed of a variety of words—nouns, adjectives, adverbs, even verbs—in a variety of combinations. However, clauses always contain two essential elements: a subject and a predicate.

Independent Clauses

A clause that can stand alone, making sense by itself, is called an **independent clause.** It needs nothing else to be complete; it has a subject and a predicate. Its subject explains *who* or *what* performs the action. The predicate consists of the main verb and any words that follow it to complete its meaning. Every complete sentence must contain at least one independent clause, as the following sentences do:

	Subject	Predicate
Independent clauses	Robert	fishes.
	We	planned things very carefully.
	Robert's English teacher	asked him to revise his paper.

Dependent Clauses

Unlike independent clauses, **dependent clauses** cannot stand alone as complete sentences. Dependent clauses contain subjects and verbs, but certain words that begin dependent clauses make them subordinate to the independent clause. Therefore, a dependent or subordinate clause must be connected to an independent clause to become meaningful and complete.

Consider this clause: *When I was 15.* You and I know this clause is not complete. It leaves us wondering, "What happened?" To make sense, the dependent clause needs to be combined with an independent clause, as Robert did in the opening sentence of his essay: *When I was 15, Brian, my best friend, turned 16.*

Writing dependent clauses and connecting them to independent clauses is a simple process. First, you must decide what to make subordinate or secondary. Then, you need to find the best word to connect the subordinate or dependent clause to the main clause. You can use either subordinating conjunctions or relative pronouns. Here is a list of both types of words:

Subordinating Conjunctions			
after	because	since	until
although	before	so	when
as	even if	so that	whenever
as if	even though	than	where
as long as	how	that	wherever
as soon as	if	though	whether
as though	in order that	unless	while

After **Robert wrote the rough draft of his essay,** he let his mother read it.

We decided it would be great *if* **we went on a fishing trip.**

See pp. 54–55 for more information on subordinating conjunctions.

Relative Pronouns				
who	whom	whose	which	that

The next Saturday night, Brian's parents--*who* **almost never went out--** were going to be out late at a party.

See p. 45 for more information on relative pronouns.

Each of these connecting words has a slightly different meaning. So try to fit your choice as accurately as possible to what you want to say.

Exercise E2-35

Label each clause as independent *or* dependent *in the following sentences from "The Sissy."*

1. He had an arch, subtle voice that he used to good effect as an instrument of his cleverness.
2. At times I caught him looking at me expectantly, as if I were holding out on him.
3. All my life I have recognized almost at a glance those who were meant to be my friends, and they have recognized me.
4. But I had withheld my friendship, because I was afraid of what it would cost me.
5. There hadn't been a moment since the fight began when Pepper wasn't worrying me in some way, if only to bark and bounce around me, and finally it was this more than anything else that made me lose heart.

Exercise E2-36

In paragraphs 3–5 (p. 23), label each independent *and* dependent *clause in the first draft of Robert's recalling essay.*

Exercise E2-37

Complete each clause by filling in the blanks with words that will make each sentence complete.

Matt, who (1) _____ , sells his artwork in local galleries and

at art shows. Whenever (2) _____ , he puts at least

half of his earnings in his savings account. The rest goes to pay for supplies

that (3) _____ . The most recent drawing

(4) _____ . He says he will never sell it because

(5) _____ . (6) People always seem to

like what (7) _____ . I sometimes move around and listen to

their comments. I also like to watch Matt at work. He says he draws whatever

(8) _____ . But he always uses bright colors that

(9) _____ . (10) _____ that Matt's artwork is
never dull.

Exercise E2-38

Write five independent clauses. Then add at least one dependent clause to each independent clause.

COLLABORATIVE WORK

After you revise your recalling essay, exchange papers with a classmate, and do the following tasks:

A.   Search for words that are used incorrectly, and circle them.

B.   Read the essay again, underlining any problem phrases.

C.   Read the essay once more, finding dependent clauses and making sure they are connected to independent clauses. Put an X in the margin where you find a problem with a dependent clause.

Then return the paper to its writer, and use the information in this section to edit your draft.

TIPS FOR EDITING

CHAPTER THREE

Observing

Reading and Writing for a Reason

When you show, you get out of the readers' way and let them come right at the experience itself.

—DONALD MURRAY

How aware are you of what is happening around you right now? Your answer depends on how careful an observer you are. Your ability to observe is not limited to what you can see, however. **Observing** means receiving impressions on many levels and involves all the senses: seeing, hearing, touching, smelling, and even tasting. Your senses help you gather the material you will need—facts, details, descriptions, and impressions—to write a clear, accurate, and convincing account of an event or person in your environment.

When you write an observation, however, simply recording literally what you see isn't enough. You must use your writing skills to help your readers see your observation *through your eyes*. You should give your readers enough information to let them share the impact of your experience—how it changed you or perhaps how it helped you discover something about yourself, about other people, about society, or even about the world.

Of course, it would be impossible for a writer to record every observation about a person, place, incident, or situation; the result would be nothing but an endless, boring list of every detail the writer saw, heard, smelled, tasted, or touched. As a writer, you need to focus on a single **dominant impression,** the one feeling, mood, or message you are trying to relay to your readers. You must decide what details to include or eliminate in order to avoid leaving your readers with a collection of confusing impressions that don't add up to a single theme or message.

Creating a dominant impression, however, is not the same as simply summarizing or passing judgment on the material you are observing. As the old writing strategy says, "Show, don't tell." Try to recreate the scene in words for your readers so that they can experience the event directly and draw their own conclusions.

In her memoir *Girl, Interrupted,* for example, Susanna Kaysen wants her readers to realize how unpleasant it was for her to be confined to a mental institution for two years of her life. She makes the following observation about one of the nurses:

Mrs. McWeeney was dry, tight, small, and pig-eyed. She had hard gray hair pressed into waves that grasped her scalp like a migraine. . . . She wore a creaky white uniform and spongy ripple-soled nurse shoes that she painted white every week; we could watch the paint cracking and peeling off between Monday and Friday. . . .

Mrs. McWeeney was unpredictable. She'd gnarl her face up for no reason while giving us our bedtime meds and slam back into the nursing station without a word. We'd have to wait for her to calm down before getting our nightly [medicine]; sometimes we waited for as long as half an hour.

This careful selection of descriptive details produces a much more effective observation than a flat summary statement like "Mrs. McWeeney was mean and ugly." Kaysen's details provide readers with enough information to draw this conclusion on their own. Letting your readers participate in the experience of your observation heightens their interest in the dominant impression you are trying to create.

LEARNING FROM PUBLISHED WRITERS

In the following published observation, the writer provides her readers with specific, vivid descriptions that enable us to observe for ourselves the scene and events she is describing. In this excerpt, taken from the novel *The Joy Luck Club* by Amy Tan, the young girl observes the new sights, sounds, smells, textures, and tastes that she encounters when she arrives at the home of her mother's new husband, where she and her mother will live. The home is far more splendid than anything she is used to, which becomes evident to the reader through the young girl's descriptions. This excerpt creates a memorable word picture of an exotic setting that few of Tan's readers have experienced firsthand.

Before You Read

Focusing Your Attention

Before you read this observation, take a few moments to respond to the following questions in your journal:

1. Think of a place you are very familiar with: your room, your home, your school, your place of employment, a garden, a restaurant. Then make a list of the sights, sounds, smells, textures, and tastes that come into your mind as you think of that place.

2. In the excerpt you are about to read, the young girl recounts the many sights, sounds, smells, textures, and tastes that she encountered when she first arrived at her new home. Think of a time when you entered a place for the first time. What sights, sounds, smells, textures, and tastes made the strongest impressions on you?

Expanding Your Vocabulary

Here are some words and their meanings that are important to your understanding of the essay. You might want to review them before you begin to read.

"this man . . . lived in a mansion located in the **British Concession** [areas where the British permitted Chinese to live] of Tientsin" (paragraph 1)

"the other **concubines** [women recognized as part of a man's household, who were expected to cater to his needs and to satisfy his sexual desires] who were called Second Wife and Third Wife" (paragraph 15)

"we cooked small eggs and sweet potatoes on top of the *houlu* [a small charcoal grill that could be used indoors]" (paragraph 18)

Amy Tan

Magpies*

I knew from the beginning our new home would not be an ordinary house. My mother had told me we would live in the household of Wu Tsing, who was a very rich merchant. She said this man owned many carpet factories and lived in a mansion located in the British Concession of Tientsin, the best section of the city where Chinese people could live. We lived not too far from Paima Di, Racehorse Street, where only Westerners could live. And we were also close to little shops that sold only one kind of thing: only tea, or only fabric, or only soap.

The house, she said, was foreign-built; Wu Tsing liked foreign things because foreigners had made him rich. And I concluded that was why my mother had to wear foreign-style clothes, in the manner of newly rich Chinese people who liked to display their wealth on the outside.

And even though I knew all this before I arrived, I was still amazed at what I saw.

The front of the house had a Chinese stone gate, rounded at the top, with big black lacquer doors and a threshold you had to step over. Within the gates I saw the courtyard, and I was surprised. There

1

2

3

4

*Amy Tan, *The Joy Luck Club* (pp. 250–255). New York: Random House, 1989.

were no willows or sweet-smelling cassia trees, no garden pavilions, no benches sitting by a pond, no tubs of fish. Instead, there were long rows of bushes on both sides of a wide brick walkway, and to each side of those bushes was a big lawn area with fountains. And as we walked down the walkway and got closer to the house, I saw this house had been built in the Western style. It was three stories high, of mortar and stone, with long metal balconies on each floor and chimneys at every corner.

When we arrived, a young servant woman ran out and greeted my **5** mother with cries of joy. She had a high scratchy voice: "Oh Taitai, you've already arrived! How can this be?" This was Yan Chang, my mother's personal maid, and she knew how to fuss over my mother just the right amount. She had called my mother Taitai, the simple honorable title of Wife, as if my mother were the first wife, the only wife.

Yan Chang called loudly to other servants to take our luggage, **6** called another servant to bring tea and draw a hot bath. And then she hastily explained that Second Wife had told everyone not to expect us for another week at least. "What a shame! No one to greet you! Second Wife, the others, gone to Peking to visit her relatives. Your daughter, so pretty, your same look. She's so shy, eh? First Wife, her daughters . . . gone on a pilgrimage to another Buddhist temple . . . Last week, a cousin's uncle, just a little crazy, came to visit, turned out not to be a cousin, not an uncle, who knows who he was. . . ."

As soon as we walked into that big house, I became lost with too **7** many things to see: a curved staircase that wound up and up, a ceiling with faces in every corner, then hallways twisting and turning into one room then another. To my right was a large room, larger than I had ever seen, and it was filled with stiff teakwood furniture: sofas and tables and chairs. And at the other end of this long, long room, I could see doors leading into more rooms, more furniture, then more doors. To my left was a darker room, another sitting room, this one filled with foreign furniture: dark green leather sofas, paintings with hunting dogs, armchairs, and mahogany desks. And as I glanced in these rooms I would see different people, and Yan Chang would explain: "This young lady, she is Second Wife's servant. That one, she is nobody, just the daughter of cook's helper. This man takes care of the garden."

And then we were walking up the staircase. We came to the top of **8** the stairs, and I found myself in another large sitting room. We walked to the left, down a hall, past one room, and then stepped into another. "This is your mother's room," Yan Chang told me proudly. "This is where you will sleep."

And the first thing I saw, the only thing I could see at first, was a **9** magnificent bed. It was heavy and light at the same time: soft rose silk and heavy, dark, shiny wood carved all around with dragons. Four posts held up a silk canopy, and at each post dangled large silk ties holding back curtains. The bed sat on four squat lion's paws, as if the weight of it had crushed the lion underneath. Yan Chang showed me how to use a small step stool to climb onto the bed. And when I tumbled onto the silk coverings, I laughed to discover a soft mattress that was ten times the thickness of my bed in Ningpo.

Sitting in this bed, I admired everything as if I were a princess. **10** This room had a glass door that led to a balcony. In front of the window door was a round table of the same wood as the bed. It too sat on carved lion's legs and was surrounded by four chairs. A servant had already put tea and sweet cakes on the table and was now lighting the *houlu*, a small stove for burning coal.

It was not that my uncle's house in Ningpo had been poor. He was **11** actually quite well-to-do. But this house in Tientsin was amazing. And I thought to myself, My uncle was wrong. There was no shame in my mother's marrying Wu Tsing.

While thinking this, I was startled by a sudden clang! clang! clang! **12** followed by music. On the wall opposite the bed was a big wooden clock with a forest and bears carved into it. The door on the clock had burst open, and a tiny room full of people was coming out. There was a bearded man in a pointed cap seated at a table. He was bending his head over and over again to drink soup, but his beard would dip in the bowl first and stop him. A girl in a white scarf and blue dress was standing next to the table, and she was bending over and over again to give the man more of this soup. And next to the man and girl was another girl with a skirt and short jacket. She was swinging her arm back and forth, playing violin music. She always played the same dark song. I can still hear it in my head after these many years—ni-ah! nah! nah! nah! nah-ni-nah!

This was a wonderful clock to see, but after I heard it that first **13** hour, then the next, and then always, this clock became an extravagant nuisance. I could not sleep for many nights. And later, I found I had an ability: to not listen to something meaningless calling to me.

I was so happy those first few nights, in this amusing house, **14** sleeping in the big soft bed with my mother. I would lie in this comfortable bed, thinking about my uncle's house in Ningpo, realizing how unhappy I had been, feeling sorry for my little brother. But most of my thoughts flew to all the new things to see and do in this house.

I watched hot water pouring out of pipes not just in the kitchen   15
but also into washbasins and bathtubs on all three floors of the house. I saw chamber pots that flushed clean without servants having to empty them. I saw rooms as fancy as my mother's. Yan Chang explained which ones belonged to First Wife and the other concubines, who were called Second Wife and Third Wife. And some rooms belonged to no one. "They are for guests," said Yan Chang.

On the third floor were rooms for only the men servants, said Yan   16
Chang, and one of the rooms even had a door to a cabinet that was really a secret hiding place from sea pirates.

Thinking back, I find it hard to remember everything that was in   17
that house; too many good things all seem the same after a while. I tired of anything that was not a novelty. "Oh, this," I said when Yan Chang brought me the same sweet meats as the day before. "I've tasted this already."

My mother seemed to regain her pleasant nature. She put her   18
old clothes back on, long Chinese gowns and skirts now with white mourning bands sewn at the bottoms. During the day, she pointed to strange and funny things, naming them for me: bidet, Brownie camera, salad fork, napkin. In the evening, when there was nothing to do, we talked about the servants: who was clever, who was diligent, who was loyal. We gossiped as we cooked small eggs and sweet potatoes on top of the *houlu* just to enjoy their smell. And at night, my mother would again tell me stories as I lay in her arms falling asleep.

If I look upon my whole life, I cannot think of another time when   19
I felt more comfortable: when I had no worries, fears, or desires, when my life seemed as soft and lovely as lying inside a cocoon of rose silk.

 ## QUESTIONS FOR CRITICAL THINKING

THINKING CRITICALLY ABOUT CONTENT

1. What are some of the most vivid descriptive words Amy Tan uses to help the reader "see" the new house?

2. What effect does the phrase "as if the weight of it had crushed the lion underneath" (paragraph 9) have on you?

THINKING CRITICALLY ABOUT PURPOSE

3. Why do you think the main character says, "Thinking back, I find it hard to remember everything that was in that house; too many good things all seem the same after a while" (paragraph 17)?

4. Why do you think Amy Tan described the sound the big wooden clock made (paragraph 12)? How does this description help her readers understand the dominant impression she is trying to communicate?

THINKING CRITICALLY ABOUT AUDIENCE

5. Do you think that readers who have never been to China can appreciate and enjoy this observation? Explain your answer.

6. What specific observations are most interesting to you? Why? In what ways do these observations help you imagine the scene as fully as possible?

THINKING CRITICALLY ABOUT POINT OF VIEW

7. Describe in one or more complete sentences the main character's point of view.

8. Write a paragraph explaining how the observation would be different if the writer's main character had been accustomed to great wealth and luxury when she first arrived at the house.

LEARNING FROM YOUR PEERS

In Chapter 2, we saw how details help us recall specific events and the feelings associated with them. Observing can also make us more aware of the day-to-day elements of the world around us. By looking intently at commonplace objects or people in our everyday lives, we may begin to identify patterns that we did not previously see. In response to the following assignment, we are going to follow the writing process of a student named Nathalie Johnson.

Nathalie's Writing Assignment: Observing

This is the topic Nathalie's instructor assigned:

What personality characteristics are required to perform well in a specific job? A worker in a fast-food restaurant needs to be dependable and friendly; a salesperson in a bookstore should have a variety of interests and knowledge of popular authors; a roofer should be nimble, strong, and unafraid of heights. Think of two people you know who have the same job but different personalities. They may work in the convenience store where you pick up your morning newspaper, or they may be ministers at your church, clerks at your local dry cleaner, or co-workers at your job. (The two people must have the same job but do not have to work at the same place.) Write an observing essay contrasting your impressions of their personalities.

Nathalie goes through the writing process as outlined in Chapter 1: *thinking, planning, developing, organizing, drafting, revising,* and *editing.*

Thinking

After class, Nathalie goes home and tries to think of people she comes into contact with frequently. She draws a map of the routes she normally takes to school and work. She thinks about the people who work at each place. Nathalie usually starts her day by going to the drive-up window at the fast-food restaurant near her house; she thinks about the restaurant workers. After eating breakfast during her drive to campus, she usually goes to the college library to study for two or three hours before her classes; she thinks about the reference librarians in the library. She decides that she does not know any of these people well enough to make judgments about their personalities. She lists other people she knows well, but she doesn't know how they behave at work. Then she makes a list of her instructors. Some are really interesting, and some, she thinks, are very strange! She decides to think about ways to describe her instructors.

Planning

Nathalie decides to make a comparison list, so she divides her paper into two columns. At the tops of the columns, she writes the names of two instructors who seem different to her in many ways. Under each person's name, she lists some of their characteristics, skipping several lines in each column. Her list looks something like this:

Physics Instructor	Art Instructor
Scruffy	Fashionable
Organized, prepares for tests	Spontaneous
All business, lectures	Friendly, likes to joke around
Impersonal, doesn't seem to care	Nice person, gives good advice
Does care, though	Students take advantage of her--or think they do.

Developing

Nathalie decides that she has enough ideas to develop an essay from her comparison list, so she spends some time adding information to the list and then freewriting about each point. Then she takes the freewriting to the members of her writing group, some of whom have the same instructors, and asks them about adding details to her descriptions. They tell her to work on the visual details because they are the most obvious differences between the two, but they also tell her that she has made some good observations about the way the two instructors behave around students. They decide that one way of behaving is not necessarily better than the other; both people are able to teach their students about their areas of expertise.

After considering her classmates' reactions, Nathalie develops her list more fully:

Art Instructor

Blond, pale, hair like dandelion fluff

Friendly--smiles--invites you into her classroom

Trendy dresser--except for her hippie sandals

Flowery skirts and wild jackets--unlikely combinations

Artistic jewelry--either she makes it or other artists do

Doesn't seem like she has a system in the classroom, but she does--

method in her madness

Physics Instructor

Looks like his clothes came from the Great Depression--threadbare

Wears suspenders! And his pants are already too short

Eyeglasses are always broken--he sits on them all the time

Seems gruff, but really cares about students

Systematic in the classroom--takes attendance, etc.

Organizing

Nathalie takes her notes to the library and maps out the main points that she wants to make about each instructor, paragraph by paragraph. Her notes are based on her comparison list, but now they are more detailed, and she has added some visual details based on her group's suggestions. She also decides to use pseudonyms for her instructors, even though she knows that she cannot disguise their identities completely.

This is what Nathalie's notes look like after she expands her comparison list into paragraphs:

My physics teacher wears suits that are almost threadbare.

His collars are frayed. His pants are too short. His clothes never

match. His glasses are always broken because he is the true

absent-minded professor and sits on them. His head looks like he shaves all over with an electric razor. He is very formal in class. He always takes attendance.

My art instructor wears clothes that are fun to look at. She wears flowery skirts and jackets with animal patches on them. Her shoes are hippie sandals right out of the 1960s. Her clothes are colorful and fun. Her hair is pale, like a dandelion gone to seed. Her eyes are blue and her skin is almost white. She is friendly to students and calls them by their first names (unlike Mr. Physics--he calls everyone "Mr. This" and "Miss That.")

Students sometimes think that my art teacher is an easy teacher because she is so friendly. She makes people work for their grades. Most students do their work, but some think they can get away without doing any work.

Mr. Physics is very traditional and structured in his approach to students. Everything goes by the book. He is organized and students know what to expect. So a person should not be judged on appearance. You can't judge a book by its cover, etc.

Drafting

Once the paragraphs are planned, Nathalie surrounds herself with the comparison lists and freewriting that she has completed, and she starts drafting her essay. She concentrates on describing each instructor as clearly as possible, using figures of speech and descriptive language whenever she can. Here is the draft of the essay that she wrote.

Nathalie's Essay: First Draft

Main Idea: Teachers can control the attitudes of their students by the clothes they wear.

Two of my instructors show that it is possible to change the attitudes of students just by wearing different types of clothing. Mr. Traditional is my physics instructor. He is a very good teacher, but when you first meet him, it is hard not to stare at his clothing all the time. Ms. Trendy, my art instructor, is also fun to stare at, but for different reasons. We may not like it, but we are always judged by our appearance.

Mr. Traditional is no exception. Some people might call him a geek. He wears outdated, almost threadbare suits. There are small holes at the elbows of his coats. He is a bachelor and probably has not gone shopping for clothing in ten years. His collars are frayed. His pants and his coat sleeves are too short. His wide, dark-striped ties never match his suits. Splattered on his ties are usually spots of ink. He wears suspenders that make his pants even shorter, and he always wears black socks that bunch up around his ankles. To add to his traditional look, he wears glasses that are so thick his eyes seem to bug out. The frames usually have tape on them because he has a habit of sitting on them. He has his hair cut so short that he looks bald. Mr. Traditional is also very traditional in his behavior. He calls his students "Mr. Gomez," "Miss Partridge," and so on. He stands rigidly at a podium and takes attendance at the beginning of every class. He counts students absent if they are not there on time. He also lectures to the class. Never does he have conversations. I am not sure if he has conversations with anyone. Most people would label him odd, to say the least.

Ms. Trendy, my art instructor, is just the opposite. If we come to class late, she just smiles and motions to us to get to work. She is always wearing something interesting to look at. There are many things to admire about her wardrobe. She looks like she spends half an hour every morning deciding what to wear. She has flowery skirts and jackets that have huge animal patches on them. Sometimes she will wear the most unlikely combinations. The only thing she should work on is her shoes. She wears them for comfort, but they never quite go with everything else that she is wearing. After all, can anyone be perfect? Her wispy, almost white hair looks like a dandelion in full seed. Her eyes are pale blue, and her skin is so pale you can see blue veins in her face. Most people would call her pretty. When she talks to students, she calls them by their first names, and she smiles a lot. She says that we are welcome to call her by her first name, but no one does.

When students first meet Ms. Trendy, they think she is an easy teacher because she is so friendly. But it is easy to mistake friendliness for not caring. She does care about every student's work, and she encourages all the students to work as hard as they can. Most students do, because they want to make her happy, but some students think they do not have to do anything because she will just smile at them. They are usually disappointed when they realize they are way behind in their work. But she gives us plenty of help outside class.

Mr. Traditional, however, cares more about the students than most students think he does. He helps them get ready for tests. He tells them what to study, and he always remembers what he talked about at the last class meeting. Students know that he will probably not be their best friend; however, they will learn from him.

A person should not be judged only on appearance. Sometimes a friendly person dresses like a dusty old couch at your grandmother's house. Sometimes the prettiest teacher can be the meanest one. It is best to go to class and listen and learn, regardless of the instructor's appearance.

Revising

Nathalie has carefully completed a draft of her essay about two people she has observed at their jobs. When she goes to class the next day, she finds that the instructor wants the students to continue their work with paragraphs and believes they are ready to look at how topic sentences work. If a topic sentence contains the main idea for a paragraph and is placed properly, all the material in the paragraph will communicate much more effectively to the readers.

First, Nathalie reviews the Checklist for Composing Topic Sentences at the beginning of the Tips for Revising section in this chapter. Then she reads all of the Tips for Revising and does the exercises her instructor assigns. Nathalie realizes that the topic sentence is an important part of every paragraph in the body of her essay, so she sets out to make sure that each of her paragraphs has one.

Returning to her essay, Nathalie looks closely at her paragraphs sentence by sentence, identifying topic sentences and checking their placement in the paragraph. She finds that some of her body paragraphs (paragraphs between the introduction and conclusion) are missing topic sentences and others have topic sentences buried in the middle. She begins to correct these problems paragraph by paragraph.

COLLABORATIVE WORK

PEER GROUP ACTIVITY

After you read the portions of the Tips for Revising your instructor assigns, turn to Nathalie's first draft (pp. 75–77), and complete the following tasks in small groups:

A. Put a caret (∧) in front of any paragraph that does not contain a topic sentence (for a definition, see p. 85).

B. Underline any topic sentences that do not appear as the first or last sentence in their paragraphs.

Compare the marks your group recorded with those your instructor will show you. Where do your marks differ from your instructor's? What do you need to review before writing your own essay?

CLASS ACTIVITY

As an entire class, look at the underlined portions of Nathalie's revised draft (pp. 80–82) to see how she changed each sentence.

A. Did you identify the **revision** problems that Nathalie corrected?

B. Do you think her changes are good ones? Discuss her changes.

Editing

Now that the body paragraphs in Nathalie's essay contain topic sentences, she needs to do some final editing and proofreading before handing in her essay. During class, the instructor explains that at this point all the students in the class should have the same working knowledge of basic sentence structure so they will have complete control over their sentences. So Nathalie reads this chapter's Tips for Editing, and she goes over the questions on the Checklist for Editing Sentences one by one to make sure she understands them. After doing the editing exercises her instructor assigns, she notices that she has a combination of sentence problems in her first draft. First, she needs to make sure that all of her sentences have subjects and predicates. Moreover, her writing gets monotonous at points. Now she knows why. In some cases, she needs to vary her sentence patterns. In others, the basic structure of her sentences should be altered. She sets out to fix each of the problems she detects.

 ## COLLABORATIVE WORK

PEER GROUP ACTIVITY

After you read the portions of the Tips for Editing that your instructor assigns, turn to Nathalie's first draft (pp. 75–77), and complete the following tasks in small groups:

A. Label every subject and every predicate (for definitions, see pp. 93–97).

B. Label each clause (or subject-verb set) as *independent* if it can stand alone or as *dependent* if it is introduced by a subordinating conjunction or relative pronoun. (For definitions, see pp. 62–64.)

C. Circle any dependent clauses that are not attached to an independent clause.

D. Put brackets around any sentences that contain multiple independent clauses that are not connected by a coordinating conjunction.

Compare the marks your group has recorded with those your instructor will show you. Where do your marks differ from your instructor's? What do you need to review before writing your own essay?

CLASS ACTIVITY

As an entire class, look at the underlined portions of Nathalie's revised draft (pp. 80–82) to see how she changed each sentence.

A. Did you identify the **editing** problems that Nathalie corrected?

B. Do you think her changes are good ones? Discuss her changes.

Nathalie's Revised Essay

Mr. Traditional and Ms. Trendy: Fashion's Influence on the College Classroom

Two of my instructors show that it is possible to change the attitudes of students just by wearing different types of clothing. Mr. Traditional is my physics instructor. He is a very good teacher, but when you first meet him, it is hard not to stare at his clothing all the time. Ms. Trendy, my art instructor, is also fun to stare at, but for different reasons. We may not like it, but we are always judged by our appearance.

~~Mr. Traditional is no exception.~~ Mr. Traditional's clothes might lead some people to label him as old-fashioned. ~~Some people might call him a geek~~. He wears outdated, almost threadbare suits. There are small holes at the elbows of his coats. He is a bachelor and probably has not gone shopping for clothing in ten years. His collars are frayed. His pants and his coat sleeves are too short. His wide, dark-striped ties never match his suits. Splattered on his ties are usually spots of ink. He wears suspenders that make his pants even shorter, and he always wears black socks that bunch up around his ankles. To add to his traditional look, he wears glasses that are so thick his eyes seem to bug out. The frames usually have tape on them because he has a habit of sitting on them. He has his hair cut so short that he looks bald.

Mr. Traditional is also very traditional in his behavior. He calls his students "Mr. Gomez," "Miss Partridge," and so on. He ~~stands rigidly at a podium and~~ takes attendance at the beginning of every class/, and h~~He~~ counts students absent if they are not there on time. He also lectures to the class. Never does he have conversations. ~~I am not sure if he has conversations with anyone. Most people would label him odd, to say the least.~~

Ms. Trendy, my art instructor, is just the opposite of Mr.

Traditional in appearance. ~~If we come to class late, she just smiles and~~ ~~motions to us to get to work.~~ She is always wearing something interesting to look at. There are many things to admire about her wardrobe. She looks like she spends half an hour every morning deciding what to wear. She makes some of her own jewelry and buys some from other artists. She has flowery skirts and jackets that have huge animal patches on them. Sometimes she will wear the most unlikely combinations. The only thing she should work on is her shoes. She wears them for comfort, but they never quite go with everything else that she is wearing. After all, can anyone be perfect? Her wispy, almost white hair looks like a dandelion in full seed. Her eyes are pale blue, and her skin is so pale you can see blue veins in her face. Most people would call her pretty. ~~When she talks to~~ ~~students, she calls them by their first names, and she smiles a lot.~~ ~~She~~ ~~says that we are welcome to call her by her first name, but no one~~ ~~does.~~

Ms. Trendy's behavior toward students matches her colorful, informal wardrobe. If we come to class late, she just smiles and motions us to get to work. When she talks to students, she calls them by their first names, and she smiles a lot. She says that we are welcome to call her by her first name, but no one does.

When students first meet Ms. Trendy, they think she is an easy teacher because she is so friendly. But it is easy to mistake friendliness for not caring. She does care about every student's work, and she encourages all the students to work as hard as they can. Most students do, because they want to make her happy, but some students think they do not have to do anything because she will just smile at them. They are usually disappointed when they realize they are way behind in their work. But she gives us plenty of help outside class.

Mr. Traditional, however, cares more about the students than most students think he does. He helps them get ready for tests. He tells them what to study, and he always remembers what he talked about at the last class meeting. Students know that he will probably not be their best friend; however, they will learn from him.

A person should not be judged only on appearance. Sometimes a friendly person dresses like a dusty old couch at your grandmother's house. Sometimes the prettiest teacher can be the meanest one. It is best to go to class and listen and learn, regardless of the instructor's appearance.

WRITING YOUR OWN OBSERVING ESSAY

So far, you have seen a professional writer and a fellow student at work trying to explain an observation or experience they feel is worth talking about. As you read the published essay and then followed the writing process of another student from first to final draft, you absorbed ideas to work with and ways of giving those ideas a form of their own. These reading and writing activities have prepared you to write your own essay focusing on an observation that is meaningful to you.

What Have you Discovered?

Before you begin your own writing task, let's review what you have learned in this chapter so far:

- Observing involves all the senses: seeing, hearing, touching, smelling, and tasting.

- Good observing demands that you use your writing skills to help your reader see through your eyes.

- Good observing *shows* rather than *tells* readers what you have seen or experienced.

- Good observing not only shows what you saw but also expresses the impact it had on you.

- You should focus your observing essay on a dominant impression you want to communicate.

- To present your observation effectively, you need to organize your ideas.

- To help you shape your essay, you should learn as much as possible about your readers.

- Before you write a draft, you need to decide on a point of view toward your subject.

- After you write a draft, you should revise your essay for meaning and organization.

- After you revise your essay, you should edit its grammar, usage, and sentence structure.

Your Writing Topic

Choose one of the following topics for your observing essay.

1. In the excerpt from *The Joy Luck Club,* Amy Tan drew on impressions from all the senses to show how her young main character observed her new home: She saw the magnificent bed; she heard the sudden clang and the music of the big wooden clock; she remembered the feel of the big bed with its soft mattress and silk coverings; she smelled (and tasted) the small eggs and sweet potatoes roasting on the indoor grill. Think of a place that is very important to you, a place that is a part of your life now or that was a part of your life in the past. Write an essay about that place, drawing on as many of the senses as possible—seeing, hearing, smelling, touching, and even tasting—so that your reader can experience that place the way you did.

2. Over your lifetime, you have observed how people approach and solve problems. Think of two people close to you who are dealing with a similar problem in completely different ways. To learn as much as you can from this experience, record your observations about these two people in a letter to a friend.

3. You have been asked to write an article for your school newspaper on student attitudes toward study habits, class participation, and attendance. Interview different types of people about these issues. Make sure you get a good sampling of students' ages, class levels, backgrounds, and reasons for coming to college. Write up your discoveries for your school newspaper.

4. Create your own observing assignment (with the assistance of your instructor), and write a response to it.

When you have selected one of these topics, you should begin your writing process in the same way Nathalie did. (You may want to review the discussion of her writing process.) This time your purpose is to write your own observing essay. If some tasks occur out of order, that adjustment is probably part of your personal writing ritual. Follow your instincts, and let them mold your own writing process. But make sure you've worked through all the stages to your final draft.

YOUR WRITING PROCESS

THINKING   Generate as many ideas on your subject as you can in as many different ways as possible: rereading, listing, freewriting, brainstorming, clustering, discussing, and questioning.

PLANNING   Begin to give your ideas shape by deciding on your approach to your topic (your content, your purpose, your audience, and your point of view). Make a list of points you want to include in your essay.

DEVELOPING   Add more details on three or four specific, focused topics that you have chosen from your list of general points.

ORGANIZING   Organize your material in a way that will be most interesting to your audience.

DRAFTING   Write a working draft of your essay in complete sentences.

REVISING   Consulting the Tips for Revising in this chapter (pp. 85–92), revise your first draft—paying special attention to your topic sentences.

EDITING   Consulting the Tips for Editing in this chapter (pp. 93–110), edit your draft for grammar and correctness—paying special attention to your basic sentence structure.

Turn in your revised draft to your instructor.

Some Final Thoughts

When you have completed your own essay, answer these four questions in your journal:

1. What was most difficult about this assignment?
2. What was easiest?
3. What did I learn about observing by completing this assignment?
4. What did I learn about my own writing process from this assignment—how I prepared to write, how I wrote the first draft, how I revised, and how I edited?

Composing Topic Sentences

Checklist for Composing Topic Sentences

✓ Does each paragraph have a **topic sentence?**
✓ Does each topic sentence explain the **main idea** of its paragraph?
✓ Is each topic sentence the **first or last sentence** in its paragraph?
✓ Is each topic sentence **clear, focused, and specific?**

In school clubs, business firms, and the military, people are organized in a chain of command to conduct the group's daily activities as well as to determine its procedures and goals. The president of a corporation, for instance, sets its overall goals; the other officers plan specific projects and assign the detail work to specific workers. In a similar way, the title of an essay generally states its overall subject, the thesis statement (usually in the first paragraph) provides the controlling idea that shapes and directs the entire essay, and topic sentences introduce the controlling idea for each body paragraph. Topic sentences, like the middle managers of a business, give shape and direction to the middle paragraphs of an essay. The supporting sentences of each paragraph are the workers that take care of specific tasks.

As you may remember from the section on revising in the previous chapter, essays usually include three different types of paragraphs: an introductory paragraph, most often the first one; a conclusion, typically the last paragraph; and body paragraphs, those that fall between the introduction and the conclusion. In this section, we are concerned mostly with body paragraphs and their topic sentences.

Clear Topic Sentences

A **topic sentence** should clearly express the main idea in its paragraph. A topic sentence should usually be the first or last sentence in a body paragraph, and it should set out the idea that the rest of the paragraph develops. Unlike a title—which can be a single word, phrase, or clause—a topic sentence, like all the sentences in an essay, should be complete: It should have a subject, a predicate, and a complete thought. For example, the title of Amy Tan's well-known novel about Chinese mothers and daughters is *The Joy Luck Club*, while the controlling idea of each paragraph in the excerpt included in this chapter is stated in a clear, complete sentence.

Look at paragraph 7 as an example. The topic sentence makes a statement about all the new things to see in the new house. The rest of the paragraph describes details of the grand house the girl and her mother have just entered for the first time.

As soon as we walked into that big house, I became lost with too many things to see: a curved staircase that wound up and up, a ceiling

85

with faces in every corner, then hallways twisting and turning into one room then another. To my right was a large room, larger than I had ever seen, and it was filled with stiff teakwood furniture: sofas and tables and chairs. And at the other end of this long, long room, I could see doors leading into more rooms, more furniture, then more doors. To my left was a darker room, another sitting room, this one filled with foreign furniture: dark green leather sofas, paintings with hunting dogs, armchairs, and mahogany desks. And as I glanced in these rooms I would see different people, and Yan Chang would explain: "This young lady, she is Second Wife's servant. That one, she is nobody, just the daughter of cook's helper. This man takes care of the garden."

This rich description is held together by the controlling idea presented in the first sentence, which is the topic sentence for the whole paragraph.

As Nathalie Johnson revised her observing essay, she decided that the topic sentence for paragraph 2 did not clearly state the controlling idea for the paragraph—a description of Mr. Traditional's wardrobe.

First Draft: Mr. Traditional is no exception.

Revision: Mr. Traditional's clothes might lead some people to label him as old-fashioned.

In this revision, the topic sentence specifically states Nathalie's impression of Mr. Traditional's wardrobe. Notice how the revised topic sentence focuses the readers' attention.

~~Mr. Traditional is no exception.~~ **Mr. Traditional's clothes might lead some people to label him as old-fashioned.** ~~Some people might call him a geek.~~ He wears outdated, almost threadbare suits. There are small holes at the elbows of his coats. He is a bachelor and probably has not gone shopping for clothing in ten years. His collars are frayed. His pants and his coat sleeves are too short. His wide, dark-striped ties never match his suits. Splattered on his ties are usually spots of ink. He wears suspenders that make his pants even shorter, and he always wears black socks that bunch up around his ankles. To add to his traditional look, he wears glasses that are so thick his eyes seem to bug out. The frames usually have tape on them because he has a habit of sitting on them. He

has his hair cut so short that he looks bald.

The new topic sentence introduces the content of the paragraph much more clearly than the original sentence did.

Exercise R3-1

State the controlling idea for paragraph 8 of the excerpt from Amy Tan's The Joy Luck Club *(pp. 69–70).*

Exercise R3-2

Read paragraph 3 of Nathalie's first draft (pp. 76–77), and compose a clear topic sentence for it.

Exercise R3-3

Underline any of the following topic sentences that could be developed in one paragraph.

1. Children who watch television every day are exposed to the highest-pressure advertising in mass media.
2. I have tried several relaxing hobbies.
3. Bear Mountain University was the best choice for me.
4. Universities often have different areas of strength and weakness.
5. I learned one easy way to make friends.
6. Cats make better pets than dogs.
7. There are several ways to avoid being disappointed in love.
8. Lasting relationships are built on a foundation of mutual interests and mutual respect.
9. I will never forget the day I got my driver's license.
10. Dogs make better pets than cats.

Exercise R3-4

Compose a topic sentence for the following paragraph.

For example, we spent a great deal of time generating ideas about something or someone we had observed closely. Then, we chose the idea that we felt we could develop with a great many relevant details. After settling on a controlling idea for the essay, we planned the body of the paper.

Focused Topic Sentences

Remember the story of Goldilocks and the three bears? She was searching for porridge that was "just right." This principle can be applied to topic sentences. A topic sentence should state an idea that can be adequately developed in one paragraph. The topic sentence thus offers shape and direction to the details in the paragraph.

As Nathalie Johnson began revising her observing essay, using the Checklist for Composing Topic Sentences, she found that she had not limited the paragraph about her art teacher to a single controlling idea. As she read her paragraph on Ms. Trendy, she decided that two ideas were included—the instructor's appearance and her behavior.

First Draft: Ms. Trendy, my art instructor, is just the opposite. If we come to class late, she just smiles and motions to us to get to work. She is always wearing something interesting to look at. There are many things to admire about her wardrobe. She looks like she spends half an hour every morning deciding what to wear. She has flowery skirts and jackets that have huge animal patches on them. Sometimes she will wear the most unlikely combinations. The only thing she should work on is her shoes. She wears them for comfort, but they never quite go with everything else that she is wearing. After all, can anyone be perfect? Her wispy, almost white hair looks like a dandelion in full seed. Her eyes are pale blue, and her skin is so pale you can see blue veins in her face. Most people would call her pretty. When she talks to students, she calls them by their first names, and she smiles a lot. She says that we are welcome to call her by her first name, but no one does.

As Nathalie began revising this paragraph, she first deleted all the details about Ms. Trendy's behavior and saved them for the next paragraph. Then she composed a new topic sentence for her paragraph that gives it a clear sense of direction.

Revision: Ms. Trendy, my art instructor, is just the opposite **of Mr. Traditional in appearance.** ~~If we come to class late, she just smiles and motions to us to get to work.~~ She is always wearing something interesting to look at. There are many things to admire about her wardrobe. She looks like she spends half an hour every morning deciding what to wear. **She makes some of her own jewelry and buys some from other artists.** She has flowery skirts and jackets that have huge animal patches on them. Sometimes she will wear the most unlikely combinations. The only thing she should work on is her shoes. She wears them for comfort, but they never quite go with everything else she is wearing. After all, can anyone be perfect? Her wispy, almost white hair looks like a dandelion in full seed. Her eyes are pale blue, and her skin is so pale you can see blue veins in her face. Most people would call her pretty. ~~When she talks to students, she calls them by their first names, and she smiles a lot. She says that we are welcome to call her by her first name, but no one does.~~

With these revisions, the topic sentence is focused and the entire paragraph is more effective.

Exercise R3-5

State the controlling idea of paragraph 2 of the excerpt from Amy Tan's The Joy Luck Club *(p. 68).*

Exercise R3-6

Read paragraph 2 of Nathalie's first draft (p. 76). Decide where the paragraph should be divided, and compose topic sentences for each new paragraph.

Exercise R3-7

Write a topic sentence that would give shape and direction to a paragraph developing each of the subjects listed below.

1. The best feature of my college
2. The ideal spot to study
3. The most entertaining sport
4. The sport that is the best to participate in
5. The most misleading advertising claim
6. The cleverest ad on Super Sunday

T I P S   F O R   R E V I S I N G

7.   Choosing an outfit
8.   My favorite musicians
9.   My least favorite musicians
10.   A good book

Exercise R3-8

Write a topic sentence for the following paragraph to make the controlling idea as clear as possible.

At Glenville College, classes are small enough for your professors to know you personally, yet the college has enough students to offer a wide variety of courses. Because Glenville is in a rural setting, peace and quiet surround you; however, Jackson, a city of 200,000, is only a half-hour drive away. Glenville's students are motivated to achieve without feeling pressure to compete.

Specific Topic Sentences

The words in topic sentences should be chosen carefully so that the controlling idea is plain to the reader. The topic sentence in paragraph 12 of the excerpt from Amy Tan's book *The Joy Luck Club* is a good example: "On the wall opposite the bed was a big wooden clock with a forest and bears carved into it." Note that this is the second sentence in the paragraph, surrounded before and after by specific details.

> While thinking this, I was startled by a sudden clang! clang! clang! followed by music. **On the wall opposite the bed was a big wooden clock with a forest and bears carved into it.** The door on the clock had burst open, and a tiny room full of people was coming out. There was a bearded man in a pointed cap seated at a table. He was bending his head over and over again to drink soup, but his beard would dip in the bowl first and stop him. A girl in a white scarf and blue dress was standing next to the table, and she was bending over and over again to give the man more of this soup. And next to the man and girl was another girl with a skirt and short jacket. She was swinging her arm back and forth, playing violin music. She always played the same dark song. . . .

Without the clear statement in the second sentence referring to a clock, readers might easily believe they are reading about a bearded man and a real girl ladling soup, not the carved figures emerging from the clock when the hour strikes.

All words in a topic sentence should be as exact as possible. In revising the topic sentences in her essay. Nathalie realizes that her new paragraph on Ms. Trendy's behavior needs a topic sentence. Here are the sentences she cut from the previous paragraph.

TIPS FOR REVISING

New Paragraph:	If we come to class late, she just smiles and motions to us to get to work. When she talks to students, she calls them by their first names, and she smiles a lot. She says that we are welcome to call her by her first name, but no one does.
Revision:	**Ms. Trendy's behavior toward students matches her colorful, informal wardrobe.** If we come to class late, she just smiles and motions to us to get to work. When she talks to students, she calls them by their first names, and she smiles a lot. She says that we are welcome to call her by her first name, but no one does.

Now the controlling idea for Nathalie's paragraph on Ms. Trendy's behavior is clearly stated, and all the supporting sentences supply further information about this topic.

Exercise R3-9

Read paragraph 7 of "Magpies" (p. 69), and underline all the specific words in the topic sentence that contribute to the paragraph's main idea.

Exercise R3-10

Go back to paragraph 4 in Nathalie's first draft (p. 77), and add more specific words and details for her topic sentence.

Exercise R3-11

Rewrite the following sentences, using specific, descriptive words from your own experience so that your reader gets a better picture of your controlling idea for the paragraph that might follow.

1. My first pet was cute.
2. My favorite class seems to go quickly.
3. One of my friends seems very unusual.
4. Our neighbors are noisy.
5. I like to relax.

Exercise R3-12

Compose five topic sentences, using specific words and phrases for paragraphs that you might write to fulfill your observing assignment.

COLLABORATIVE WORK

After writing a draft of your own observing essay, exchange papers with a classmate, and do the following tasks:

A. Underline each topic sentence.

B. Put brackets around any topic sentences that do not make the controlling idea clear.

C. In the margin, suggest changes to make the topic sentences clearer and more meaningful.

Then return the paper to its writer, and use the information in this section to revise your draft.

Sentence Structure and Sentence Combining

Checklist for Editing Sentences

✓ Does each sentence have a **complete subject** and a **complete predicate?**
✓ Does each complete subject have a **simple subject?**
✓ Does each complete predicate have a **simple predicate?**
✓ Does your writing offer a variety of the following sentence patterns: **subject-verb, subject–verb–direct object, subject–verb–indirect object–direct object,** and **subject–verb–complement?**
✓ Do you vary your sentences with **introductory elements, inverted subjects and verbs,** and **expletives?**
✓ Does the writing offer a variety of sentence structures: **simple, compound, complex,** and **compound-complex?**

Writing is a building-block process. Writers use words to make phrases and clauses, which work together to provide the foundation for sentences. Then they put together the related sentences to form paragraphs that in turn make up an essay. The whole process sounds pretty simple, doesn't it? But writers—whether they are professionals or eager students—know that effort and energy goes into producing written work that communicates clearly and effectively.

Sentences convey complete thoughts, and good sentences provide the basis of a successful essay. Learning about sentences and their structure is definitely a cornerstone of good writing. Learning how to combine sentences so that your thoughts flow smoothly will make your writing even stronger. After working with the information in this part of Chapter 3, you will be a more confident writer because the writing you produce will rest on a more solid foundation.

Subjects

Every sentence must have a subject to be complete. The **subject** is a group of words—nouns and pronouns and their modifiers—that tells who or what is performing the action in the sentence or who or what exists in a state of being. The key word that identifies exactly who or what the sentence is about is called the **simple subject.** The subject plus all of the words that describe or relate to it is called the **complete subject.** If the subject has no modifiers, sometimes the complete subject and the simple subject are one and the same. As these examples from Nathalie's observing essay illustrate, the subject usually comes first in a sentence. (The simple subjects are in italics here.):

Subjects: *Mr. Traditional* is my physics instructor.

                  His *collars* are frayed.

T I P S F O R E D I T I N G

Ms. Trendy, **my art instructor,** is just the opposite.

His wide, dark-striped *ties* never match his suits.

To add to his traditional look, *he* wears glasses that are so thick his eyes seem to bug out.

Some sentences have more than one simple subject. When two or more words in the complete subject describe who or what the sentence is about, the sentence has a **compound subject.** Look at this sentence from paragraph 2 of Nathalie's essay:

His *pants* **and his coat** *sleeves* are too short.

The words *pants* and *sleeves* function as the simple subject, both words explaining what is short. The additional words in the complete subject further describe the subject, telling whose pants and sleeves and what kind of sleeves.

In some sentences, the complete subject appears after the verb, near the middle or end of the sentence. The words in these sentences are in **inverted order.** To isolate the complete and simple subjects, rearrange the sentence, putting the complete subject before the verb.

Inverted:	Splattered on his ties are usually *spots* **of ink.**
Rearranged:	*Spots* **of ink** are usually splattered on his ties.

Spots of ink is the complete subject, with the noun *spots* functioning as the subject.

Sometimes sentences begin with *It* or *There*—expressions that we call **expletives.** These have no grammatical function. They simply begin a sentence, forcing the complete subject to follow the verb. To help identify the subject and verb, eliminate the expletive and put the sentence in natural order.

Expletive:	There are **small** *holes* at the elbows of his coats.
Rearranged:	**Small** *holes* are at the elbows of his coats.

It often functions as a pronoun serving as the subject of a sentence. In addition, *there* can function as an adverb, telling where. So don't assume that *it* and *there* will always be expletives.

One final word about subjects: Sometimes a subject does not actually appear in its sentence but is understood, such as in commands and requests. The implied subject—the person spoken to—may be obvious to the reader, or the command may be addressed to whoever is reading the sentence. Often, the understood subject is simply *you*—meaning either someone specific or anyone in general. Of course, in these cases the complete subject and the simple subject are the same:

Nathalie, read over your essay once again. Pay close attention to punctuation and capitalization. (*You* read over your essay once again. *You,* meaning Nathalie, pay close attention.)

Pass me the salt. (*You*, someone specific, pass me the salt.)

Wear gloves before applying the dye to wet hair. (*You*, meaning anyone using the product, wear gloves.)

Subjects are easy to identify once you understand all of their special characteristics.

Exercise E3-1

Underline the complete subjects in all the sentences in paragraphs 2 through 4 of "Magpies" by Amy Tan (pp. 68–69). Then circle the simple subjects.

Exercise E3-2

Write out the complete subjects from each sentence in paragraph 3 of Nathalie's first draft observing essay (pp. 76–77). Then circle the simple subjects.

Exercise E3-3

Finish the following paragraph by supplying a complete subject in each blank. Then circle the simple subject in each case.

A few years ago (1) _____ traveled to a small town in southern Illinois that had been flooded. When they arrived at Alton,

(2) _____ saw a town literally swept off the map.

(3) _____ filled low-lying yards, and (4) _____ had even taken refuge in trees and atop sheds and houses.

(5) _____ had to use boats to get to their houses.

(6) _____ were completely destroyed. In the downtown area,

(7) _____ were salvaging what they could. Several feet of water had been siphoned from the buildings, but (8) _____ of mud remained in most businesses. Overall, however, (9) _____ were in good spirits as they pitched in and helped each other.

(10) _____ were particularly helpful as they came from miles around to put Alton, Illinois, back together again.

Exercise E3-4

Write 10 sentences of your own. Then underline the complete subject and circle the simple subject in each sentence.

Predicates

Just as every sentence must have a subject, each complete thought must also have a **predicate,** a word or group of words that tells what the subject does. The key word that reveals the subject's action or state of being is called the **simple predicate** or the **verb.** The **complete predicate** includes the verb plus any modifiers or additional words and phrases that furnish more information about the verb. The predicate usually follows the subject. Look again at these examples from Nathalie's essay. The complete predicates are in boldface type with the verbs in boldface italics.

Predicate: Mr. Traditional *is* **my physics teacher.**

His collars *are* **frayed.**

Ms. Trendy, my art instructor, *is* **just the opposite.**

His wide, dark-striped ties **never** *match* **his suits.**

To add to his traditional look, he *wears* **glasses that are so**

thick his eyes seem to bug out.

In the first four examples, the complete predicate is found at the end of the sentence. In the last sentence, however, part of the complete predicate begins the sentence.

These additional examples from Nathalie's first draft illustrate other ways the complete predicate may be interrupted by the subject:

Interrupted   **When students first meet Ms. Trendy,** they *think* **she is**
Predicates:
an easy teacher because she is so friendly.

Never *does* he *have* **conversations.**

The order of these words gives variety and vitality to their sentences and makes reading them interesting.

Exercise E3-5

Underline the complete predicates and circle the verbs in all the sentences in paragraphs 2 through 4 of Amy Tan's "Magpies" (pp. 68–69).

Exercise E3-6

In Nathalie's first draft, underline the complete predicates and circle the verbs in each sentence in paragraph 3 (pp. 76–77).

Exercise E3-7

Fill in the blanks with words or phrases that will complete each predicate in the following paragraph.

My best friend, who is a very easy person to frighten, stayed

(1) _____ . We knew she would be by herself. So we decided

(2) _____ . First, we called (3) _____ .

After she said, "Hello," we hung up. Finally, after four calls, she

(4) _____ . Then we decided (5) _____ .

We could see her (6) _____ . Then we started

(7) _____ , which we knew she heard because she

started asking, "Who's there?" We didn't (8) _____ . Then

we decided that we had tortured her enough. So we yelled our names through

the open window. At first she was (9) _____ . But we vowed

(10) _____ .

Exercise E3-8

Write ten original sentences. Then underline the complete predicates and circle the verbs in your sentences.

Basic Sentence Patterns

Most sentences made up of only one clause follow one of four basic sentence patterns: Subject-Verb, Subject-Verb-Direct Object, Subject-Verb-Indirect Object-Direct Object, and Subject-Verb-Complement.

Subject-Verb (S-V)

The simplest pattern consists of only two elements, a subject followed by a verb.

	S	V
S-V:	Nathalie	left.

Often, adding words and phrases does not affect the subject-verb sentence pattern.

	S	V
S-V:	Nathalie	left yesterday.

	S	V
S-V:	Nathalie	left today for Nashville, hoping to find a new job.

Subject–Verb–Direct Object (S-V-DO)

Some sentences rely on words called **direct objects** to complete the action of their verbs (see p. 38). The following subject-verb combination, for example, does not make sense by itself: *He wears*. This sentence requires at least one more word, a direct object, that will identify what he wears: *He wears outdated, almost threadbare suits*. In this sentence from Nathalie's essay, *suits* is the direct object, the word that completes the action of the verb, telling what *he* wears.

Simply asking the questions *Who?* or *What?* after the verb will help you determine whether a sentence has a direct object. Here is another sentence from Nathalie's essay:

	S	V		DO	
S-V-DO:	He has	his	**hair**	cut so short that he looks bald.	

He has *what?* He has *hair*, the direct object, the word that completes the action of the verb.

Subject–Verb–Indirect Object–Direct Object (S-V-IO-DO)

Some transitive verbs require an **indirect object.** This word or group of words helps complete the verb's action by revealing to whom or to what (or for whom or for what) something is done or given. The indirect object always appears before the direct object, as in the following example from Nathalie's essay:

	S	V	IO	DO	
S-V-IO-DO:	But she gives		*us*	**plenty**	of help outside class.

She is the subject; *gives* is the verb. What does she give? *Plenty of help*, the direct object. To whom does she give plenty of help? To *us*, the indirect object.

To identify indirect objects, simply insert the preposition *to* or *for* before the word you think is an indirect object, creating a prepositional phrase. Look for the following verbs, which often precede indirect objects: *ask, assign, award, do, give, leave, make, promise, send, throw.*

Subject-Verb-Complement (S-V-C)

A **complement** is a word that further identifies another word, supplying information that expands the sentence's meaning. Sentences can have one of two types of complements: object complements or subject complements.

Object complements always follow direct objects. Note these examples from Nathalie's first draft:

	S	V	DO	OC	
S-V-DO-OC:	Some people	might call	him	a **geek.**	

	S	V	DO	OC	
S-V-DO-OC:	Most people	would label	him	**odd,**	to say the least.

In both examples, the object complements expand upon or *complement* the direct object.

Subject complements are words that refer to the subject, describing and giving additional identifying information. Direct objects, indirect objects, and object complements follow transitive active verbs, but subject complements always follow linking verbs, state-of-being verbs that connect the complement to the subject. (For a definition and a list of linking verbs, see p. 38).

          s   **v**   **sc**

S-V-SC: Mr. Traditional is **my physics instructor.**

          s   **v**   **sc**

S-V-SC: Mr. Traditional is also **very traditional in his behavior.**

Both these examples show the placement and function of subject complements in a sentence.

Pattern Variations

In some instances, identifying the sentence's pattern may prove more difficult than our previous discussion may lead you to believe. Sometimes introductory words and phrases cloud your view. Other times, the word order is changed, and the sentence structure may be complicated and confusing. The following guidelines will help you handle sentences that stray from the five basic patterns.

Introductory Elements

Just as adding elements to the end of a sentence does not affect its basic pattern, adding introductory words, phrases, and clauses does not change the pattern either. In the following example from Nathalie's essay, note how the original sentence pattern remains unaffected by the additions:

   s   **v**   **sc**
Mr. Traditional is also very traditional in his behavior.

      s   **v**   **sc**
Honestly, Mr. Traditional is also very traditional in his behavior.

      s   **v**   **sc**
Most of the time Mr. Traditional is very traditional in his behavior.

      s   **v**   **sc**
Even on Halloween, Mr. Traditional is very traditional in his behavior.

Inverted Order

Sometimes introductory elements result in inverted sentence patterns, causing the subject to follow the verb. Look at these sentences in inverted order:

Inverted order:	There **sat** Nathalie's **keys,** right where she left them.

(V above "sat", S above "keys")

Inverted order:	On the table near the door **sat** Nathalie's **keys.**

(V above "sat", S above "keys")

Questions are simply statements that have been changed into questions. In a question, the verb is split by the subject, producing a V-S-V pattern. The helping verb precedes the subject, and the remainder of the verb follows the subject.

Question:	**Did Nathalie write** the first draft of her essay last night?

(V above "Did", S above "Nathalie", V above "write")

The helping verb *did* comes before the subject *Nathalie,* while the main verb *write* follows the subject. Putting the question in statement form produces an S-V pattern.

Statement:	**Nathalie did write** the first draft of her essay last night.

(S above "Nathalie", V above "did", V above "write")

Expletives

As discussed on page 94, some sentences begin with words we call expletives—*It* and *There*. Expletives function as sentence starters but do not serve as subjects. In sentences that begin with expletives, the subject comes after the verb.

Expletive:	*There* are many ways to improve your writing.

(V above "are", S above "ways")

Expletive:	*It* is a mystery to all of us.

(V above "is", S above "mystery")

Remember that *it* can function as a pronoun, as in this sentence: *It squirmed across the floor, making us recoil in horror.* In this sentence, *it* is doing the action, or the squirming, so *it* is a pronoun.

Exercise E3-9

Determine the pattern for the following clauses taken from "Magpies" by Amy Tan.

1. The front of the house had a Chinese stone gate.
2. This man takes care of the garden.

3. The house, she said, was foreign-built.
4. Yan Chang showed me how to use a small step stool to climb onto the bed.
5. This was a wonderful clock to see.

Exercise E3-10

Label each sentence in paragraphs 3 and 4 of Nathalie's first daft (pp. 76–77) according to the pattern it follows. Consider each of the five basic patterns, along with any variations.

Exercise E3-11

Complete the following paragraph by supplying words of the type indicated in parentheses.

(1) _____ (verb) you ever wanted to just disappear for a couple of days? My friend Dave did. First, he let his (2) _____ (direct object) in on the plan because he really wanted to get away from certain friends and school pressures. His (3) _____ (subject) okayed his (4) _____ (direct object) of camping out in a forest preserve about twenty-five miles from his house. But he had to fake everyone else out. Basically, he just told his (5) _____ (indirect object) (6) _____ (direct object). Sometimes he was just (7) _____ (subject complement), giving answers like "I don't know" when people asked him what he was doing for the weekend. Some of his friends got really (8) _____ (subject complement) with him. A couple even called (9) _____ (direct object) a (10) _____ (object complement). But he didn't (11) _____ (verb). He just called himself (12) _____ (object complement) because he was able to disappear without anyone finding him. There were so many (13) _____ (subject) that he thought about that weekend that all the trouble was worth it. (14) _____ (verb) Dave disappear again? He says he will, if life ever weighs him down and he needs some time to himself.

Exercise E3-12

Write original sentences or questions using the following sentence patterns.

1. V-S-V
2. S-V-SC
3. V-S
4. S-V-DO-OC
5. S-V-IO-DO

Sentence Structure

You may have noticed in working with the basic sentence patterns that some sentences have more than one subject-verb pair. Sometimes these subject-verb combinations appear in an **independent clause,** a collection of words that can stand alone as a sentence. On other occasions the subject-verb combination appears in a **dependent clause,** a group of words that cannot stand by itself as a complete thought.

One common way of categorizing sentences is by determining how many independent and dependent clauses they contain. These clauses can appear in combinations that produce four different kinds of sentence structures: (1) simple, (2) compound, (3) complex, and (4) compound-complex.

Simple Sentences

The simplest (and shortest) sentence is one that consists of one word: *Quit! Leave! Retreat!* The subject in each of these sentences is understood to be *you: (You) quit! (You) leave! (You) retreat!* Besides sharing the same subject, each of these simple sentences consists of one subject-verb combination that expresses a single thought.

The following simple sentences from Nathalie's essay are longer. Each sentence consists of a single independent clause, a group of words containing only one subject and one verb that work together to form a single idea.

Simple:	**s** **v** **Mr. Traditional is** my physics instructor.

              s   **v**   **v**
Some **people might call** him a geek.

           s   **v**
His **collars are** frayed.

                         s   **v**
His wide, dark-striped **ties** never **match** his suits.

Sometimes sentences have more than one subject or verb. As long as subjects and verbs work together as one unit or combination within one independent clause, the sentence is still classified as simple. Remember, even with a compound subject or verb, the simple sentence has one complete thought and nothing more.

$$\overset{S}{} \qquad \overset{S}{} \quad \overset{V}{}$$

Compound Subject: His **pants** and his coat **sleeves are** too short.

$$\overset{S}{} \quad \overset{V}{} \qquad\qquad \overset{V}{}$$

Compound Verb: **He stands** rigidly at a podium and **takes** attendance at the beginning of every class.

Exercise E3-13

Underline the simple sentences in paragraphs 8 and 12 of "Magpies" (pp. 69–70).

Exercise E3-14

Write out the simple sentences in paragraphs 3 and 4 of Nathalie's first draft (pp. 76–77).

Exercise E3-15

Fill in the blanks of the following paragraph with either a subject or a verb to make each simple sentence complete.

One of my favorite activities in the fall is our county fair. Usually,

(1) _____ and I go several times during the week. We

(2) _____ enough money for a couple of rides and

something to eat and drink. Sometimes we play the games of chance. Julie

(3) _____ dimes at milk bottles and (4) _____

a huge stuffed tiger. (5) _____ and (6) _____

like to throw darts at balloons. That (7) _____ a pretty easy

game to win. At least once we (8) _____ the animal exhibits.

The (9) _____ are my favorites. They look so harmless and

lovable. My cousin Carmen never (10) _____ the poultry

houses. She says it's because they smell, but I think it's because she's really scared of

birds. Anyway, we usually (11) _____ enough food to make us

want more. There are so many (12) _____ to see at the fair.

(13) _____ you like to go?

Exercise E3-16

Write ten original simple sentences.

Compound Sentences

When two independent clauses are combined using certain words and punctuation, a **compound sentence** results. Thus, a compound sentence has two subject-verb pairs in separate independent clauses. You might think of compound sentences as two simple sentences that join forces to make a longer, more interesting, more complicated sentence structure.

The easiest and most common way to combine independent clauses and produce a compound sentence is through **coordination**—the process of joining together two independent clauses. First, you need words that function as connectors, the **coordinating conjunctions** *for, and, nor, but, or, yet,* and *so.* Then, you need a comma before the conjunction. Look at this compound sentence from Nathalie's essay:

	Independent	Independent
	S V V	S V V
Coordinating Conjunction:	We may not like it, **but** we are always judged by our appearance.	

Here is another example:

	Independent	Independent
	S V	S V
Coordinating Conjunction:	He tells them what to study, **and** they always learn	

Another way to combine independent clauses and form a compound sentence is by using **conjunctive adverbs.** These special adverbs are similar to coordinating conjunctions in that both types of words perform connecting duties. However, conjunctive adverbs require different punctuation—usually a semicolon and one comma. Look at these sentences that contain conjunctive adverbs:

	Independent
	S V
Conjunctive Adverb:	Nathalie wanted to turn in her paper early; **however,**

	Independent
	S V V	V V V V
	she had to work late two nights and didn't get to finish it as planned.

Note that everything before *however* is an independent clause, as is everything after it. Also, the punctuation marks are in their correct places—a semicolon before *however* with a comma after. Here is another example that follows the same format:

	Independent	
	S V	S V
Conjunctive Adverb:	Nathalie missed an entire week of school; **consequently,** she got	
	Independent	
	behind in all her classes.	

Note that some of the common conjunctive adverbs in the following list consist of more than one word:

Common Conjunctive Adverbs		
accordingly	hence	nevertheless
also	henceforth	next
anyway	however	nonetheless
as a result	in addition	now
at the same time	incidentally	on the other hand
besides	in contrast	otherwise
certainly	ideed	similarly
consequently	in fact	still
conversely	instead	subsequently
finally	likewise	therefore
for example	meanwhile	thus
furthermore	moreover	

Exercise E3-17

Underline each compound sentence in paragraphs 8 through 12 of Amy Tan's "Magpies" (pp. 69–70), and label the words connecting the independent clauses as either coordinating conjunctions or conjunctive adverbs.

Exercise E3-18

Underline the compound sentence in paragraph 1 of Nathalie's first draft (pp. 75–76).

Exercise E3-19

Nathalie's essay contains several simple sentences that could be combined, thus producing compound sentences. Combine several pairs of sentences, making at least five new compound sentences.

Exercise E3-20

Write four compound sentences using coordinating conjunctions and four compound sentences using conjunctive adverbs.

TIPS FOR EDITING

Complex Sentences

So far, our discussion of sentence structure has mentioned only independent clauses. When dependent clauses appear, sentences become more complex in structure; hence the term *complex sentence*. A **complex sentence** consists of one independent clause and one or more dependent clauses. Complex sentences become easier to identify and compose when you understand the process of subordination.

To *subordinate* means to make something unequal or not as important as something else. In writing, **subordination** refers to the process of using subordinating words to show unequal relationships between two or more ideas. Basically, a writer starts out with two independent clauses and then makes one of the clauses dependent, adding a word at the beginning that makes it impossible for that clause to stand alone as a complete thought. Look at this example:

	S V	S V
Independent Clauses:	Nathalie revised her essay three times.	She earned a good grade.

Add the word *because* to subordinate the first independent clause.

	S V
Subordination:	Because Nathalie revised her essay three times. . . .

Add the new dependent clause to the remaining independent clause, producing a complex sentence.

	Dependent	Independent
	S V	S V
Complex Sentence:	Because Nathalie revised her essay three times, she earned a good grade.	

In the previous example, the word *because* is a **subordinating conjunction.** (For a complete list of subordinating conjunctions, see p. 54.) Writers use subordinating conjunctions to make dependent clauses that work logically with main or independent clauses. As you can see, subordinating conjunctions help writers express connections between ideas, explaining time, comparisons, contrasts, and cause/effect relationships.

Another type of subordinating word is a **relative pronoun.** As you learned in Chapter 2, there are only five relative pronouns: *that, which, who, whom,* and *whose.* These words help subordinate ideas that give additional identification and description.

	S V	S V
Independent Clauses:	Nathalie is the most studious girl in our glass.	She always finds time for social activities.

Use one of the relative pronouns and subordinate the first independent clause.

                                   S V

Subordination: **who** is the most studious girl in our class

Combine the new dependent clause with the remaining independent clause, making a complex sentence.

Dependent	Independent
S V	**V**

Complex Sentence: Nathalie, **who** is the most studious girl in our class, always finds time for social activities.

Notice that when you use relative pronouns to subordinate ideas and combine dependent and independent clauses, you may have to omit or move words. Nevertheless, the result is a complex sentence that is more interesting than two short simple sentences. Look at how subordination produces complex structures that flow with ease:

                       S   **V**   **S V**

Simple Sentences: Mr. Traditional is my physics instructor. He is a very good teacher.

Independent		Dependent	
S	**S V**		**V**

Complex Sentence: Mr. Traditional, **who is** my physics instructor, is a very good teacher.

                      S   **V**   **S**   **V**

Simple Sentences: Some people might call him a geek. He wears outdated, almost threadbare suits.

Dependent	
S **V**	

Complex Sentence: **Since he wears** outdated, almost threadbare suits,

Independent	
S **V** **V**	

some people might call him a geek.

Adding subordinating clauses to your writing is another good way to vary your sentence structure and make your sentences as accurate as possible.

Exercise E3-21

Underline each complex sentence in paragraphs 2 through 5 of Amy Tan's "Magpies" (pp. 68–69).

TIPS FOR EDITING

Exercise E3-22

Beginning with paragraph 3, underline the complex sentences in the first draft of Nathalie's observing essay (pp. 76–77).

Exercise E3-23

Combine the following pairs of sentences, producing complex sentences by subordinating one of the independent clauses.

1. Jay had a throbbing headache and a sore throat.
    Jay worked a regular shift.
2. We stripped the paper from the kitchen walls.
    We smoothed the walls with an electric sander.
3. Fernando starts work next week.
    He must buy black pants, a white shirt, and black shoes.
4. We must send in our order within two weeks.
    We may not get tickets for the season opener.
5. The Flying Zombies won the national band competition.
    The contest was held in Miami.

Exercise E3-24

Combine sentences from Nathalie's first draft essay (pp. 75–77), using subordinating conjunctions or relative pronouns to produce at least five new complex sentences.

Exercise E3-25

Write ten original complex sentences, making sure each sentence has at least one independent clause and at least one dependent clause that begins with a subordinating conjunction or a relative pronoun.

Compound-Complex Sentences

The final type of sentence is really a combination of two others. A **compound-complex sentence** contains two or more independent clauses and one or more dependent clauses. Quite often, these sentences are longer than their counterparts, simply because compound-complex sentences require three clauses at the very minimum. The clauses can appear in any order as long as the relationships between them are logical and clear.

Nathalie's first compound-complex sentence appears in paragraph 2.

Independent		Dependent		Independent
S V		S V		S

He wears suspenders that make his pants even shorter, and he always

	Dependent	
V	S V V	

wears black socks that bunch up around his ankles.

He wears suspenders is the first independent clause, followed by the dependent clause *that make his pants even shorter*. The second independent clause, *he always wears black socks*, is followed by the dependent clause *that bunch up around his ankles*. Thus, this sentence consists of two independent and two dependent clauses, fulfilling the criteria for a compound-complex sentence.

The following original sentences provide additional examples of how clauses can be arranged in a variety of ways to create compound-complex sentences:

Dependent	Independent	Independent
S V	S V	S V V

Before Nathalie went home, she stopped at the new bookstore, **but** she didn't buy anything.

Independent	Dependent	
S V	S V	

Nathalie often cooks dinner for her family **because** her mother works late, **and**

Independent
S   V   V

sometimes she will even manage to do the laundry.

Independent	Independent	Dependent
S V V	S V V	S V

Nathalie plans to attend college, **but** she wants to go to Purdue **if** she can get a scholarship.

All of these are compound-complex sentences with the minimum number of clauses (one dependent and two independent). But remember that this type of sentence can include more of both types of clauses.

Exercise E3-26

Underline the compound-complex sentences in Amy Tan's "Magpies" (pp. 68–71). Then label the independent and dependent clauses that make up each sentence.

Exercise E3-27

Underline the compound-complex sentences in paragraphs 3 through 6 of Nathalie's revised draft (pp. 80–82). Then label the independent and dependent clauses that make up each sentence.

Exercise E3-28

Add either an independent clause or a dependent clause in each blank to make compound-complex sentences.

1. Dante usually does whatever he wants; however, _____

2. _____ , Regina called her best friend, but Stephanie said she had never heard of the guy.

3. Doug, _____ , starts a new job tomorrow, and he plans to go shopping for a new car after he gets off work.

4. When the waiter brought the dessert tray, I chose a piece of cake _____ , but my date selected pie _____ .

5. If you want to lose weight, _____ , and _____ .

Exercise E3-29

Write ten original compound-complex sentences, making sure that each sentence has at least two independent clauses and at least one dependent clause.

 ## COLLABORATIVE WORK

After you revise your observing essay, exchange papers with a classmate, and do the following tasks:

A. Circle any sentences that do not have a subject.

B. Select one paragraph and label each sentence according to its pattern: S-V, S-V-DO, S-V-IO-DO, or S-V-C.

C. Choose another paragraph and label each sentence according to its structure: simple, compound, complex, or compound-complex.

Then return the paper to its writer, and use the information in this section to edit your draft.

Explaining
Reading and Writing for a Reason

When I began to write, I found it was the best way to make sense out of my life.

—JOHN CHEEVER

Imagine trying to get through even one day of your life without being able to say, "Just let me explain." When you are late for school, work, or an appointment, you need to explain why. When you don't do something you promised to do, you must explain. Often (but not always), explanations help others realize you had good reasons for being late or for other actions. You also use explaining for far more important reasons than simply giving an account of why you were late or unable to do something. You use explaining to help others understand clearly and completely what you know, think, and feel about matters that are important to you. You also use explaining to help others understand how something happened or how to perform a process.

Explaining is an essential part of all forms of communication. Whether we are interested in the latest news in the stock market or the fashion industry, we are always reading explanations of these trends. News reports speculate about events; textbooks explain the process of photosynthesis or fossil formation. The ability to explain through writing may be one of the most important skills we possess as human beings. Through explaining, we communicate and share ideals and values—we help others know, understand, and respect our ideas or feelings.

When Elie Wiesel won the Nobel Peace Prize in 1986, he wrote a speech in which he explained why he had spent his entire life as a human-rights activist and why, as a Holocaust survivor who lost his entire family in concentration camps, he works to locate and bring to justice those people who were responsible for the Holocaust. Wiesel stated that we cannot simply let injustice exist anywhere in the world; we must interfere. He then went on to explain in detail what he meant by "interfering"—taking immediate action to stop human suffering, no matter where it occurs.

When human lives are endangered, when human dignity is in jeopardy, national borders and sensitivities become irrelevant. Wherever men or women are persecuted because of their race, religion or political views, that place must—at that moment—become the center of the universe. . . .

What all these victims need above all is to know that they are not alone; that we are not forgetting them, that when their voices are stifled we shall lend them ours, that while their freedom depends on ours, the quality of our freedom depends on theirs.

In offering this explanation, Elie Wiesel helps us recognize and understand the importance of preventing injustice. Even though we may never be faced with the serious threats to dignity and freedom that he describes, Wiesel has shown us that we all have a role to play in ensuring the freedom of all human beings.

LEARNING FROM PUBLISHED WRITERS

The published writing that follows explains the effect that race had on one of America's tennis players, and in so doing gives us new insights into prejudice. It was written by Arthur Ashe, an African-American tennis star whose dignity and intelligence both on and off the tennis court won him worldwide respect. In 1992, the press reported that Ashe was HIV-positive and suffering from AIDS, even though the champion tennis player did not want the information to be made public, preferring to enjoy his last days with his family in privacy. Soon after his situation was announced, Arthur Ashe decided to write a book, *Days of Grace*, explaining his views about life in general, about being the first African-American tennis player to win several major tennis titles, about the effect of having the whole world know he had AIDS, and other related topics. He died in 1993, a few months before the book was published. In this passage, Arthur Ashe explains how the prejudice and racism that has existed (and still exists) in this country often cast a shadow over his life.

Before You Read

Focusing Your Attention

Before you read this explaining essay, take a few moments to respond to the following questions in your journal:

1. Have you or any of your friends or family ever experienced the "burden of race" that Ashe describes? How did it make you feel?

2. In the excerpt you are about to read, Arthur Ashe explains a time when he had to do something that was against what he believed in. Have you ever had to do something against your principles? What was it? Why did you have to do it? How did it make you feel?

Expanding Your Vocabulary

Here are some words and their meanings that are important to your understanding of the essay. You might want to review them before you begin to read.

"The reporter's questions had been **probing** [penetrating]" (paragraph 1)

"she was **groping** [struggling] for the right words" (paragraph 1)

"Race is for me a more **onerous** [unpleasant, hard to bear] burden than AIDS." (paragraph 8)

"other people have been **baffled** [confused] by it" (paragraph 9)

"Isn't AIDS **inevitably** [unavoidably] fatal?" (paragraph 9)

"I do not mean to appear **fatalistic** [believing that the worst will happen], **self-pitying** [feeling sorry for oneself], **cynical** [scornful], or **maudlin** [overly sentimental]." (paragraph 11)

"The shadow fell across me . . . **literally** [in actual fact] and **metaphorically** [symbolically, speaking figuratively]" (paragraph 13)

"What could **mar** [ruin] such a day?" (paragraph 14)

"my sensitivity, or perhaps **hypersensitivity** [extreme sensitivity], to its **nuances** [delicate shades of meaning or feeling]" (paragraph 14)

"I imagined insistent, **clamorous** [noisy] callers" (paragraph 14)

"I do not want Austin's gift to be **sullied** [ruined, made dirty]" (paragraph 19)

"She is **pensive** [thoughtful]" (paragraph 27)

"the slightest semblance of '**Eurocentric**' [viewing European culture as dominant] influence" (paragraph 30)

Arthur Ashe

The Burden of Race*

I had spent more than an hour talking in my office at home with a   1
reporter for *People* magazine. Her editor had sent her to do a story
about me and how I was coping with AIDS. The reporter's questions
had been probing and yet respectful of my right to privacy. Now, our

*Arthur Ashe and Arnold Rampersad, *Days of Grace: A Memoir* (pp. 126–131). New York: Knopf, 1993.

interview over, I was escorting her to the door. As she slipped on her coat, she fell silent. I could see that she was groping for the right words to express her sympathy for me before she left.

"Mr. Ashe, I guess this must be the heaviest burden you have ever had to bear, isn't it?" she asked finally.   **2**

I thought for a moment, but only a moment. "No, it isn't. It's a burden, all right. But AIDS isn't the heaviest burden I have had to bear."   **3**

"Is there something worse? Your heart attack?"   **4**

I didn't want to detain her, but I let the door close with both of us still inside. "You're not going to believe this," I said to her, "but being black is the greatest burden I've had to bear."   **5**

"You can't mean that."   **6**

"No question about it. Race has always been my biggest burden. Having to live as a minority in America. Even now it continues to feel like an extra weight tied around me."   **7**

I can still recall the surprise and perhaps even the hurt on her face. I may even have surprised myself, because I simply had never thought of comparing the two conditions before. However, I stand by my remark. Race is for me a more onerous burden than AIDS. My disease is the result of biological factors over which we, thus far, have had no control. Racism, however, is entirely made by people, and therefore it hurts and inconveniences infinitely more.   **8**

Since our interview (skillfully presented as a first-person account by me) appeared in *People* in June 1992, many people have commented on my remark. A radio station in Chicago aimed primarily at blacks conducted a lively debate on its merits on the air. Most African Americans have little trouble understanding and accepting my statement, but other people have been baffled by it. Even Donald Dell, my close friend of more than thirty years, was puzzled. In fact, he was so troubled that he telephoned me in the middle of the night from Hamburg, Germany, to ask if I had been misquoted. No, I told him, I had been quoted correctly. Some people have asked me flatly, what could *you*, Arthur Ashe, possibly have to complain about? Do you want more money or fame than you already have? Isn't AIDS inevitably fatal? What can be worse than death?   **9**

The novelist Henry James suggested somewhere that it is a complex fate being an American. I think it is a far more complex fate being an African American. I also sometimes think that this indeed may be one of those fates that are worse than death.   **10**

I do not want to be misunderstood. I do not mean to appear fatalis-   **11** tic, self-pitying, cynical, or maudlin. Proud to be an American, I am also proud to be an African American. I delight in the accomplishments of fellow citizens of my color. When one considers the odds against which we have labored, we have achieved much. I believe in life and hope and love, and I turn my back on death until I must face my end in all its finality. I am an optimist, not a pessimist. Still, a pall of sadness hangs over my life and the lives of almost all African Americans because of what we as a people have experienced historically in America, and what we as individuals experience each and every day. Whether one is a welfare recipient trapped in some blighted "housing project" in the inner city or a former Wimbledon champion who is easily recognized on the streets and whose home is a luxurious apartment in one of the wealthiest districts of Manhattan, the sadness is still there.

In some respects, I am a prisoner of the past. A long time ago, I   **12**
made peace with the state of Virginia and the South. While I, like other blacks, was once barred from free association with whites, I returned time and time again, under the new rule of desegregation, to work with whites in my hometown and across the South. But segregation had achieved by that time what it was intended to achieve: It left me a marked man, forever aware of a shadow of contempt that lays across my identity and my sense of self-esteem. Subtly the shadow falls on my reputation, the way I know I am perceived; the mere memory of it darkens my most sunny days. I believe that the same is true for almost every African American of the slightest sensitivity and intelligence. Again, I don't want to overstate the case. I think of myself, and others think of me, as supremely self-confident. I know objectively that it is almost impossible for someone to be as successful as I have been as an athlete and to lack self-assurance. Still, I also know that the shadow is always there; only death will free me, and blacks like me, from its pall.

The shadow fell across me recently on one of the brightest days,   **13**
literally and metaphorically, of my life. On August 30, 1992, the day before the U.S. Open, the USTA and I together hosted an afternoon of tennis at the National Tennis Center in Flushing Meadows, New York. The event was a benefit for the Arthur Ashe Foundation for the Defeat of AIDS. Before the start, I was nervous. Would the invited stars (McEnroe, Graf, Navratilova, et al.) show up? Would they cooperate with us, or be difficult to manage? And, on the eve of a Grand Slam tournament, would fans pay to see light-hearted tennis? The answers were all a resounding yes (just over ten thousand fans

turned out). With CBS televising the event live and Aetna having provided the air time, a profit was assured. The sun shone brightly, the humidity was mild, and the temperature hovered in the low 80s.

What could mar such a day? The shadow of race, and my sensitivity, or perhaps hypersensitivity, to its nuances. Sharing the main stadium box with Jeanne, Camera [Ashe's wife and young daughter], and me, at my invitation, were Stan Smith [a former tennis champion], his wife Majory, and their daughter Austin. The two little girls were happy to see one another. During Wimbledon in June, they had renewed their friendship when we all stayed near each other in London. Now Austin, seven years old, had brought Camera a present. She had come with twin dolls, one for herself, one for Camera. A thoughtful gesture on Austin's part, and on her parents' part, no doubt. The Smiths are fine, religious people. Then I noticed that Camera was playing with her doll above the railing of the box, in full view of the attentive network television cameras. The doll was the problem, or rather, the fact that the doll was conspicuously a blond. Camera owns dolls of all colors, nationalities, and ethnic varieties. But she was now on national television playing with a blond doll. Suddenly I heard voices in my head, the voices of irate listeners to a call-in show on some "black format" radio station. I imagined insistent, clamorous callers attacking Camera, Jeanne, and me: **14**

"*Can you believe the doll Arthur Ashe's daughter was holding up at the AIDS benefit? Wasn't that a shame?*" **15**

"*Is that brother sick or what? Somebody ought to teach that poor child about her true black self!*" **16**

"*What kind of role model is Arthur Ashe if he allows his daughter to be brainwashed in that way?*" **17**

"*Doesn't the brother* understand *that he is corrupting his child's mind with notions about the superiority of the white woman? I tell you, I thought we were long past that!*" **18**

The voices became louder in my head. Despite the low humidity, I began to squirm in my seat. What should I do? Should I say, To hell with what some people might think? I know that Camera likes her blond dolls, black dolls, brown dolls, Asian dolls, Indian dolls just about equally; I know that for a fact, because I have watched her closely. I have searched for signs of racial partiality in her, indications that she may be dissatisfied with herself, with her own color. I have seen none. But I cannot dismiss the voices. I try always to live practically, and I do not wish to hear such comments on the radio. On the other hand, I do not want Austin's gift to be sullied by an ungracious response. Finally, I act. **19**

"Jeanne," I whisper, "we have to do something."   20

"About what?" she whispers back.   21

"That doll. We have to get Camera to put that doll down."   22

Jeanne takes one look at Camera and the doll and she understands   23
immediately. Quietly, cleverly, she makes the dolls disappear. Neither
Camera nor Austin is aware of anything unusual happening.
Smoothly, Jeanne has moved them on to some other distraction.

I am unaware if Margie Smith has noticed us, but I believe I owe   24
her an explanation. I get up and go around to her seat. Softly I tell
her why the dolls have disappeared. Margie is startled, dumbfounded.

"Gosh, Arthur, I never thought about that. I never *ever* thought   25
about anything like that!"

"*You* don't have to think about it," I explain. "But it happens to us,   26
in similar situations, all the time."

"All the time?" She is pensive now.   27

"All the time. It's perfectly understandable. And it certainly is not   28
your fault. You were doing what comes naturally. But for us, the dolls
make for a bit of a problem. All for the wrong reasons. It shouldn't be
this way, but it is."

I return to my seat, but not to the elation I had felt before I saw   29
that blond doll in Camera's hand. I feel myself becoming more and
more angry. I am angry at the force that made me act, the force of
racism in all its complexity, as it spreads into the world and creates
defensiveness and intolerance among the very people harmed by
racism. I am also angry with myself. I am angry with myself because I
have just acted out of pure practicality, not out of morality. The
moral act would have been to let Camera have her fun, because she
was innocent of any wrongdoing. Instead, I had tampered with her
innocence, her basic human right to act impulsively, to accept a gift
from a friend in the same beautiful spirit in which it was given.

Deeply embarrassed now, I am ashamed at what I have done. I   30
have made Camera adjust her behavior merely because of the likeli-
hood that some people in the African-American community would
react to her innocence foolishly and perhaps even maliciously. I know
I am not misreading the situation. I would have had telephone calls
that very evening about the unsuitablity of Camera's doll. Am I being
a hypocrite? Yes, definitely, up to a point. I have allowed myself to
give in to those people who say we must avoid even the slightest semblance of "Eurocentric" influence. But I also know what stands behind the entire situation. Racism ultimately created the state in
which defensiveness and hypocrisy are our almost instinctive responses, and innocence and generosity are invitations to trouble.

This incident almost ruined the day for me. That night, when   **31**
Jeanne and I talked about the excitement of the afternoon, and the
money that would go to AIDS research and education because
of the event, we nevertheless ended up talking mostly about the incident of the dolls. We also talked about perhaps its most ironic aspect.
In 1954, when the Supreme Court ruled against school segregation in
Brown v. Board of Education, some of the most persuasive testimony
came from the psychologist Dr. Kenneth Clark concerning his research on black children and their pathetic preference for white dolls
over black. In 1992, the dolls are still a problem.

Once again, the shadow of race had fallen on me.   **32**

QUESTIONS FOR CRITICAL THINKING

THINKING CRITICALLY ABOUT CONTENT

1. Why do you think Arthur Ashe says that race has been more of a burden in his
    life than AIDS?

2. Why do you think Ashe described so thoroughly (paragraphs 14–19) the
    difficulty he had in making the decision to do something about the blond doll
    his daughter was holding?

THINKING CRITICALLY ABOUT PURPOSE

3. In your opinion, what is Arthur Ashe's purpose in this essay? Explain your
    answer.

4. Why do you think Arthur Ashe explained to Marjory Smith his reasons for
    wanting the doll out of view of the television cameras?

THINKING CRITICALLY ABOUT AUDIENCE

5. Do you think this chapter is written primarily for African-American audiences,
    white audiences, or both? Explain your answer.

6. Does Ashe convince you that he did the right thing in having his wife remove
    the dolls? Explain your answer.

THINKING CRITICALLY ABOUT POINT OF VIEW

7. Describe in a complete sentence the writer's point of view.

8. Ashe's friend Marjory Smith, who is white, was surprised at Arthur Ashe's
    reaction to the blond doll. Retell the story of Camera and the doll from Marjory
    Smith's viewpoint.

LEARNING FROM YOUR PEERS

Explaining through speaking is often easier than explaining through writing. When you have conversations with teachers, friends, or employers, you know from their expressions when they need more information. When you write, however, you don't have face-to-face contact to let you know when to make changes, add information, or clarify facts. Your readers have the words you have written and no more. If you don't explain yourself fully, clearly, and convincingly, your readers will be confused and frustrated. To see how one person learned to compose an explanation, we will follow the writing process of a student named Victor Cantanzaro.

Victor's Writing Assignment: Explaining

This is the topic Victor's instructor assigned:

All of us have many skills that we take for granted. We may not consider it unusual to know how to organize a storeroom or plant a flower garden or prepare a restaurant for the evening rush, yet if we take stock of what we know and what we have learned over time, we find that we all possess an amazing variety of skills. Explain a complicated process that you learned over a long period of time to an audience of your peers. Your purpose is not to tell them how to perform a particular action, but to explain how the process works.

Victor went through the process as outlined in Chapter 1: *thinking, planning, developing, organizing, drafting, revising,* and *editing.*

Thinking

Victor's class spends several minutes brainstorming ideas, and the students list them on the chalkboard:

rollerblading

grooming a golf course

decorating a Christmas tree

preparing a holiday meal

preparing a picnic to take to the park

rebuilding an engine

reupholstering a couch

opening a restaurant in the morning

making eighty dozen doughnuts before 6 a.m.

planning a month's employee schedule at a convenience store

planning the perfect ski vacation

Victor can see that the people in his class have many skills. He is unsure about what he is going to include on his list, but he thinks about his experiences in scouting and camping. He decides that he will carry a small notepad around with him for a few days so he can jot down his skills whenever he thinks of them.

Planning

Over the next few days, Victor writes down a list of his skills:

preparing a romantic spaghetti dinner

camping and backpacking in the woods

navigating in wilderness areas

singing 27 silly campfire songs

scheduling furniture deliveries

finding the best deals on used CDs

finding great furniture at the flea market

obedience training for stubborn dogs

Victor looks over the list and decides that he does not want to write about scouting or camping activities because he has not been involved in them for a long time. He certainly does not want to put himself in the position of being asked to sing those 27 silly campfire songs, and he is no longer interested in training dogs. That leaves flea markets, romantic dinners, and the furniture delivery business. His surefire romantic dinners revolve around setting the mood as much as preparing the food, so he decides that he would be too embarrassed to reveal all his secrets. He knows about finding bargains at the flea market, but he is sure that two other people are doing their papers on that topic. Victor decides to concentrate on his furniture delivery business. After all, most people have something delivered to their homes sooner or later, and he can help them understand the process.

Developing

Victor starts drawing diagrams of the warehouse and trucking offices of the delivery business he works for. He writes out schedules and lists of people who work there. In trying to imagine how to explain the process to people who have never been there, he decides to cluster his ideas about the work he does for this business.

His cluster looks like this:

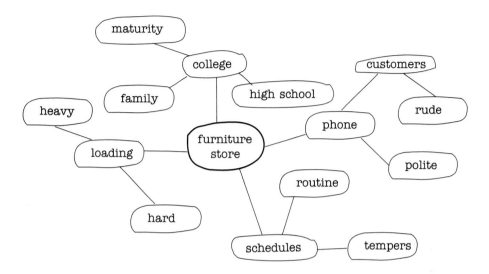

Victor is not sure how to go about developing his ideas, so he puts his writing aside until he can get some help. When Victor's class meets, the students break into groups and discuss the work they have done so far. Victor's classmates ask him several questions, which he writes down. They want to know what he likes best about the job, what he hates about the job, what is most interesting, and what is most difficult. Victor knows the answers to these questions, so all he has to do is allow time to write them down.

Organizing

When he goes to the library that afternoon, Victor takes out his freewriting and the group's questions and begins organizing his ideas. First he answers the questions one by one. Then he decides to introduce the topic by explaining why he decided to work instead of go to college after high school. Then he can talk about his experiences on the job and how he has learned more and more about the business with time.

This is his question-and-answer sheet with all his notes on it:

What do I like best about the job? We have a great system, good

trucks, and hard workers. I don't have to go to the gym because I get so

much exercise on the job.

What is the most interesting? I have learned the complicated

business of scheduling deliveries.

What is the most difficult? I hate having to be cheerful when I answer the phone. People are often angry and upset when they call. I have to say, "Yes, sir--we'll take care of it right away," even when I have no clue how we will fix the problem. Salespeople make promises that they know they can't keep, and they blame their problems on us. When we get to a house to make a delivery, sometimes the people are nowhere to be seen.

Why I went to work instead of college: My family wanted me to go to college, so I decided to do the opposite. I was hardheaded in those days. I was also sick of studying. I wanted to make some money.

Drafting

Victor continues writing according to the plan he made, adding details and background as he writes. Before he knows it, he has completed a draft.

Victor's Essay: First Draft ....

Main Idea: You will be surprised to find out how furniture gets from the store to your door.

When I graduated from high school. I did not want to go college right away. My family said that I should go to the local community college. But my family's wishes weren't my own I was stubborn, more stubborn than they thought I would be. I did not know what I wanted to study, I thought I should work for a while. So that is what I did.

I was the first one in my family. Who did not go on to college after high school. I got a job working at a delivery company. My first job was to take orders. It was kind of boring. I had to sit by the telephone and make sure. To answer it cheerfully and promptly. When people want something delivered, they want it now. The biggest part of our business was delivering furniture for stores to customers. Most customers think that the stores in our area all have their own trucks, but in our town, almost all the furniture was delivered. By our company. We had the best trucks and the best workers.

Started teaching me how to schedule the deliveries. This is easier said than done. Some pushy salesperson would promise a customer anything--that we could definitely have a truck to her front door at nine sharp the next morning. We would have to argue with the salesperson and repeat that we had a one-week wait. We had to say, "Look, there are other customers waiting." But the salespeople were promising things we couldn't deliver. Sure, I liked scheduling the trucks, but not arguing with the customers. My boss, a pretty cool guy about the age of my oldest brother. By that time, it was winter. It was getting cold out. But I decided to give it a try because the money was good. Besides, I was simply tired of the hassles. Arguing constantly with salespeople and customers. That made my job especially nerve-racking.

Loading the truck was hard work. We had to go around to a bunch of stores and load stuff so that we could deliver it without having to unload other furniture. Sometimes my back hurt, that made the day more difficult. Every day's weather outlook was really important, especially if it was snowy or rainy. The furniture was covered with plastic, foam, and paper, the extra protection wasn't enough if we had to deliver in snowy, windy, or rainy weather. I really like the snow when I am not delivering furniture. Some of my fondest memories are from the snow--especially when my family took trips into a winter wonderland. Since I was raised in the Southwest, we had no snow at home the only time I saw snow was when we traveled. I developed a real appreciation for those beautiful white flakes. I lost that appreciation with this job. Other bad stuff that happened was not having people at home when they said they would be there. We always called and confirmed the directions and delivery time, sometimes people would decide at the last minute that they did not want the furniture. Then they would act like it was our mistake. Then we had to charge the store for the delivery, so no one was happy.

I worked at that business for about two years. Got very strong from lifting all that furniture. Learned how to be polite to people when I didn't feel like it. I earned a lot of money, and I think I know more about how the business world operates than my brother, who is finishing his M.B.A. He thinks he learned a lot from books, but I learned a lot from doing business. I think that working for that business was the best decision for me. Now I have enough money saved so that I did not have to do something I didn't want to do. To borrow money for school. My business whiz brother, however, has several thousand dollars in student loans. My ambition is to graduate from college with no debts.

Revising

Victor feels fairly confident about his first draft. Putting onto paper his reasons for his actions during a crucial time in his life was a good exercise for his psyche. In fact, writing about these events gave him a feeling of assurance about his decision to work after high school. But he knows he still has to revise his writing. At this point in the term, Victor's instructor has asked the class to focus on how the sentences in their paragraphs work together to form a unified whole. The instructor is careful to explain that if the student writers make sure their work is unified and logical now, they can build on this ability as their writing gets more and more complex throughout the term.

Victor's task right now is to review the Checklist for Writing Focused Paragraphs at the beginning of the Tips for Revising section in this chapter. Then he reads the Tips for Revising and does all the exercises his instructor assigns. Victor learns that the class is supposed to focus on the content rather than the structure of their paragraphs. In this case, the process involves getting the basic ideas onto paper and then making sure the ideas are clearly related to one another so the audience can share these observations as accurately as possible.

Victor returns to his draft and approaches his revision, determined to make each paragraph a logical unit. In some instances, he is able to add transitions to his sentences to help his readers picture what he sees. In other cases, he finds sentences that do not fit into their paragraphs. Victor looks closely at his essay for both types of problems.

 ## COLLABORATIVE WORK

PEER GROUP ACTIVITY

After you read the portions of the Tips for Revising your instructor assigns, turn to Victor's first draft (pp. 122–124), and complete the following tasks in small groups:

A.   Underline sentences that your group thinks do not logically fit in their current paragraphs.

B. Put a slash between sentences that are not related to each other.

Compare the marks your group recorded with those your instructor will show you. Where do your marks differ from your instructor's? What do you need to review before writing your own essay?

CLASS ACTIVITY

As an entire class, look at the underlined portions of Victor's revised draft (pp. 126–128) to see what changes he made.

A. Did you identify the **revision** problems that Victor corrected?

B. Do you think his changes are good ones? Discuss his changes.

Editing

Now that the paragraphs in Victor's essay are logical, he needs to do some final proofreading and editing before handing in his essay. In the next class meeting, the instructor explains how important it is to recognize and correct fragments and run-on sentences. When Victor reads the Tips for Editing section in this chapter, he is reminded that fragments and run-ons are both serious sentence errors. A fragment is a piece of a sentence punctuated as a complete sentence; a run-on is more than one sentence punctuated as a single sentence. Victor goes over the questions in the Checklist for Correcting Fragments and Run-ons one by one, and he continues to work on his draft until it fulfills all the requirements on the checklist.

 ## COLLABORATIVE WORK

PEER GROUP ACTIVITY

After you read the portions of the Tips for Editing your instructor assigns, turn to Victor's first draft (pp. 122–124), and complete the following tasks in small groups:

A. Read each of the sentences for completeness, and put brackets around any fragments (for a definition, see p. 139).

B. Read Victor's first draft again, looking for multiple sentences that are run together as one. Separate these run-on sentences (for a definition, see p. 144) with a slash.

Compare your group's marks with those your instructor will show you. Where do your marks differ from your instructor's? What do you need to review before writing your own essay?

CLASS ACTIVITY

As an entire class, look at the underlined portions of Victor's revised draft (pp. 126–128) to see what changes he made.

A.   Did you identify the **editing** problems that Victor corrected?

B.   Do you think his changes are good ones? Discuss his changes.

Victor's Revised Essay

How Furniture Gets from the Store to Your Door

When I graduated from high school/, I did not want to go to college right away. My family said that I should go to the local community college. But my family's wishes weren't my own. I was stubborn, more stubborn than they thought I would be. Because I did not know what I wanted to study, I thought I should work for a while. So that is what I did.

~~I was the first one in my family. Who did not go on to college after high school.~~ I got a job working at a delivery company. ~~My first job was to take orders. It was kind of boring. I had to sit by the telephone and make sure. To answer it cheerfully and promptly. When people want something delivered, they want it now.~~ The biggest part of our business was delivering furniture for stores to customers. Most customers think that the stores in our area all have their own trucks, but in our town, almost all the furniture was delivered/ bBy our company. We had the best trucks and the best workers.

My first job was to take orders. It was kind of boring. When people want something delivered, they want it now. I had to sit by the telephone and make sure/ tTo answer it cheerfully and promptly. Some customers were courteous, but most were very short with me.

After a few months, the manager, Mr. Kobler. sStarted teaching me how to schedule the deliveries. This is easier said than done. Some pushy salesperson would promise a customer anything--that we could definitely have a truck to her front door at nine sharp the next morning. We would have to argue with the salesperson and repeat that we had a one-week wait. We had to say, "Look, there are other customers waiting." But the salespeople were promising things we couldn't deliver. Sure, I liked scheduling the trucks, but not arguing with the customers. My boss, a pretty cool guy about the age of my oldest brother/,then said, "Maybe you're ready to help load the trucks." By that time, it was winter. It was getting cold out. But I decided to give it a try because the money was good. Besides, I was simply tired of the hassles. Arguing constantly with salespeople and customers/ ~~That~~ made my job especially nerve-racking.

Loading the truck was hard work. We had to go around to a bunch of stores and load stuff so that we could deliver it without having to unload other furniture. ~~Sometimes my back hurt, that made the day more difficult.~~ Every day's weather outlook was really important, especially if it was snowy or rainy. The furniture was covered with plastic, foam, and paper/. T/he extra protection wasn't enough if we had to deliver in snowy, windy, or rainy weather. ~~I really like the snow when I am not delivering furniture. Some of my fondest memories are from the snow--especially when my family took trips into a winter wonderland. Since I was raised in the Southwest, we had no snow at home the only time I saw snow was when we traveled. I developed a real appreciation for those beautiful white flakes. I lost that appreciation with this job.~~ Other bad stuff that happened was not having people at home when they said they would be there. Even though w/We always called and confirmed the directions and delivery time, sometimes people would decide at the last minute that they did not want the furniture. Then they would act like it was our mistake.

Then we had to charge the store for the delivery, so no one was happy.

I worked at that business for about two years. I g~~G~~ot very strong from lifting all that furniture. I l~~L~~earned how to be polite to people when I didn't feel like it. ~~I earned a lot of money, and~~ I think I know more about how the business world operates than my brother, who is finishing his M.B.A. He thinks he learned a lot from books, but I learned a lot from doing business.

My ambition is to graduate from college with no debts. ~~I think that working for that business was the best decision for me.~~ Now I earned a lot of money at my job; therefore, I have enough money saved so that I did not have to ~~do something I didn't want to do. To~~ borrow money for school. My business whiz brother, however, has several thousand dollars in student loans. ~~My ambition is to graduate from college with no debts.~~ I think that working for that business was the best decision for me.

WRITING YOUR OWN EXPLAINING ESSAY

So far, you have seen a professional writer and a fellow student at work trying to explain an experience or process they felt was worth writing about. As you read and followed the writing process of another student from first to final draft, you absorbed ideas to work with and ways of giving those ideas a form of their own. These reading and writing activities have prepared you to write your own essay explaining an experience or process that is meaningful to you.

What Have You Discovered?

Before you begin your own writing task, let's review what you have learned in this chapter so far:

- We use explaining to help others understand what we know, what we think, and what we feel about certain matters.
- Explaining in writing is more difficult than explaining in speech because you cannot respond to the gestures and facial expressions of your readers.

- To present your explanation effectively, you need to organize your ideas.

- To help you shape your essay, you should learn as much as possible about your readers.

- Before you write a draft, you need to decide on a point of view toward your subject.

- After you write a draft, you should revise your essay for meaning and organization.

- After you revise your essay, you should edit its grammar, usage, and sentence structure.

Your Writing Topic

Choose one of the following topics for your explaining essay:

1. In the professional essay that you read at the beginning of this chapter, Arthur Ashe explains why he had to do something that was against his principles. Although it was a very difficult thing for him to do, he believed that he had no choice. He explained that if he had followed his beliefs, his actions would have been misinterpreted, causing even greater misunderstandings between blacks and whites. Reflect on your own experiences with members of a different race either in school, at work, or in public places. Write an essay explaining an event or a period in your life when the issue of race caused you to behave in a particular way or to do something that you would ordinarily not do. Explain fully and clearly the circumstances that existed, the way you acted or responded, and why you acted or responded that way.

2. Explain to your classmates a complicated hobby you have, including what it takes to get started in this hobby and what the satisfactions are. For example, how would a person get started in stamp collecting, and what could it lead to?

3. Your college newspaper is running a special edition on study habits, and the editor has asked you to write an article explaining how you manage all the demands on your time, including studying, socializing, working, and keeping family obligations. Prepare the essay for the next edition of the paper.

4. Create your own explaining assignment (with the assistance of your instructor), and write a response to it.

When you have selected one of these topics, you may begin your writing process in the same way Victor did. (You may find his experience helpful in giving you ideas.) This time your purpose is to write your own explaining essay. If some tasks occur out of order, that adjustment is probably part of your personal writing ritual. Follow your instincts, and let them mold your own writing process. But make sure you've worked through all the stages to your final draft.

YOUR WRITING PROCESS

THINKING   Generate as many ideas on your subject as you can in as many different ways as possible: rereading, listing, freewriting, brainstorming, clustering, discussing, and questioning.

PLANNING   Begin to give your ideas shape by deciding on your approach to your topic (your content, your purpose, your audience, and your point of view). Make a list of points you want to include in your essay.

DEVELOPING   Add more details on three or four specific, focused topics that you have chosen from your list of general points.

ORGANIZING   Organize your material in a way that will be most interesting to your audience.

DRAFTING   Write a working draft of your essay in complete sentences.

REVISING   Consulting the Tips for Revising in this chapter (pp. 131–137), revise your first draft—paying special attention to the unity and logic of each paragraph.

EDITING   Consulting the Tips for Editing in this chapter (pp. 138–148), edit your draft for grammar and correctness—paying special attention to sentence fragments and run-on sentences.

Turn in your revised draft to your instructor.

Some Final Thoughts

When you have completed your own essay, answer these four questions in your journal:

1. What was most difficult about this assignment?
2. What was easiest?
3. What did I learn about explaining by completing this assignment?
4. What did I learn about my own writing process from this assignment—how I prepared to write, how I wrote the first draft, how I revised, and how I edited?

Writing Focused Paragraphs

Checklist for Writing Focused Paragraphs

✓ Do all paragraphs **focus** on a single controlling idea?
✓ Should any paragraphs be **divided** into additional paragraphs?
✓ Are the sentences in each paragraph related to the topic sentence to form a **unified** whole?
✓ Are the sentences in each paragraph related to one another, following a **logical** train of thought?

Have you ever tried to find a single document in a filing cabinet drawer so packed that you couldn't move the file folders? To restore order to a filing cabinet, you need to sort all the papers into piles by category, throw out the useless or outdated items, then sort the piles into logical groups. Sometimes the paragraphs in your essays can resemble an overloaded filing cabinet. Just as organizing a filing cabinet makes important papers easier to find, clearing your paragraphs of unrelated ideas, organizing essential ideas logically, and connecting ideas with supporting details will help an audience understand the important contents of your essay.

Focus

To organize a filing cabinet, you might begin by sorting the contents into three piles: papers to put back in the cabinet, papers to store elsewhere, and papers to discard. Writers often use a similar method to focus their body paragraphs (the paragraphs that fall between the introduction and conclusion of an essay) on a single **controlling idea.** For many writers, the first step in revising is making sure the controlling idea for each paragraph is clear to their audience. Usually, they state this idea in a topic sentence at the beginning of the paragraph. Then they sort the sentences in that paragraph into (1) those that contribute to the controlling idea, (2) those that support another idea and need a separate paragraph, and (3) those that need to be thrown out entirely.

Look at paragraph 9 of Arthur Ashe's "The Burden of Race":

Since our interview (skillfully presented as a first-person account by me) appeared in *People* in June 1992, many people have commented on my remark ["Race is for me a more onerous burden than AIDS."]. A radio station in Chicago aimed primarily at blacks conducted a lively debate on its merits on the air. Most African Americans have little trouble understanding and accepting my statement, but other people have been baffled by it. Even Donald Dell, my close friend of more than thirty years, was puzzled. In fact, he was so troubled that he telephoned me in the middle of the night from Hamburg, Germany, to ask if I had been misquoted. No, I told him, I had been quoted correctly. Some people have asked me flatly, what could *you*, Arthur Ashe, possibly have to complain about? Do you want more money or fame than you already have? Isn't AIDS inevitably fatal? What can be worse than death?

Ashe focuses this entire paragraph on the controlling idea stated in the first sentence, people's reactions to his remark (explained in the previous paragraph) that race was his heaviest burden.

After rereading the first draft of his explaining essay, Victor realized he had to rework his second paragraph to focus more clearly on a single controlling idea.

First Draft: I was the first one in my family. Who did not go on to college after high school. I got a job working at a delivery company. My first job was to take orders. It was kind of boring. I had to sit by the telephone and make sure. To answer it cheerfully and promptly. When people want something delivered, they want it now. The biggest part of our business was delivering furniture for stores to customers. Most customers think that the stores in our area all have their own trucks, but in our town, almost all the furniture was delivered. By our company. We had the best trucks and the best workers.

After studying this paragraph, Victor dropped the first sentence and divided the rest of the paragraph into two paragraphs, one that explained the furniture delivery business and one that outlined his first duty, answering the phones. This revision also reflects some other corrections he made in the Editing section of this chapter.

Revision: ~~I was the first one in my family. Who did not go on to~~ college after high school. I got a job working at a delivery company. My first job was to take orders. It was kind of ~~boring. I had to sit by the telephone and make sure.~~ ~~To~~ answer it cheerfully and promptly. When people want ~~something delivered, they want it now.~~ The biggest part of our business was delivering furniture for stores to customers. Most customers think that the stores in our area all have their own trucks, but in our town, almost all the furniture was delivered by our company. We had the best trucks and the best workers.

> **My first job was to take orders. It was kind of boring. When people want something delivered, they want it now. I had to sit by the telephone and make sure to answer it cheerfully and promptly. Some customers were courteous, but most were very short with me.**

TIPS FOR REVISING

Now the ideas for these two topics are classified into two categories, so both paragraphs are clearer and more focused.

Exercise R4-1

State the controlling idea that focuses paragraph 8 of Arthur Ashe's "The Burden of Race" (p. 114).

Exercise R4-2

Read paragraph 3 of Victor's first draft (pp. 122–123), and decide how to focus it more clearly.

Exercise R4-3

Find the sentence that states the controlling idea for paragraph 5 in Victor's first draft (pp. 123–124), and move or delete any sentences in that paragraph that do not explain that idea.

Exercise R4-4

Rewrite the following paragraph, deleting all irrelevant material so that the paragraph focuses on one controlling idea.

Astronomy is the oldest of all the sciences. It began several thousand years ago, when people first wondered about the stars at night. Life was simple then. I sometimes enjoy using a telescope to look at the stars. Most of the people who used to wonder about the stars were hunters and shepherds, although I'll bet people from other professions also wondered about the stars. Shepherds and hunters could not write then, perhaps because they did not have a school system like we have today, and we do not know much about their thoughts. Yet they used the stars as guides on their journeys. Those days must have been interesting.

Unity

To be unified, a paragraph develops one point, and all the sentences in that paragraph stick to that point. Each paragraph should form a unified whole, with all its sentences relating to its topic sentence. In paragraph 12 of "The Burden of Race,"

Arthur Ashe writes a unified paragraph that focuses on his sense of being "a prisoner of the past":

> In some respects, I am a prisoner of the past. A long time ago, I made peace with the state of Virginia and the South. While I, like other blacks, was once barred from free association with whites, I returned time and time again, under the new rule of desegregation, to work with whites in my hometown and across the South. But segregation had achieved by that time what it was intended to achieve: It left me a marked man, forever aware of a shadow of contempt that lays across my identity and my sense of self-esteem. Subtly the shadow falls on my reputation, the way I know I am perceived; the mere memory of it darkens my most sunny days. I believe that the same is true for almost every African American of the slightest sensitivity and intelligence. Again, I don't want to overstate the case. I think of myself, and others think of me, as supremely self-confident. I know objectively that it is almost impossible for someone to be as successful as I have been as an athlete and to lack self-assurance. Still, I also know that the shadow is always there; only death will free me, and blacks like me, from its pall.

A good way to check for unity at this point is to make a **scratch outline.** To do this, read each paragraph and jot down its controlling idea. If a paragraph isn't focused on one idea, consider your options for achieving unity. Should some ideas be moved to other paragraphs? Do you need to divide the material into two paragraphs? Do some of the ideas need to be deleted altogether?

When Victor reread paragraph 4 of his draft, he realized it was not unified at all because he had included details about more than one topic. The unnecessary details are underlined.

First Draft: Loading the truck was hard work. We had to go around to a bunch of stores and load stuff so that we could deliver it without having to unload other furniture. Sometimes my back hurt, that made the day more difficult. Every day's weather outlook was really important, especially if it was snowy or rainy. The furniture was covered with plastic, foam, and paper, the extra protection wasn't enough if we had to deliver in snowy, windy, or rainy weather. I really like the snow when I am not delivering furniture. Some of my fondest memories are from the snow--especially when my family took trips into a winter wonderland. Since I was

raised in the Southwest, we had no snow at home the only
time I saw snow was when we traveled. I developed a real
appreciation for those beautiful white flakes. I lost that
appreciation with this job. Other bad stuff that happened
was not having people at home when they said they would
be there. We always called and confirmed the directions
and delivery time, sometimes people would decide at the
last minute that they did not want the furniture. Then
they would act like it was our mistake. Then we had to
charge the store for the delivery, so no one was happy.

As Victor tried to identify the main topic, he realized that he really went off on a
tangent about the snow. Because of this tangent, this particular paragraph is not unified. It has a focus in its clear topic sentence: *Loading the truck was hard work.* But to
give this paragraph unity, Victor had to delete all the irrelevant details that don't directly relate to the paragraph's topic sentence. He also corrected some sentence
structure errors that he learned about in Tips for Editing in this chapter.

Revision: Loading the truck was hard work. We had to go
around to a bunch of stores and load stuff so that we
could deliver it without having to unload other furniture.
~~Sometimes my back hurt, that made the day more difficult.~~ Every day's weather outlook was really
important, especially if it was snowy or rainy. The
furniture was covered with plastic, foam, and paper. The
extra protection wasn't enough if we had to deliver in
snowy, windy, or rainy weather. ~~I really like snow when I
am not delivering furniture. Some of my fondest memories
are from the snow especially when my family took trips
into a winter wonderland. Since I was raised in the
Southwest, we had no snow at home the only time I saw
snow was when we traveled. I developed a real
appreciation for those beautiful white flakes. I lost that
appreciation with this job.~~ Other bad stuff that happened

was not having people at home when they said they would

be there. Even though we always called and confirmed the

directions and delivery time, sometimes people would

decide at the last minute that they did not want the

furniture. Then they would act like it was our mistake.

Then we had to charge the store for the delivery, so no

one was happy.

Victor has made this paragraph unified as well as focused, strengthening the main ideas and making the paragraph more effective.

Exercise R4-5

Read paragraph 12 of Ashe's essay (p. 115), and write down the topic sentence and the details that relate to that topic.

Exercise R4-6

Read paragraph 4 of Victor's revised essay (pp. 126–127). Write out the topic sentence, and list the supporting details.

Exercise R4-7

Read the following sentences, and group them into two unified paragraphs. Drop sentences that don't fit into either paragraph.

1. The first day of classes is always a confusing time at my campus.
2. Today, we know a great deal more about the ways in which diseases can be transmitted than was known in the nineteenth century.
3. Finding new buildings and locating classrooms takes a lot of time.
4. The bookstore is inevitably a crowd scene, with long lines going out the door and around the corner.
5. We know that mosquitoes, not noxious fumes in the air, carry malaria.
6. It's fun seeing old friends in classes again, though.
7. We know that typhoid comes from an unclean water or food supply.
8. For instance, we would never casually drink water from an old well.
9. Old wells can be dangerous if children play near them and fall in.
10. Long ago people had some funny ideas.

Exercise R4-8

Read the following paragraph, and write down the unifying idea. Then delete any sentences that do not belong in this paragraph.

Country music is finally coming into its own. It's gaining respectability as an important part of our culture. For instance, the Piney Woods Opry in Abita Springs recently received an NEA grant to record many of the songs they have written based on Louisiana's rural history. Steel guitars revolutionized music. Much of our folklore from other parts of the nation is preserved in such country music tunes as "Casey Jones" and "Barbara Allen." Abita Springs also has a microbrewery.

 ## COLLABORATIVE WORK

After writing a draft of your own explaining essay, exchange papers with a classmate, and do the following tasks:

A. Put brackets around each sentence that seems unrelated to its paragraph's controlling idea.

B. Draw an arrow to another paragraph if any sentences you found in task A seem to belong somewhere else, or put a question mark beside sentences you think should be deleted.

C. Place a paragraph symbol (¶) where a division should be made in a paragraph to form two paragraphs.

Then return the paper to its writer, and use the information in this section to revise your draft.

Fragments and Run-ons

Checklist for Correcting Fragments and Run-ons

✓ Is each sentence **complete?**
✓ Does each **noun phrase** that functions as a subject have a verb?
✓ Are **verb phrases** paired with subjects?
✓ Are **prepositional phrases** connected to independent clauses?
✓ Do **verbal phrases** function as subjects, have their own verbs, or work correctly with independent clauses?
✓ Is each **dependent clause** joined in some way to an **independent clause?**
✓ Does each sentence connect thoughts appropriately to **avoid run-on sentences?**

Writing is a game of catch-up. Our minds often race at a dizzying pace as we struggle to record our thoughts on paper or on the computer screen. Even if we were wizards with a pen or speed demons on the keyboard, we could never write as fast as we think. But we try. And in making these noble efforts, we transform ideas into writing. Sometimes we produce the material that thoughts are made of—simple words and phrases, fragmentary responses, strings of sentences that stop only when we get tired.

Because we often do not think in complete thoughts in our first drafts, we must pay close attention when editing for sentence errors. The most common sentence faults are fragments and run-ons. In this section, you will learn how to identify and correct fragments and run-ons. Even with close attention to these critical areas, you still may find that you think in fragmentary responses and seemingly endless sentence jumbles. But you will also discover that your sentences will communicate clearly if you keep completeness and correctness in mind as you edit your first draft.

Fragments

Of the two kinds of sentence errors, fragments are the more frustrating because they are so familiar. Our ears and eyes are bombarded with fragments every day. People speak in fragments: "Your score on the test?" "Ninety." Advertisers sell products with fragments. "The best deal in town!" "The most for your money." Journalists write in fragments: "Sox 2, Rangers 1 in 12 innings."

In certain instances—usually in everyday, informal situations—speaking in fragments is acceptable. In writing, fragments are sometimes used to create special effects—for example, when professional writers want to reproduce the sounds and rhythms of spoken language in fiction, newswriting, or advertising. For academic writing, however, and most writing on the job, only complete sentences make the grade.

As you learned in Chapter 2, a complete sentence requires two basic elements: a subject and a verb. If either of these elements is missing, you have a **fragment.** Don't be fooled by a fragment trying to pass as a sentence. Even if it begins with a capital letter and ends with a period, a question mark, or an exclamation point, a string of words isn't necessarily a sentence. Remember that a fragment is nothing more than a phrase or dependent clause, a nonsentence that must be corrected by supplying the missing parts or by connecting the fragment to a nearby sentence. The subjects and verbs of each independent clause are in bold type in the examples that follow, and the fragments are underlined.

Phrase Fragments

Four different types of phrases produce fragments when they are punctuated like a sentence: noun phrases, verb phrases, prepositional phrases, and verbal phrases.

Noun Phrases

Inexperienced writers often write fragments with noun phrases. The first draft of Victor's explaining essay includes a noun phrase that tries to pass as a complete sentence:

Fragment:	My boss, a pretty cool guy about the age of my oldest brother.

As you can see, this phrase has a subject, but there is no action or state of being. Victor's boss is not doing anything. To make a complete sentence, Victor can choose one of two options: (1) Add a verb, or (2) join the fragment to a nearby sentence (or to another fragment that includes a verb).

Possible Revision:	$\overset{\text{S}}{\text{My }}\overset{}{\textbf{boss}},\overset{\text{V}}{/\textbf{ is}}$ a pretty cool guy about the age of my oldest brother.
Victor's Revision:	$\overset{\text{S}}{\text{My }}\textbf{boss}$, a pretty cool guy about the age of my oldest brother$\overset{\text{V}}{/}$, then **said**, "Maybe you're ready to help load the trucks."

Verb Phrases

As you learned in Chapter 2, a **verb phrase** consists of a verb plus any modifiers that help complete its meaning. However, a verb phrase does not contain a subject. So a verb phrase cannot be capitalized and punctuated as a sentence because it is incomplete. Together, a verb phrase and a subject make a complete sentence.

The second "sentence" in paragraph 5 of Victor's first draft is a verb phrase fragment:

Fragment: Got very strong from lifting all that furniture.

We don't know *who* got strong from lifting furniture. But we know from the previous paragraphs that Victor is the person explaining his job at a furniture delivery company. To correct the verb phrase fragment, Victor can either supply a missing subject to make the fragment complete or connect the fragment to the previous sentence.

Possible Revision:
S   V   V
I worked at that business for about two years and g**Got**

very strong from lifting all that furniture.

Victor's Revision:
S V
I gGot very strong from lifting all that furniture.

Prepositional Phrases

As you remember, a preposition connects a noun or pronoun to the remainder of its sentence. We call the noun or pronoun the *object of the preposition*. The preposition plus its object and modifiers make up a **prepositional phrase.** Because the prepositional phrase is missing both a subject and a verb, it cannot stand alone as a complete sentence. However, prepositional phrases often try to pass themselves off as sentences. Look at this example from Victor's first draft:

Fragment: Most customers think that the stores in our area all have

their own trucks, but in our town, almost all the

furniture was delivered. By our company.

One prepositional phrase is capitalized and punctuated as a complete sentence: *By our company.* To make it complete, simply connect the phrase to a nearby sentence.

Victor's Revision: Most customers think that the stores in our area all have

S
their own trucks, but in our town, almost **all** the furniture

V
was delivered/ bBy our company.

Verbal Phrases

Like prepositional phrases, **verbal phrases** do not contain subjects and main verbs. As a result, they must be connected to independent clauses. You need to watch for three different types of verbal phrases: present participle, past participle, and infinitive.

Present participle: Studying until midnight, Victor finally went to bed.

Past participle: Tired and worn out from a 12-hour workday, Victor stumbled into the shower.

Infinitive: To succeed as a student, Victor has to plan his time carefully.

The boldfaced phrases in these examples are punctuated correctly, enhancing the meaning of the independent clauses. However, in paragraph 3 of his draft, Victor finds a present participial phrase left as a complete sentence.

Fragment: Besides, I was simply tired of the hassles. <u>Arguing constantly with salespeople and customers.</u> That made my job especially nerve-racking.

Arguing constantly with salespeople and customers cannot stand alone because it contains no subject and main verb. To correct this fragment, you can join the phrase to a nearby sentence or supply the missing subject and verb to make a separate sentence.

Possible Revision: Arguing constantly with salespeople and customers, **I was** simply tired of the hassles.

Possible Revision: **I** really **hated** arguing with salespeople and customers.

Victor's Revision: **Arguing constantly with salespeople and customers/** ~~**That**~~ **made** my job especially nerve-racking.

Here is another verbal phrase from Victor's first draft that is punctuated as a sentence. This time the verbal phrase is an infinitive (*to* + the base form of the verb).

Fragment: I had to sit by the telephone and make sure. <u>To answer it cheerfully and promptly.</u>

To correct the fragment, simply connect the infinitive phrase to the previous sentence or give it a subject and verb of its own.

Victor's Revision: **I had** to sit by the telephone and make sure/ t~~T~~o answer it cheerfully and promptly.

Subordinate Clause Fragments

Writers sometimes capitalize and punctuate subordinate clauses as complete sentences. Although these groups of words include a subject and a verb, they also contain a word that makes the clause dependent, a **subordinating conjunction** (*as, since, because, when, where,* etc.) or a **relative pronoun** (*which, that, who, whom, whose*) that begins the clause and connects it to the rest of the sentence.

sub
conj   S   V

Since his teacher gave the class an extension, Victor has time to revise his essay again.

rel
pron
S V

Jake, **who is Victor's best friend,** hopes to attend graduate school to study psychology.

Victor's draft includes two sentence fragments (underlined here) that are actually subordinate clauses.

Fragments:	When I graduated from high school. I did not want to go to college right away.
	I was the first one in my family. Who did not go on to college after high school.

Most of the time the best way to correct clause fragments is by attaching them to a sentence before or after them.

S V

Revisions:	When I graduated from high school/, **I did** not want to go to college right away.

S V

I was the first one in my family/, wWho did not go on to college after high school.

Exercise E4-1

Each of the following fragments is part of a complete sentence taken from paragraphs 9 through 13 of "The Burden of Race" by Arthur Ashe. Refer to the essay, and complete each sentence as it appears in its original form. After you copy the rest of the sentence, explain what each fragment needed to become complete—a subject, a verb, or both.

Fragment:	Of my right to privacy.

TIPS FOR EDITING

Correction: The reporter's questions had been probing and yet respectful of my right to privacy. (The fragment needed both a subject and a verb.)

1. Since our interview (skillfully presented as a first-person account by me) appeared in *People* in June 1992.
2. Even Donald Dell, my close friend of more than thirty years.
3. Suggested somewhere that it is a complex fate being an American.
4. To overstate the case.
5. On one of the brightest days, literally and metaphorically, of my life.

Exercise E4-2

Underline the ten fragments in the following paragraphs.

My English teacher made us watch a classic movie and write a paper about it. A critical analysis essay where we had to do more than just summarize the plot. The movie was *Rebel Without a Cause* from 1955. Starring James Dean, Natalie Wood, and Sal Mineo. It was Dean's last film. Actually released after his death in a car crash.

Dean, Wood, and Mineo play three teenagers who are having trouble. With their families. Dean plays Jim, who has a wimp for a father. And a mother who wears the pants in the family. They move from town to town whenever Jim gets in trouble. Wood plays the part of Judy. Her problem lies with her father. He won't kiss her or show physical affection. Because he thinks Judy is too old and mature for such displays. She turns to a gang and later to Jim. For the affection she needs. Mineo portrays the most disturbed teenager, Plato. Shooting puppies to get attention. Plato basically lives on his own. With only a maid to show him attention. His parents are divorced. His father lives in another city, and his mother travels all the time. To avoid dealing with Plato. The movie covers a day in the lives of these troubled teens as they turn to each other for support.

Exercise E4-3

Rewrite the fragments you found in Exercise E4-2 to make them complete sentences.

Exercise E4-4

Rewrite each of the following phrases and clauses as a complete sentence.

1. running down the street
2. which is the best option
3. although we don't talk much anymore
4. feels the same way I do
5. Tonya, the girl I talked to at the game,

Run-on Sentences

Our brains think in bits and pieces of thoughts. But our minds also generate ideas so fast that it's hard to tell where one thought ends and the next begins. Sometimes when we transform these ideas into written words, our thoughts are still hard to separate, and so we produce sentences that flow forward without stopping. We call such sentences run-ons.

Run-on sentences present two or more independent thoughts as a single unit. Writers, in their haste, capitalize and punctuate a run-on as one sentence. Basically, run-ons can be divided into two types: fused sentences and comma splices. Both are easy to identify and correct.

Fused Sentences

A **fused sentence** is a run-on sentence that includes two or more independent clauses punctuated as one sentence, with no punctuation between the clauses. Look at the following example from Victor's explaining draft:

                                       S   V   S V

Fused Sentence: But my family's **wishes weren't** my own/**I was** stubborn,

more stubborn than they thought I would be.

To correct fused sentences, you can choose from one of six options explained in this section.

Comma Splices

The only difference between a fused sentence and a comma splice is the punctuation. When two or more independent clauses are separated with a comma, they produce a **comma splice.** Victor's first draft has several comma splices, including this example from paragraph 4:

                              S   V   V

Comma Splice: The **furniture was covered** in plastic, foam, and paper,/the

                            S   V

extra **protection wasn't** enough if we had to deliver in

snowy, windy, or rainy weather.

The comma splice occurs after the word *paper*.

Correcting Run-on Sentences

Using no punctuation at all or using a comma by itself is not sufficient to connect two independent clauses. Therefore, you can choose one of the following six correction options to make the comma splice a grammatically correct sentence:

1. *Make two complete sentences by placing a period between the independent clauses.* Marking the break between independent clauses with a period is probably the easiest way to correct a run on.

   Revisions: But my family's **wishes weren't** my own. **I was** stubborn, more stubborn than they thought I would be.

   The **furniture was covered** in plastic, foam, and paper.

   The

   extra **protection wasn't** enough if we had to deliver in snowy, windy, or rainy weather.

2. *Add a coordinating conjunction and a comma between the independent clauses.*   Do you remember the coordinating conjunctions—*for, and, nor, but, or, yet, so?* (For a definition, see p. 53.) They connect equal sentence elements, in this case independent clauses. Simply choose the coordinating conjunction that accurately explains the connection between the clauses, and place the conjunction after a comma.

   Revisions: But my family's **wishes weren't** my own, *and* **I was**

                    Coor
                    Conj

   stubborn, more stubborn than they thought I would be.

                    Coor
                    Conj

   The **furniture was covered** in plastic, foam, and paper, *but* the extra **protection wasn't** enough if we had to deliver in snowy, windy, or rainy weather.

3. *Use just a semicolon.*   Writers often use semicolons interchangeably with periods. But semicolons should be used to connect independent clauses only when they are closely related and the relationship is clear. Otherwise, a period would be a better choice.

   Revisions: But my family's **wishes weren't** my own; **I was** stubborn, more stubborn than they thought I would be.

   The **furniture was covered** in plastic, foam, and paper; the extra **protection wasn't** enough if we had to deliver in snowy, windy, or rainy weather.

4. *Insert a semicolon, a conjunctive adverb or a transitional expression, and a comma.* You may remember from Chapter 2 that conjunctive adverbs and transitional expressions are words that help one idea flow to the next. When conjunctive

adverbs and transitional expressions (see p. 55) connect two independent clauses, a semicolon is effective.

Revisions:

$\overset{\textbf{Conj}}{\underset{\textbf{Adv}}{}}$

But my family's **wishes weren't** my own; *besides,* **I was** stubborn, more stubborn than they thought I would be.

The furniture was covered in plastic, foam, and paper;

$\overset{\textbf{Conj}}{\underset{\textbf{Adv}}{}}$

however, the extra **protection wasn't** enough if we had to deliver in snowy, windy, or rainy weather.

5. *Make one independent clause dependent.* Still another correction option involves subordination (see p. 63). You can make one clause dependent by adding either a subordinating conjunction or a relative pronoun. (For a list of subordinating conjunctions, see p. 56; for a list of relative pronouns, see pp. 45 and 63.)

Before you add the subordinating conjunction or relative pronoun, you must first decide which clause to subordinate or make dependent. Just remember that the more important idea should remain in the independent clause. Look at these examples from Victor's draft:

Revisions:

$\overset{\textbf{Sub}}{\underset{\textbf{Conj}}{}}$

Because my family's **wishes weren't** my own, **I was** stubborn, more stubborn than they thought I would be.

$\overset{\textbf{Sub}}{\underset{\textbf{Conj}}{}}$

Even though the **furniture was covered** in plastic, foam, and paper, the extra **protection wasn't** enough if we had to deliver in snowy, windy, or rainy weather.

6. *Put both independent clauses into one independent clause.* Sometimes the two independent clauses can be rewritten and combined into one independent clause.

Revisions:

I was more stubborn than my family expected, with wishes of my own.

The furniture's extra **covering** of plastic, foam, and paper **did not provide** enough protection during deliveries in snowy, windy, or rainy weather.

Exercise E4-5

The following run-on sentences are made up of correct sentences that appear in "The Burden of Race." Underline the independent clauses in each.

1. During Wimbledon in June, they had renewed their friendship when we all stayed near each other in London now Austin, seven years old, had brought Camera a present.
2. The Smiths are fine, religious people, then I noticed that Camera was playing with her doll above the railing of the box, in full view of the attentive network television cameras.
3. I do not mean to appear fatalistic, self-pitying, cynical, or maudlin, proud to be an American, I am also proud to be an African American.
4. The moral act would have been to let Camera have her fun, because she was innocent of any wrongdoing instead, I had tampered with her innocence, her basic human right to act impulsively, to accept a gift from a friend in the same beautiful spirit in which it was given.
5. We also talked about perhaps its most ironic aspect in 1954, when the Supreme Court ruled against school segregation in *Brown v. Board of Education*, some of the most persuasive testimony came from the psychologist Dr. Kenneth Clark concerning his research on black children and their pathetic preference for white dolls over black.

Exercise E4-6

The following run-on sentences are made up of sentences that appear in the final draft of Victor's restating essay. Underline the independent clauses in each run-on sentence.

1. When I graduated from high school, I did not want to go to college right away, my family said that I should to the local community college.
2. After a few months, the manager, Mr. Kobler, started teaching me how to schedule the deliveries this is easier said than done.
3. But I decided to give it a try because the money was good besides, I was simply tired of the hassles.
4. Even though we always called and confirmed the directions and delivery time, sometimes people would decide at the last minute that they did not want the furniture then they would act like it was our mistake.
5. My business whiz brother, however, has several thousand dollars in student loans, I think that working for that business was the best decision for me.

Exercise E4-7

Underline and correct the run-ons (both fused and comma splices) in the following paragraphs.

Making a good impression is important, especially when going on a job interview. Most people agree that there are several things you can do, these things will ensure that you put your best foot forward.

First, you should take a copy of your resume with you, this will show the interviewer that you are prepared and serious. Even if you have already submitted a resume, it won't hurt to have one in hand when you walk through the door. The resume should be neatly typed, it should also have your education and work histories along with names, addresses, and phone numbers of references.

You should also be punctual, plan to arrive at least ten minutes early. You can relax and take note of your surroundings. Don't be too early, you may become bored and nervous while waiting. Above all, don't be late, if an emergency comes up, just call and explain your situation. People are usually understanding.

Dress neatly, make sure your clothes are clean and pressed. Pay close attention to details, many interviewers look at shoes and accessories for clues about your personality and habits. Also, dress appropriately, for example, if you are interviewing for a position where you will have to dress up, such as a bank teller, you will want to wear dress-up clothes. But if you are interviewing for a maintenance worker position, school clothes will be fine.

When you greet the interviewer, smile and give a firm handshake. Then sit back, relax, and answer questions confidently and clearly, the rest is up to you as you try to make your first impression count.

Exercise E4-8

Correct the run-on sentences you identified in Exercises E4-5 and E4-6.

 ## COLLABORATIVE WORK

After you have revised your explaining essay, exchange papers with a classmate, and do the following tasks:

A. Circle any fragments.

B. Underline any run-on sentences.

Then return the paper to its writer, and use the information in this section to edit your draft.

CHAPTER FIVE

Investigating
Reading and Writing for a Reason

**But it is part of the business of the writer—to examine
attitudes, to go beneath the surface, to tap the source.**
—JAMES BALDWIN

We all know what the term *investigator* means. From Sherlock Holmes, the fictional British private investigator who solved the most complex crime cases, to characters on TV detective series today, these private eyes solved crimes by investigating— finding relevant and important information about their cases.

Students need to investigate as well, though not necessarily by following criminals in dark alleys. Most research papers, in fact, are based on investigation. **Investigating** in this sense involves gathering as much information as possible about a person, a place, event, or topic. This information can be gathered through interviews with people; through library research; through visits to archives (places where books, letters, personal papers, maps, documents, and other records are kept); through books, newspapers, and magazines; or through the Internet. In fact, as technology advances, more of this information is available right on your computer—whether you visit a person, a place, or a library on-line. During your college career, you will probably write research papers in many different classes.

As you investigate for your own papers, you must be certain to answer the six journalist's questions—*who, what, where, when, why,* and *how.* As you answer each of these questions, you must constantly ask yourself what information your reader needs to know to gain a full understanding of your topic. You cannot assume that your readers are familiar with your subject or that they will be able to figure out what you are trying to say. You must remember that the more information you provide, the better and deeper your readers' understanding and appreciation will be. If you do a very thorough and careful job of investigating and explaining, you will then find the answer to the most important questions: *why* and *how.*

Investigating includes not only finding the answers to questions but presenting the information in such a way that your readers have enough facts to come to the same conclusions you did. Your readers will do this not because you told them what to think but because you *showed* them—through information, facts, details, examples, and quotations—all the information they need to understand the topic for themselves.

In a book titled *Young Men and Fire,* writer Norman Maclean investigates the causes and effects of a terrible forest fire that killed twelve fire fighters in Mann Gulch, Montana, in 1949. The fire fighters were dropped from a plane into the burning forest, wearing parachutes developed by a man named Frank Derry. Maclean gathered information about the Derry parachute by reading newspapers and reports, by interviewing fire fighters, and by examining the parachutes himself.

> The parachute developed by Frank Derry became the standard Smoke-jumpers' parachute for many years and is the parachute used by the crew that dropped on the Mann Gulch fire. The rocking motion had been reduced by three openings through which air could be released—an opening in the top and two slots on opposite sides. On the outside of the chute attached to the slots were "tails," pieces of nylon that acted as rudders to guide the flow of air coming through the slots, and to them guide lines were attached so that the direction of the flight was ultimately determined by the jumper. . . . It had a speed of seven or eight knots, and, as soon as the jumper could, he turned his face to the wind and looked over his shoulder to see, among other things, that he didn't smash into a cliff.

Through the process of investigating, Maclean discovered *who* used the parachute, *what* the parachute was used for, *why* the parachute was designed in a particular way, and *where, when,* and *how* it was used. This knowledge allowed him to add considerable depth to his account of the fire fighters' parachute jump. It also allows us as readers to realize that even well-designed equipment was not enough to save the fire fighters from their fate.

LEARNING FROM PUBLISHED WRITERS

The following professional essay, "America's New Merchants of Death," was written by William Ecenbarger and published in *Reader's Digest* in April 1993. Using investigation to support his conclusions, Ecenbarger reveals how American tobacco companies encourage youngsters in other nations to smoke. The companies use this strategy to make up for declining cigarette sales in the United States.

Before You Read

Focusing Your Attention

Before you read this investigating essay, take a few moments to respond to the following questions in your journal:

1. Think of a topic or issue that has been reported in the news recently. If you were asked to give an investigative report on this topic, what questions would you ask to gather the necessary information?

2.   In the article you are about to read, the writer investigates the ways cigarette manufacturing companies encourage young people in other countries to smoke. Make a list of the things that you suspect these companies do to encourage new young customers to begin smoking.

Expanding Your Vocabulary

Here are some words and their meanings that are important to your understanding of the essay. You might want to review them before you begin to read.

"children are being **lured** [tempted] into nicotine addiction" (paragraph 2)

"companies have been fighting legislation that **curtails** [decreases or stops] cigarette use by minors" (paragraph 2)

"children are being **seduced** [unfairly persuaded] into smoking" (paragraph 3)

"Smoking rates in the **Third World** [developing nations of the world] are climbing" (paragraph 4)

"**Philip Morris** [one of the leading U.S. tobacco companies, maker of Marlboro cigarettes] assured stockholders" (paragraph 6)

"Developing countries are unusually **vulnerable to** [open to attack by] cigarette advertising." (paragraph 12)

"Into this climate of **naïveté** [innocence and/or ignorance]" (paragraph 14)

"Tobacco advertising is more **pervasive** [widespread]" (paragraph 16)

"speaking **on condition of anonymity** [with the guarantee that one's identity will not be revealed]" (paragraph 18)

"It's **ludicrous** [ridiculous]" (paragraph 18)

"Sports sponsorship is even more **insidious** [persuasive but harmful]" (paragraph 24)

"Tobacco logos are **blazoned** [prominently displayed] on events of every description" (paragraph 24)

"Tobacco companies **skirt** [avoid] laws against TV commercials." (paragraph 25)

"many of the children who **succumb** [give in, surrender]" (paragraph 27)

"U.S. tobacco companies **capitalize** [make a profit] on this by associating smoking with **affluence** [wealth]." (paragraph 35)

"American cigarettes are considered a **gauge** [measurement] of style and **panache** [flair]" (paragraph 38)

"The weapon Washington **wielded** [used]" (paragraph 42)

"It empowers the USTR to **retaliate** [get revenge]—with **punitive** [punishing] tariffs" (paragraph 42)

William Ecenbarger

America's New Merchants of Death*

In Germany, three women in black miniskirts set up a display table   **1**
beside a Cadillac in the center of Dresden. In exchange for an empty
pack of local cigarettes, they offer passers-by a pack of Lucky Strikes
and a leaflet that reads: "You just got hold of a nice piece of America.
Lucky Strike is the original . . . a real classic." Says German physician Bernhard Humburger, who monitors youth smoking, "Adolescents time and again receive cigarettes at such promotions."

- A Jeep decorated with the yellow Camel logo pulls up in front of a
  high school in Buenos Aires. The driver, a blond woman wearing
  khaki safari gear, begins handing out free cigarettes to 15- and 16-
  year-olds on their lunch recess.

- In Malaysia, a man responds to a television commercial for "Salem
  High Country Holidays." When he tries to book a trip, he is refused
  by the office manager, who later admits that the $2.5-million-a-year
  operation exists only to advertise Salem on TV. This promotes Salem
  cigarettes without technically breaking the law.

- At a video arcade in Taipei, free American cigarettes are strewn atop
  each game. "As long as they're here, I may as well try one," says a
  pony-tailed high-school girl in a Chicago Bears T-shirt. Before the
  United States entered the Taiwanese cigarette market, such
  giveaways were uncommon at spots frequented by adolescents.

A *Reader's Digest* investigation covering 20 countries on four conti-   **2**
nents has revealed that millions of children are being lured into nicotine addiction by American cigarette makers. In several nations, U.S.
tobacco companies have been fighting legislation that curtails cigarette
use by minors and are cleverly violating the spirit of curbs on advertising. Their activities clearly show a cynical disregard for public health.

But the most shocking finding is that children are being seduced   **3**
into smoking in the name of America itself. In some countries, tobacco companies never would have gained a foothold without the
help of a powerful ally: the U.S. government.

*William Ecenbarger, "America's New Merchants of Death." *Reader's Digest* (Apr., 1993),
pp. 50–57.

Although domestic sales have dropped for eight straight years, and   **4**
by the year 2000 only one in seven Americans will likely smoke, sales
elsewhere have more than tripled since 1985. Smoking rates in the
Third World are climbing more than two percent a year. Most alarming is the rise in youth smoking. In the Philippines, 22.7 percent of
people under 18 now smoke. In some Latin American cities, the
teen-age rate is an astonishing 50 percent. In Hong Kong, children as
young as seven are smoking.

Why are the young so important? Because millions of adult smok-   **5**
ers either kick their habit or die each year, the cigarette industry depends on attracting new customers. Most smokers begin between ages
12 and 16; if a young person hasn't begun by 18, he or she is unlikely
ever to smoke.

"Tobacco is a growth industry, and we are gaining in volume and   **6**
share in markets around the world," Philip Morris assured stockholders in its 1991 annual report.

"Growth prospects internationally have never been better," gushed   **7**
Dale Sisel, chief executive officer of R. J. Reynolds (RJR) Tobacco
International at last summer's international tobacco conference in
Raleigh, N.C. "We all produce and sell a legal product that more
than one billion consumers around the world use every single day."

Unmentioned at the conference was the fact that smoking is one   **8**
of the leading causes of premature death, linked to cancers of the
mouth, lung, esophagus, kidney, pancreas, bladder and cervix, as well
as to heart disease. Or that, according to The World Health Organization, tobacco will prematurely kill 200 million who are now children and eventually wipe out ten percent of the world's population.
This grim prospect is due in no small part to the spectacular U.S. invasion of overseas markets.

More than 50,000 medical studies have demonstrated these haz-   **9**
ards. Yet the tobacco gurus assembled at Raleigh referred to the "debate" and "controversy" over smoking.

"The American people need to know precisely how their compa-   **10**
nies and government are promoting smoking among the world's children," says Dr. Carlos Ferreyra Nuñez, president of the Argentine Association of Public Health. "If they knew the full story, I believe they
would stop this outrage."

Here is that story.   **11**

Developing countries are unusually vulnerable to cigarette adver-   **12**
tising. Until recently, some of them sold tobacco only through government monopolies, with little or no attempt at persuasion. And be-

cause most of these countries don't have effective anti-smoking campaigns, many of their people are surprisingly innocent of the link between tobacco and disease. In Manila, we even found cigarettes sold at a snack bar operated by the local Boy Scouts.

Many governments, moreover, are reluctant to wage anti-smoking wars because they're addicted to tobacco taxes. Argentina gets 22.5 percent of all its tax revenue from tobacco; Malawi, 16.7 percent.   **13**

Into this climate of naïveté and neglect, American tobacco companies have unleashed not only the marketing wizardry that most of us take for granted, but other tactics they wouldn't dare use here.   **14**

In Malaysia, *Gila-Gila*, a comic book popular with elementary-school students, carried a Lucky Strike ad. Teen-agers going to rock concerts or discos in Budapest are regularly met by attractive women in cowboy outfits who hand them Marlboros. Those who accept a light on the spot also receive Marlboro sunglasses.   **15**

Tobacco advertising is more pervasive in other parts of the world than here. African merchants can get their shops painted to look like a pack of Marlboros. The Camel logo adorns store awnings and taxis in Warsaw. Christmas trees in Malaysian discos are trimmed free by Kent—with balls and stars bearing the Kent logo. In Mexico, one in five TV commercials is for cigarettes. On an average day, 60 spots for American brands appear on Japanese TV, many of them during programs watched by teens.   **16**

Although their marketing budgets are secret, tobacco companies have bolstered their spending for international advertising, adding substantially to the $4 billion allocated yearly for the United States. "It's crucial for them," says Richard Pollay, professor of marketing at the University of British Columbia. "Familiarity in advertising breeds trust."   **17**

Tobacco spokesmen insist that cigarette advertising draws only people who already smoke. But an ad executive who worked until recently on the Philip Morris account, speaking on condition of anonymity, disagrees. "You don't have to be a brain surgeon to figure out what's going on. Just look at the ads. It's ludicrous for them to deny that a cartoon character like Joe Camel isn't attractive to kids."   **18**

Dr. John L. Clowe, president of the American Medical Association, says, "It is clear that advertising fosters tobacco use among children. And, despite tobacco-industry denials, ads like Joe Camel are especially appealing to adolescents, equating smoking with sexual prowess, athleticism, even success."   **19**

Numerous independent studies support this view. Time and again   **20** they have shown that cigarette advertising creates an environment in which young people are more likely to smoke. That may explain why the U.S. Centers for Disease Control found that smokers between ages 12 and 18 prefer Marlboro, Newport and Camel—three of the most advertised brands.

Like the United States, some of the more progressive developing countries have banned cigarette commercials on TV and radio. This doesn't stop the tobacco companies, however. To keep their logos before the public, they resort to "brand-stretching"—advertising non-tobacco products and services named after their brands. Most of these items have special appeal to young people: Marlboro jeans and jackets, for example. **21**

In Malaysia, a music store called Salem Power Station wraps customers' tapes and CDs in plastic bags bearing the Salem logo, and television carries an MTV-like show called "Salem Powerhits." A Budapest radio station broadcasts a rock program called the Marlboro Hit Parade, and in China Philip Morris sponsors the Marlboro American Music Hour. **22**

Rock concerts are especially effective. One of the live performances under tobacco sponsorship (Salems in Seoul) was by Paula Abdul, who is popular among teens. Stars who have appeared in televised concerts underwritten by the industry include Madonna (Salems in Hong Kong) and Dire Straits (Kents in Malaysia). **23**

Sports sponsorship is even more insidious, for it implies that smoking and fitness mix. Tobacco logos are blazoned on events of every description, from cycling in Morocco to badminton in Indonesia. There's the Salem Open Tennis Tournament in Hong Kong and the Kent International Sailing Regatta, to name just a couple. U.S. tobacco companies spent $100 million sponsoring sports in 1992—double the 1985 total. **24**

Tobacco companies regularly skirt laws against TV commercials. In Shanghai, Philip Morris airs spots for "The World of Marlboro" at the end of American sitcom reruns. Except that cigarettes aren't mentioned, the ad is identical to a Marlboro commercial: the Marlboro man and his horse splash across a stream, the man dismounts and gazes toward mountains that look like the Rockies. **25**

One of the most misleading forms of brand-stretching is the "travel" ad. In Thailand, where all cigarette advertising is forbidden, an ad appeared in the Bangkok *Post* for "Kent Leisure Holidays." It showed the company's logo and offered "A Pleasure Trip." A Thai **26** doctor phoned to book the trip, but was turned down and told the cruise ship was in the Caribbean and wouldn't be in Bangkok for at least two years.

Unfortunately, many of the children who succumb to brand-stretching find habits that begin as cobwebs end up as steel cables. At a McDonald's in Malaysia, Sunil Ramanathan, 16, finishes off a Big Mac, lights a Marlboro and inhales deeply. He says he's smoked since he was ten.   **27**

"I know smoking is bad for me, but I can't stop. I try to quit, but after one day I start again."   **28**

Just off Taipei's bustling Keelung Road, high-school students begin filing into the Whisky A Go-Go disco about 9 p.m., and soon the room is a sea of denim. On each table are free packs of Salems. Before long, overhead fans are fighting a losing battle with the smoke.   **29**

"American tobacco companies spend more than a quarter of a billion dollars every year giving away cigarettes, many of which are smoked by children and teen-agers," says Joe Tye, editor of the newsletter *Tobacco Free Youth Reporter*. "If they can get a youngster to smoke a few packs, chances are he'll be a customer for life."   **30**

The companies say adult establishments, such as discos, cannot legally admit minors. The industry insists it instructs distributors of free samples to screen out the underaged. "It doesn't work," says Cecilia Sepulveda, a tobacco expert with Chile's Ministry of Public Health. "We estimate that 40 percent of 13-year-olds in Santiago smoke."   **31**

Of seven under-18 students assembled at the Beltram High School in Buenos Aires, five say they have been offered free Camels. None was asked his age. One, Ruben Paz, 16, said he got his from a "blond, American-looking girl" handing out cigarettes from "the Camel Jeep" at the school door.   **32**

Young black-marketers hawk single cigarettes to their peers. Ten-year-olds in the tin-roofed *kampungs* of the Malaysian jungle can buy a Salem for eight cents. Students at the St. Ignatius School in Santiago buy cigarettes for ten cents at *carritos*, handcarts that also sell candy and soft drinks near the school.   **33**

Although increasingly controlled in America, vending machines are used widely abroad. They were rare in East Germany, but since reunification U.S. and British companies have installed tens of thousands. In parts of Japan, machines sit on almost every corner.   **34**

"Many African children have two hopes," says Paul Wangai, a   **35**
physician in Nairobi, Kenya. "One is to go to heaven, the other to
America. U.S. tobacco companies capitalize on this by associating
smoking with affluence. It's not uncommon to hear children say they
start because of the glamorous life-style associated with smoking."

Cigarette advertising outside the United States focuses heavily on   **36**
our life-styles; indeed, the ads are seen as a way of learning about
America itself. A letter from secretarial students in China appeared
in the Petaluma, Calif., *Argus-Courier:* "Every day we listen to the
Marlboro American Music Hour. We enjoy Elvis Presley and Michael
Jackson. We smoke American cigarettes and wear American clothes.
We are eager to gain more information about American life."

To hear the children of the rest of the world tell it, everyone in   **37**
America smokes. The truth is, the United States has one of the *lowest*
smoking rates — 25.5 percent of the population.

Yet because of U.S. advertising, American cigarettes are considered   **38**
a gauge of style and panache. In Bangkok, young Thais sew Marlboro
logos on their jackets and jeans to boost their status. At the city's
Wat Nai Rong High School, 17-year-old Wasana Warathongchai says
smoking makes her feel "sophisticated and cosmopolitan, like America." She lumps Marlboros with "jeans and denim jackets, Pizza Hut,
everything we like about America."

The theme of last summer's Raleigh conference was "The Tobacco   **39**
Industry to the Year 2000," and on hand were two experts from the
U.S. Department of Agriculture to help the industry sell tobacco
overseas.

. . . Wait a minute. Didn't the American government decide in   **40**
1964 that cigarettes are a major cause of death and disease, and
doesn't the U.S. government discourage its own citizens from smoking? Then how can we encourage people of other nations to smoke?

For many years, Japan, Korea, Taiwan and Thailand imposed stern
trade restrictions on imported cigarettes. But in the early 1980s,
American tobacco companies joined forces with the Office of the
U.S. Trade Representative (USTR) to crack these Asian markets.

The weapon Washington wielded was Section 301 of the Trade   **42**
Act of 1974. It empowers the USTR to retaliate — with punitive tar-
iffs — against any nation thought to have imposed unfair barriers on
American products.

In September 1985, the USTR began an investigation of Japanese   **43**
trading practices. Sen. Jesse Helms (R., N.C.) then stepped in on be-

half of the tobacco industry. Helms dispatched a letter to Prime Minister Yasuhiro Nakasone, intimating he could not support a substantial U.S. defense presence in the Pacific or help stem the tide of anti-Japanese trade sentiment in Congress unless Japan opened its cigarette market.

"I urge that you establish a timetable for allowing U.S. cigarettes a specific share of your market," Helms wrote. "I suggest a total of 20 percent within 18 months." Three months later, the Japanese government agreed to open its markets more.

During this same period, tobacco companies enlisted two former aides to President Reagan—Michael Deaver and Richard Allen—as lobbyists. Deaver received $250,000 for pressing Philip Morris's case in South Korea and in a meeting with President Chun Doo Hwan. That country yielded to a 301 action in May 1988. By 1990, tobacco-industry clout had opened markets in Taiwan and Thailand.

The results have been devastating. Before the Americans arrived, smoking rates were declining slightly in Japan, but since 1987 cigarette consumption by minors has increased 16 percent. Among Taiwanese high-school students, the smoking rate climbed from 19.5 percent in 1985 to 32.2 percent in 1987. Between 1988 and 1991, the number of Thai smokers ages 15 to 19 increased 24 percent, with similar increases for Korean high-school boys.

"We were making headway in discouraging smoking, but all has been washed away by the flood of American advertising," says David D. Yen, chairman of an anti-smoking group in Taiwan. "We want your friendship, but not your tobacco."

The cigarette lobby will have significant access to the Clinton Administration. A number of high-level Clinton appointees have had financial ties to the tobacco industry, including U.S. Trade Representative Mickey Kantor, who represented smoking interests and whose former law firm lobbies for Philip Morris. Says University of California at San Francisco medical-school professor Stanton Glantz: "It's like the fox guarding the henhouse."

The U.S. cigarette business is booming. Exports are soaring, factories being built. And at the end of the rainbow lies China, with 300 million smokers—30 percent of the world market.

"This vastly larger marketplace means a whole new world of opportunities," RJR's Dale Sisel told the Raleigh conference. Expansion abroad, he continued, would "pave the way for a bigger and brighter future."

That kind of talk makes Argentina's Dr. Ferreyra Nuñez quake   51
with anger. "American tobacco companies know their product causes
death. Yet they promote smoking among children. What must these
people think? Don't they have children of their own?"

 ## QUESTIONS FOR CRITICAL THINKING

THINKING CRITICALLY ABOUT CONTENT

1. Why do you think the writer includes so many statistics (numbers and
    percentages)? Which statistics do you think are most effective?

2. Why do you think the writer begins his article with several anecdotes
    (descriptions of true incidents)?

THINKING CRITICALLY ABOUT PURPOSE

3. What do you think Ecenbarger's purpose is in this essay?

4. Why do you think the writer quotes children in this essay?

THINKING CRITICALLY ABOUT AUDIENCE

5. What group or groups of readers do you think would most benefit from reading
    this article?

6. What effect might the closing quote have on the readers of this article?

THINKING CRITICALLY ABOUT POINT OF VIEW

7. What evidence does the writer give to prove that children are being victimized
    by both cigarette companies and the U.S. government? Is the evidence
    convincing?

8. If an article about children smoking in other countries were being written by
    someone who supported the tobacco industry, what arguments might he or she
    make in defense of tactics such as strong advertising and free cigarettes? Write a
    summary of these arguments.

LEARNING FROM YOUR PEERS

Satisfying your curiosity about an unfamiliar subject often requires some kind of investigation. You may go to the library or the telephone directory seeking the answers
to a particular question. When you ask friends and neighbors about how to find a
good used car or what restaurants have the best meals, you are investigating. In response to an investigating assignment, we are going to follow the writing process of a
student named LaKesha Montgomery.

LaKesha's Writing Assignment: Investigating

This is the topic LaKesha's instructor assigned:

When we meet people who have occupations that interest us, we often wonder what led them to pursue that line of work and what we can learn from them. This writing assignment will give you an opportunity to ask questions of people who work in fields that you find interesting. You may interview anyone for this assignment, but you might prefer to investigate a subject that is closely related to your future profession. You might ask questions like these: How does this profession help other people? How will this profession affect your day-to-day life? What interesting types of work or people will this profession expose you to? Organize the results of your interview into an investigating essay.

LaKesha goes through the writing process as outlined in Chapter 1: *thinking, planning, developing, organizing, drafting, revising,* and *editing.*

Thinking

LaKesha knows exactly what she wants to investigate for this assignment. She's been planning her own apartment for about two years. She is living at home with her parents to save money, but she wants her first apartment to reflect her strong interest in interior design. Not knowing exactly where to start her search, LaKesha browses through the classified advertisements under "Furniture" and "Estate Sales" in the Sunday newspaper. She notices that a few furniture stores advertise free design consultations. She writes down their telephone numbers.

Planning

The next day, LaKesha makes several telephone calls to find some people willing to be interviewed. She tells them that she has a list of questions she would like to ask them about planning for a first apartment. LaKesha asks them what time is convenient for them and then makes appointments for later in the week. She plans to interview a designer for a furniture store and a person who manages estate sales.

The next time her writing class meets, LaKesha works with some of her classmates to develop a list of questions to ask her interviewees. LaKesha plans to meet with the designer and the estate sales manager for about 15 minutes each, so she decides that she does not need more than ten general questions.

1. What are the most important items to buy for my first apartment?

2. Are there some items I should avoid buying?

3. How can I decide what color scheme to use?

4. What is the biggest mistake people make when they move into their first apartment?

5. What items should I purchase new?

6. What items should I look for at thrift shops and estate sales?

7. What items are especially important for students to own?

8. How can I plan my apartment so that it will have enough storage space for books?

9. What is the best way to organize limited storage space for clothes and accessories?

10. How can I make the apartment reflect my own personality and feel like home?

Before she conducts the interviews, LaKesha writes her questions on a notepad, leaving plenty of space for the answers. She also leaves a blank space at the end of her questions where she can expand her notes after the interviews.

Developing

After LaKesha meets with the designer, Marjorie Bliss, and the estate sale manager, Joyce Dotson, she has several pages of notes. Marjorie talked about what kind of furniture to buy first and what to spend the most money on; she also discussed designing the apartment, planning color schemes, and allowing for seasonal decorations. Joyce emphasized ways to save money on items that most people wouldn't think of, such as kitchen utensils and dish towels. She also told LaKesha that sometimes estate sales offer an opportunity to find unusual decorating items at reduced prices.

LaKesha decides that her questions have given her plenty of material for her essay. She just needs to spend some time expanding her notes before she forgets any important details. She goes back over her interview notes and writes down additional comments that Marjorie and Joyce made. Here are some of the notes she took:

1. What are the most important items to buy for my first apartment?

   • mattress

   • box springs--old ones from home are broken down--should buy new ones to get a good night's sleep

2. Are there some items I should avoid buying?

   • expensive couch

   • living room furniture

   • major appliances--too hard to move--try to find apartment with appliances furnished

3. How can I decide what color scheme to use?

   - Choose one basic color that I like--then coordinate with two accent colors
   - Red, white, and blue is versatile--can be contemporary or country
   - Make sure I love something--don't just buy it for function

4. What is the biggest mistake that people make when they move into their first apartment?

   - They spend too much money on furniture that others will use and not enough on things for themselves--like a good mattress, a back-supporting chair, a desk with plenty of nooks and crannies.
   - They spend a lot of money on things like shiny pots and pans and dishes when they could get by on things purchased from estate sales and garage sales.
   - They spend too much on items like lamps that they will probably get tired of after a few years.

5. What items should I purchase new?

   - Definitely the mattress and box springs
   - A good desk chair--unless I can find one at an estate sale
   - A computer is more important than furniture these days

6. What items should I look for at thrift shops and estate sales?

   - pots, pans, kitchen equipment
   - sheets, dish towels, unusual decorating items at reasonable prices

7. What items are especially important for students to own?

   - desk, bookshelves, a good chair

8. How can I plan my apartment so that it will have enough storage space for books?

   - Don't skimp when buying functional book storage. Maybe buy plastic crates from thrift stores and stack them up to make bookshelves.

9. What is the best way to organize limited storage space for clothes and accessories?

   - Rotate clothes by season

- Throw away, give away, or sell clothes I don't wear. Have a yard sale.

10. How can I make the apartment reflect my own personality and feel like home?

- Buy only things I love
- Save a little money for an occasional extravagance
- Shop at estate sales for things just like my grandmother's--or completely unlike my grandmother's--depending on what I like
- Look through magazines and find pictures of rooms that I love. Magazines are newer and trendier than decorating books.

Organizing

LaKesha meets with her writing group and tells them about her interviews. Others in her group have also found people who were willing to talk about their jobs. The members of the writing group agree that LaKesha should mention her career goal first, then explain the advice given to her by the people she interviewed.

This is the framework that LaKesha came up with after meeting with her group:

1. Introduction--my career goal--commercial interior design. Plus who I interviewed.

2. Marjorie--how I got in touch with her and what she told me. Stuff about magazines and a desk and bookshelf and chairs.

3. Important--mattress, box springs, and reason why.

4. About style and color schemes. How to do research on these.

5. Then Joyce Dotson--about estate sales. What to buy. How to buy it.

6. Conclusion--what I learned and what I will do to plan my apartment.

Drafting

Here is the draft that LaKesha wrote.

LaKesha's Essay: First Draft

Main Idea: I learned how to start designing my own apartment from an interior decorator and an estate salesperson.

For this assignment, I wanted to investigate ways to decorate my first apartment on a budget. One should always try to get the most from their money. I plan to major in commercial interior design. I interviewed one woman who is a designer for an upscale furniture store (or gallery, as they call it). I also interviewed another interesting woman. This one sells entire estates. People should respect these ladies' opinions and admire their work. They were happy to give me some good advice, which I plan to use when I finally move into my own place. I learned that if a person plans ahead, you can be prepared to move out.

First I went to see Marjorie Bliss, an interior designer. She has been working in this field for 10 years. Few disagree with her advice. I called Marjorie for an appointment and told her that I would not likely be buying anything. She scheduled me for a weekday morning when the store is not busy. She told me that I should start looking through magazines now to decide what kind of look I would like to live with. Marjorie said that making things comfortable is her priority. It is especially important in working with small places. Clutter is always a problem when students do not have enough places to put things away. She suggested that I might want to think about a desk and large bookshelf first. Although these pieces of furniture do not have to be new, they should be functional. Marjorie said that the chair is the most important purchase, because they will determine how long I am willing to sit and study.

She said the next thing to consider buying new would be a mattress, box springs, and bed frame. According to Marjorie, some people who move out of their parents' house just take these items with them. However, often the furniture is worn out because the pieces were bought for a much younger person or were passed down from someone else in the family. When I looked at the prices of the mattresses, I decided that I should start saving now! Six hundred dollars is a lot to pay for something to sleep on--not even the headboard. None of the mattresses could make their way into my pocketbook.

I told her I was very interested in making my apartment look nice, not just comfortable. Everybody wants their place to be neat and presentable. She said that once I decide on a style, I should choose one color to dominate. One or two colors to coordinate are the best. What do you think is the easiest combination to work with? According to Marjorie, very easy colors to work with are red, white, and blue. Those colors can be contemporary, traditional, or it can be country. Just a change in accessories can sometimes change the whole mood of the room if the furniture has a basic line to them. She said I could even change some inexpensive accessories to match the season. For example, a candle and a centerpiece can make its decorating presence known subtly and cheaply. Marjorie also showed me several magazines to look for at the library and told me that I should save my money and purchase only things that I absolutely need (like the desk, chair, and bed) until I have my basic furnishings. She said that I could start putting items on layaway and making payments about a year before I am ready to move into my apartment.

The next day I went to the library and spent several hours looking at the magazines that she recommended. Some of the magazines had its "helpful hints" grouped together in special sections. Anyway, I think I have enough ideas now to help me furnish several houses. A good thing that is, considering my major.

The next person I interviewed was Joyce Dotson. She sells estates when people die or retire or move out of state. She sells everything that no one in the family wants. Sometimes there are valuable pieces of furniture, often antiques. However, there are always items that are very low cost, because most people already have enough of them. She told me that items like towels, sheets, dishcloths, and kitchen items are always good buys. Joyce said that I should make a list of everything that I need and go to the part of the house where those items are located as soon as the estate sale opens. I should look through things closely. Each room and closet offers potential savings bonanzas. There will usually be a line, but the first people being antique dealers and collectors. The majority are coming for the expensive items. Joyce said that I could buy many useful things for a small fraction of the price of similar new items. Like Marjorie, she advised me to start buying items for my apartment about a year ahead of time and to keep crossing things off my master list as I buy them. She said it is easy to buy impulse items at estate sales and spend money on things I do not really need. She said that if I see something I really like that goes with my decorating scheme, it's not a bad idea to buy it at an estate sale because the price will never be better. She said if I change my mind later, I can always have a yard sale.

These interviews have made me more excited than ever about getting my own apartment. Neither the designers nor I are interested in outlandish ideas. I have started a list of the things I need and things I like. I've even encouraged my boyfriend, Ryan, to start his own list for when he moves out. I believe that I was lucky to interview two people who know so much. This decorating duo offer good advice. Marjorie and Joyce have helped me think about the things I will need every day. Everything they have told me has been helpful. Joyce, who has access to all kinds of furniture, plans to let me know if she is going to be selling a desk and bookcase and bed at reasonable prices. I know that I will be watching the classified advertisements for her sales. I will also be spending long hours in the library, looking at pictures and imagining how perfect my first apartment will be with its carefully selected furniture and accessories.

Revising

LaKesha was really charged up from these two interviews and was anxious to put her discoveries into readable form. She was amazed at how fast she wrote. She knows that revising this essay will take more time than usual because she didn't pay much attention to how she made her statements; she just wanted to put the ideas from her interviews onto paper. But now the time has come to revise. As usual, the instructor gives the class some guidelines to follow for their revising process. This time, the instructor wants the class members to focus on developing their paragraphs as fully as possible.

LaKesha turns to the Checklist for Developing Paragraphs on page 176. She sees quickly that this set of revision questions is designed to help her develop her ideas fully within her paragraphs and say exactly what she means in the best way possible. So she welcomes this list to start her on her revising process. She reads the Tips for Revising and completes the exercises her instructor assigns.

When she returns to her own paper, LaKesha approaches her revision cautiously because she knows she has a lot of work to do. When she writes fast without revising along the way, her paragraphs usually stop before they should, and she doesn't include enough examples and explanations. So the Checklist for Developing Paragraphs comes her way at an opportune time. And it's a good checklist to apply to any essay she composes. As she rereads her draft against the checklist, she finds several problems and begins noting changes she wants to make. In one paragraph she finds a topic sentence that is not well developed, and in another she finds a line of reasoning that doesn't make sense. Another paragraph doesn't have a closing remark. LaKesha continues to survey her draft with special attention to these three types of errors.

 ## COLLABORATIVE WORK

PEER GROUP ACTIVITY

After you read the portions of the Tips for Revising your instructor assigns, turn to LaKesha's first draft (pp. 163–166), and complete the following tasks in small groups:

A. Put a star by any paragraphs that would be more effective if they followed another line of reasoning.

B. Put an X by any paragraph that is not fully developed.

Compare the marks your group recorded with those your instructor will show you. Where do your marks differ from your instructor's? What do you need to review before writing your own essay?

CLASS ACTIVITY

As an entire class, look at the underlined portions of LaKesha's revised draft (pp. 169–172).

A.   Did you identify the **revision** problems that LaKesha corrected?

B.   Do you think her changes are good ones? Discuss her changes.

Editing

Now that LaKesha has expanded her paragraphs to more accurately represent her individual thoughts and her logical reasoning, she needs to do some final proofreading and editing before handing in her essay. The instructor explains that at this point all the students in the class need to have some basic knowledge about agreement—between subjects and verbs and between pronouns and their antecedents. So LaKesha shifts her focus from the content of her sentences to specific points of grammar. She reads the Tips for Editing section in this chapter to learn about both types of agreement. After she finishes the exercises her instructor assigns, she goes over the questions in the Checklist for Correcting Agreement Problems one by one and makes changes so that her revised draft fulfills all these requirements.

 COLLABORATIVE WORK

PEER GROUP ACTIVITY

After you read the portions of the Tips for Editing your instructor assigns, turn to LaKesha's first draft (pp. 163–166), and complete the following tasks in small groups:

A.   Underline all the subjects and verbs (for definitions, see p. 187) that do not agree.

B.   Circle any pronouns and antecedents (for definitions, see p. 199) that do not agree.

Compare the marks your group recorded with those your instructor will show you. Where do your marks differ from your instructor's? What do you need to review before writing your own essay?

CLASS ACTIVITY

As an entire class, look at the underlined portions of LaKesha's revised draft (pp. 169–172) to see how she changed each sentence.

A. Did you identify the **editing** problems that LaKesha corrected?

B. Do you think her changes are good ones? Discuss her changes.

LaKesha's Revised Essay

Designing Decisions

For this assignment, I wanted to investigate ways to decorate my first apartment on a budget. One should always try to get the most from ~~their~~ his or her money. I plan to major in commercial interior design. I interviewed one woman who is a designer for an upscale furniture store (or gallery, as they call it)~~./~~, and I also interviewed another interesting woman./ ~~This one~~ who sells entire estates. People should respect these ~~ladies'~~ women's opinions and admire their work. Marjorie Bliss, who works in the furniture store, has a very different job, however, from Joyce Dotson, who sells furniture and other decorative items when heirs no longer want them. Both women gave me good advice based on their different approaches to decorating. ~~They were happy to give me some good advice, which I plan to use when I finally move into my own place.~~ I learned that if a person plans ahead, ~~you~~ he or she can be prepared to move out.

First I went to see Marjorie Bliss, an interior designer. For a fee, interior designers help people plan, furnish, and decorate their homes. They take into consideration an individual's taste, life-style, and pocketbook when advising clients. Since s~~S~~he has been working in this field for 10 years/, ~~f~~Few disagree with her advice. I called ~~Marjorie~~ her for an appointment and told her that I would not likely be buying anything. She scheduled me for a weekday morning when the store is not busy--neither she nor any of the employees had customers at their desks. She told me that I should start looking through magazines now to decide what kind of look I would like to live with. Marjorie said that making things comfortable is her priority/, because iIt is especially important in working with small places. Since cØlutter is always a problem when students do not have enough places to put things away/. sŞhe suggested that I might want to think first about a desk and a large bookshelf .first/ Although these pieces of furniture do not have to be new, they should be functional. Marjorie said that the chair is the most important purchase, because ~~they~~ it will determine how long I am willing to sit and study.

She said the next thing to consider buying new would be a mattress, box springs, and bed frame. According to Marjorie, some people who move out of their parents' house just take these items with them. However, often the furniture is worn out because the pieces were bought for a much younger person or were passed down from someone else in the family. When I looked at my bed at home, I discovered Marjorie was right. Years of curling up in the very center had made a crater in my mattress center, and underneath the box springs sagged and metal protruded in half a dozen places. When I looked at the prices of the mattresses, I decided that I should start saving now!. Six hundred dollars is a lot to pay for something to sleep on--not even the headboard. None of the mattresses could make ~~their~~ its way into my pocketbook.

I told her I was very interested in making my apartment look nice, not just comfortable. Everybody wants ~~their~~ his or her place to be neat and presentable. She said that once I decide on a style, I should choose one color to dominate. One or two colors to coordinate are the best. What do you think is the easiest combination to work with? According to Marjorie, very easy colors to work with are red, white, and blue. Those colors can be contemporary, traditional, or ~~it can be~~ country. Just a change in accessories can sometimes change the whole mood of the room if the furniture has a basic line to ~~them~~ it. She said I could even change some inexpensive accessories to match the season. For example, a candle and a centerpiece can make ~~its~~ their decorating presence known subtly and cheaply. Marjorie also showed me several magazines to look for at the library and told me that I should save my money and purchase only things that I absolutely need (like the desk, chair, and bed) until I have my basic furnishings. She said that I could start putting items on layaway and making payments about a year before I am ready to move into my apartment. If people plan ahead, they can be prepared to move out.

The next day I went to the library and spent several hours looking at the magazines that she recommended. Some of the magazines had ~~its~~ their "helpful hints" grouped together in special sections. In the *Walls and Windows* hint section, I found useful information about painting. The magazine provided instructions for marbleizing, sponging, combing, and rag rolling to provide specialized finishes on walls. The hint included tools, paints, and approximate costs for each method as well as instructions on how to do the job. Anyway, I think I have enough ideas now to help me furnish several houses. A good thing that is, considering my major.

The next person I interviewed was Joyce Dotson. She sells estates when people die or retire or move out of state. She sells everything that no one in the family wants. Sometimes there are valuable pieces of furniture, often antiques. However, there are always items that are very low cost, because most people already have enough of them. She told me that items like towels, sheets, dishcloths, and kitchen items are always good buys. Towels that cost from $5 to $8 even at a discount store often sell for less than half that at most estate sales. Pots and pans often sell in sets for a few dollars rather than the $89 that I saw marked on all stainless steel cookware on sale last week. Joyce said that I should make a list of everything that I need and go to the part of the house where those items are located as soon as the estate sale opens. I should look through things closely. Each room and closet offers a potential savings bonanza$. There will usually be a line, but the first people ~~being~~ are antique dealers and collectors. The majority are coming for the expensive items. Joyce said that I could buy many useful things for a small fraction of the price of similar new items. First, I will need new linens and pots and pans. I can make do with plastic plates and cheap flatware for a while. Curtains, rugs, and decorative items can wait until I have more money. Like Marjorie, she advised me to start buying items for my apartment about a year ahead of time and to keep crossing things off my master list as I buy them. She said it is easy to buy impulse items at estate sales and spend money on things I do not really need. She said that if I see something I really like that goes with my decorating scheme, it's not a bad idea to buy it at an estate sale because the price will never be better. She said if I change my mind later, I can always have a yard sale.

These interviews have made me ~~more~~ as excited ~~than ever~~ about getting my own apartment as I was the day I received the acceptance letter and scholarship from my college. Neither the designers nor I am ~~are~~ interested in outlandish ideas. I have started a list of the things I need and things I like. For instance, I know now that I like Art Deco furniture and accessories. During the 1920s and 1930s modern furniture with clean lines and simple design became very popular. I saw a Swedish chair in blond wood that I would like to buy. I also like Tiffany glass lamps, which are very elaborate with shades that look like the stained glass windows in my church. I've even encouraged my boyfriend, Ryan, to start his own list for when he moves out. I believe that I was lucky to interview two people who know so much. This decorating duo offers good advice. Marjorie and Joyce have helped me think about the things I will need every day. Everything they have told me has been helpful. Joyce, who has access to all kinds of furniture, plans to let me know if she is going to be selling a desk and bookcase and bed at reasonable prices. I know that I will be watching the classified advertisements for her sales. I will also be spending long hours in the library, looking at pictures and imagining how perfect my first apartment will be with its carefully selected furniture and accessories.

WRITING YOUR OWN INVESTIGATING ESSAY

So far, you have seen a professional writer and a fellow student at work trying to investigate an idea, impression, or experience they feel is worth studying. As you read and followed the writing process of another student from first to final draft, you absorbed ideas to work with and ways of giving those ideas a form of their own. These reading and writing activities have prepared you to write your own essay investigating a special person from your point of view.

What Have You Discovered?

Before you begin your own writing task, let's review what you have learned in this chapter so far:

- Investigating involves finding relevant and important information about a subject.

- Investigating means learning not only *who, what, why, when,* and *where* something happened but also *how* it happened.

- Investigating means *showing* rather than just *telling* your readers the answers to these questions.

- To present your investigation effectively, you need to organize your ideas.

- To help you shape your essay, you should learn as much as possible about your readers.

- Before you write a draft, you need to decide on a point of view toward your subject.

- After you write a draft, you should revise your essay for meaning and organization.

- After you revise your essay, you should edit its grammar, usage, and sentence structure.

Your Writing Topic

Choose one of the following topics for your investigating essay:

1. In the article that you read in the beginning of this chapter, "America's New Merchants of Death," the writer investigated the ways cigarette companies encourage young people in other countries to begin smoking. Conduct your own investigation of the ways cigarette companies encourage people (particularly young people) to smoke in the United States. Carefully study the cigarette advertisements that appear in newspapers and magazines and on billboards, and then write an essay reporting the results of your investigation. Be sure to cover such issues as the visual images and wording used to make smoking seem appealing and the publications and other places where these ads appear.

2.   Interview people who are employed in a profession that you plan to pursue, and write an essay about why this field suits your own goals and objectives.

3.   Interview someone who holds a responsible position in your student community, such as an officer in a student organization or in student government. Try to find out what motivates this person to do this work, and then discover what difficulties and satisfactions are involved. Then write an essay summarizing your findings and highlighting the achievements of the person you interviewed.

4.   Create your own investigating essay (with the assistance of your instructor), and write a response to it.

When you have selected one of these topics, you may begin your writing process in the same way LaKesha did. (You may find rereading her experience helpful in giving you ideas.) This time your purpose is to write your own investigating essay. If some tasks occur out of order, that adjustment is probably part of your personal writing ritual. Follow your instincts, and let them mold your own writing process. But make sure you've worked through all the stages to your final draft.

YOUR WRITING PROCESS

THINKING   Generate as many ideas on your subject as you can in as many different ways as possible: rereading, listing, freewriting, brainstroming, clustering, discussing, and questioning.

PLANNING   Begin to give your ideas shape by deciding on your approach to your topic (your content, your purpose, your audience, and your point of view). Make a list of points you want to include in your essay.

DEVELOPING   Add more details on three or four specific, focused topics that you have chosen from your list of general points.

ORGANIZING   Organize your material in a way that will be most interesting to your audience.

DRAFTING   Write a working draft of your essay in complete sentences.

REVISING   Consulting the Tips for Revising in this chapter (pp. 176–186), revise your first draft—paying special attention to developing your paragraphs as fully as possible.

EDITING   Consulting the Tips for Editing in this chapter (pp. 187–206), edit your draft for grammar and correctness—paying special attention to agreement problems.

Turn in your revised draft to your instructor.

Some Final Thoughts

When you have completed your own essay, answer these four questions in your journal:

1. What was most difficult about this assignment?
2. What was easiest?
3. What did I learn about investigating by completing this assignment?
4. What did I learn about my own writing process from this assignment—how I prepared to write, how I wrote the first draft, how I revised, and how I edited?

Developing Paragraphs

Checklist for Developing Paragraphs

✓ Are the methods of reasoning used in the essay best for what is being said at different points: **definition, description, classification, cause-effect, comparison-contrast, and analysis?**
✓ Does each paragraph contain enough **examples, facts, and numbers?**

Urban planners, important members of the teams that develop or renew cities, look for the most logical ways to meet citizens' needs. Then they create the spaces, streets, and buildings that are appropriate for the many different people and activities of a given city. You may find that developing paragraphs is a bit like the procedure urban planners follow. For example, if your readers need to understand an unfamiliar word, you might build a paragraph that defines that word for them. If you want to bring to mind a special place, you might write a descriptive paragraph.

Kinds of Paragraphs

One way of developing paragraphs is to use specific patterns that capture the way we think about different issues and topics. For instance, if you want to communicate the atmosphere of a wonderful restaurant, you might use a description that appeals to your readers' senses. Or if your investigating essay deals with a topic unfamiliar to your audience, you might compare your topic to something they are already familiar with. The following methods are widely used for developing paragraphs logically. Each represents a different way of thinking about a topic. Sometimes you will use several of these methods in a single paragraph; other times, you will use one method for an entire paragraph.

Definition

When you explain the meaning of a term for your audience, you are **defining.** In paragraph 21 of "America's New Merchants of Death," William Ecenbarger uses definition to familiarize his audience with the strategies tobacco companies use to keep their product in the public eye.

> Like the United States, some of the more progressive developing countries have banned cigarette commercials on TV and radio. This doesn't stop the tobacco companies, however. To keep their logos before the public, they resort to "brand-stretching"—advertising non-tobacco

products and services named after their brands. Most of these items have special appeal to young people: Marlboro jeans and jackets, for example.

As LaKesha began to revise her essay, she decided that her paragraph about her interview with Marjorie Bliss would be clearer if she included a definition of *interior designer*.

TIPS FOR REVISING

First Draft:	First I went to see Marjorie Bliss, an interior designer. She has been working in this field for 10 years. Few disagree with her advice.
Revision:	First I went to see Marjorie Bliss, an interior designer. **For a fee, interior designers help people plan, furnish, and decorate their homes. They take into consideration an individual's taste, life-style, and pocketbook when advising clients.** Since she has been working in this field for 10 years, few disagree with her advice.

Now LaKesha's audience will better understand her paragraph, because she has defined what might be an unfamiliar term for them.

Description

A **description** draws a verbal picture for your audience of a place, object, person, group, or situation. In paragraph 1 of "America's New Merchants of Death," William Ecenbarger provides a list of vivid snapshots illustrating tobacco marketing around the world.

- A Jeep decorated with the yellow Camel logo pulls up in front of a high school in Buenos Aires. The driver, a blond woman wearing khaki safari gear, begins handing out free cigarettes to 15- and 16-year-olds on their lunch recess.

- In Malaysia, a man responds to a television commercial for "Salem High Country Holidays." When he tries to book a trip, he is refused by the office manager, who later admits that the $2.5-million-a-year operation exists only to advertise Salem on TV. This promotes Salem cigarettes without technically breaking the law.

- At a video arcade in Taipei, free American cigarettes are strewn atop each game. "As long as they're here, I may as well try one," says a pony-tailed high-school girl in a Chicago Bears T-shirt. Before the

United States entered the Taiwanese cigarette market, such giveaways were uncommon at spots frequented by adolescents.

LaKesha decided that she could develop paragraph 3 of her draft by describing the state of her own bedroom furniture to support Marjorie's point about worn mattresses.

First Draft:

She said the next thing to consider buying new would be a mattress, box springs, and bed frame. According to Marjorie, some people who move out of their parents' house just take these items with them. However, often the furniture is worn out because the pieces were bought for a much younger person or were passed down from someone else in the family. When I looked at the prices of mattresses, I decided that I should start saving now! Six hundred dollars is a lot to pay for something to sleep on--not even the headboard. None of the mattresses could make their way into my pocketbook.

Revision:

She said the next thing to consider buying new would be a mattress, box springs, and bed frame. According to Marjorie, some people who move out of their parents' house just take these items with them. However, often the furniture is worn out because the pieces were bought for a much younger person or were passed down from someone else in the family. **When I looked at my bed at home, I discovered Marjorie was right. Years of curling up in the very center had made a crater in my mattress center, and underneath the box springs sagged and metal protruded in half a dozen places.** When I looked at the prices of the mattresses, I decided that I should start saving now. Six hundred dollars is a lot to pay for something to sleep on--not even the headboard. None of the mattresses could make its way into my pocketbook.

Thanks to LaKesha's description, her readers can visualize the state of her mattress and box springs and can understand why she needs to start saving.

Classification

Another way of developing an idea is by **classifying** or grouping similar items in a paragraph. For instance, people can be grouped by similar occupations, hobbies, regions where they live, political beliefs, and so on. In paragraph 45 of his essay, William Ecenbarger classifies some of the former government figures involved in lobbying for the tobacco industry.

> During this same period, tobacco companies enlisted two former aides to President Reagan—Michael Deaver and Richard Allen—as lobbyists. Deaver received $250,000 for pressing Philip Morris's case in South Korea and in a meeting with President Chun Doo Hwan.

LaKesha decided she could improve her essay by grouping the accessories that she hopes to obtain at estate sales in the order of necessity. She added the following categories to paragraph 6:

First Draft:	Joyce said that I could buy many useful things for a small fraction of the price of similar new items.
Revision:	Joyce said that I could buy many useful things for a small fraction of the price of similar new items. **First, I will need new linens and pots and pans. I can make do with plastic plates and cheap flatware for a while. Curtains, rugs, and decorative items can wait until I have more money.**

Cause-Effect

Writers often need to explain causes that lead to a particular effect or an effect that comes from a particular cause. Explaining is an important tool. The papers that you will need to write for your other courses in college—history and science, for example—often draw on this ability. William Ecenbarger uses **cause-effect reasoning** in paragraph 12 to explain why American tobacco companies are able to succeed in the overseas market.

> And because most of these countries don't have effective anti-smoking campaigns, many of their people are surprisingly innocent of the link between tobacco and disease.

In paragraph 2 of her essay, where she mentioned the importance of a comfortable chair, LaKesha found two places where the relationships between her ideas could be better conveyed using cause-effect reasoning.

First Draft: Marjorie said that making things comfortable is her priority. It is especially important in working with small places. Clutter is always a problem when students do not have enough places to put things away. She suggested that I might want to think about a desk and a large bookshelf first.

Revision: Marjorie said that making things comfortable is her priority./ , **because i**It is especially important in working with small places. **Since c**Ølutter is always a problem when students do not have enough places to put things away./, **s**She suggested that I might want to think **first** about a desk and a large bookshelf. first.

By using the words *because* and *since* to point out the cause-effect relationships, LaKesha made the topic in the revised paragraph much clearer.

Comparison-Contrast

When you point out similarities, you use **comparisons** to develop your ideas. When you emphasize differences, you use **contrasts.** This skill will prove to be especially useful in other courses such as literature or political science. Paragraph 4 of "America's New Merchants of Death" contrasts tobacco sales in the United States and the rest of the world.

Although domestic sales have dropped for eight straight years, and by the year 2000 only one in seven Americans will likely smoke, sales elsewhere have more than tripled since 1985. Smoking rates in the Third World are climbing more than two percent a year. Most alarming is the rise in youth smoking. In the Philippines, 22.7 percent of people under 18 now smoke. In some Latin American cities, the teen-age rate is an astonishing 50 percent. In Hong Kong, children as young as seven are smoking.

LaKesha decided to use comparison-contrast to make her introduction more informative. She realized that the similarities and differences between the two women she interviewed were important.

First Draft: I interviewed one woman who is a designer for an upscale furniture store (or gallery, as they call it). I also interviewed another interesting woman. This one sells entire estates. People should respect these ladies' opinions and admire their work.

Revision: I interviewed one woman who is a designer for an upscale furniture store (a gallery, as they call it), and I also interviewed another interesting woman who ~~This lady~~ sells entire estates. People should respect these ~~ladies'~~ women's opinions and admire their work. **Marjorie Bliss, who works in the furniture store, has a very different job, however, from Joyce Dotson, who sells furniture and other decorative items when heirs no longer want them. Both women gave me good advice based on their different approaches to decorating.**

Now, LaKesha's audience gets a clearer picture of the backgrounds of the two people she interviewed for her investigation into furnishing an apartment.

Analysis

To analyze an idea, you must break it into its basic parts, then show the relationships between those parts. As in the article on tobacco companies, **analysis** is a major component of essays on many serious topics. You will find this skill useful in sociology, biology, and many other fields. In paragraph 25 of "America's New Merchants of Death," William Ecenbarger uses analysis effectively to clarify how American tobacco companies get around other countries' laws against cigarette advertising.

> Tobacco companies regularly skirt laws against TV commercials. In Shanghai, Philip Morris airs spots for "The World of Marlboro" at the end of American sitcom reruns. Except that cigarettes aren't mentioned, the ad is identical to a Marlboro commercial: the Marlboro man and his horse splash across a stream, the man dismounts and gazes toward mountains that look like the Rockies.

LaKesha decided that analyzing the helpful hints she found in one magazine would develop her essay even further.

First Draft: The next day I went to the library and spent several hours looking at the magazines that she recommended. Some of the magazines had its "helpful hints" grouped together in special sections. Anyway, I think I have enough ideas now to help me furnish several houses. A good thing that is, considering my major.

Revision: The next day I went to the library and spent several hours looking at the magazines that she recommended. Some of the magazines had their "helpful hints" grouped together in special sections. **In the** *Walls and Windows* **hint section, I found useful information about painting. The magazine provided instructions for marbleizing, sponging, combing, and rag rolling to provide specialized finishes on walls. The hint included tools, paints, and approximate costs for each method as well as instructions on how to do the job.** Anyway, I think I have enough ideas now to help me furnish several houses. A good thing that is, considering my major.

Exercises R5-1

In "America's New Merchants of Death" (pp. 152–159), find at least one paragraph that illustrates each of the methods of development you studied in this chapter.

Exercise R5-2

Find paragraphs in LaKesha's first draft (pp. 163–166) that could be developed further, using at least three of the methods of development that were used in "America's New Merchants of Death."

Exercise R5-3

Using the methods of paragraph development that you have just reviewed, write additional sentences that give supporting details for each of the topic sentences below.

1. Many people do not understand exactly what the mass media are.
2. Most people have a sense of right and wrong.
3. Wages control a firm's cost of doing business.
4. My down jacket is a useful item of apparel.

5. A library is like a gold mine in many ways.
6. Rock and country are both popular types of music at my school.
7. The study methods that work for me might not be the right ones for you.
8. Every one of us has the potential for improving his or her daily life.
9. Strong paragraphs can be logically developed in several ways.
10. Who needs big business in America?

Exercise R5-4

Develop the following paragraph, using at least one of the methods of development you have reviewed in this section.

Basically, details are building blocks that you combine to construct a paragraph. The following techniques can help you develop your topic sentences with details that provide information in several ways.

Supporting Details

Urban planners need to ensure that the city facilities they develop for different activities are adequate. For example, a baseball park that seats only 10,000 people would need to be expanded in Cleveland, but an opera house of the same size would work admirably in that city. Like these planners, you need to build not only the right kinds of support into your paragraphs but also enough details to develop your main ideas adequately. Often you will need to furnish different types of support within a single paragraph; the amount of support may also vary. But one guideline remains constant: *Specific details are the building blocks of well-developed paragraphs.* Some ideas may need a great many details; others will not. If you cram too many details into one paragraph, you may confuse your readers rather than clarify your thoughts for them. On the other hand, using too few details leaves your essay weak and unclear.

Examples

Giving examples of what you are writing about is an effective way to make your ideas clear to your audience. **Examples** support your ideas by making them specific, interesting, and memorable. In paragraph 16 of "America's New Merchants of Death," the writer uses examples to support his topic sentence.

> Tobacco advertising is more pervasive in other parts of the world than here. African merchants can get their shops painted to look like a pack of Marlboros. The Camel logo adorns store awnings and taxis in Warsaw. Christmas trees in Malaysian discos are trimmed free by Kent—with balls and stars bearing the Kent logo. In Mexico, one in five TV commercials is for cigarettes. On an average day, 60 spots for American brands appear on Japanese TV, many of them during programs watched by teens.

LaKesha decided that she could make her essay more interesting with the addition of some specific examples in paragraph 7 of her first draft. So she described some of the decorating styles she likes and furnished details about them.

Revision: I have started a list of things I need and things I like. **For instance, I know now that I like Art Deco furniture and accessories. During the 1920s and 1930s, modern furniture with clean lines and simple design became very popular. I saw a Swedish chair in blond wood that I would like to buy. I also like Tiffany glass lamps, which are very elaborate with shades that look like the stained glass windows in my church.**

Now LaKesha's readers have a detailed sense of what her decorated apartment will be like, and they can share her excitement over her discoveries.

Facts and Numbers

Providing your audience with facts and numbers about your topic is another way to develop your paragraphs. In paragraph 32 of his essay, William Ecenbarger uses numbers and facts so that his readers will understand the scope of the problem that American tobacco companies are causing by selling to underage consumers in foreign countries.

> Of seven under-18 students assembled at the Beltram High School in Buenos Aires, five say they have been offered free Camels. None was asked his age. One, Ruben Paz, 16, said he got his from a "blond, American-looking girl" handing out cigarettes from "the Camel jeep" at the school door.

The proportion of underage students who have been approached supports the author's contention that cigarettes are being openly hawked to minors in other countries.

When LaKesha checked the paragraph development in her essay, she decided that adding the estimates she received for furniture and other goods would strengthen paragraph 6 on estate sales.

First Draft: The next person I interviewed was Joyce Dotson. She sells estates when people die or retire or move out of state. She sells everything that no one in the family wants. Sometimes there are valuable pieces of furniture, often antiques. However, there are always items that are very low cost, because most people already have enough of them. She told me that items like towels, sheets, dishcloths, and kitchen items are always good buys.

Revision: The next person I interviewed was Joyce Dotson. She sells estates when people die or retire or move out of state. She sells everything that no one in the family wants. Sometimes there are valuable pieces of furniture, often antiques. However, there are always items that are very low cost, because most people already have enough of them. She told me that items like towels, sheets, dishcloths, and kitchen items are always good buys. **Towels that cost from $5 to $8 even at a discount store often sell for less than half that at most estate sales. Pots and pans often sell in sets for a few dollars rather than the $89 that I saw marked on all stainless steel cookware on sale last week.**

Now, LaKesha's audience has a clear picture of the savings possible at estate sales.

Exercise R5-5

Find three paragraphs in "America's New Merchants of Death" (pp. 152–159) in which examples, facts, or numbers develop the topic.

Exercise R5-6

Find three places in LaKesha's first draft (pp. 163–166) where she might add examples, facts, or numbers to further develop her topic.

Exercise R5-7

For each of the following topic sentences, write examples, facts, or numbers that further develop the idea.

1. Crowded classrooms make learning difficult in some subjects that are part of my school's core curriculum.
2. For example, in my biology lab, we are often unable to have hands-on experiences with certain experiments.

3. We are the most disadvantaged because of the low teacher-to-student ratio.
4. Limiting class size seems to be the only answer.
5. In some subjects, however, large numbers of students in the same class are not as much of a problem.

Exercise R5-8

Rewrite the following paragraph, using examples, facts, and numbers to develop the topic.

Children who watch television are exposed daily to some of the highest-pressure advertising in mass media. They hear about toys, candy, and new kinds of gum until they essentially become salespeople to their parents for the children's market in America.

 ## COLLABORATIVE WORK

After writing a draft of your own investigating essay, exchange papers with a class-mate, and do the following tasks:

A. List the different ways paragraphs can be developed. Then, in the margins, suggest alternative ways to develop specific paragraphs.

B. Put a checkmark by each paragraph that needs more examples, facts, or numbers.

Then return the paper to its writer, and use the information in this section to revise your draft.

Agreement

Checklist for Correcting Agreement Problems

✓ Do **singular subjects** agree with **singular verbs?**
✓ Do **plural subjects** agree with **plural verbs?**
✓ Do **pronouns and antecedents** agree in **number, person, and gender?**
✓ Do **pronouns that have no antecedents** refer to themselves?
✓ Do you **avoid sexist references** with indefinite pronouns?

Disagreement can sometimes be healthy. When individuals or groups of people calmly and rationally express opposing viewpoints, positive changes can often result. When emotions run rampant, however, disagreement can escalate to the point that communication becomes extremely difficult, if not impossible.

In writing, grammatical disagreement can also cause problems in communicating effectively and clearly. In this section, you will learn that agreement between sentence elements is essential in writing grammatically correct prose that pleases writers and readers alike.

Subject-Verb Agreement

Every sentence must have a subject and a main verb, two necessary elements that work together to make complete thoughts. Another necessary requirement is that the subject and verb **agree** in number. Simply stated, a singular subject—only one person, place, thing, or idea—needs a singular verb. A plural subject—more than one person, place, thing, or idea—needs a plural verb.

In Chapter 2, you learned that pronouns and nouns can function as subjects. To refresh your memory about singular and plural pronouns, turn to page 44. You probably remember that writers usually just add an *-s* or *-es* when changing nouns from singular to plural: *car, cars; room, rooms; match, matches.* Verbs, however, usually form plurals in the opposite way. Most verbs ending in *-s* are singular, whereas the verb in its basic form (without an *-s*) is plural: *we go, he goes; we paint, he paints.* Look at these sentences from the first draft of LaKesha's investigating essay:

	S	**V**	
Singular:	This **one sells** entire estates.		

	S	**V**	**V**	**V**
Plural:	**People should respect** these women's opinions and **admire** their work.			

Remember that some verbs undergo spelling changes when shifting number. Look at the verbs in the following chart:

Singular	Plural
is	are
was	were
has	have
does	do

These additional examples from LaKesha's first draft illustrate how subjects and verbs should always agree in number:

S   V
I plan to major in commercial interior design.

S   V   **S   V**
They were happy to give me some good advice, which **I plan** to use
        S   V
when **I** finally **move** into my own place.

S   V   **S   V**
I interviewed one woman **who is** a designer for an upscale furniture
                              S   V
store (or gallery, as **they call** it).

Exercise E5-1

In the following sentences taken from William Ecenbarger's investigating essay "America's New Merchants of Death," underline each subject once and each verb twice, and label these words as either singular or plural.

1. In Malaysia, a man responds to a television commercial for "Salem High Country Holidays."
2. In several nations, U.S. tobacco companies have been fighting legislation that curtails cigarette use by minors and are cleverly violating the spirit of curbs on advertising.
3. This grim prospect is due in no small part to the spectacular U.S. invasion of overseas markets.
4. More than 50,000 medical studies have demonstrated these hazards.
5. Of seven under-18 students assembled at the Beltram High School in Buenos Aires, five say they have been offered free Camels.

Exercise E5-2

In paragraph 2 of LaKesha's first draft on page 165, underline the main subject once and the main verb twice in each sentence, and label the words as singular or plural.

Exercise E5-3

Underline the correct forms of the verbs in parentheses to make the following sentences complete.

I (1) (*knows, know*) a woman who spends about two hours a day answering inquiries on the Internet. Ms. Sheridan, who works in admissions, (2) (*talk, talks*) to students via her computer terminal. Sometimes she (3) (*get, gets*) to talk to foreign exchange students. Often these students, after talking with her on the Internet, (4) (*call, calls*) Ms. Sheridan at her office to get more information about the various departments at our college. They (5) (*try, tries*) to keep informed so that they (6) (*has, have*) all the necessary course work completed before they apply to a specific program. Ms. Sheridan also (7) (*talk, talks*) with high school seniors about entrance prerequisites. Her conversation subjects, while talking on the Internet, (8) (*range, ranges*) from SAT scores to college sports programs. She (9) (*do, does*) what she can to answer students' questions about college. Ms. Sheridan believes that students who (10) (*is, are*) better informed about college have a better chance of attaining their goals.

Exercise E5-4

Write ten original sentences using different subjects and verbs from the following lists.

Subjects		Verbs	
we	friend	is	are
you	computers	get	gets
jogging	children	take	takes
schedules	they	has	have
she	flower	confuse	confuses
directions	I	cost	costs
habits	book	understand	understands
		make	makes

Hard-to-Find Subjects

The first step in making sure that subjects and verbs agree is finding the subject. If you make an error in identifying the subject, determining its number will be difficult. The following discussion will help you isolate subjects that are hard to pinpoint because of their location within the sentence.

Separated Subjects and Verbs

Normally, people have little difficulty with subject-verb agreement when the sentence is in natural order—that is, when the subject comes before the verb. However, when phrases or dependent clauses wedge themselves between the main subject and verb, problems may arise. Sometimes people are tempted to make the verb agree with a noun that appears in a phrase or a dependent clause.

Separated   **S**   **V**
Subjects   **One** [of LaKesha's classmates] **is meeting** her in the
and Verbs: library this morning to read over her draft.

The subject is *one*, not *classmates* (*classmates* is the object of the preposition *of*). Thus, the subject is singular, requiring the singular verb *is meeting*.

                    S   **V**
            The **keys** [lying on the counter] **are** LaKesha's.

The subject is *keys*, not *counter* (*counter* is the object in the propositional phrase *on the counter*). *Keys* is plural and needs the plural verb *are*.

                                    S
            The grammatical **errors** [that LaKesha made after writing the
                                    V
            first draft] **have been corrected.**

Errors is the plural subject, which agrees with the verb *have been corrected*. The dependent clause *that LaKesha made after writing the first draft* has no effect on the subject and verb's number.

Inverted Order

Normally, the subject comes before the verb, even when other words separate the two elements. However, sometimes the verb appears before the subject; this inverted order may cause problems in subject-verb agreement.

                                                    V   **S**
    Inverted: At the bottom of the stack of papers **sits** LaKesha's **essay**.

Simply change the sentence around, shifting words and phrases so that the sentence appears in natural order—subject first, then verb.

                                S   **V**
    Natural: LaKesha's **essay sits** at the bottom of the stack of papers.

Now it is easy to see that the subject is *essay*, a singular noun that requires the singular verb *sits*.

Expletives

When words such as *there* and *it* introduce a sentence, we call them **expletives.** When they serve as sentence starters, they do not function as subjects.

	V	S

Expletive: There **is** only one **paragraph** still giving me problems.

The subject is *paragraph*, a singular noun that requires the singular verb *is*. Dropping *there* and rearranging the sentence in natural order produces this result:

	S	V

Statement: Only one **paragraph is** still giving me problems.

There functions as a subject only when it refers to itself as a word, but those occasions are rare.

S   V
There **appears** too many times in LaKesha's draft.

Unlike *there*, *it* is always considered the subject of the sentence when used as an expletive. *It* is always singular, thus requiring a singular verb.

S V
It is good to know that LaKesha learned how to correct her errors.

S V
It is Mrs. Johnson who suggested that we read each other's papers.

Questions

Questions are usually sentences in inverted order, since a part of the verb normally comes before the subject. If you cannot easily identify the subject, simply make the question a statement. Then locating the subject and making it agree with the verb should be a much easier task, as the following examples illustrate:

V   S
Question: **Is** LaKesha's **teacher** one of the tough graders?

Rearrange the question to produce this statement:

S   V
Statement: LaKesha's **teacher is** one of the tough graders.

The singular subject *teacher* agrees with the singular verb *is*.

                                   V   S   V

Question: Are your **friends planning** to turn in their assignments soon?

In statement form, the question reads like this:

                         S   V

           Your **friends are planning** to turn in their assignments soon.

The subject *friends* requires the plural verb *are planning.*

Exercise E5-5

Underline the main subjects once and the main verbs twice in the following sentences from the essay "America's New Merchants of Death." Then label the subjects and verbs as either singular or plural.

1. In Hong Kong, children as young as seven are smoking.
2. But an ad executive who worked until recently on the Phillip Morris account, speaking on condition of anonymity, disagrees.
3. In Shanghai, Phillip Morris airs spots for "The World of Marlboro" at the end of American sitcom reruns.
4. At a McDonald's in Malaysia, Sunil Ramanathan, 16, finishes off a Big Mac, lights a Marlboro and inhales deeply.
5. And at the end of the rainbow lies China, with 300 million smokers—30 percent of the world market.

Exercise E5-6

The following sentences come from LaKesha's first draft. Underline the main subjects once and the main verbs twice, and label them as singular or plural.

1. Although these pieces of furniture do not have to be new, they should be functional.
2. According to Marjorie, some people who move out of their parents' house just take these items with them.
3. What do you think is the easiest combination to work with?
4. A good thing that is, considering my major.
5. Sometimes there are valuable pieces of furniture, often antiques.

Exercise E5-7

From the choices in parentheses, underline the verb that agrees with the subject of each sentence in the following paragraph.

    If you want to stretch your dollars, you might consider buying secondhand clothes. There (1) (*is, are*) many places you can shop in most cities. The Salvation Army, which operates some of the nation's most popular secondhand stores, usually (2) (*offer, offers*) a good selection of men's, women's, and children's clothing. The clothing items that the Salvation Army accepts (3) (*is, are*) usually in good shape, with no tears, discoloration, or excessive wear. The prices are usually good, too. At the local thrift store, a decent pair of jeans (4) (*go, goes*) for as little as $2. People who are willing to take the time (5) (*is, are*) often surprised at what they can find. Once my efforts paid off when I was browsing around. Sitting at the bottom of a pile of sweatshirts (6) (*was, were*) a Polo T-shirt that looked brand new. I got it for 50 cents. My friend Carmen, who is one of the sharpest dressers at school, always (7) (*find, finds*) bargains. There (8) (*is, are*) many occasions when she comes away with a brand-new outfit for under $10. Privately owned businesses that sell "gently used" clothing usually (9) (*charge, charges*) more for certain items. But you can find some good deals at those places, too. (10) (*Are, Is*) the people I hang out with critical of my secondhand wardrobe? No, they're not, because they're wearing used clothing too.

Exercise E5-8

Write 10 original sentences—four sentences with a phrase or a clause separating the subject and verb, two sentences in inverted word order with the verb before the subject, two sentences beginning with an expletive, and two questions in which part of the verb precedes the subject.

Compound Subjects

When two or more persons, places, things, or ideas perform the verb's action (or state of being), we call the subject compound. **Compound subjects** are joined by coordinating conjunctions that help determine the subject's number.

And is the most common coordinating conjunction. When *and* joins two subjects, they are usually considered plural (See p. 53 for a list of more coordinating conjunctions.)

Compound **Subjects:**	**LaKesha and Randy** hope for good grades. **LaKesha and Randy** are two people who **both** hope for good grades. **My two sisters and LaKesha** have the same birthday.

In the last example, *sisters* and *LaKesha* form the compound subject, thus requiring the plural verb *have*. Even though *LaKesha* is a singular noun and is next to the verb, the subject is still plural.

In some cases, a compound subject joined by *and* may be treated as singular. All of these situations have unusual circumstances:

1.   *When the two subjects joined by* and *are considered a single unit, the subject is considered singular.*

>   s   v
> **Ice cream and cake is** my dad's favorite dessert.

>   s   v
> **Hunt-and-peck is** the best way to describe my typing strategy.

2. *When* every *or* each *comes before a compound subject, the subject is singular.*

> **S**   **V**
> **Singular:**   **Each essay and magazine article** that LaKesha reads **gives** her
>   more information for her research paper.

Each means every single essay and article. Thus, each one *gives* information, not *give* information.

> **S**   **V**
> **Singular:**   **Every student and teacher needs** a parking permit.

The word *every* implies that every single one of the students and teachers *needs* a permit.

3. *When each part of the compound subject refers to the same person, place, thing, or idea, a singular verb is needed.*

> **S**   **V**
> **Singular:**   **LaKesha's best friend and biggest fan is** her mom.

The compound subject *friend and fan* refers to one person, *mom*. Therefore, the subject is singular, requiring the singular verb *is*.
   Compound subjects can also be joined by other conjunctions: *or, nor, either . . . or, neither . . . nor, not only . . . but also, whether . . . or*. When these conjunctions perform their linking functions with subjects, the verb should agree with the closest subject.

> **S**   **V**
> **Plural:**   **Neither LaKesha, her friends, nor her parents** ever **expect**
>   her to stay out past her curfew.

The compound subject is *LaKesha, friends*, and *parents*. Since *parents* is closest to the verb, the verb must be plural—*expect*.

> **S**   **V**
> **Singular:**   **Either mashed potatoes or hash brown casserole is** going to
>   be the starch of the day.

The compound subject is *potatoes* and *casserole*. Since *casserole* is singular and closer to the verb, the verb must be singular—*is*.

Indefinite Pronouns

As you learned in Chapter 2, a pronoun refers to or replaces a specific noun or pronoun. However, some pronouns refer to a noun or pronoun that is not specific. These are **indefinite pronouns.** Some indefinite pronouns are always singular, others are always plural, and still others may be either singular or plural. The best strategy is to familiarize yourself with the following categories:

Indefinite Pronouns

Singular	Plural	Both
another, anybody, anyone, anything each, either, everybody, everyone, everything, neither, no one, nobody, nothing, one, somebody, something	both, few, many, several	all, any, more, most, none, some

Using the singular and plural pronouns poses few problems, as the following sentences illustrate:

                  s   v

Singular: **Everyone** in LaKesha's English class **was** on time.

          s   v

      Neither wants to go first.

           s   v

      Somebody knows what happened to the missing computer disks.

         s v

Plural: **Both feel** that LaKesha's thesis statement is clear and specific.

         s v

      Many say that this will be a hard winter.

         s   v

      Several plan to speak during the meeting.

To decide whether an indefinite pronoun is singular or plural, you must determine what the pronoun means. If the indefinite pronoun refers to a singular noun, a singular verb is needed. Likewise, if the indefinite pronoun refers to a plural pronoun, a plural verb is required.

         s   v

Singular: **None** of LaKesha's time **was spent** daydreaming.

None refers to time, a singular noun. Thus, the verb must be singular, *was spent*.

                                        S   V

Plural: **None** of LaKesha's grammatical errors **were** critical.

None refers to *errors*, a plural noun, which matches up with the plural verb, *were*.

                                          S   V

Singular: **None is** lost.

None by itself is always singular.

    Here is a final hint about indefinite pronouns, a good rule to remember. If the indefinite pronoun means *how much* of something, a singular verb is needed (*None of LaKesha's time was . . .*). However, if the indefinite pronoun tells *how many*, then a plural verb is required (*None of LaKesha's grammatical errors were . . .*).

Collective Nouns

Certain nouns cause confusion because they appear to be singular in form when they actually name several persons, places, or things. These words, called **collective nouns,** include the following: *army, audience, band, chorus, class, committee, couple, crew, crowd, faculty, family, flock, gang, herd, jury, majority, navy, orchestra, senate, team,* and *troop.*

    The guidelines governing agreement of collective nouns and verbs are simple. When the noun clearly refers to a group that functions as a single unit, a singular verb is required.

                                        S   V

Singular: The team **plans** to win this afternoon.

                                      S   V

                      The **jury has reached** a verdict.

If the collective noun refers to a group in which members act individually, a plural verb is needed.

                                      S   V

Plural: The **team are getting** their physical examinations this afternoon.

                                      S   V

                      The **jury have eaten** the lunches that were delivered to the courthouse.

If the sentences sound awkward, replace the subject with another subject that is clearly plural.

                                      S   V

Plural: The **players are getting** their physical examinations this afternoon.

      s   **v**

The jury members have eaten the lunches that were delivered to the courthouse.

Other Agreement Rules

These additional guidelines will help you solve agreement problems that arise in your writing:

1. *Some nouns appear to be plural, ending in -s, when they are singular in meaning:* measles, mumps, news, molasses, checkers, physics, mathematics.

             s **v**
    Singular: The **news is** something my grandmother can't live without.

          s   **v**
    Physics has confused students for generations.

    Some words that appear to be plural can be singular or plural, depending on their meaning: *statistics, athletics, politics, ethics, economics, ceramics.* If the word refers to a field of study or a profession, it usually takes a singular verb. However, in some instances a plural verb may be needed.

             s **v**
    Singular: **Politics is** an interesting sideline for many people.

            s   **v**
    Plural: The **politics** involved in obtaining the government contract **are** mind-boggling.

2. *Words that refer to amounts*—money, time, distance, measurement, or percentage—*can be singular or plural.* If the word refers to a single unit functioning as one group, the verb is singular. If the word refers to individual units, a plural verb is needed.

             s **v**
    Singular: **Ten years is** a long time with no word from your daughter.

             s   **v**
    Plural: **Ten years have passed** since she heard from her daughter.

3. *Words that refer to themselves are singular.*

             s   **v**
    Singular: **"Peaches" is** what we call my friend Brenda.

             s   **v**
    "Monkeys" was the password for our clubhouse when we were in elementary school.

4. *The title of a book, play, movie, television show, article, song, album, video, or computer program is singular.*

              S   V

Singular: **"Broken Bottles" is** a new country song that LaKesha likes.

                                 S   V

                              The Flintstones was Elizabeth Taylor's only movie appearance during 1994.

Exercise E5-9

Underline the subjects once and the verbs twice in the following sentences from "America's New Merchants of Death." Then explain why the author chose a singular or plural verb.

1. Why are the young so important?
2. On an average day, 60 spots for American brands appear on Japanese TV, many of them during programs watched by teens.
3. One of the live performances under tobacco sponsorship (Salems in Seoul) was by Paula Abdul, who is popular among teens.
4. Sports sponsorship is even more insidious, for it implies that smoking and fitness mix.
5. None was asked his age.

Exercise E5-10

Underline the subjects once and the verbs twice in the following sentences taken from LaKesha's revised essay, and label the subjects and verbs as singular or plural.

1. Six hundred dollars is a lot to pay for something to sleep on—not even the headboard.
2. This decorating duo offers good advice.
3. Each room and closet offers a potential savings bonanza.
4. The majority are coming for the expensive items.
5. She scheduled me for a weekday morning when the store is not busy—neither she nor any of the employees had customers at their desks.

Exercise E5-11

Choose one of the verbs in parentheses to successfully complete each sentence in the following paragraph.

    I am currently serving on the student activities committee. Everyone on the committee (1)(*want, wants*) to make this year's activities the most exciting ever. I'm on the Spring Fling subcommittee, which (2) (*meet, meets*) every Tuesday afternoon. Lamar and Debra, two friends I know from pep band, (3) (*is, are*) also on the committee, along with four other people. Right now we are trying to decide which clubs will participate in the food concessions and which in the outdoor game booths. Two weeks before Spring Fling, all clubs (4) (*is, are*) notified of our final choices. The dunking booth (5) (*is, are*) Spring Fling's most popular activity, and it is difficult to choose the club to run it. The committee (6) (*has, have*) their own ideas about who should run the dunking booth, but I'm sure the decision will come to a vote. Each club (7) (*offer, offers*) a bid proposal for the booth that they want to run. Our committee has already spent six hours going over all of the various ideas submitted by campus clubs. It seems that six hours (8) (*is, are*) too much time to spend meeting about food and game booths. The majority of our committee members (9) (*is, are*) eager to get things decided so we can go on to other business. We will vote on booth designations at our next meeting. So everyone (10) (*is, are*) asking students what they think so we can get as much input as possible.

Exercise E5-12

Write original sentences using the following words and phrases as subjects and using is, are, was, *or* were *as verbs.*

1. all of the pie
2. neither the cat nor the dogs
3. five gallons
4. red beans and rice
5. the community chorus

Pronoun-Antecedent Agreement

We make additional demands on pronouns in terms of agreement. While pronouns functioning as subjects must match up with verbs, each pronoun must also agree with the noun that it refers to or replaces. We call that noun an **antecedent.** Note that in the following sentences from LaKesha's draft, each pronoun has an antecedent that can be clearly identified, either in the same sentence or in a previous one:

Antecedent

I called Marjorie for an appointment and told **her** that **I** would not likely

be buying anything.

She scheduled **me** for a weekday morning when the store is not busy.

The first-person pronouns, *I* and *me*, refer to LaKesha, the author of the essay. The pronoun *her* refers to Marjorie, as does *she*, which begins the second sentence.

Once you have identified the pronoun's antecedent, you should make sure that the two words agree in three ways: number, person, and gender.

Number simply refers to whether the words are singular (one) or plural (more than one).

Person refers to someone's relationship to the speaker.

First person:	The person speaking (*I*)
Second person:	The person spoken to (*you*)
Third person:	The person, place, or thing spoken about (*he, she, it, they*)

Gender refers to **masculine** *(he, his)*, **feminine** *(she, her)*, or **neuter** (referring to nouns that have no male or female qualities—*it, its)*.

Look at these sentences from LaKesha's revised essay. They all feature pronouns and antecedents that agree in all three ways.

Correct Agreement:	**Marjorie** said that making things comfortable is **her** priority, because it is especially important in working with small places.

The pronoun *her* is singular, feminine, and third-person, agreeing with the proper, singular, feminine, third-person noun *Marjorie*.

Correct Agreement:	Although these **pieces** of furniture do not have to be new, **they** should be functional.

The pronoun *they* is plural, neuter, and third-person, referring to the plural, neuter, third-person noun *pieces*.

Correct Agreement:	Marjorie said that the **chair** is the most important purchase, because **it** will determine how long **I** am willing to sit and study.

It is a singular, neuter, third-person pronoun referring to the singular, neuter, third-person noun *chair. I* is a first-person pronoun that refers to the writer.

Exercise E5-13

List each pronoun and its antecedent in paragraphs 24 through 27 of "America's New Merchants of Death (pp. 152–159).

Exercise E5-14

List each pronoun and its antecedent in paragraph 6 of LaKesha's first draft on page 164. Remember that some pronouns may not have antecedents.

Exercise E5-15

Complete the sentences in the following paragraph by supplying the correct pronouns. Then underline each pronoun's antecedent.

Hector and Morgan recently came up with a plan to make some extra money.

(1) _____ decided to offer baby-sitting on Saturdays.

(2) _____ called (3) _____ service "Parents'
Day Out." After I decided to help (4) _____ ,

(5) _____ got a city permit for day care and made up flyers and

posted (6) _____ on billboards in grocery stores, malls, and

churches, on telephone poles, wherever (7) _____ could find a

place. (8) _____ plan was a good one because on the first

Saturday of operation, (9) _____ had 12 kids to take care of.

Morgan and I agreed to give Hector more of the profits because

(10) _____ cleaned up and stayed late at Morgan's house, where

we kept the kids.

Exercise E5-16

Write original sentences using the following pronouns. Also, make sure each pronoun has an antecedent.

1. his
2. their
3. it
4. she
5. them

Specific Agreement Problems

Making sure pronouns agree with their antecedents can be difficult. Some special problems can occur in one of three areas: *number, person,* or *gender.* Determining the basic qualities of a noun or pronoun can be tricky. However, if you read closely and analyze carefully, you can make pronouns agree with their antecedents. This should be an easy task to accomplish once you know what you are looking for.

Problems in Number

1. *Compound antecedents.*

    a. Two or more antecedents joined by *and* require a plural pronoun, even if one of the antecedents is singular.

    Plural: For a surprise, **LaKesha and her sisters** took **their** parents out to eat.

    One exception occurs when the two antecedents refer to the same person. Then the pronoun should be singular.

Singular: LaKesha's best friend and strongest supporter had no doubt that **she** could keep her secret.

Another exception occurs when the adjective *each* or *every* precedes the compound antecedent. Then a singular pronoun is needed.

Singular: Each cat and dog in the pound had received **its** shots.

b.   When two or more antecedents are joined by *or, nor, either . . . or, whether . . . or, neither . . . nor,* or *not only . . . but also,* the pronoun agrees with the closer noun.

Singular: Either LaKesha or her sister April has not paid **her** share of **her** parent's surprise restaurant outing.

Plural: Neither LaKesha nor her sisters spent **their** entire allowances last week.

Singular: Whether the cats or the dog received **its** shots last year is a good question because the vet can't find the records.

Plural: Whether the dog or the cats received **their** shots last year is a good question because the vet can't find the records.

2.   *Collective nouns as antecedents.*   Words such as *class, team, couple,* and *band* often are confusing because they can refer either to a single unit or to the individuals that make up that unit. So collective nouns can be either singular or plural, depending on the intended meaning of the word. If the collective noun names a group that functions as a unit, a singular pronoun is needed.

Singular: The team conducts **its** practices in the afternoon.

If the collective noun names a group whose members act separately, a plural pronoun is needed.

Plural: The team listed **their** goals for the season.

3.   *Indefinite pronouns as antecedents.*   Pronouns may refer to other pronouns. When indefinite pronouns serve as antecedents, we must remind ourselves which words are always singular, which pronouns are always plural, and match them up accordingly. (See p. 195 for a complete list of indefinite pronouns.)

a.   Indefinite pronoun antecedents that are always singular require singular pronouns. This rule holds true even when the indefinite pronoun is followed by a prepositional phrase with a plural object.

Singular: Everyone is hoping that **his or her** grades arrive soon.
        Each took **its** turn at the feeding pan.
        Each of the pigs took **its** turn at the feeding pan.

b.   Indefinite pronoun antecedents that are always plural require plural pronouns.

Plural: **Both** turned in **their** papers early.
              Few sent **their** money in on time.

c.   Some indefinite pronouns may be singular or plural. First you must determine the word's number by how it is used in the sentence. Then you will be able to match the indefinite pronoun antecedent to a pronoun that agrees with it.

Plural: **Most of the students** took **their** seats when the bell rang.

Most is clearly plural because it refers to *students*. Therefore, *their* is the correct pronoun choice.

Singular: **Most of the play** gets **its** inspiration from mythology.

Most refers to *play*, a singular noun, thus determining that the pronoun choice is singular, *its*.

d.   Some indefinite pronouns may not require antecedents (*everyone, everybody, someone, somebody*). Look at this example:

      Everyone could benefit from the hints LaKesha collected.

Everyone does not need an antecedent because it is self-explanatory. No additional words are needed to explain who is meant.

Problems in Person

A pronoun may fail to agree with its antecedent in person. Usually this problem occurs when the second person *you* is used to refer to third person nouns or indefinite pronouns.

Shift: If **a person** does not exercise regularly, **you** can easily lose flexibility and strength.
              No one should turn in **your** key until the week is over.

To correct such problems, rewrite the sentences, using either third-person singular or plural pronouns.

Revisions: If **a person** does not exercise regularly, **he or she** can easily lose flexibility and strength.
              If **people** do not exercise regularly, **they** can easily lose flexibility and strength.

No one should turn in **his or her** key until the week is over. **Students** should not turn in **their** keys until the week is over.

Sometimes a shift in person occurs from the first person to the second.

Shift:	I decided to consult a financial adviser because **you** can consolidate **your** bills and save money in interest payments.
Revision:	I decided to consult a financial adviser because **I** can consolidate **my** bills and save money in interest payments.

Problems in Gender

Third-person singular personal pronouns are the only pronouns that exhibit differences in gender. The **masculine pronouns** are *he, him,* and *his;* the **feminine pronouns** are *she, her,* and *hers.* The **neuter pronouns,** which exhibit neither masculine nor feminine characteristics, are *it* and *its.*

Generally, identifying an antecedent as masculine, feminine, or neuter is an easy task, as the following sentences from LaKesha's first draft illustrate:

Masculine:	I've even encouraged my boyfriend, **Ryan,** to start **his** own list for when **he** moves out.
Feminine:	I called **Marjorie** for an appointment and told **her** that I would not likely be buying anything.
Neuter:	I will also be spending long hours in the library, looking at pictures and imagining how perfect my first **apartment** will be with **its** carefully selected furniture and accessories.

Sometimes identifying gender is difficult, particularly with certain indefinite pronouns like *anyone, someone,* or *everybody.* Historically, writers have used the masculine pronouns to refer to the indefinite pronouns. In recent years, however, we have realized that such practices are sexist because they exclude women. Therefore, you should avoid using the masculine pronouns if there is any question about gender. Instead, adopt one of the following strategies:

1. *Use* his or her, *but don't overdo it.* His or her can quickly become monotonous and awkward.

Incorrect:	**Everyone** paid **his** dues this month.
Revision:	**Everyone** paid **his or her** dues this month.

2. *Rewrite the sentence to make the antecedent plural.*

Incorrect:	**Everyone** paid **his** dues this month.
Revision:	**All** the students paid **their** dues this month.

3. *Rewrite the sentence, omitting the personal pronoun.*

Incorrect:	**Everyone** sent **his** best wishes on Granny's birthday.
Revision:	**Everyone** sent Granny best wishes on her birthday.

Exercise E5-17

In the following sentences taken from "America's New Merchants of Death," underline each pronoun and draw a line to its antecedent.

1. The driver, a blond woman wearing khaki safari gear, begins handing out free cigarettes to 15- and 16-year-olds on their lunch recess.
2. Most smokers begin between the ages of 12 and 16; if a young person hasn't begun by 18, he or she is unlikely ever to smoke.
3. On an average day, 60 spots for American brands appear on Japanese TV, many of them during programs watched by teens.
4. Although their marketing budgets are secret, tobacco companies have bolstered their spending for international advertising, adding substantially to the $4 billion allocated yearly for the United States.
5. "If they can get a youngster to smoke a few packs, chances are he'll be a customer for life."

Exercise E5-18

Correct the pronoun-antecedent agreement errors in the following sentences taken from LaKesha's first draft.

1. One should always try to get the most from their money.
2. None of the mattresses could make their way into my pocketbook.
3. Everybody wants their place to be neat and presentable.
4. Just a change in accessories can sometimes change the whole mood of the room if the furniture has a basic line to them.
5. I learned that if a person plans ahead, you can be prepared to move out.

Exercise E5-19

Underline the pronouns in parentheses that will correctly complete the sentences in the following paragraph.

Our English class recently took a field trip to see *Romeo and Juliet* performed by a national touring company. Everyone voted to pay for (1) (*his or her, their*) own ticket instead of asking the administration to fund the trip. On the morning of the trip, surprisingly no one had forgotten (2) (*his or her, their*) money. After our instructor reminded us of the day's activities, the class boarded the bus and took (3) (*its, their*) seats. I sat by Melanie and Melinda. Neither of them had brought (4) (*her, their*) copy of the play, and I hadn't either. So I borrowed our teacher's book so I could skim over Shakespeare's tragedy before we got to the theater. I wanted to refresh my memory because (5) (*you, I*) could find things to look for before seeing the "live" play. Both Melanie and Melinda had brought (6) (*her, their*) headphones, so they listened to music while I read. After about forty-five minutes, we arrived at the theater where the play was being performed. A couple of guys asked if they could take (7) (*his, their*) headphones, and the instructor said "Certainly not!" Since the play didn't start for an hour, we were free to explore the campus. Melanie, Melinda, and I decided to go to the bookstore. We had seen an advertisement about (8) (*its, their*) semiannual book clearance sale. We browsed around for a while. But neither one of us had brought (9) (*her, our*) checkbook, so we didn't buy anything. Then we went to the theater and found the rest of our classmates, who each had (10) (*his or her, their*) own story to tell.

Exercise E5-20

Make the following noun phrases and clauses complete sentences by adding a verb phrase that includes a pronoun.

> Everybody in the room
> Everybody in the room sipped his or her drink.

1. Many of the club members
2. The new jazz band performing tomorrow night
3. Either Anthony or Darnell
4. Susie, Molly, and Maya each
5. Not only birds but also squirrels

 ## COLLABORATIVE WORK

After you revise your investigating essay, exchange papers with a classmate, and do the following tasks:

A. Circle any subjects and verbs that disagree in number.

B. Underline any pronouns that disagree with their antecedents in number, person, or gender.

Then return the paper to its writer, and use the information in this section to edit your draft.

Restating
Reading and Writing for a Reason

Suit the action to the word, the word to the action.
—WILLIAM SHAKESPEARE

Although much of what we write is inspired by our own ideas, experiences, thoughts, attitudes, and responses to events and circumstances, another type of writing, called restating, is crucial to success in college. **Restating** is just a fancy way of saying, "Put it in your own words," and it is a very natural form of communication. You restate all the time—when you give an account of your day, when you describe a movie you saw, when you summarize a book you read, or when you tell someone about a conversation you had. You put the information into your own words while striving to retain the meaning and the flavor of the original version.

Restating in writing means taking the information provided in some other source—a textbook, a lecture, a graph, an illustration, a map, a movie, or documentary—and recording the material in your own words. The result is a summary of the material that allows readers to understand it almost as completely as if they were previewing the original source of information.

Think of the last time you took an essay examination in school. When you took the exam, you were restating the information you read in your textbook or heard in a class discussion or lecture. For example, if you were asked in a psychology class to write an essay describing Sigmund Freud's major contributions to the field of psychology, your instructor would not expect you to record Freud's own words exactly as you had read them; in fact, if you did that, you would either be praised for having a photographic memory or be accused of cheating! Rather, you would be expected to sum up Freud's theories in your own words, allowing your instructor to judge whether you had read and understood the assigned course material.

In fact, restating is the basis of all research papers. Once you choose your topic and begin to read your sources of information, your main job, until you write a draft of your paper, is to restate information from other sources. You may restate in note form or in complete sentences. But in order to avoid **plagiarizing,** which is copying someone else's words or ideas without acknowledging your sources, you should never take any phrases or sentences from another source without putting them in quotation marks and recording the title and author of the source. (For information on quotation marks, see pp. 299–302.) This chapter will help you practice restating for paper assignments using sources.

When you restate something you read, you should concentrate first on identifying the main idea, then on organizing and summarizing the rest of the material to show how it supports the main idea. By restating, you accomplish several important goals: You develop a better understanding of the material; you are able to see the relationship of ideas to one another; and you let your reader know that you understand and can analyze the original material. The primary goal in restating is *not* to be as brief as possible (restating is not a note-taking exercise) but to explain the content, the purpose, and the meaning of the material using your own words.

LEARNING FROM PUBLISHED WRITERS

To see how restating works, you will read a professional article about Hispanic enrollment in public schools and view a chart about the age of college students. Each of these pieces is followed by a restatement of the information they contain. The essay titled "Surge in Hispanic Student Enrollment Predicted," written by Jeff Archer and published in 1996 in *Education Week*, discusses the predicted increase in the number of Hispanic students in the United States by the year 2030. The restatement following Archer's essay begins with the main idea of the passage and then summarizes the information in the essay that supports the main idea.

Before You Read

Focusing Your Attention

Before you read this essay, take a few moments to respond to the following questions in your journal:

1.   Recall the last time you were required to restate information—either in writing or in speaking—in school, at work, or in a social situation. Did you have any difficulty restating? Were your readers or listeners able to fully comprehend the material? Explain your answer.

2.   In the article you are about to read, the writer describes the predicted increase in the number of Hispanic students who will be attending schools in the United States by the year 2030. Think about the racial and ethnic makeup of your college classes. Do the students in your classes reflect the racial and ethnic diversity that exists in the United States today?

Expanding Your Vocabulary

Here are some words and their meanings that are important to your understanding of the essay. You might want to review them before you begin to read.

"one in four . . . will likely be of **Hispanic** [people from Spanish-speaking cultures] origin" (paragraph 1)

"the nation's education system will need major **retooling** [overhauling, changing]" (paragraph 5)

"The U.S. House . . . **opted** [decided] against greater restrictions on legal immigration." (paragraph 9)

"**demographic** [pertaining to human population] shifts . . . have left districts scrambling . . . to serve an **influx** [a sudden surge or increase] of Hispanic and Asian immigrants" (paragraph 11)

Jeff Archer

Surge in Hispanic Student Enrollment Predicted*

By 2030, nearly one in four school-age children in the United States will likely be of Hispanic origin, a new report from the U.S. Bureau of the Census predicts.   **1**

The report shows that Hispanics will make up 24.5 percent of the overall U.S. population by 2050. But the high birthrate among Hispanics means the growth in the Hispanic population will be even faster among people age 18 and under and thus will be seen in school enrollments well before the midcentury mark.   **2**

The first such projection issued since 1993, the report also foresees a sharp increase in the percentage of Asian-Americans.   **3**

The percentage of non-Hispanic whites in the country's school-age   **4**

*Jeff Archer, "Surge in Hispanic Student Enrollment Predicted." *Education Week* (Mar. 27, 1996), p. 3.

population will fall below 50 percent for the first time in history between 2030 and 2040, the Census Bureau figures show.

The projections released this month strengthened the view of   5
many educators that the nation's education system will need major retooling to meet the needs of an increasingly diverse population.

"We continue to prepare teachers for nonexistent students: mid-   6
dle-class students who speak English and have plenty of resources
at home," said Maria Robledo Montecel, the executive director of
the Intercultural Development Research Association, a nonprofit
education-research and training organization based in San Anto-
nio.

Even if immigration ceased, the Hispanic share of the U.S. popu-   7
lation would jump from about 10 percent to about 18 percent by
2050, according to Census Bureau projections. The agency defines
the term Hispanic as anyone of Spanish culture or origin, regardless
of race.

"These trends are so substantial, it would take tremendous social   8
changes to stop them," said Gregory Spencer, the chief of the popula-
tion-projections branch at the bureau. Mr. Spencer's projections assume a continuation of the current annual immigration rate of about
820,000 people.

The U.S. House last week approved tougher measures dealing with   9
illegal aliens, but opted against greater restrictions on legal immigration. In another vote last week, the lawmakers approved a measure to
allow states to deny a free public education to illegal-immigrant children.

Hispanic students already make up the largest ethnic category in   10
the schools of some of the nation's biggest cities.

In Texas, demographic shifts over the past 10 years have left dis-   11
tricts scrambling for bilingual teachers and other resources to serve an
influx of Hispanic and Asian immigrants.

"The toughest part is the teacher shortage, but we have to also do   12
an enormous amount of staff development with teachers just to catch
up," said José Hernandez, the Houston schools' assistant superintendent for special programs.

The Houston district needs about 300 more teachers for its   13
English-as-a-second-language programs, he said, and immigration
has swelled enrollments at some schools to nearly double their capacity.

Troubling Dropout Rates

A chief concern among many advocates for Hispanic students is the dropout rate, a problem experts say could grow worse if the population growth is not met with additional resources.   **14**

"What is ironic is that as the Hispanic population continues to grow, we are seeing a decline in the availability of bilingual services," said Ms. Robledo Montecel.   **15**

Nationwide, about 33 percent of Hispanics ages 18 to 24 were high school dropouts in 1993, according to a recent report from the Institute for Educational Leadership, a Washington-based think tank.   **16**

Ms. Robledo Montecel said schools need more programs that will encourage greater parental involvement among Hispanics, discourage the tracking of Hispanic students into nonacademic programs, and increase participation of such families in preschool programs.   **17**

Only about 17 percent of 3- and 4-year-old Hispanic children in the United States enter preschool programs or kindergarten, compared with about 30 percent for blacks and about 34 percent for whites of the same age, according to the U.S. Education Department.   **18**

While the census projections have focused attention on the growing Hispanic school-age population, the number of Asian-American students is also expected to climb rapidly, from about 4 percent now to about 9 percent in 2050.   **19**

Restatement of "Surge in Hispanic Student Enrollment Predicted"

According to the U.S. Census Bureau, by the year 2030, 25 percent of school-age children in this country will be of Hispanic origin. In addition, because of the high birth rate among Hispanics, there will be even faster growth among those Hispanics who are under the age of 18. The same report predicts a sharp rise in the percentage of Asian Americans as well. In contrast, the number of non-Hispanic whites among the country's school-age population will fall below 50 percent for the first time in history.

As a result of these predictions, educators have begun to realize that more changes will have to be made in order to properly educate this "increasingly diverse population"; in particular, teachers will have to be trained to meet the needs of these students.

While a large number of Hispanic people immigrate to this country, about 820,000 per year, even if immigration stopped, the percentage of Hispanics in the United States would still increase to about 18 percent by the year 2050.

In fact, Hispanic students make up the largest ethnic category in some cities, particularly in Texas, where the large number of non-English-speaking students has caused a serious shortage of bilingual teachers and teachers who have the necessary training and knowledge to serve the needs of Hispanic and Asian immigrants.

Because there is a higher dropout rate for Hispanic students than for other groups, experts fear that unless more resources are put in place, particularly in bilingual education, the dropout rate will get even worse. In addition, experts believe that more involvement by Hispanic parents is needed, along with a decrease in the use of tracking and an increase in the use of preschool programs by Hispanic families.

Although attention is now being paid to the growing number of Hispanic children entering the school system, the number of Asian-American students in this country is expected to double within the next 50 years.

QUESTIONS FOR CRITICAL THINKING

THINKING CRITICALLY ABOUT CONTENT

1. Does the writer of the original essay give sufficient statistics to prove that the Hispanic student population will increase dramatically in this country in the next thirty years?

2. Is the restatement of the original essay equally effective in convincing the reader that the Hispanic population will increase sharply?

THINKING CRITICALLY ABOUT PURPOSE

3. What is Jeff Archer's main idea? How does the writer of the restatement essay express this main idea?

4. If you were writing the restating essay, what would you do differently to communicate the purpose of the original essay? Explain your answer.

THINKING CRITICALLY ABOUT AUDIENCE

5. Who do you think Archer's intended audience is? (Remember, the article was first published in *Education Week*.) Do you think the restating essay is addressed to the same type of audience? Explain your answer.

6. Do you think readers would prefer to read the original version rather than the restating essay? Explain your reasoning.

THINKING CRITICALLY ABOUT POINT OF VIEW

7. If you were the superintendent of a school district in a large urban area, what immediate changes would you make in your schools as a result of the information contained in this article?

8. Do you think Hispanic people are portrayed favorably, unfavorably, or in a neutral manner in both the original and restating essays? Explain your answer in a complete paragraph.

Interpreting Graphics

A type of restating that is particularly useful in college involves summarizing and interpreting information that is presented in graphic form. The term *graphic* refers to illustrations such as drawings, maps, charts, or graphs. Much of the material that you will read in college will contain *visuals* (another word for graphs and charts). Your ability to interpret these graphics or visuals will help you better understand the material contained in your textbooks. Graphics are not useful simply for interpreting textbook material, however. If you look in any newspaper or magazine, you will notice that many of the articles include graphics that contain statistics, percentages, costs—information that is much easier to present in a chart or graph than in words. Furthermore, information is often more dramatic when it is presented in graphic form rather than in words, because large changes in percentages or numbers are clearly highlighted.

A graph published in *The New York Times* in August 1994 gave data (information) about students who attended college from 1972 to 1992. Notice how much useful information can be contained in a very small space when it is presented graphically. Following the graph is a restating essay in which the information and meaning contained in the graph are expressed in words.

Before You Read

Focusing Your Attention

Before you study this graph and restatement, take a few moments to respond to the following questions in your journal:

1. As a student, do you find that visual aids help you understand the information being presented? Explain your answer.

2. Think about some written material that you had to study and understand for a recent examination. Would this material have been easier to understand if it had been presented in graphic form? Explain your answer in detail.

When the Juniors Are Senior

More than two million Americans 35 and older were enrolled in colleges in 1992.

Women are leading the way. In 1992, they were two-thirds of the college students age 35 and older, up from 53.4 percent in 1972, the first year in which the Census Bureau surveyed older students.

A love for learning is certainly helpful to older students in search of sheepskins, but the real incentive may be money. The 1990 census found that college graduates earn an average of $2,116 a month compared with $1,077 a month for those with only a high school diploma.

ANNE CRONIN

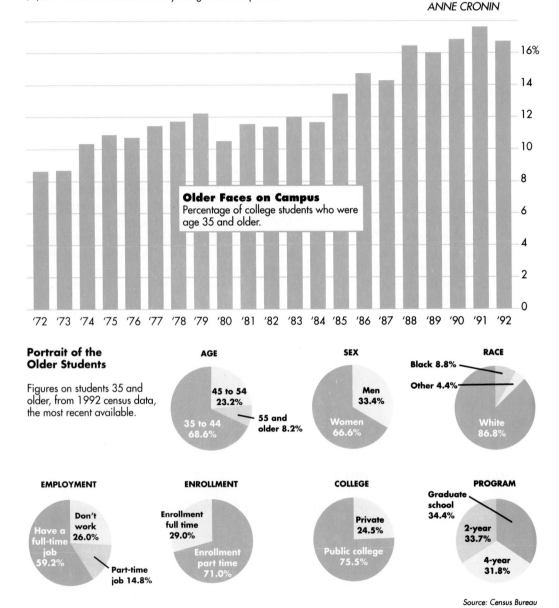

Older Faces on Campus
Percentage of college students who were age 35 and older.

Portrait of the Older Students

Figures on students 35 and older, from 1992 census data, the most recent available.

AGE
- 45 to 54 23.2%
- 35 to 44 68.6%
- 55 and older 8.2%

SEX
- Men 33.4%
- Women 66.6%

RACE
- Black 8.8%
- Other 4.4%
- White 86.8%

EMPLOYMENT
- Don't work 26.0%
- Have a full-time job 59.2%
- Part-time job 14.8%

ENROLLMENT
- Enrollment full time 29.0%
- Enrollment part time 71.0%

COLLEGE
- Private 24.5%
- Public college 75.5%

PROGRAM
- Graduate school 34.4%
- 2-year 33.7%
- 4-year 31.8%

Source: Census Bureau

*Anne Cronin, "When the Juniors Are Senior," (text and graphics), The New York Times (August 17, 1994), Education page.

Restatement of "When the Juniors Are Senior"

The bar graph at the top of the previous page shows that the percentage of college students who were 35 years old or older has been steadily increasing since 1972, the first year the Census Bureau began to sur-vey older students. Although there were slight drops in enrollment by students over 35 in certain years, particularly from 1980 to 1985, the *percentage* climbed steadily from about 9 percent in 1972 to over 16 percent in 1992, with an all-time high of almost 18 percent in 1991.

The pie graphs at the bottom of the previous page give a breakdown or "portrait" of the students over 35 according to age, sex, race, employment status, enrollment status, type of college, and type of program.

In terms of age, the largest percentage (68.6%) of older students in college are between the ages of 35 and 44. The second-largest percentage of students (23.2%) are between the ages of 45 and 54, and the smallest percentage of students (8.2%) are 55 and older.

In terms of gender, women outnumber men by far; 66.6 percent of college students 35 or older are women, compared with 33.4 percent who are men.

In terms of race, 86.8 percent of the older college students are white, comprising an enormous majority, while blacks comprise 8.8 percent of the older students and "other" races comprise the smallest percentage, 4.4 percent.

As for employment, 59.2 percent of the older students work full time, while 14.8 percent of the students work part time and 26 percent of the older students do not work.

In terms of enrollment, 71 percent of the older students attend college part time, an enormous majority. In contrast, only 29 percent are enrolled as full-time students.

In terms of the type of college the older students are attending, 75.5 percent attend public colleges, while only 24.5 percent of the older students attend private colleges.

The type of program the older students are enrolled in is divided somewhat equally: 33.7 percent of the students are enrolled in a two-year program; 34.4 percent of the students are enrolled in graduate school programs; and 31.8 percent of the students are enrolled in four-year programs.

The explanation at the top of the page suggests that the reason older students are returning to college in increasing numbers may not be simply because of a love of learning. According to the census report, college graduates earn an average of $2,116 a month compared to $1,077 a month for those with only a high school diploma, a difference of $1,039 a month.

QUESTIONS FOR CRITICAL THINKING

THINKING CRITICALLY ABOUT CONTENT

1. In your opinion, does the writer express the full meaning and purpose of the visual aids in the restating essay?

2. Which format is more effective, the visual aids or the restating essay? Explain your answer.

THINKING CRITICALLY ABOUT PURPOSE

3. Why do you think the creator of the visual aids used both a bar graph and pie charts?

4. Why do you think the writer of the restating essay described each visual aid separately?

THINKING CRITICALLY ABOUT AUDIENCE

5. Who do you think was the original audience for the visual aids? Do you think the restating essay is addressed to the same audience? Explain your answer.

6. If you were restating these visuals, what would you do differently to make your restatement interesting to your readers?

THINKING CRITICALLY ABOUT POINT OF VIEW

7. Are these visual aids an effective way to encourage people to attend college? Explain your answer.

8. Even if you are not one of the "older students" described in the visual aids and in the restating essay, would this information convince you that you should attend college? Explain your answer in a paragraph.

LEARNING FROM YOUR PEERS

The writing tasks in this chapter are slightly different from those you have completed so far. Instead of composing an essay about your own ideas, you must restate information or experiences that someone else has written about. Restating another writer's ideas and research in your own words allows you to find out whether you completely understand those ideas. This skill will help you whenever you have to summarize another writer's main points. It will also benefit you in writing short-answer or essay tests. To observe the process of restating in action, we are going to follow the writing process of a student named Inez Morales.

Inez's Writing Assignment: Restating Information from a Professional Essay

This is the first part of the topic Inez's instructor assigned:

Explain the following article by Lawrence Kutner in your own words. The purpose of this assignment is to make sure you understand what the author is saying and are able to analyze the content of the essay. Because this restatement is part of a larger research project, it is very important to complete this assignment accurately and thoroughly.

The second part of Inez's assignment will test her ability to understand and restate the information contained in a graph. (See p. 222).

Inez goes through the writing process as outlined in Chapter 1: *thinking, planning, developing, organizing, drafting, revising,* and *editing.*

Lawrence Kutner

Teaching About Racial and Ethnic Differences*

The 4-year-old white girl studied the photographs the researcher   **1**
had given her. Each picture showed pairs of children—one black and one white—in ambiguous, nonthreatening situations, like two children in a playground. The researcher asked the girl questions about what she saw, such as: "Which child is the bad child?" or "Which child will win the game of checkers?"

"Every time there was something good, she picked the white   **2**
child," said Dr. Phyllis A. Katz, a developmental psychologist who conducted this research and who is the director of the Institute for Research on Social Problems in Boulder, Colorado. "Every time there was something bad, she picked the black child.

"The mother was mortified."   **3**

*Lawrence Kutner, "Teaching About Racial and Ethnic Differences." *The New York Times* (Oct. 7, 1993), p. C4.

While the preschool girl's reactions were extreme for those chil-   **4**
dren tested, they reflect the biases clearly shown by many children
her age. The mother was shocked because her daughter's words con-
tradicted everything she had consciously hoped the girl would believe.

We like to think that young children pay no attention to the   **5**
racial and ethnic differences they see and hear. But recent research
by Dr. Katz has shown that many children categorize people by
race—or at least by skin color—as early as 6 months of age. In
those studies, infants were shown color photographs of people's
faces, either all men or all women. The first four showed people of
the same race. The children quickly "habituated" to the photographs, looking at each new image for less time than the previous
ones.

The fifth photograph showed the face of someone of a differ-   **6**
ent race. Most 6-month-old children spent more time studying
this photograph than the previous few. Developmental psychologists interpret this result as showing that the children recognized
that there was something different about this fifth person—that
he or she did not fit into the same category as the earlier photographs.

But noticing differences is very different from assigning values or   **7**
interpretations to those differences.

"One of the reasons why young children may form biases against   **8**
certain people of different races is because their parents are not helping them understand the differences those children are noticing," Dr.
Katz said. "Children aren't color-blind. To act as if they are will probably confuse children enormously."

One powerful source of early information and misinformation   **9**
about people who look and sound different is television. Many
programs that appeal to young children, especially the older cartoons and slapstick comedies, are filled with racial and ethnic
stereotypes. Villains speak with heavy accents. Many ethnic and
cultural groups are presented as inherently stupid or incompetent.
Children who live in communities where almost everyone looks
and sounds like they do are the most likely to accept those portray-
als as true.

"The children who have only occasional experiences with other   **10**
races are most likely to develop prejudices and believe in racial
stereotypes," said Vivian Jenkins Nelsen, the president of Inter-

Race, a research and consulting group in Minneapolis devoted to race relations. She added that there's a big difference between going to school with children of other races, where you may interact with them relatively little, and living in the same neighborhood.

Young children are also very sensitive to the unspoken information **11** from their parents about racial and cultural differences. Do their parents appear tense or sound condescending with certain people? What do their parents' friends look and sound like?

Children's concepts of themselves also influence how they inter- **12** pret racial and ethnic differences. Those who feel worthless, oppressed or unappreciated often try to cast blame on others. They are suspicious and fearful instead of curious about people who are different.

"Children who have poor self-esteem tend to be more prejudiced; **13** those with higher self-esteem are more open-minded," said Verna Simpkins, the director of membership and program services for the Girls Scouts of the U.S.A. in Manhattan and an author of its "Valuing Differences" curriculum. "Children who feel comfortable with their own cultural background feel more comfortable exploring someone else's."

Thinking

Inez's first task is to read the article by Lawrence Kutner, which she does several times. As she reads each paragraph, she tries to understand the author's ideas and their arrangement so she can restate them in her own words.

Planning

After reading and rereading the article, Inez jots down the essay's main ideas in her own words. Since her entire restatement must be in her own words, she rereads her work to make sure that she is accurately restating the essay. Then she makes sure that she has not added any of her own opinions about the subject.

Inez's list of main ideas looks like this:

1. Dr. Phyllis A. Katz is director of the Institute for Research on Social

Problems in Boulder, Colorado.

2. Young children think that people with dark skin or heavy accents—from TV, slapstick comedies—make some ethnic or racial groups look stupid or bad.

3. Vivian Jenkins Nelsen—president of Inter-Race in Minneapolis (a research and consulting group)—believes that attending school with children from other groups does not change racial stereotypes of children who live in neighborhoods where everyone is of the same skin color. I think this is true.

4. What parents say influences beliefs in young children.

6. Self-esteem may also form a child's prejudices—Verna Simpkins.

Developing

Next, Inez checks over her list to see whether she has repeated or left out any important points that need to be included in the restatement. She finds that she has missed some material and misrepresented other information. The additions she makes to her list are in bold type here:

1. Dr. Phyllis A. Katz, director of the Institute for Research on Social Problems in Boulder, Colorado, **says babies and little children see differences in skin color--as early as six months of age!**

2. **By four years old children start making value judgments about people of other races.**

3. Young children think that people with dark skin or heavy accents--from TV, slapstick comedies--make some ethnic or racial groups look stupid or bad. **If parents do not explain that these are stereotypes, their children accept what they see on TV as true.**

4. Vivian Jenkins Nelsen--president of Inter-Race in Minneapolis (a research and consulting group)--believes that attending school with children from other groups does not change racial stereotypes of children who live in neighborhoods where everyone is of the same skin color. ~~I think this is true.~~

5. **Parents' behavior** influences beliefs in young children. **Kids see how their parents behave with others and the kids form their own opinions.**

6. Self-esteem may also form a child's prejudices--Verna Simpkins, **director of membership and program services for the Girl Scouts of the U.S.A. She believes that children with high self-esteem are more open-minded and willing to learn about the cultural backgrounds of other kids.**

Organizing

In a restatement, material should be explained in the order in which it is presented in the original source. So Inez uses her list of main ideas as a guide in organizing her material. She does not rearrange any ideas.

Drafting

Inez now feels ready to restate the essay. As she writes, she realizes that she is sticking closely to her list. She changes a few words to make her points clear, and she adds verbs or modifiers that she left out when she was making her list. She finds herself naturally following the sequence of the original article. Here is Inez's restatement:

Inez's Essay: First Draft
Restating Information from an Essay

Main Idea: Children learn about ethnic differences from television and from their living environment.

Dr. Phyllis A. Katz, director of the Institute for Research on Social Problems in Boulder, Colorado, has been studying children and their perceptions about people. She found that children begin to notice differences in skin color at about six months old. Her research shows that they start making value judgments about those differences just a few years later. For example, one white girl had decided by the time she was four years old that blacks were "bad."

Dr. Katz firmly believes that television programs misinform young children about people with dark skin or heavy accents. Programs which appeal to children present certain ethnic or racial groups as stupid or bad. If parents do not clearly explain that these are stereotypes, children begin to accept what they see on television as true.

Another researcher, Vivian Jenkins Nelsen, the president of Inter-Race in Minneapolis (a research and consulting group), believes that attending school with children from other groups does not change racial stereotypes of children who go home to neighborhoods where all the children look alike. Living in racially mixed neighborhoods appears to help break down stereotypes.

The behavior of their parents is another influence that does shape beliefs in young children. They see how their parents interact with others and form opinions based on those interactions. If they are biased and prejudiced, young children are affected.

Self-esteem may also influence children's prejudices, according to Verna Simpkins, the director of membership and program services for the Girl Scouts of the U.S.A. So parents who instill self-esteem in their children also combat prejudice in the best way. She believes that children with high self-esteem are more open-minded and willing to learn about the cultural backgrounds of other children.

Inez's Writing Assignment: Restating Information from a Graph

This is the second part of the topic Inez's instructor assigned:

Restate in your own words the information contained in the following graph, which appeared in the Chronicle of Higher Education *in January 1994. Do not worry about the length of your restating essay; just be as thorough and as informative as possible so that your reader will know that you interpreted and understood all the information in the graph.*

Federal Spending on AIDS Research

FISCAL YEARS 1982-1994 (IN MILLIONS)

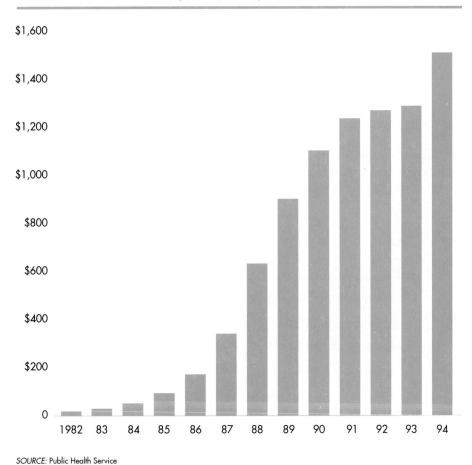

SOURCE: Public Health Service

Chronicle of Higher Education (Jan. 5, 1994), p. A36.

Thinking

Inez studies the graph and makes sure that she understands the information presented in it. Then she thinks about the best way to express this visual information in words. She looks at the years shown on the graph and thinks about events that were happening during those years. She tries to discover a relationship between the events and the amount of money spent on research.

Planning

Inez decides that the clearest way to present the ideas is to divide the years into groups that match presidential terms in the United States. She knows that the AIDS epidemic began in the early 1980s, when she was in preschool. She checks with her older brother to find out who was president at that time. Then she lists the amount of money spent on AIDS research in each president's term.

Inez's list looks like this:

1. 1982 to 1987--President Reagan (really 1988--but dollars show an abrupt jump in 1988)

2. 1988 to 1992--Bush

3. 1992 to 1994--Clinton

Inez looks at her list and wonders what she can add to this. She thinks that maybe the graph has more information, but she also knows that she has already started interpreting the information and drawing some conclusions.

Developing

Inez starts adding information to her list. This is what it looks like:

1. 1982 to 1987--President Reagan (really 1988--but dollars show an abrupt jump in 1988)--funding gradually increased--at the end of his term--$300 million per year (slightly more than $1 per U.S. citizen).

2. 1988 to 1992--Bush--funding level doubled from about $600 million in f. y. 1988--to about $1,300 million in 1992.

3. 1992 to 1994--Clinton--increased slightly to about $1,500 million a year.

Organizing

Inez decided at the very early stages of developing her restatement that the best way to present this material is chronologically—from past to present. Since she generated her list in this order, she can simply use it now as a guide to write the first draft of her restatement.

Drafting

Inez decides that she has understood and interpreted all the information in the graph, so she begins her draft, following her second list very closely. She is surprised at how quickly the writing is finished and realizes that her prewriting activities were very helpful. Here is Inez's draft.

Inez's Essay: First Draft
Restating Information from a Graph

Main Idea: Federal spending on AIDS research has increased an enormous amount since 1982.

According to the Public Health Service, federal spending on AIDS research grew from almost nothing in fiscal year 1982 to nearly $1,600 million ($1 billion, 600 million) in fiscal year 1994. During the early years of the AIDS epidemic (1982-1987), when President Reagan was in the White House, funding increased from minimal levels gradually to about $300 million per year (slightly more than $1 per U.S. citizen). Since President Clinton has been in the White House, funding has increased slightly to about $1,500 million a year. During President Bush's term, the funding level doubled from about $600 million in fiscal year 1988 to about $1,300 million in 1992. The government has increased its total cost of federal research on the AIDS epidemic over slightly more than a decade to about $8,500 million, or around $34 per U.S. citizen.

Revising

Inez has written her restatements as clearly as possible. She believes that she has figured out the main ideas of the article and the graph and that she has stated the information pretty well. But now she needs to review what she has said and smooth it out so that it represents the author's thoughts as accurately as possible. As the class members get stronger in their writing, they are able to move to more complex issues in their revisions. The focus this time is on organizing paragraphs.

Inez reviews the Checklist for Organizing Paragraphs at the beginning of the Tips for Revising section in this chapter. Inez knows that each item on the checklist will move her closer to a revised draft that is well organized and consistent. In the first phase of this particular revision process, she chooses an effective method for expanding on the ideas in each paragraph. In the second phase, she varies these methods so that the final draft is not monotonous in any way.

Inez reads the Tips for Revising and does all the exercises her instructor assigns. Then she works through the checklist carefully, first identifying the methods of organization she uses in each paragraph and then making sure she uses a variety of methods in her essay. She finds problems in both areas and tries to resolve them in her revised draft.

COLLABORATIVE WORK

PEER GROUP ACTIVITY

After you read the portions of the Tips for Revising your instructor assigns, turn to Inez's first drafts (pp. 221–222 and 225), and complete the following tasks in small groups:

A.   List the organizing method (for definitions, see pp. 232–239) Inez uses in each paragraph of her restatement of an essay.

B.   List the organizing method Inez uses in each paragraph of her restatement of information from a graph.

Compare your group's lists with the ones your instructor will show you. Where do your marks differ from your instructor's? What do you need to view before writing your own essay?

CLASS ACTIVITY

As an entire class, look at the underlined portions of Inez's revised essays (pp. 227–229) to see what changes she made.

A.   Did you identify the **revision** problems that Inez corrected?

B.   Do you think her changes are good ones? Discuss her changes.

Editing

Now that the information in Inez's paragraphs is organized effectively, she needs to do some final proofreading and editing before handing in her assignment. The instructor wants the students to notice how the meaning of specific words in the English language can change with their forms. Noticing these fine points of language, the instructor explains, helps everyone see how even a letter or a single punctuation mark can change a word's meaning and role in its sentence. So Inez reads the Tips for Editing section in this chapter to learn about verb forms, noun forms, and modifiers. Returning to her draft, she goes over the questions in the Editing Checklist one by one and makes changes so that her revised draft fulfills all the requirements.

COLLABORATIVE WORK

PEER GROUP ACTIVITY

After you read the portions of the Tips for Editing your instructor assigns, turn to Inez's first drafts (pp. 221–222 and 225), and complete the following tasks in small groups:

A.   Underline all the verbs (for a definition, see p. 37) in this essay.

B.   Put brackets around all the nouns (for a definition, see p. 40) in this essay.

C.   Put squares around all the adjectives and adverbs (for definitions, see pp. 46 and 49) in this essay.

D.   Circle any incorrect forms of the words you have highlighted on this draft.

Compare your group's marks with those your instructor will show you. Where do your marks differ from your instructor's? What do you need to review before writing your own essay?

CLASS ACTIVITY

As an entire class, look at the underlined portions of Inez's revised drafts (pp. 227–229) to see what changes she has made.

A.   Did you identify the **editing** problems that Inez corrected?

B.   Do you think her changes are good ones? Discuss her changes.

Inez's Revised Essay
Restating Information from an Essay

Learning About Stereotypes

Dr. Phyllis A. Katz, director of the Institute for Research on

Social Problems in Boulder, Colorado, has been studying children and their perceptions about people. She found that children begin to notice differences in skin color at about six months old. Her research shows that they start making value judgments about those differences just a few years later. For example, one white girl had decided by the time she was four years old that blacks were "bad."

Dr. Katz firmly believes that television programs misinform young children about people with dark skin or heavy accents. ~~Programs~~ Slapstick comedies and older cartoons, which appeal to children, present certain ethnic or racial groups as acting stupidly or badly. For example, *The Little Rascals,* a famous series from earlier in this century, is often rerun on television, and it gives a terrible impression of its one African-American character. If parents do not clearly explain that these are stereotypes, children begin to accept ~~what they see~~ these false images seen on television as true.

Another researcher, Vivian Jenkins Nelsen, the president of Inter-Race in Minneapolis (a research and consulting group), believes that attending school with children from other groups does not change racial stereotypes of children who go home to neighborhoods where all the children look alike. Living in racially mixed neighborhoods appears to help break down stereotypes.

The behavior of their parents toward people of other ethnic groups is another influence that does shape beliefs in young children. If parents are biased and prejudiced, young children are affected. For instance, if parents appear tense or condescending, children will imitate these behaviors. ~~They~~ Children see how their parents interact with others and form opinions based on those interactions. ~~If they are biased and prejudiced, young children are affected.~~

Self-esteem may also influence children's prejudices, according to Verna Simpkins, the director of membership and program services for the Girl Scouts of the U.S.A. ~~So parents who instill self-esteem in their~~

~~children also combat prejudice in the best way.~~ She believes that children with high self-esteem are more open-minded and willing to learn about the cultural backgrounds of other children. <u>So parents who instill self-esteem in their children also combat prejudice in the best way.</u>

Inez's Revised Essay
Restating Information from a Graph

Funding of AIDS Research

According to the Public Health Service, federal spending on AIDS research grew from almost nothing in fiscal year 1982 to nearly $1,600 million ($1 billion, 600 million) in fiscal year 1994. During the early years of the AIDS epidemic (1982–1987), when President Reagan was in the White House, funding increased from minimal levels gradually to about $300 million (slightly more than $1 per U.S. citizen). ~~Since President Clinton has been in the White house, funding has increased slightly to about $1,500 million a year.~~ During President Bush's term, the funding level doubled from about $600 million in fiscal year 1988 to about $1,300 million in 1992. <u>Since President Clinton has been in the White House, funding has increased slightly to about $1,600 million a year.</u> The government has increased its total cost of federal research on the AIDS epidemic over slightly more than a decade to about $8,500 million, or around $34 per U.S. citizen.

WRITING YOUR OWN RESTATING ESSAY

So far, you have seen a professional writer and a fellow student at work trying to restate an idea or body of information as accurately as possible. As you read the published essay and followed the writing process of another student from beginning to end, you absorbed ideas and ways of giving those ideas a form of their own. These reading and writing activities have prepared you to write your own restatement of an essay and a graph.

What Have You Discovered?

Before you begin your own writing task, let's review what you have learned in this chapter so far:

- Restating is crucial to success in college.
- Restating entails putting information from another source (for example, a textbook, a lecture, a graph, an illustration, or a map) into your own words.
- Restating helps you develop a better understanding of the material and see relationships among the ideas more clearly.
- Restating lets you show your reader you are able to comprehend and analyze the material in question.
- To present your restatement effectively, you need to organize your ideas.
- To help you shape your essay, you should learn as much as possible about your readers.
- Before you write a draft, you need to understand the original author's point of view toward the subject.
- After you write a draft, you should revise your essay for meaning and organization.
- After you revise your essay, you should edit its grammar, usage, and sentence structure.

Your Writing Topic

Choose one of the following topics for your restating essay:

1. Find a short editorial or comic strip in a newspaper or newsmagazine, and restate it. Include a photocopy of the original, and highlight the section you have chosen to restate.

2. Find a scientific or technical article that interests you, and interpret one of its accompanying graphs or charts. Include a photocopy of the original, and highlight the section you have chosen to restate.

3. Find a difficult section of a textbook for a course you are now taking, and restate it clearly. Include a photocopy of the original, and highlight the section you have chosen to restate.

4. Create your own restating essay (with the assistance of your instructor). Include a photocopy of the original, and highlight the section you have chosen to restate.

When you have selected one of these topics, you may begin your writing process in the same way Inez did. (You may find her experience helpful in giving you ideas.)

This time your purpose is to write your own restating essay. If some tasks occur out of order, that adjustment is probably part of your personal writing ritual. Follow your instincts, and let them mold your own writing process. But make sure you've worked through all the stages to your final draft.

YOUR WRITING PROCESS

THINKING   Paraphrase the original source as accurately as possible.

PLANNING   Make sure you understand the order of the original material and know as much as you can about the author's approach to the topic.

DEVELOPING   Decide which topics you will develop most fully in your restatement.

ORGANIZING   Organize your material so that it follows the original as closely as possible.

DRAFTING   Write a working draft of your essay in complete sentences.

REVISING   Consulting the Tips for Revising in this chapter (pp. 232–240), revise your first draft—paying special attention to ways of organizing your paragraphs.

EDITING   Consulting the Tips for Editing in this chapter (pp. 241–259), edit your draft for grammar and correctness—paying special attention to verbs, nouns, and modifiers.

Turn in your revised draft to your instructor.

Some Final Thoughts

When you have completed your own essay, answer these four questions in your journal:

1.   What was most difficult about this assignment?
2.   What was easiest?
3.   What did I learn about restating by completing this assignment?
4.   What did I learn about my own writing process from this assignment—how I prepared to write, how I wrote the first draft, how I revised, and how I edited?

Organizing Paragraphs

Checklist for Organizing Paragraphs

✓ Are the ideas organized in a way that is most effective for the purpose of each paragraph: **general-to-particular order, particular-to-general order, time order, space order, movement from one extreme to another?**
✓ Is a **combination** of these methods used when appropriate?

Imagine you have just moved to a new apartment that has the kitchen you've always dreamed of. Surrounded by furniture, boxes, and odds and ends, you could simply start unpacking and stowing utensils anywhere, or you could work out a plan first. What things should you consider before you begin unpacking? Every utensil has a specific function. Items for everyday use need to be easily accessible, for example, while items reserved for special occasions can be stowed in places that are harder to get to. If you plan in this way, you won't put your best dishes in the most accessible cabinet and your pots and pans in the highest cabinet over your built-in double oven and microwave.

Organizing paragraphs can be like arranging your possessions in a new apartment. You need to consider the purpose of your essay and decide how each paragraph will serve that purpose, then arrange the details in a logical manner. The most common ways of organizing paragraphs are (1) general-to-particular order, (2) particular-to-general order, (3) time order, (4) space order, and (5) movement from one extreme to another.

Let's say you are writing about vegetable gardens. If the purpose of one of your paragraphs is to explain how to grow compatible plants near each other, you would want to arrange most of the details in *space order,* beginning with one row of the garden and working to the others. If, however, you want to convince a reader of the value of growing organic vegetables, you might arrange the paragraph by using *movement from one extreme to another*—for example, from the least important detail to the most important ones. When you choose a method of organizing a paragraph, you should consider the purpose of the paragraph and the types of details you are using.

General-to-Particular Order

General-to-particular order will probably be the most useful method of organization at this stage of your writing life. Paragraphs arranged in this way usually begin with a general statement, then move to particular details to develop that statement.

The following paragraph from Tobias Wolff's "The Sissy" (in chapter 2) uses a general-to-particular organization to describe the identifying features of spring:

It was springtime. The earth was spongy with melted snow, and on the warmest days, if you listened for it, you could hear a faint, steady sibilance of evaporation, almost like a light rain. The trees were hazy with new growth. Bears had begun to appear on the glistening granite faces of the mountainsides above us, taking the sun and soaking up heat from the rock; at lunchtime people came out onto their steps and watched them with upturned, benevolent faces. My mother was with me again. The nuts were all husked and drying in the attic. What did I need trouble for?

This paragraph begins with a general statement: *It was springtime.* The writer then provides specific details that explain how he can tell it is spring.

As Inez Morales reviewed her essay, she decided that her second paragraph, which contains only three general statements, would be much better if she added specific details to develop the first general statement about how television influenced children's images of others.

First Draft: Dr. Katz firmly believes that television programs misinform young children about people with dark skin or heavy accents. Programs which appeal to children present certain ethnic or racial groups as stupid or bad. If parents do not clearly explain that these are stereotypes, children begin to accept what they see on television as true.

Revision: Dr. Katz firmly believes that television programs misinform young children about people with dark skin or heavy accents. ~~Programs~~ **Slapstick comedies and older cartoons,** which appeal to children, present certain ethnic or racial groups as **acting** stupid**ly** or bad**ly**. **For example,** *The Little Rascals,* **a famous series from earlier in this century, is often rerun on television, and it gives a terrible impression of its one African-American character.** If parents do not clearly explain that these are stereotypes, children begin to accept ~~what they see~~ **these false images seen** on television as true.

Now, Inez's paragraph is logically organized, proceeding from one general statement to three detailed supporting statements. The logical organization and more developed ideas give her audience a much clearer picture of Inez's idea in this paragraph than the original essay did.

Particular-to-General Order

When you reverse the first method of organization, you arrange your paragraph so that it proceeds from particular statements to a general one. If you feel a topic may be hard for your audience to understand or difficult for readers to agree with, you may choose to use **particular-to-general order.** The following paragraph from "The Sissy" by Tobias Wolff (the published essay in Chapter 2), describes the writer's view of the fight that he cannot avoid, beginning with details and ending with a general statement:

> His first swing caught me dead on the ear. There was an explosion inside my head, then a continuous rustling sound as of someone crumpling paper. It lasted for days. When he swung again I turned away and took his fist on the back of my head. He threw punches the way he threw balls, sidearm, with a lot of wrist, but he somehow got his weight behind them before they landed. This one knocked me to my knees. He drew back his foot and kicked me in the stomach. The papers in my bag deadened the blow but I was stunned by the fact that he had kicked me at all. I saw that his commitment to this fight was absolute.

The specifics in this paragraph lead up to the author's conclusion about his opponent's "commitment" to the fight.

As Inez inspected her restating essay, she decided that her fourth paragraph, which already began with a specific detail, would be best organized from particular to general.

First Draft: The behavior of their parents is another influence that does shape beliefs in young children. They see how their parents interact with others and form opinions based on those interactions. If they are biased and prejudiced, young children are affected.

Revision: The behavior of their parents **toward people of other ethnic groups** is another influence that does shape beliefs in young children. **If parents are biased and prejudiced, young children are affected. For instance, if parents appear tense or condescending, children will imitate these behaviors.** ~~They~~ **Children** see how their parents interact with others and form opinions based on those interactions. ~~If they are biased and prejudiced, young~~

~~children are affected.~~

Now that it ends with a statement about parental interactions in general, Inez's paragraph is more effectively organized, saving its main idea for the end of the paragraph.

Time Order

Time order (also called **chronological order**) is a third way to organize the material in your paragraphs. You probably used this method in your recalling essay, which discussed a past experience; you may have also used it in your explaining essay if you described a process.

In paragraphs arranged according to a time sequence, words that express time indicate to your reader the order in which events occurred or the order in which they should be performed. The following paragraph, taken from Corky Clifton's essay "Life Sentences," which appears in Chapter 7, is organized according to time. The author uses chronological order to discuss his appeals to the prison Pardon Board:

> If Jesus Christ himself was in here with a life sentence, he couldn't get out unless he had money to put in the right places. I've always been a pretty stubborn person, so even though I was told how the political and Pardon Board system works, I freely submitted to all the prison rules and discipline. After twelve years with a perfect record—no disciplinary reports—I applied to the Pardon Board and was denied any consideration for relief. So I waited ten more years and applied again, with still an excellent prison record. This time they wouldn't even hear my case. In 1983 I applied to the board for the third time and the Pardon Board cut my time to fifty years. However, the judge and D.A., retired, simply called the governor's legal staff and told them they don't want me to be free—so, end of case. When I applied for my pardon in 1983, the D.A. published an article in the newspaper saying I was a very dangerous man that would kill anyone who got into my way. He said a lot of things which were all designed to turn public opinion against me and justify his reason for protesting my release.

By following a time order, this paragraph allows readers to understand both the time involved in getting a sentence changed and the seriousness of the request.

In her summary of graph data on AIDS research, Inez placed the information on President Clinton's spending before her reference to George Bush, so she revised her draft to keep the time order logical.

First Draft: According to the Public Health Service, federal

spending on AIDS research grew from almost nothing in

fiscal year 1982 to nearly $1,600 million ($1 billion, 600

million) in fiscal year 1994. During the early years of the AIDS epidemic (1982–1987), when President Reagan was in the White House, funding increased from minimal levels gradually to about $300 million per year (slightly more than $1 per U.S. citizen). **Since President Clinton has been in the White House, funding has increased slightly to about $1,500 million a year.** During President Bush's term, the funding level doubled from about $600 million in fiscal year 1988 to about $1,300 million in 1992. The government has increased its total cost of federal research on the AIDS epidemic over slightly more than a decade to about $8,500 million, or around $34 per U.S. citizen.

Revision: According to the Public Health Service, federal spending on AIDS research grew from almost nothing in fiscal year 1982 to nearly $1,600 million ($1 billion, 600 million) in fiscal year 1994. During the early years of the AIDS epidemic (1982–1987), when President Reagan was in the White House, funding increased from minimal levels gradually to about $300 million per year (slightly more than $1 per U.S. citizen). ~~Since President Clinton has been in the White House, funding has increased slightly to about $1,500 million a year.~~ During President Bush's term, the funding level doubled from about $600 million in fiscal year 1988 to about $1,300 million in 1992. **Since President Clinton has been in the White House, funding has increased slightly to about $1,600 million a year.** The government has increased its total cost of federal research on the AIDS epidemic over slightly more than a decade to about $8,500 million, or around $34 per U.S. citizen.

Now the paragraph is easy to follow because it presents the material in the graph in a logical manner.

Space Order

Space order, or organizing details in a paragraph using their relationship to each other in space, helps you describe a favorite outfit from head to toe or a trip you took to Alaska or Florida. The following paragraph is taken from Amy Tan's novel *The Joy Luck Club* reprinted in Chapter 3:

> The front of the house had a Chinese stone gate, rounded at the top, with big black lacquer doors and a threshold you had to step over. Within the gates I saw the courtyard, and I was surprised. There were no willows or sweet-smelling cassia trees, no garden pavilions, no benches sitting by a pond, no tubs of fish. Instead, there were long rows of bushes on both sides of a wide brick walkway, and to each side of those bushes was a big lawn area with fountains. And as we walked down the walkway and got closer to the house, I saw this house had been built in the Western style. It was three stories high, of mortar and stone, with long metal balconies on each floor and chimneys at every corner.

Tan takes her readers step by step from the gate to the entrance of a stately house in Tientsin, China, giving her paragraph a unified spatial organization.

To help herself stay awake to generate her second restatement, Inez found herself having to move from room to room in her small apartment. Here is a description of her prewriting activity that also illustrates space order:

> Inez sat in a green love seat in the center of her quiet apartment. This room was where she usually started brainstorming for essays and school projects. Her mind started to wander, however, from the restatement due on Friday to the freshly baked cookies sitting on her kitchen counter only a few feet to her right. Inez couldn't concentrate with those cookies tempting her. She jumped up and walked around the coffee table and into the kitchen. She realized that she was thirsty, so she walked to the other side of her kitchen to the refrigerator, where she poured a cold glass of milk. With her hunger and thirst under control, she walked out of the kitchen, to her right, and down the hallway to her bedroom. Inez finally settled down at her desk by the window on the far side of her bedroom and started to work on her rough draft.

This description of Inez's movement around her apartment uses spatial order.

Movement from One Extreme to Another

Another method of organizing details in a paragraph, **movement from one extreme to another,** can follow any line of reasoning that makes sense of the details you have chosen for your essay. You might explain how to choose a dog, for example, by moving from most important to least important considerations. For a city apartment, the most important feature would be the dog's size and exercise needs. (For instance, a Dalmation needs running space while a Lhasa Apso is quite content in a 10-by-12-

foot room.) Least important to an apartment dweller would be a dog's hunting ability or usefulness in herding sheep. You can also reverse the order and begin with the least important; this is a good method to use in persuasive writing because readers often remember best the information they read last.

In the following paragraph from Robert Lee's essay "The Death Penalty Is an Effective Punishment, which appears in Chapter 8, Lee works up to the most important issue, "Has the accused *earned* the penalty?":

> Deterrence should never be considered the *primary* reason for administering the death penalty. It would be both immoral and unjust to punish one man merely as an example to others. The basic consideration should be: Is the punishment deserved? If not, it should not be administered regardless of what its deterrent impact might be. After all, once deterrence supersedes justice as the basis for a criminal sanction, the guilt or innocence of the accused becomes largely irrelevant. Deterrence can be achieved as effectively by executing an innocent person as a guilty one (something that communists and other totalitarians discovered long ago). If a punishment administered to one person deters someone else from committing a crime, fine. But that result should be viewed as a bonus of justice properly applied, not as a reason for the punishment. The decisive consideration should be: Has the accused *earned* the penalty?

This method of organization makes this information easy to understand and emphasizes the last question—the most important consideration for assigning a penalty, as far as the author is concerned.

As Inez reviewed her essay, she decided that paragraph 5 should have its most important point at the end.

First Draft: Self-esteem may also influence children's prejudices, according to Verna Simpkins, the director of membership and program services for the Girl Scouts of the U.S.A. ~~So~~ parents who instill self-esteem in their children also combat prejudice in the best way. She believes that children with high self-esteem are more open-minded and willing to learn about the cultural backgrounds of other children.

Revision: Self-esteem may also influence children's prejudices, according to Verna Simpkins, the director of membership and program services for the Girl Scouts of the U.S.A. ~~So parents who instill self-esteem in their children also combat prejudice in the best way~~. She believes that children with high self-esteem are more open-minded and willing to learn about the cultural backgrounds of other children. **So parents who instill self-esteem in their children also combat prejudice in the best way.**

Exercise R6-1

Identify the method of development in paragraphs 4 and 11 in Lawrence Kutner's essay, "Teaching About Racial and Ethnic Differences" (pp. 218 and 219).

Exercise R6-2

Identify the method of development Inez uses in paragraph 1 of her revised restatement of an essay (p. 238).

Exercise R6-3

1. Make up a topic sentence that introduces the following details in a paragraph. Then arrange the details in logical order.

    Wake up early.   Wash up.

    Go to class.   Turn off the alarm.

    Get out of bed.   Eat breakfast.

2. Choose a logical method of development and make up a topic sentence for a paragraph that includes the following details.

    I am failing math.

    I don't understand differential equations.

    I still do not understand when to use semicolons in my essays.

    My English instructor says I don't include enough specific, concrete details in my essays.

    I am barely passing astronomy.

    I got it mixed up with astrology.

    I can't tell rocks apart in geology.

    My drama coach is mad at me.

    I hate my folk-dancing class.

Exercise R6-4

List the best method of development for paragraphs on the following topics.

1. How to make candles
2. We should keep affirmative action.

3. What I will wear to the prom
4. Today, scientists question some of Darwin's theories.
5. Some people put their time to good use.

 ## COLLABORATIVE WORK

After writing a draft of your own restating essay, exchange papers with a classmate, and do the following tasks:

A. Look at each paragraph, and decide whether it is organized in a logical way or could be improved through another method of organization.

B. Mark the paragraphs that need revising, and make suggestions for new methods of organization in the margin.

Then return the paper to its writer, and use the information in this section to revise your draft.

Verb Forms, Noun Forms, and Modifiers

Checklist for Editing Verbs, Nouns, and Modifiers

✓ Are **verbs** in their **correct forms**?
✓ Are **verbs** in their **correct tenses,** changing to show differences in time?
✓ Are **nouns** used correctly according to **case**?
✓ Are **adjectives** close to the words they **modify**?
✓ Are **comparative adjective forms** used correctly?
✓ Are **adverbs** located near the words they modify?
✓ Are **comparative adverb forms** used correctly?

In English, verbs, nouns, adjectives, and adverbs change forms to play different roles in their sentences. Verbs change their forms to show tense or time; nouns to show singular, plural, and ownership; and adjectives and adverbs to highlight comparisons or contrasts. In these particular parts of speech, even small differences, like a single letter added to a word, mean something; all such changes make our attempts to communicate with others more interesting and more accurate.

Verb Forms

Now that you've organized your kitchen in your new apartment, you want to start using some of your equipment. From food blender to electric knife, each kitchen tool has specific rules governing its proper use. Parts of speech in language also follow specific rules for their correct usage. We could spend our time arguing whether or not verbs are the most important words in sentences. However, most people do agree that the chances of making errors in verb usage are greater than with almost any other part of speech. Think about all the words that function as verbs, the different forms these verbs can take, and the variations in time and tense that verbs express. It's no surprise that using verbs correctly takes concentrated effort. "I seen my friend yesterday" is a verb usage mistake that would create a very negative impression on readers and listeners. By reviewing the principal parts and tenses of verbs, you will communicate more clearly and correctly and your writing will become more confident overall.

Principal Parts

Every verb in the English language can appear in four different forms: present, present participle, past, and past participle. The **present** or *base form* expresses action that occurs now, in the present: *I run. We run. You run. They run. He, she,* or *it runs.*

Note that the third person singular—*he, she, it,* or any singular noun—requires the addition of an *-s* to the verb.

Here is a verb in its present form in Inez's first draft:

> Dr. Katz firmly **believes** that television programs misinform young
>
> children about people with dark skin or heavy accents.

The **present participle** expresses action that continues in both the past and present. Simply add *-ing* to the present verb form: *running, learning, moaning, singing.* Every verb in the English language forms the present participle this way. But the present participle form cannot function alone in a sentence. A present participle must be paired with one or more helping verbs, forming the main verb in the sentence: *I am running. We were running. You are running. They have been running. He, she,* or *it is running.* (See p. 59 for a list of helping verbs.) The following sentence features a verb that consists of a present participle plus a helper:

> Dr. Phyllis A. Katz, director of the Institute for Research on Social
>
> Problems in Boulder, Colorado, **has been studying** children and their
>
> perceptions about people.

The **past tense** and **past participle** forms both express action that has happened in the past. Regular verbs form the past tense and past participle forms by adding *-d* or *-ed: lived, died, learned, moaned.* However, irregular verbs form the past and past participles by changing their spellings entirely: *run, ran; know, known; see, saw.* Of course, past forms of verbs can function as main verbs, as this sentence from Inez's essay illustrates:

> **Past Tense:**   She **found** that children begin to notice differences in skin
>
> color as early as six months old.

Like present participles, past participles require helping verbs, forms of *be* and *have,* before they can function as the main verbs of sentences: *I have run. We had run. You were known. They were seen. He, she* or *it is known.* The following sentence from Inez's first restating essay depends on a past participle and a helper as its main verb:

> **Past Participle:**   For example, one white girl **had decided** by the time
>
> she was four years old that blacks were "bad."

Forming the principal parts of a regular verb should be a simple task. However, irregular verbs offer wide variations in forming the past and past participle forms. The best advice is to refer to lists such as the following chart so you can be certain to use verbs correctly.

Irregular Verbs

Present	Past	Past Participle
am	was	been
be	was	been
bear	bore	borne
beat	beat	beaten, beat
begin	began	begun
bend	bent	bent
bid	bid	bid
bind	bound	bound
bite	bit	bitten
blow	blew	blown
break	broke	broken
bring	brought	brought
build	built	built
burst	burst	burst
buy	bought	bought
catch	caught	caught
choose	chose	chosen
come	came	come
cost	cost	cost
cut	cut	cut
deal	dealt	dealt
dive	dived, dove	dived
do	did	done
draw	drew	drawn
drink	drank	drunk
drive	drove	driven
drown	drowned	drowned
eat	ate	eaten
fall	fell	fallen
feed	fed	fed
feel	felt	felt
fight	fought	fought
find	found	found
flee	fled	fled
fly	flew	flown
forget	forgot	forgotten
forgive	forgave	forgiven
freeze	froze	frozen
get	got	got, gotten
give	gave	given
go	went	gone
grow	grew	grown
hang (execute)	hanged	hanged

Present	Past	Past Participle
hang (suspend)	hung	hung
hide	hid	hidden
hear	heard	heard
know	knew	known
lay	laid	laid
lead	led	led
leave	left	left
lie (recline)	lay	lain
lose	lost	lost
meet	met	met
pay	paid	paid
prove	proved	proved, proven
put	put	put
raise	raised	raised
read	read	read
ride	rode	ridden
ring	rang	rung
rise	rose	risen
run	ran	run
see	saw	seen
set	set	set
shake	shook	shaken
shine	shone, shined	shone, shined
shrink	shrank	shrunk
sing	sang	sung
sink	sank	sunk
sit	sat	sat
sleep	slept	slept
speak	spoke	spoken
spend	spent	spent
spread	spread	spread
spring	sprang	sprung
stand	stood	stood
steal	stole	stolen
stick	stuck	stuck
stink	stank	stunk
strike	struck	struck
strive	strove, strived	striven, strived
swear	swore	sworn
sweep	swept	swept
swell	swelled	swollen, swelled
swim	swam	swum
swing	swung	swung
take	took	taken
teach	taught	taught

Present	Past	Past Participle
tear	tore	torn
tell	told	told
think	thought	thought
throw	threw	thrown
understand	understood	understood
wake	woke, waked	woken, waked, woke
wear	wore	worn
weave	wove	woven
wring	wrung	wrung
write	wrote	written

Exercise E6-1

Choose ten verbs from the essay "Surge in Hispanic Student Enrollment Predicted" (pp. 209–211), and make a chart like the one that follows in Exercise E6-2, identifying the present form, present participle, past tense, *and* past participle *of each verb.*

Exercise E6-2

Complete the following chart, providing the correct forms for these verbs from the draft of Inez's first restating essay.

Present	Present Participle	Past	Past Participle
1. _____	_____	fought	_____
2. _____	_____	remembered	_____
3. promise	_____	_____	_____
4. _____	covering	_____	_____
5. _____	_____	_____	called
6. get	_____	_____	_____
7. _____	becoming	_____	_____
8. _____	_____	_____	sat
9. drive	_____	_____	_____
10. see	_____	_____	_____

TIPS FOR EDITING

Exercise E6-3

Fill in the blanks with the correct forms of the italicized verbs to make each sentence in the following paragraph complete.

Last summer I (1) _____ (*spend*) a week with my great-aunt, who lives in the Ozark Mountains in northern Arkansas. I had (2) _____ (*ride*) a train for 16 hours, so I (3) _____ (*sleep*) for 12 hours when I got to her house. I had (4) _____ (*lie*) down on an old four-poster bed with a down-filled mattress. I (5) _____ (*dream*) about lying in a field of daisies, but I (6) _____ (*wake*) up sneezing and chilled. My aunt (7) _____ (*make*) me some chicken soup, which I wolfed down as fast as I could get the spoon in my mouth. I hadn't (8) _____ (*eat*) since the night before, except for a pop and chips on the train. Anyway, I (9) _____ (*feel*) so sick. I just (10) _____ (*hang*) my head off the bed and prayed that I would get better. And I did.

Exercise E6-4

Write original sentences using the following forms of these irregular verbs.

1. throw
2. prove
3. burst
4. lead
5. strive

Time and Tense

Because verbs express action or state of being, considering time is essential. To express time relations, writers use one of six **tenses** that are formed from the verb's principal parts. The first three tenses, called the **simple tenses,** denote an action or state of being that occurs in the present, past, or future.

Present: Inez **works** on her writing assignment every night.

Past:	Inez **worked** on her writing assignment last night.
Future:	Inez **will work** on her writing assignment tomorrow night.

As you can clearly see, the present tense refers to action that happens now or immediately, while the past tense denotes action that has already occurred. Finally, the future tense expresses action that has not yet been completed.

The other tenses are called the **perfect tenses.** They denote action completed by a certain time. The past participle form of the verb—plus certain helping verbs—goes into each of the perfect tenses, as these sentences illustrate:

Present Perfect:	Inez **has worked** on her essay all week.
Past Perfect:	Inez **had worked** on her essay for a week before she turned it in.
Future Perfect:	Tomorrow Inez **will have worked** on her essay for a week.

The present perfect tense refers to action that began in the past but continues or is completed in the present. The past perfect tense indicates action that both began and ended in the past. The future perfect tense expresses action that will be completed at some specific time in the future.

The following chart will be a handy reference tool as you learn to form the six tenses of any verb. All you need to know are the verb's principal parts plus the correct words to complete the tense.

Present	Past	Future
Present or base form: add -s for third person singular—*he, she, it*	Past tense	Present + *will*

Present Perfect	Past Perfect	Future Perfect
have or *has* + past participle	*have* or *had* + past participle	*will* + *have* + past participle

Exercise E6-5

Choose ten verbs from the essay "Surge in Hispanic Student Enrollment Predicted" (pp. 209–211), and complete the following chart. The verb need *is provided as an example.*

Present	**Past**	**Future**
need	needed	will need
_____	_____	_____
_____	_____	_____
_____	_____	_____
_____	_____	_____
_____	_____	_____

Present Perfect	**Past Perfect**	**Future Perfect**
has needed	had needed	will have needed
_____	_____	_____
_____	_____	_____
_____	_____	_____
_____	_____	_____
_____	_____	_____

Exercise E6-6

List each verb in paragraphs 4 and 5 of the first draft of Inez's restatement of an essay (p. 222), and label each one as present, past, or future tense.

Exercise E6-7

Supply a verb in the correct tense to complete each of the following sentences.

My mother and father (1) _____ (*encourage*, past perfect) me

to get involved in our community, but I always (2) _____

(*think*, past) up an excuse. So this year my friend Carla and I

(3) _____ (*decide*, past) to participate in a local fundraising

drive for AIDS. We rarely (4) _____ (*take*, present) part in such events. But we (5) _____ (*feel*, past perfect) that we should do something for our community. We just never (6) _____ (*take*, past) the time. Anyway, we (7) _____ (*sign*, past) up about a month before the walkathon. Within a week, Carla and I (8) _____ (*collect*, past perfect) over $200 in pledges. By the day of the event, we (9) _____ (*gather*, past perfect) almost $750 in pledges. We then (10) _____ (*walk*, past) the entire six miles with our heads held high.

Exercise E6-8

Write sentences using the following verbs. Then identify each verb's tense.

1. will grow
2. rejected
3. will have sent
4. has notified
5. had applied

Emphatic and Progressive Forms

Besides the basic forms covered in our discussion of tense, verbs have two other forms: emphatic and progressive. **Emphatic** is the shortest, simplest, and least used form, appearing only in the present and past tenses.

Present emphatic: *do* + present or base form

Past emphatic: *did* + present or base form

Writers use the emphatic form in three different cases: for emphasis, for negative sentences, and for questions.

Emphasis:	Inez **did finish** her essay on time.
Negative:	However, Inez **did not complete** her history project.
Question:	**Do you think** Inez will pass her math exam?

Progressive forms are used to express action or state of being that continues or is in progress. For example, this sentence from Inez's first restating essay features a verb in the progressive form:

Dr. Phyllis A. Katz, director of the Institute for Research on Social Problems in Boulder, Colorado, **has been studying** children and their perceptions about people.

Notice that the verb *has been studying* implies two things: action that occurred in the past (because of the helping verb *has been*) and action that continues to occur during the present (because of the present participle *studying*). If Dr. Katz *had* studied, it would be clear that the action had begun and ended in the past. But Dr. Katz *has been* studying. So you can see that the progressive forms refer to action in progress during whatever time or tense is specified.

Each of the six tenses has a progressive form.

Present:	*am, are, is* + present participle Inez **is planning** a camping trip later this month.
Past:	*was, were* + present participle Inez **was hoping** that her cousin Maria would go camping, too.
Future:	*will be* + present participle Inez **will be leaving** early in the morning.
Present Perfect:	*have* or *has been* + present participle Inez **has been sleeping** late this week.
Past Perfect:	*had been* + present participle Inez **had been saving** for a year when she bought her car.
Future Perfect:	*will have been* + present participle At midnight Inez **will have been studying** for five hours.

Exercise E6-9

Choose three different sentences from the essay "Surge in Hispanic Student Enrollment Predicted" (pp. 209–211), and replace the verbs with a progressive form. Change any other words necessary to make the sentences logical.

Exercise E6-10

List any verbs in the emphatic and progressive forms in Inez's revised restating essays (pp. 227–229), and label each verb's tense.

Exercise E6-11

Match each verb in the second column with the correct tense from the first column.

_____	**1.** Present		A.	will have sought
_____	**2.** Past		B.	speaks
_____	**3.** Future		C.	had been crying

_____	4.	Present perfect	D. will have been waiting
_____	5.	Past perfect	E. laid
_____	6.	Future perfect	F. had shaken
_____	7.	Present emphatic	G. did send
_____	8.	Past emphatic	H. was figuring
_____	9.	Present progressive	I. will formulate
_____	10.	Present perfect progressive	J. has been thinking
_____	11.	Past progressive	K. have been eating
_____	12.	Past perfect progressive	L. will be catching
_____	13.	Future progressive	M. do remember
_____	14.	Future perfect progressive	N. will have hidden

Exercise E6-12

Write sentences using the following verb forms.

1. leave (present emphatic)
2. forget (past progressive)
3. type (future perfect progressive)
4. upset (past emphatic)
5. operate (present perfect progressive)

Noun Forms

Nouns are not nearly as versatile as verbs. Because time really has no effect on a noun's function, studying noun forms is a shorter and simpler process than mastering the many time and tense changes that verbs undergo.

Quite simply, nouns change form according to their relationship with the words in the rest of their sentences. This noun characteristic is called **case.** Nouns have three cases: *subjective, objective,* and *possessive.* Nouns in the subjective and objective cases change neither their form nor their spelling. The difference lies in how these nouns function. Nouns in the **subjective case** function as subjects or predicate nouns in their sentences, sometimes called *subject complements.* (For more on subjects, see p. 93; on subject complements, see p. 99.) **Objective case** nouns serve as objects in sentences, either as direct objects (see p. 97), indirect objects (see p. 98), object complements (see p. 98), or objects of prepositions (see p. 51). **Possessive**

case nouns simply show ownership. Most nouns form the possessive case by adding an apostrophe (') and an -s.

The following examples from Inez's first restating essay illustrate the three noun forms:

Subjective: If parents do not clearly explain that these are stereotypes, **children** begin to accept what they see on television as true.

She believes that **children** with high self-esteem are more open-minded and willing to learn about the cultural backgrounds of other children.

Objective: Dr. Phyllis A. Katz, director of the Institute for Research on Social Problems in Boulder, Colorado, has been studying **children** and their perceptions about people.

Programs which appeal to **children** present certain ethnic or racial groups as stupid or bad.

Possessive: Self-esteem may also influence **children's** prejudices, according to Verna Simpkins, the director of membership and program services for the Girl Scouts of the U.S.A.

Note that the noun *children* changes form only for the possessive case. Its other form, *child*, shows the singular. To make sure you form the possessive case correctly, refer to the guidelines for apostrophe usage on pp. 306–307.

Exercise E6-13

List each noun and its appropriate case in paragraphs 3 through 5 of "Surge in Hispanic Student Enrollment Predicted" (pp. 209 and 210).

Exercise E6-14

List each noun and its case in the first two paragraphs of Inez's first draft restatement of "Teaching about Racial and Ethnic Differences" (pp. 221–222).

Exercise E6-15

Complete the sentences in the following paragraph by adding a noun in each blank. Then identify each noun's case.

My (1) _____ owns two (2) _____

that are located in different towns. Sometimes I help out.

(3) _____ largest (4) _____ is located in a
town about 20 miles from my home. The (5) _____ customers
come from all around because it's the only (6) _____ for several
miles. Everyone is really friendly, but one (7) _____ is especially
nice. Mrs. Paulson is her name. She always smiles and asks how I've been since she
last saw me. (8) _____ face and hair are always fixed very nicely,
and she dresses like she's ready for church every time she comes in. Often she will
give me a (9) _____ when I take her
(10) _____ out to her car. I wish all customers were as nice as
Mrs. Paulson.

Exercise E6-16

Write original sentences using the following nouns in the cases that are indicated.

1. vacation (objective)
2. game (possessive)
3. paycheck (subjective)
4. computer (objective)
5. week (possessive)

Modifiers

Words that **modify**—normally called adjectives and adverbs—add details to sentences, either describing, limiting, or identifying so that sentences become more vivid and interesting. Without modifiers, our writing would be bland, boring, and listless. However, to use adjectives and adverbs correctly, you need to learn about their different forms and how each form functions.

Adjective Forms

As you remember from Chapter 2, **adjectives** are words that modify nouns or pronouns (see p. 46). We often think of adjectives as words that tell how something or someone looks: *dark, light, tall, short, large, small.* For example, look at the last sentence in Inez's second restating essay:

Adjectives: The government has increased its **total** cost of **federal**
research on the **AIDS** epidemic over slightly more than a
decade to about $8,500 million, or around $34 per **U.S.**
citizen.

Adjectives often follow linking verbs, modifying the subjects of sentences. (For more on linking verbs, see p. 38.)

Adjective:	Inez was **confident** that she had done a good job on her paper.
	Inez felt **certain** that she would receive a good grade.

Adjectives can appear in one of three different forms: *positive, comparative,* and *superlative*. The **positive form** is the basic form used to describe a person, place, or thing: *dark, light, tall, short, large, small, early, confident, certain*. Adjectives in this form either precede the nouns or pronouns they modify or follow linking verbs and modify subjects.

Many adjectives can appear in other forms—comparative and superlative. **Comparative adjectives,** used to show similarities and differences between two nouns or pronouns, require either an *-er* ending or the words *more* or *less*.

Comparative:	Inez is **older** than her brother Tony.
	Inez is also **more studious** than Tony, who likes to spend most of his time drag racing.
	But Inez is **less muscular** than Tony, who lifts weights four times a week.

The **superlative form** is used to compare three or more persons, places, or things. To form the superlative, add *-est* or the words *most* or *least* before the adjective.

Superlative:	Inez is the **tallest** person in her family.
	Inez was also the **most dependable** worker in the office because she was never late or absent from a day of work.
	Inez is the **least responsible** of all her family members when it comes to keeping up with things because she is always losing something.

In deciding whether to add *-er* or *more, -est* or *most,* go by this general rule: For adjectives of three or more syllables, place the words *more* or *most* (or *less* or *least*) before the adjective.

Positive	Comparative	Superlative
considerate	more considerate	most considerate
beautiful	more beautiful	most beautiful
agreeable	less agreeable	least agreeable
interesting	more interesting	most interesting

However, all rules have exceptions. For one- or two-syllable words, you can also use *more* or *most* when *-er* or *-est* sounds strange or awkward.

Positive	Comparitive	Superlative
active	more active	most active
just	less just	least just
nervous	more nervous	most nervous
helpless	more helpless	most helpless

Absolute Adjectives		
complete	horizontal	supreme
dead	impossible	unanimous
empty	infinite	unique
endless	parallel	vacant
eternal	pregnant	vertical
everlasting	round	whole

Some words cannot be compared at all. For example, **absolute adjectives**—words such as *equal* or *square*—have no degrees. Something cannot be *more equal* or *more square*. However, one thing can be *more nearly equal* than another or *more nearly square* than something else. Keep in mind that the adjectives in the following list cannot be compared:

Irregular Forms

Some adjectives do not take the *-er* or *-est* suffixes. Neither can they form comparisons by adding *more, most, less,* or *least.* We call these adjectives **irregular,** meaning they change forms entirely. Refer to the following list, and try to memorize the adjective forms that you think will give you trouble.

Positive	Comparative	Superlative
bad	worse	worst
good	better	best
far	farther, further	farthest, furthest
ill	worse	worst
many, much	more	most
little	less	least
well	better	best

Here's a word of caution: Adjectives should not be doubly compared. If an adjective takes an *-er* or *-est* ending, you should not use *more, most, less,* or *least*. Likewise, if you add *more, most, less,* or *least* before an adjective, you should not add the *-er* or *-est* suffixes (not *more longer* or *least beautifulest*).

Exercise E6-17

Circle the adjectives in paragraphs 8 through 11 of "Surge in Hispanic Student Enrollment Predicted" (p. 210), and underline the nouns they modify. Do not include articles (a, an, the).

Exercise E6-18

In Inez's first draft of her restatement of "Teaching about Racial and Ethnic Differences" on page 222, circle the adjectives in paragraphs 2 and 3 and underline the words they modify. Do not include articles (a, an, the).

Exercise E6-19

Fill in the blanks in the following paragraph with the appropriate adjective forms indicated in parentheses.

We went car shopping last week and looked at several different models. The first salesman told us that the Jeep was the (1) _____ (superlative form of *popular*) four-wheel drive vehicle in the country. He said it was (2) _____ (comparative form of *roomy*) than a Blazer. Maybe he was telling the truth, but we looked at a Blazer and thought it might be a (3) _____ (comparative form of *good*) deal. But there wasn't a great deal of difference in price and options. We weren't (4) _____ (positive form of *content*) with just two stops. We decided to look at something (5) _____ (comparative form of *expensive*). We checked out an Amigo, which is much (6) _____ (comparative form of *small*) than either a Jeep or a Blazer. The (7) _____ (superlative form of *sharp*) one on the lot was black with green and white pinstripes. I thought it was the (8) _____ (superlative form of *cool*) thing I'd ever seen. But dad still wasn't ready to settle, so we looked at a Geo Tracker. It was (9) _____ (comparative form of *attractive*) as far as price. Of course, it didn't have all of the options or the size of the Jeep or Blazer. But it gets great gas mileage, and it's easy to handle. For travel purposes, it would be the

(10) _____ (superlative form of *good*). What did we choose?
Nothing yet. My dad is still holding on to his down payment money, and I've still
got my bus pass.

Exercise E6-20

*Choose five of the adjectives you identified in Exercise E6-18, and write original sentences
using each of their comparative and superlative forms.*

> **Example:**   reliable
>
> When it comes to keeping promises, my sister is **more reliable**
> than my brother.
>
> Marcie is the **most reliable** worker in the office.

Adverb Forms

Adverbs most often modify verbs, as you learned in Chapter 2. Even when adverbs
modify adjectives and other adverbs, the adverb is usually located near a verb. Look
at these examples:

> **Adverb:**   Dr. Katz **firmly** believes that television programs
>
> misinform young children about people with dark skin or
>
> heavy accents.

The adverb *firmly* modifies the verb *believes*. Notice that *firmly* can also follow the
verb: *Dr. Katz believes firmly that television programs misinform young children about people with dark skin or heavy accents.*

Look at another example from Inez's first draft:

> **Adverb:**   If parents do not **clearly** explain that these are
>
> stereotypes, children begin to accept what they see on
>
> television as true.

The adverb *clearly* modifies the verb *explain*. *Clearly* can also appear after the verb: *If
parents do not explain clearly that these are stereotypes, children begin to accept what they
see on television as true.*

Occasionally adverbs follow linking verbs. However, when this happens, the adverb will modify a predicate adjective.

> **Adverb:**   Inez was **very** tired after working on her paper until 2 a.m.

Words such as *very, rather, somewhat, extremely,* and *totally* are **intensifiers.** They
tell how much or to what degree. When intensifiers are used with action verbs, they
modify other adverbs.

> **Intensifiers:**   Inez read her paper **very** slowly as she looked for errors.

Adverbs have the same degrees of comparison as adjectives: *positive, comparative,* and *superlative.* Most regular adverbs form comparisons by adding the words *more, most, less,* and *least.* However, some regular adverbs can take *-er* and *-est* suffixes. Other irregular adverbs change spelling entirely, as do certain irregular adjectives.

The following list illustrates the comparative forms of selected adverbs:

	Positive	**Comparative**	**Superlative**
Regular	early*	earlier	earliest
	fast*	faster	fastest
	straight*	straighter	straightest
	carefully	less carefully	least carefully
	quietly	more quietly	most quietly
Irregular	badly	worse	worst
	well**	better	best

Early, fast, and *straight* can function as either adverbs or adjectives. Simply look at how the words are used in the sentence.

**Well* can function as an adverb or adjective. When *well* means how something or someone performs, it functions as an adverb. When *well* refers to how someone feels, it is an adjective.

Writers should avoid unnecessary comparisons. For example, no adverb has two ways of comparing. Therefore, double comparisons like *more worse* and *most earliest* are incorrect.

Like absolute adjectives, **absolute adverbs** defy comparison because the positive or original form implies the superlative. For example, if something continues *endlessly,* how can it continue *more endlessly*? *Endlessly* means "continuing without stopping," so comparison is impossible. Other adverbs that cannot be compared include *equally, eternally, impossibly, infinitely, invisibly, perfectly, totally, uniquely,* and *universally.*

Double Negatives

Writers sometimes use two negative words in one sentence. These **double negatives** are normally unacceptable because they are confusing and grammatically incorrect.

Double Negative:	Inez does**n't** want **no** help with her assignment.
Revision:	Inez does**n't** want **any** help with her assignment.
Double Negative:	Inez did**n't hardly** take a break today at work.
Revision:	Inez **hardly** took a break today at work.

Other common negatives include *barely, no, neither, never, nothing, nobody, no one, nowhere,* and *scarcely.*

Exercise E6-21

Underline each adverb in paragraphs 1, 2, 10, and 19 in the article "Surge in Hispanic Student Enrollment Predicted" (pp. 209–211). Then supply the comparative and superlative forms for each adverb that can be logically compared.

Exercise E6-22

List each adverb in the first draft of Inez's restatement of "Teaching about Racial and Ethnic Differences" on pages 221 to 222. List the comparative and superlative forms for each adverb that can be logically compared.

Exercise E6-23

Read the following paragraph, and list any faulty adjective and adverb forms.

Several friends and I went to the basketball game last night. I felt badly, but I didn't want to make no excuses. I just tried to act like nothing was hardly bothering me. Anyway, my friend Ernesto wanted to sit in the most farthest seat he could find. But everyone else wanted to sit more closer. The visiting team had on most unique uniforms that looked like paint splashed against a black background. During the first half, our team played miserable. But in the second half, the Tigers started playing good. We started yelling loud each time one of our players had the ball. Finally, our team tied the game with 12 seconds left. Our best player shot the ball from 30 feet out. There wasn't nobody near him. The ball swished through the net, the most perfect ending we could have asked for.

Exercise E6-24

Write sentences using each of the following adverbs in the degree specified.

1. infinitely (positive)
2. neatly (superlative)
3. early (comparative)
4. bad (comparative)
5. rudely (superlative)

COLLABORATIVE WORK

When you have revised your restating essay, exchange papers with a classmate, and do the following tasks:

A.   Circle all verbs and nouns that are incorrect according to form and tense.

B.   Underline adjective or adverb forms that are used incorrectly.

Then return the paper to its writer, and use the information in this section to edit your draft.

Analyzing
Reading and Writing for a Reason

When I began to write, I found that it was the best way to make sense out of my life.

—JOHN CHEEVER

Every time we think, we are engaging in the process of **analyzing.** We consider a topic from different perspectives, we evaluate the available information, we weigh the quality of the alternatives—then we decide what we think about the topic. Analyzing allows us to have a deeper and richer understanding of the world around us. We don't simply let our feelings or first impressions guide our thinking. Instead, we engage in a conscious process of considering and evaluating a number of factors so that we can reach conclusions that are logical and useful.

In much the same way, when you write an analyzing essay, your purpose is to give your reader—and yourself—a deeper understanding of the topic than you had before. When you analyze, you are not simply describing something to your reader; you are not simply presenting information to your reader; you are not simply giving your opinion to your reader; you are not simply trying to persuade your reader to do something; and you are not necessarily offering a solution to a problem. In analyzing, you often perform *all* of these tasks. And as a result of your analysis, your readers will have an expanded vision of your topic.

In his memoir *Second Sight*, Robert Hine writes about what his life was like when surgery restored his eyesight after many years of blindness. In this passage, written soon after he saw the faces of friends for the first time, Hine analyzes the way we think of the human face.

> Faces raise so many questions. We assume that the face is the primary means of human contact. "Face-to-face" is a basic term in the language. . . . It refers to one-on-one relationships, fundamental in the building of strong traditional communities. What then for the blind? Because they do not see faces, are they excluded from community? Obviously not. The blind do not need to "face" one another (though they often do so, turning toward the voice as a gesture of respect or an effort to conform). Theirs is the special bonding based either on their own inter-

nal images from voices or on some spiritual sense. Though faces are newly precious to me, for myself or for my community, I realize that the blind have their own form of face-to-face relationships.

Notice here that the writer does not simply recall, observe, or explain the way that blind people think about the human face and the way it affects relationships. Hine presents his information in a way that makes him, and his readers, consider the topic in a deeper way.

LEARNING FROM PUBLISHED WRITERS

The following published writing is part of a chapter of a book titled *Life Sentences,* written by Corky Clifton, a prisoner in the Louisiana State Penitentiary. In this excerpt, Clifton analyzes his reasons for making a desperate attempt to escape from prison. He wrote *Life Sentences* after he was recaptured in 1989. A year later, Corky Clifton died in prison.

Before You Read

Focusing Your Attention

Before you read this account, take a few moments to respond to the following questions in your journal:

1.   Think of a time when you acted or did something without carefully analyzing the situation. What were the results?

2.   In the essay you are about to read, the writer analyzes his reasons for risking his life to escape from prison. Think of the most difficult decision you have ever had to make. In what way did you analyze the situation and circumstances before you made the decision? Did you think about it for a long time? Discuss it with others? Write about it?

Expanding Your Vocabulary

Here are some words and their meanings that are important to your understanding of the essay. You might want to review them before you begin to read.

"I could not even **inflict** [carry out] revenge on my enemies within prison." (paragraph 5)

"I have only two **disciplinary reports** [reports of misconduct] in 27 years." (paragraph 6)

Corky Clifton

Life Sentences: Rage and Survival Behind Bars*

Why did I escape? I suppose it was for the same reason that men have fought wars and died for throughout history. I wanted to be free.   **1**

For 27 years I have submitted to discipline, the rules, the harsh conditions, the torment of my children growing from babies into men—without ever seeing them. I've never had a visit from any of my family during these 27 years because, being from Ohio, no one could afford the trip here to Louisiana.   **2**

I once thought, as most people do, that all you had to do in order to get out of prison was just be good and they'll let you out someday. One does not have to be in the prison system very long to learn what a joke that is.   **3**

If Jesus Christ himself was in here with a life sentence, he couldn't get out unless he had money to put in the right places. I've always been a pretty stubborn person, so even though I was told how the political and Pardon Board system works, I freely submitted to all the prison rules and discipline. After 12 years with a perfect record—no disciplinary reports—I applied to the Pardon Board and was denied any consideration for relief. So I waited 10 more years and applied again, with still an excellent prison record. This time they wouldn't even hear my case. In 1983 I applied to the board for the third time and the Pardon Board cut my time to 50 years. However, the judge and D.A., retired, simply called the governor's legal staff and told them they don't want me to be free—so, end of case. When I applied for my pardon in 1983, the D.A. published an article in the newspaper saying I was a very dangerous man that would kill anyone who got into my way. He said a lot of things which were all designed to turn public opinion against me and justify his reason for protesting my release.   **4**

In spite of having to endure the torment of prison life all these years without hope, I was still determined to better myself, no longer with any hope that a nice record would get me my freedom but because the years of discipline and hardships had molded my personality   **5**

---

*Wilbert Rideau and Ron Wikberg, eds., *Life Sentences: Rage and Survival Behind Bars.* (pp. 251–254). New York: Times Books, 1992.

to the extent that I no longer desired to do anything criminal. I could not even inflict revenge on my enemies within prison.

I taught myself how to repair watches, and for more than 20 years I repaired watches for other prisoners as well as guards. I also taught myself how to paint pictures. At the 1988 Angola Arts & Crafts Festival, I won a second place for one of my watercolors. Aside from all my other accomplishments within prison, I have only two disciplinary reports in 27 years. I proved my honesty and sincerity many times over. Every time I made a friend through correspondence, one of the first things they wanted to know is how come I'm still in prison. I'm always tempted to use up several legal pads trying to explain about the corrupt legal and political system here in Louisiana. But who's gonna believe a man can be kept in here all his life just because some big shot out there don't want him out? Well, I am one example of it, and there are hundreds more lifers in here, many of them I know personally, who are in here for no other reason than because some big shot out there don't want them to go free. The only way you can get around that is *money*—in the right places.   **6**

Since the sheriff, the D.A. and/or the judge can dictate who can get out and who can't, then what's the purpose of a pardon board? Why the waste of taxpayers' money? I spent many years in here struggling for freedom. There are many people here in prison, as well as outside, who believe I should be free, but the judge and D.A. say they intend to see that I never go free, as long as I live. How am I supposed to handle that?   **7**

I'm not Charles Manson or some other mass murderer. I didn't torture or mutilate some child. When I was 23 years old, I killed a man in a robbery. That's bad enough. But the point is, hundreds of prisoners in here for the same, and even worse crimes have been pardoned throughout all the years I been here. The majority of them served only half or less time than I have.   **8**

Of course, it's no mystery to me why I'm still in prison. The judge and D.A. are keeping me here. But I say that's unfair; should, in fact, be illegal. They prosecuted and sentenced me 27 years ago, and that should be the end of their involvement in my case. They justify keeping me in here by claiming I am still the same dangerous man I was 27 years ago. If this were true, then I would like for someone to explain why, when I escaped a few weeks ago, I did not steal a car, knock someone in the head, or break into one of the many houses I passed.   **9**

On the night of April fifteenth, when I finally made up my mind to escape, I knew the odds were against me. I was fifty-two years old and had already suffered two heart attacks. In those final few days be-   **10** fore April fifteenth, I fought many emotional battles with myself. I had a lot to lose, and I'd be letting down a lot of good people who'd put their trust in me. But desperation is pretty hard to win a rational argument with. My time was running out. Had run out, really, because I was certainly in no condition to run through that jungle in the Tunica Hills. But even against all odds, I went for it anyway.

I struggled through those hills, mountains really, for five days and six   **11**
nights, sleeping on the ground, with no food and very little water. I ended up in Mississippi. I seen a lot of people and I even talked to a few.

After a couple days I knew it would be impossible for me to get   **12**
away unless I stole a car or knocked someone in the head. Not far from Woodville, Mississippi, I came across a house trailer. I sat in the bushes watching the trailer from about 50 yards away. I watched a woman drive up and unlock the door and go in alone. A few minutes later, she came out and washed her car. I could have knocked her in the head, or even killed her, took her car, and been long gone. But I couldn't bring myself to do that.

I discovered that in reality I could no longer commit the crimes   **13**
that I once did. So here I stood in those bushes, watching that house trailer, that car, and that lady—my ticket to freedom—and discover I can't pay the price. I can't think of any words that could truly describe the dejection and hopelessness I felt at that moment. There was no way I could continue on as I had those five days past. There was just no strength left in my legs to go on. Resigned to my fate, I walked several hundred yards to the highway and gave myself up.

So now I am left with only two ways left to escape my torment.   **14**
Just sit here for God knows how many more years, and wait on a natural death. Or I can avoid all those senseless years of misery and take my own life now.

Having to sit in this cell now for several weeks with nothing—even   **15**
being denied my cigarettes—I have thought a lot about suicide, and it seems to be the most humane way out of a prison I no longer care to struggle in. Suicide, or endless torment. Which would you choose?

 ## QUESTIONS FOR CRITICAL THINKING

THINKING CRITICALLY ABOUT CONTENT

1. What are some of the factors and conditions Corky Clifton analyzed in reaching his decision to escape?

2. What are some of the factors and conditions Clifton analyzed as he watched the woman enter her house alone (paragraphs 12 and 13)?

THINKING CRITICALLY ABOUT PURPOSE

3.   What do you think Clifton's purpose is in this excerpt?

4.   Why do you think Clifton ends this excerpt with a question?

THINKING CRITICALLY ABOUT AUDIENCE

5.   Did the fact that this excerpt was written by a convicted criminal have any effect on you? Explain your answer.

6.   In paragraph 2 of his essay, the author mentions the "torment" of not being able to see his children growing up, yet he doesn't mention the crime he committed until paragraph 8. Why do you think he presents his material in this order?

THINKING CRITICALLY ABOUT POINT OF VIEW

7.   Describe in a complete sentence the writer's point of view.

8.   If you were the district attorney who prosecuted Corky Clifton, how would you respond to Clifton's analysis? Write your response to him in the form of a letter.

LEARNING FROM YOUR PEERS

Learning to write analytically is a skill that will be useful to you in many areas of life. Analyzing helps you understand why something happened and what the effects of the event are on your life. In the process of writing an analytical essay, you should make these connections very clear for yourself and for your readers. In other college classes, you may be asked to analyze a scientific process, a political or historical event, or a piece of literature. The skills you use to write essays of this type are basically the same in all contexts: Take the event apart and put it together again in a way that makes sense to you. To watch an analytical essay take shape, we are going to follow the writing process of a student named Matthew Machias.

Matthew's Writing Assignment: Analyzing

This is the topic Matthew's instructor assigned:

Some events in our lives do not seem important at the time they are happening, but when we look back on them later, we understand that they were actually turning points in our attitude toward the world. Think of an important event in your life that caused you to change your attitude toward life, and analyze the change.

Matthew goes through the process as outlined in Chapter 1: *thinking, planning, developing, organizing, drafting, revising,* and *editing.*

Thinking

In response to the assignment, Matthew begins to freewrite. He was a cross-country runner in high school, and he knows that the discipline of practice made him stretch his physical and emotional limits, but he does not think that he can analyze those changes in himself. He knows that he learned to run in any weather, that his body yearns for that daily exercise, but he can hardly remember a time when he felt any different. Then Matthew thinks about his attitude toward studying. He can see that his self-discipline has paid off, but again, he has always been the type of student who does homework right after dinner.

Matthew keeps on writing and thinking. He starts listing all the major events in his life over the past three years:

first job

first car

high school prom

graduation

starting college

sitting on a jury

taking a trip without my family for the first time

Suddenly he realizes that the experience of being on a jury really changed his perspective about justice, about drunk driving, and about being held accountable for one's actions.

Planning

Matthew begins writing notes about his experiences on the jury. He can almost feel his palms sweating in anxiety as he recalls the moment when he realized that he held the fate of another human being in his hands. Matthew starts listing the feelings he connects with each stage of the jury deliberation:

anxiety

self-doubt

anger

empathy

sympathy

questioning

acceptance

Then he decides to focus his analysis on the changes that occurred throughout the whole process of deliberation. He wants to look at how others in the group influenced his thinking, and he wants to capture the difficulty of coming to some agreement within the group. He already understands the complexity of this assignment in comparison to the writing tasks he has done so far in this book, and he is ready for the challenge of the higher level of thinking.

Developing

Matthew starts a list with two columns. In the first column, he copies down his list of feelings. In the other column, he writes down the ideas he associates with the feelings he listed. His list looks like this:

Feelings	Events
Anxiety	My heart was pounding and my hands were sweating.
Self-doubt	Could I vote to send this man to jail?
Anger	He had gone out and driven recklessly while drunk, even though his license was suspended.
Empathy	I could picture him at a party having a few cool ones.
Sympathy	He should be going to college, studying, and flipping burgers.
Questioning	Would I trust my life to him? Did he betray his friend?
Acceptance	We all voted that he was guilty.

Matthew looks over his list and knows that many ideas are there, but he also knows that he still has to go into detail about his experience. The list helps him discover how he felt during the first hour or so of jury deliberation, but he knows that he has not told the whole story. He writes down several more notes to himself, focusing on the facts that led to changes in his own thinking. Here are his notes:

The facts:

The guy had killed his best friend because of his drinking.

He had a history of drunk driving.

He had been to "drunk school."

His license was suspended.

He drove anyway.

He should have known better.

We had to decide whether it was murder or manslaughter. Accident or intentional? I was the only one who could not bring myself to pronounce him a murderer.

I changed my mind:

I couldn't feel sorry for the guy.

He knew what he was doing.

His friend had paid the price for the driver's drinking.

After he spends some more time thinking about his feelings and changed attitudes, he is ready to organize the material.

Organizing

Now Matthew has an abundance of feelings, facts, and opinions to work with. But he also needs to put this material into some kind of order that will be meaningful and interesting to his readers. So far, he has simply let one item lead into another as he followed his basic instincts for putting his paper in order. Now he decides to let "the big question" be his main focus.

The big question: Could I vote to send this man to jail?

His guilt was certain--but what was he guilty of? Was it an accident, or was it intentional?

We had to decide whether it was murder or manslaughter. I was the only one who could not bring myself to pronounce him a murderer.

The facts:

The guy had killed his best friend because of his drinking.

He had a history of drunk driving.

He had been to "drunk school."

His license was suspended.

He drove anyway.

He should have known better.

Other influences

It's hard to sort out the consequences of things like this--was his friend foolish for getting in the truck with him? He must have known about the driver's previous hassles with the law.

"Granny"--the oldest woman on the jury--asked me how I would feel if the person killed had been my best friend. She reminded me of the driver's past convictions. She said he knew very well what happened to him when he drank--he knew the consequences, and no previous punishment had changed his behavior.

My conclusions:

I knew everyone else was right.

I couldn't feel sorry for the guy.

He knew what he was doing.

His friend had paid the price for the driver's drinking.

So what changed?

This experience has made me less likely to say, "Lock 'em up and throw away the key." Seeing real people with real problems is not like seeing someone on television or in the movies. When I saw the human side of a drunk driver, it was harder to condemn his actions.

Matthew was now ready to write his first draft. He definitely has enough material to work with, and he is bursting with the emotions connected with the event.

Drafting

After adding even more detail and thinking further about the process of changing his attitude, Matthew wrote his first draft.

Matthew's Essay: First Draft

Main Idea: Analyzing a drunk driver case was more difficult than I thought it would be.

The trial was finally over, but the jury still had to deliberate.

Since I was on the jury, the most difficult part of the trial was ahead of me. Try to understand. Determining someone's future was the toughest thing I'd ever done.

As the jury walked out of the jury box, my heart was pounding I looked at the defendant out of the corner of my eye. Looking sad and alone, the man sat next to his attorney. The defendant was pretty good-looking and seemed well-mannered. Could I vote to send Allen Wayne Grant, Jr., to jail for five or ten years? What would happen to the defendant? I didn't know.

We had finished listening to both sides present evidence, examine witnesses, and summarize their arguments. We had looked at photographs of the terrible automobile accident, shots of the wreckage, close-ups of Grant's best friend, even photos of him being taken away. We heard that Grant had been driving while intoxicated on Highway 281 at 2 a.m. after a party. Yes, his blood alcohol level was .11, well over the legal limit. He had been convicted of drunk driving on previous occasions during 1994-95, and he had completed a special program in mid-May to educate drunk drivers. Grant had gone out and driven over 80 mph while drunk, even though his license was suspended. "Why did he do it?" I wondered.

As the jury walked to the room where the jurors were supposed to decide the defendant's fate, I could not help thinking how much the defendant looked like all my friends. I could picture this man at a party having a few cool ones, joking with my friends, flirting. The defendant did not seem like an evil person. He did not seem like a murderer. Yet I asked myself who would want to get into a car with him. Would I trust my life to him? The answer was "No way." Still, I did not want to have to decide how he should spend the next years of his life. He should be going to college, studying and flipping burgers to support his good times.

When we finally were sitting around the jury table, an old man volunteered to be the jury foreman. He was a retired physician, Dr.

Samuel Anderson. "Great!" I thought. "We're already agreeing." It seemed like everyone just wanted this process to be over and done. We decided to take a vote and decide if the defendant who looked like a really nice guy was guilty or innocent of murdering his friend. We all voted that he was guilty.

Then the difficult discussions came out. What exactly was he guilty of doing? Did Grant mean to kill his friend? Was he negligent? We had to decide whether he had taken his friend's life by accident or intentionally. We looked at the photographs again. We reviewed the evidence.

As we went through that process, I thought about all the parties I have been to where people drank, listening to CDs, danced, and having fun. I have seen people leave parties after they have been drinking I've seen them head for their cars. I have even tried to stop a few of them from time to time. I have had a few drinks at those parties myself but I never drank when I was the designated driver. No way! Anyway, if Grant's friend got in the car with him that night, surely he knew what Grant's history was maybe he thought he knew Grant better than he really did. So was the friend partly to blame for his own death? We were not allowed to hear any testimony about his friend's drinking habits or driving history therefore I could not answer that question. Besides, we were supposed to make our decision on the basis of the facts before us.

We took another vote. There were eleven votes for second degree murder meaning that he had intentionally killed his friend. Of course, I admitted voting for manslaughter. Everyone looked at me and asked me my reasons.

Calmly I explained that I did not think Grant meant to kill his best friend. There was a soft-spoken, grandmotherly woman there who had a friend who was a member of MADD. "Matthew, how would you feel if the person killed was a close friend of yours?" she asked. She reminded me that the defendant had been convicted of drunk driving on earlier occasions. She asked me gosh, I wanted to scream and get everything over if I would want to drive on the same road as that man when he was drunk. Then two other people middle-aged businessmen reminded me that the man knew the consequences of his actions. He knew that he was driving without a license and he knew that his past record was not a good one. If he had learned anything, he would have been riding with a friend, not driving.

In my heart, I knew they were right. Even though the twenty-two year old defendant looked like a nice person, he was guilty I still wanted to shake his hand and wish him well. His best friend's family would have to live with the image of that horrible, heartbreaking accident for many years. They would never see their loved one again. He was only 23. My responsibility was to the law and to society. Even good people make mistakes of judgment however when mistakes are made over and over, they become a pattern. Grant knew what he was doing when he drove to the party that night, and he knew what he was doing when he took that first drink. He did not know that his actions would lead to his best friend's death his friend trusted him to drive him home, that was the last decision he was ever able to make. We held the vote again, which was unanimous for second degree murder.

After we filed back into the jury box, the foreman read the jury's verdict. I knew that the group's judgment was the right one, even though I still felt sorry for the defendant. I told myself as I walked out of the room that I never wanted to be on another jury again. I was always the person who said, "Lock up those criminals and throw away the key." This experience made me realize that it is easier to say that when you do not have to look closely at the person and the situation involved.

Revising

After Matthew wrote his first draft, he felt he had learned many new things about himself and about the responsibility of judging other people's actions. In fact, he felt that writing this essay moved him closer to understanding this particular event in his life, as well as the process of analysis itself. Now it is time to revise his work. The instructor tells the class to focus the revision process on a few specific, related items that involve the unity and logic of the paragraphs in their essays.

Matthew reviews the Checklist for Writing Unified Paragraphs at the beginning of the Tips for Revising section of this chapter. He reads the Tips for Revising section and does the exercises his instructor assigns. Although some of these guidelines sound mechanical, the students in the class are reminded to focus on the meaning rather than the construction of their sentences. The instructor wants the students to look closely not only at specific phrases and sentences but also at their roles in the paragraphs.

Matthew begins his revision with a great deal of hesitation, not immediately realizing the importance of the items on this list. But after he works with his draft for a while, he starts to see how the guidelines are related and how they work together to improve the essay as a whole. When he applies these criteria to his first draft, he discovers problems in both unity and logic. He sets out to remedy these problems one by one.

 ## COLLABORATIVE WORK

PEER GROUP ACTIVITY

After you read the portions of the Tips for Revising your instructor assigns, turn to Matthew's first draft (pp. 269–272), and complete the following tasks in small groups:

A.   Underline any sentences that do not develop logically from the previous sentence.

B.   Put a caret (^) where your group thinks transitions between sentences are missing.

Compare the marks your group made to those your instructor will show you. Where do your marks differ from your instructor's? What do you need to review before writing your own essay?

CLASS ACTIVITY

As an entire class, look at the underlined portions of Matthew's revised draft (pp. 274–277) to see what changes he made.

A.   Did you identify the **revision** problems that Matthew corrected?

B.   Do you think his changes are good ones? Discuss his changes.

Editing

Now that the sentences in Matthew's essay are unified and logical, he needs to do some final proofreading and editing before handing in his essay. The instructor stresses the fact that the rules of punctuation help writers say exactly what they mean. Matthew already understands this, and he does not want to turn a paper in that has punctuation problems. He reads the Tips for Editing section and works on a few exercises in areas in which he knows he has problems. Because Matthew already sees a few punctuation problems as he begins to revise his paper, he goes through the Checklist for Editing Punctuation and Mechanics systematically so that he doesn't miss anything.

COLLABORATIVE WORK

PEER GROUP ACTIVITY

After you read the portions of the Tips for Editing your instructor assigns, turn to Matthew's first draft (pp. 269–272), and complete the following tasks in small groups:

A.   Circle any errors in end punctuation: periods, question marks, and exclamation points (for explanations, see pp. 289–291).

B.   Circle any errors in internal punctuation: commas, semicolons, colons, quotation marks, hyphens, dashes, parentheses, apostrophes, underlining/italics (and, for explanations, see pp. 292–309).

C.   Circle any capitalization errors (for an explanation, see pp. 310–313).

D.   Circle any abbreviation errors (for an explanation, see pp. 314–316) that you find.

E.   Circle any errors you find in writing numbers (for an explanation, see p. 318).

CLASS ACTIVITY

As an entire class, look at the underlined portions of Matthew's revised draft (pp. 274–277) to see what changes he made.

A.   Did you identify the **editing** problems that Matthew corrected?

B.   Do you think his changes are good ones? Discuss his changes.

Matthew's Revised Essay

A Matter of Life and Death

The trial was finally over, but the jury still had to deliberate.

Since I was on the jury, the most difficult part of the trial was ahead of me. Try to understand. Determining someone's future was the toughest thing I'd ever done.

As ~~the jury~~ we walked out of the jury box, my heart was pounding. I looked at the ~~defendant~~ man on trial out of the corner of my eye. Looking sad and alone, the ~~man~~ defendant sat next to his attorney. The ~~defendant~~ fellow was ~~pretty good-looking~~ fairly handsome and seemed well-mannered. Could I vote to send Allen Wayne Grant, Jr., to jail for five or ten years? What would happen to ~~the defendant~~ him? I didn't know.

~~Finally, w~~We had finished listening to both sides present evidence, examine witnesses, and summarize their arguments. Early in the trial, ~~w~~We had looked at photographs of the terrible ~~automobile accident, shots of the~~ wreckage, close-ups of Grant's best friend, even photos of ~~him~~ the body being taken away. Next, ~~w~~We heard that Grant had been driving while intoxicated on Highway 281 at 2 a.m. after a party. Yes, his blood alcohol level was .11, well over the legal limit. After ~~h~~He had been convicted of drunk driving on ~~previous~~ other occasions during 1994-95, ~~and~~ he had completed a special program in mid-May to educate drunk drivers. Still, Grant had gone out and driven over 80 mph while drunk, even though his license was suspended. "Why did he do it?" I wondered.

As the jury walked to the room where ~~the jurors~~ we were supposed to decide the defendant's fate, I could not help thinking how much ~~the defendant~~ he looked like all my friends. I could picture ~~this man~~ him at a party having a few cool ones, joking with my friends, flirting. ~~The defendant~~ He did not seem like an evil person. He did not seem like a murderer. Yet I asked myself ~~who~~ whether I would want to get into a car with him. Would I trust my life to him? The answer was, "No way." Still, I did not want to have to decide how he should spend the next years of his life. He should be going to college, studying, and flipping burgers to support his good times.

When we finally were sitting around the jury table, an old man volunteered to be the jury foreman. He was a retired physician, Dr. Samuel Anderson. "Great!" I thought. "We're already agreeing." It seemed like everyone just wanted this process to be over and done. We decided to take a vote and decide if the defendant, who looked like a really nice guy, was guilty or innocent of murdering his friend. We all voted that he was guilty.

Then the difficult discussions came out: What exactly was he guilty of doing? Did Grant mean to kill his friend? Was he negligent? We had to decide whether he had taken his friend's life by ~~accident or intentionally~~ accidentally or intentionally. We looked at the photographs again. We reviewed the evidence.

As we went through that process, I thought about all the parties I have been to where people ~~drank~~ were drinking, listening to CDs, ~~danced~~ dancing, and having fun. I have seen people leave parties after they have been drinking; I've seen them head for their cars. I have even tried to stop a few of them from time to time. I have had a few drinks at those parties myself, but I never drank when I was the designated driver. No way! Anyway, if Grant's friend got in the car with him that night, surely he knew what Grant's history was. (Maybe he thought he knew Grant better than he really did.) So was the friend partly to blame for his own death? We were not allowed to hear any testimony about his friend's drinking habits or driving history; therefore, I could not answer that question. Besides, we were supposed to make our decision on the basis of the facts before us.

We took another vote. ~~There were E~~Eleven ~~votes~~ voted for second degree murder, meaning that he had intentionally killed his friend. Of course, I admitted voting for manslaughter/, meaning that he had accidentally killed his friend. Everyone looked at me and asked me my reasons.

Calmly, I explained that I did not think Grant meant to kill his best friend. There was a soft-spoken, grandmotherly woman there

who had a friend who was a member of MADD. "Matthew, how would
you feel if the person killed was a close friend of yours?" she asked.
She reminded me that the defendant had been convicted of drunk
driving on earlier occasions. She asked me--gosh, I wanted to scream
and get everything over--if I would want to drive on the same road as
that man when he was drunk. Then two other people, middle-aged
businessmen, reminded me that the man knew the consequences of
his actions. He knew that he was driving without a license, and he
knew that his past record was not a good one. If he had learned
anything, he would have been riding with a friend, not driving.

   In my heart, I knew they were right. Even though the ~~twenty two~~
22 year old defendant looked like a nice person, he was guilty. (I still
wanted to shake his hand and wish him well.) His best friend's family
would have to live with the image of that horrible, heartbreaking
accident for many years. They would never see their loved one again.
He was only 23. My responsibility was to the law and to society. Even
good people make mistakes of judgment; however, when mistakes are
made over and over, they become a pattern. Grant knew what he was
doing when he drove to the party that night, and he knew what he was
doing when he took that first drink. He did not know that his actions
would lead to his best friend's death. H~~h~~is friend trusted him to drive
him home~~/~~; that was the last decision he was ever able to make. We
held the vote again, which was unanimous for second degree murder.

   After we filed back into the jury box, the foreman read the jury's
verdict. I knew that the group's judgment was the right one, even
though I still felt sorry for the defendant. I told myself as I walked out
of the room that I never wanted to be on another jury again. I was
always the person who said, "Lock up those criminals and throw away
the key." This experience made me realize that it is easier to say that
when you do not have to look closely at the person and the situation
involved.

WRITING YOUR OWN ANALYZING ESSAY

So far, you have seen a professional writer and a fellow student at work trying to analyze ideas, impressions, experiences, and information. As you read the published essay and followed the writing process of another student from first to final draft, you absorbed not only ideas but ways of giving those ideas a form of their own. These reading and writing activities have prepared you to write your own analysis of a topic that is meaningful to you.

What Have You Discovered?

Before you begin your own writing task, let's review what you have learned in this chapter so far:

- Analyzing involves evaluating a subject.
- Analyzing enables you to better understand the world around you.
- Analyzing involves describing, persuading, explaining, giving your opinion, and offering a solution to a problem.
- To present your analysis effectively, you need to organize your ideas.
- To help you shape your essay, you should learn as much as possible about your readers.
- Before you write a draft, you need to decide on a point of view toward your subject.
- After you write a draft, you should revise your essay for meaning and organization.
- After you revise your essay, you should edit its grammar, usage, and sentence structure.

Your Writing Topic

Choose one of the following topics for your analyzing essay:

1. In the professional essay that you read at the beginning of this chapter, the writer, Corky Clifton, analyzed his reasons for escaping from prison, describing how he considered both the potential risks and the rewards of his decision. Think about the most important decision you ever made, such as choosing a spouse, going to college, accepting a job, moving to a new place, or ending an important relationship, and write an essay analyzing the process that you went through in order to arrive at your decision. In your concluding paragraph, analyze why the decision was a good or bad one.

2. Write an essay about an important event that changed your attitude toward an

authority figure in your life (a parent, a religious leader, a teacher, a club sponsor, a supervisor or boss), and analyze the change.
3.   Write about a current event that has become significant in U.S. history, and analyze its significance.
4.   Create your own analyzing essay (with the assistance of your instructor), and write a response to it.

After you have chosen one of these topics, you should begin the writing process in the same way Matthew did. (You may find rereading Matthew's analysis helpful.) This time your purpose is to write your own analyzing essay. If some tasks occur out of order, that adjustment is probably part of your personal writing ritual. Follow your instincts, and let them mold your own writing process. But make sure you've worked through all the stages to your final draft.

YOUR WRITING PROCESS

THINKING   Generate as many ideas on your subject as you can in as many different ways as possible: rereading, listing, freewriting, brainstorming, clustering, discussing, and questioning.

PLANNING   Begin to give your ideas shape by deciding on your approach to your topic (your content, your purpose, your audience, and your point of view). Make a list of points you want to include in your essay.

DEVELOPING   Add more details on three or four specific, focused topics that you have chosen from your list of general points.

ORGANIZING   Organize your material in a way that will be most interesting to your audience.

DRAFTING   Write a working draft of your essay in complete sentences.

REVISING   Consulting the Tips for Revising in this chapter (pp. 281–288), revise your first draft—paying special attention to making your paragraphs focused and coherent.

EDITING   Consulting the Tips for Editing in this chapter (pp. 289–321), edit your draft for grammar and correctness—paying special attention to punctuation and mechanics.

Turn in your revised draft to your instructor.

Some Final Thoughts

When you have completed your own essay, answer these four questions in your journal:

1. What was most difficult about this assignment?
2. What was easiest?
3. What did I learn about analyzing by completing this assignment?
4. What did I learn about my own writing process from this assignment—how I prepared to write, how I wrote the first draft, how I revised, and how I edited?

Writing Unified Paragraphs

Checklist for Writing Unified Paragraphs

✓ Do clear **pronoun references** link sentences?
✓ Do well-chosen **transitional words, phrases, and clauses** guide readers through the essay?
✓ Do **synonyms** help emphasize ideas and unify the essay?
✓ Is **parallel structure** used correctly and effectively?
✓ Does the **repetition of key words** make the essay coherent?

A ship's captain about to embark on a long voyage always first charts a course. An important part of making this chart involves identifying and focusing on the best course from the point of departure to the destination. Similarly, for your readers to follow your thoughts in an essay, you need to chart the best course between your sentences and your paragraphs. There are various ways of showing the relationships among parts of sentences, among sentences, and among paragraphs. These include the use of pronouns, transitional words and expressions, synonyms, parallelism, and repetition. Using these strategies will allow you to produce unified paragraphs that cohere, or hold together, both within the paragraphs and with the paragraphs around them.

Pronoun Reference

Many writers link sentences in a paragraph by using a pronoun to refer to a noun in a preceding sentence. By using pronouns that refer to nouns or other pronouns in a sentence or a paragraph, you help your readers follow the course you have charted through the ideas of your essay. For example, in the following paragraph from "Life Sentences," the author uses pronouns to hold the paragraph together.

> Of course, **it**'s no mystery to **me** why **I**'m still in prison. The judge and D. A. are keeping **me** here. But **I** say **that**'s unfair; should, in fact, be illegal. **They** prosecuted and sentenced **me** 27 years ago, and **that** should be the end of **their** involvement in **my** case. **They** justify keeping **me** in here by claiming **I** am still the same dangerous man **I** was 27 years ago. If **this** were true, then **I** would like for **someone** to explain why, when **I** escaped a few weeks ago, **I** did not steal a car, knock **someone** in the head, or break into **one** of the many houses **I** passed.

The pronouns in this passage serve two purposes: They link the ideas in the paragraph, and they prevent needless repetition of nouns. Notice that it is absolutely clear in this paragraph which noun each pronoun replaces.

As Matthew Machias looked back over his essay analyzing his reactions as a juror, he decided that using pronouns in paragraph 4 would help him connect his thoughts better.

First Draft: As the jury walked to the room where the jurors were supposed to decide the defendant's fate, I could not help thinking how much the defendant looked like all my friends. I could picture this man at a party having a few cool ones, joking with my friends, flirting. The defendant did not seem like an evil person. He did not seem like a murderer.

Revision: As the jury walked to the room where ~~the jurors~~ **we** were supposed to decide the defendant's fate, I could not help thinking how much ~~the defendant~~ **he** looked like all my friends. I could picture ~~this man~~ **him** at a party having a few cool ones, joking with my friends, flirting. ~~The defendant~~ **He** did not seem like an evil person. He did not seem like a murderer.

Transitions

Words, phrases, and clauses that guide readers through your ideas are often referred to as **transitions.** Specific transition words, phrases, and clauses establish time, space or distance, contrasts, examples, additions, order, and conclusions. Here is a list of some transitions that might be useful to you:

Time: now, then, meanwhile, before, afterward, first, second, thus far, soon, next, meanwhile, immediately, eventually, currently, in the future

Space: nearby, farther, on the other side, down, above, below

Comparison: similarly, likewise, in like manner, in the same way, in comparison

Contrast: but, yet, still, however, despite this, although, on the other hand, nevertheless, nonetheless, in contrast, on the contrary, at the same time

Example: for example, in fact, for instance, thus, specifically, namely

Addition: in addition, also, besides, furthermore, even, too, moreover, and, further

Conclusion: since, thus, therefore, finally, lastly, in conclusion, in short

Result: therefore, thus, consequently, so, accordingly, as a result, hence

Transitions help your reader fit the pieces of your essay together in the way you intend because they explain the relationships between your ideas.

In the following example from Arthur Ashe's "The Burden of Race," which appears in Chapter 4, transitions guide the reader through the complexities of the author's emotions:

> I can **still** recall the surprise **and** perhaps **even** the hurt on her [the reporter's] face. I may **even** have surprised myself, **because** I simply had never thought of comparing the two conditions before. **However,** I stand by my remark. Race is for me a more onerous burden **than** AIDS. My disease is the result of biological factors over which we, **thus far,** have had no control. Racism, **however,** is entirely made by people, **and therefore** it hurts **and** inconveniences infinitely more.

All the boldfaced transitions in this paragraph serve to show the relationship between the author's ideas and, in turn, move the readers as smoothly as possible through the sentences. The result is a clear, readable, unified paragraph.

As Matthew continued revising his essay to create unified paragraphs that would link his ideas, he added transitional words, phrases, and clauses to explain the process of a trial more clearly for his audience.

First Draft: We had finished listening to both sides present evidence, examine witnesses, and summarize their arguments. We had looked at photographs of the terrible automobile accident, shots of the wreckage, close-ups of Grant's best friend, even photos of him being taken away. We heard that Grant had been driving while intoxicated on Highway 281 at 2 a.m. after a party. Yes, his blood alcohol level was .11, well over the legal limit. He had been convicted of drunk driving on previous occasions during 1994-95, and he had completed a special program in mid-May to educate drunk drivers. Grant had gone out and driven over 80 mph while drunk, even though his license was suspended. "Why did he do it?" I wondered.

Revision: **Finally,** w~~W~~e had finished listening to both sides present evidence, examine witnesses, and summarize their arguments. **Early in the trial, w**~~W~~e had looked at photographs of the terrible ~~automobile accident, shots of~~

~~the~~ wreckage, close-ups of Grant's best friend, even photos of ~~him~~ **the body** being taken away. **Next, w**~~We~~ heard that Grant had been driving while intoxicated on Highway 281 at 2 a.m. after a party. Yes, his blood alcohol level was .11, well over the legal limit. **After h**~~He~~ had been convicted of drunk driving on ~~previous~~ **other** occasions during 1994-95, ~~and~~ he had completed a special program in mid-May to educate drunk drivers. **Still,** Grant had gone out and driven over 80 mph while drunk, even though his license was suspended. "Why did he do it?" I wondered.

Synonyms

Sometimes the repetition of key words can become so monotonous that it detracts from an essay. In this case a writer may use **synonyms,** words that share a meaning or are closely related in meaning, to emphasize an idea. In the passage analyzing his escape, Corky Clifton uses synonyms to describe his state of mind when he realized he would be spending the rest of his life in prison.

> I discovered that in reality I could no longer commit the crimes that I once did. So here I stood in those bushes, watching that house trailer, that car, and that lady — **my ticket to freedom** — and discover I can't pay the **price.** I can't think of any words that could truly describe the dejection and **hopelessness** I felt at that moment. There was no way I could continue on as I had these five days past. There was just no strength in left my legs to go on. **Resigned to my fate,** I walked several hundred yards to the highway and gave myself up.

Clifton substitutes the word *price* for *ticket to freedom* and then uses *resigned to my fate* as a synonym for *hopelessness*.

Matthew decided that synonyms would break up the monotony of the following paragraph from his essay:

First Draft: As the jury walked out of the jury box, my heart was pounding. I looked at the defendant out of the corner of my eye. Looking sad and alone, the man sat next to his attorney. The defendant was pretty good-looking and seemed well-mannered. Could I vote to send Allen Wayne Grant, Jr., to jail for five or ten years? What would happen to the defendant? I didn't know.

Revision: As ~~the jury~~ **we** walked out of the jury box, my heart was pounding. I looked at the ~~defendant~~ **man on trial** out of the corner of my eye. Looking sad and alone, the ~~man~~ **defendant** sat next to his attorney. The ~~defendant~~ **fellow** was ~~pretty good looking~~ **fairly handsome** and seemed well-mannered. Could I vote to send Allen Wayne Grant, Jr., to jail for five or ten years? What would happen to ~~the defendant~~ **him?** I didn't know.

Matthew's revision here is more readable and much more interesting than his first draft.

Parallelism

Writers often write key words and phrases in **parallel form**—a series of words, phrases, and clauses that have the same grammatical structure—to show their relationship to one another and to unify sentences and paragraphs. In the following excerpt from "Life Sentences," Corky Clifton uses parallel structure to present his ideas as efficiently as possible:

> For 27 years I have submitted to
>
> **discipline,**
>
> **the rules,**
>
> **the harsh conditions,**
>
> **the torment** of my children growing from babies into men--without ever seeing them.

The parallel structure here makes us understand the importance of these features in Clifton's present life.

Matthew Machias found two places where he could improve his essay by using parallel structure. In paragraph 7, Matthew revised the following sentence:

First Draft: As we went through that process, I thought about all the parties I have been to where people drank, listening to CDs, danced, and having fun.

Revision: As we went through that process, I thought about all the parties I have been to where people ~~drank~~ **were drinking,** **listening** to CDs, ~~danced~~ **dancing,** and **having** fun.

This example focuses its parallel structure on present participles (*-ing* verb forms). This structure makes us realize we are reading a list of equivalent items.

Next, Matthew revised another sentence to be parallel.

> **First Draft:**   We had to decide whether he had taken his friend's life by accident or intentionally.
>
> **Revision:**   We had to decide whether he had taken his friend's life ~~by accident or intentionally~~ **accidentally** or **intentionally.**

Both these examples are clearer and easier to read in parallel form.

Repetitions

Repeating key words and phrases not only helps your sentences and paragraphs cohere but also emphasizes important ideas. For example, notice how the repetition of the words *freedom* and *free* make this paragraph from "Life Sentences" coherent and unified:

> Since the sheriff, the D.A. and/or the judge can dictate who can get out and who can't, then what's the purpose of a pardon board? Why the waste of taxpayers' money? I spent many years in here struggling for **freedom.** There are many people here in prison, as well as outside, who believe I should be **free,** but the judge and D.A. say they intend to see that I never go **free,** as long as I live. How am I supposed to handle that?

The focus in this paragraph is clearly on the notion of being free. Repetition illustrates the importance of this concept for the writer.

As Matthew looked back over his first draft and his first revision, he saw that he could clarify the relationship between his ideas and emphasize the difficulties in his job by repeating some key words in paragraph 8.

> **First Draft:**   We took another vote. There were eleven votes for second degree murder, meaning that he had intentionally killed his friend. Of course, I admitted voting for manslaughter.
>
> **Revision:**   We took another **vote.** ~~There were E~~**e**leven ~~votes~~ **voted** for second degree murder**, meaning that he had intentionally killed his friend.** Of course, I admitted **voting** for manslaughter/**, meaning that he had accidentally killed his friend.**

Here Matthew uses the techniques of repetition (*vote, voted, voting* and *meaning, meaning*) as well as parallel structure (*meaning that he had . . . , meaning that he had . . .*) to make the ideas in this paragraph clear and to show how they are related.

TIPS FOR REVISING

Exercise R7-1

*In paragraphs 8 and 9 of the excerpt from "Life Sentences" (p. 263), underline and iden-
tify the pronoun references, transitions, synonyms, parallelism, or repetitions that connect
his ideas logically and emphasize the importance of his ideas.*

Exercise R7-2

*Read paragraph 4 of Matthew's first draft (p. 270), and suggest some unifying devices that
might improve it.*

Exercise R7-3

*Rewrite the following sets of sentences, using pronoun references, transitions, synonyms,
parallelism, and repetitions to make the sentences coherent. You might want to combine
some of the sentences.*

1. Beth is slightly overweight. Beth is aware of her condition. Beth ate some
   cheesecake.
2. You think the world has many good qualities and it could be better. You have a
   realistic attitude about government. You might want to be a political scientist.
3. I feel sure that the American people want a forceful leader who will stick by
   decisions. This person will accept the consequences of actions.
4. Many people have good reasons for earning a college degree. One good reason is
   a better life. Another of them is to gain respect.
5. I think dogs make better pets than cats. Dogs are loyal. Cats are sneaky. Some
   people might not agree.

Exercise R7-4

*Rewrite the following paragraph, supplying logical transitions in the blanks. Use pronouns,
transitional words or phrases, synonyms, parallelism, and repetition.*

Health is important for each of us in reaching our goals. _____ ,

a sick person does not function as well as usual; _____ , some

people will learn to function at a higher level than _____ or

_____ did before becoming ill. _____ , we

are all capable of learning to function with varying degrees of health.

COLLABORATIVE WORK

After writing a draft of your own analyzing essay, exchange papers with a classmate,
and do the following tasks:

A. Mark with a caret (^) places where you feel cohesive devices are needed, either
within a sentence or paragraph or between sentences and paragraphs.

B. In the margin beside each mark, suggest a method or specific words, phrases, or clauses to use.

Then return the paper to its writer, and use the information in this section to revise your draft.

Punctuation and Mechanics

Checklist for Editing Punctuation and Mechanics

✓ Does each sentence use correct **end punctuation** (periods, question marks, and exclamation points)?
✓ Are **commas** used correctly?
✓ Are **semicolons** used correctly?
✓ Are **colons** used correctly?
✓ Are **quotation marks** used correctly?
✓ Are **hyphens** used correctly?
✓ Are **dashes** used correctly?
✓ Are **parentheses** used correctly?
✓ Are **apostrophes** used correctly?
✓ Are the appropriate words, phrases, and titles **underlined** or **italicized?**
✓ Are the appropriate words and abbreviations **capitalized?**
✓ Are **abbreviations, initialisms,** and **acronyms** used correctly?
✓ Are **numbers** appropriately spelled or written in figures?

Can you imagine streets and highways without stoplights or traffic signs? Driving would become a life-or-death adventure as motorists made risky trips with no rules to guide or protect them. Good writers, like conscientious drivers, prefer to leave little to chance. They observe the rules of punctuation and capitalization and use abbreviations and numbers correctly to ensure that their readers arrive safely (and correctly) at their destination. Without punctuation or capitalization, sentences would run together in a steady stream. Writers need to use markers—periods, commas, dashes, capitalization, abbreviations—to help their audience take pleasurable reading trips. Above all, however, by honoring guidelines for punctuation and mechanics, writers compose prose that is clear, correct, and complete.

Punctuation

Think of punctuation marks as crucial signposts that tell your readers when to start, stop, and shift gears in the course of navigating your writing. Let's look at each of these markers in turn.

End Marks

End marks signal the ends of sentences in three different ways: The period ends a statement; the question mark indicates an inquiry; and the exclamation point highlights an emphatic statement. In addition, the period has a few other functions within a sentence.

Period

The most common end punctuation is the **period,** which should be used with statements, mild commands or requests, and indirect questions. Look at the following examples from Matthew's first draft:

Statement:	The trial was finally over, but the jury still had to deliberate.
Command:	Try to understand.
Indirect question:	Yet I asked myself who would want to get into a car with him.

Besides indicating the end of a sentence, the period is used in other common instances:

1. *Use a period with most abbreviations.*   Acronyms and some other abbreviations do not require periods, so the best advice is to consult a dictionary when questions arise. Also, note that when an abbreviation ends a sentence, only one period is required.

   Kim's new address is 104 Seventh St., Boulder, CO 80322.
   The defendant worked two part-time jobs—as an office trainee at IBM and as a swimming instructor at the YMCA.
   At the trial, the county coroner—Dr. James Richfield—testified that he reached the accident scene at 3:07 a.m.

2. *Use periods with numerals when expressing money amounts and decimals.*

   1.5   .033 $4.65 $849.50

3. *Use three spaced periods (. . .) to indicate a pause or words that have been omitted from the text.*

   Let's see . . . I think I'll order the diet plate.

   We had finished listening to both sides present evidence . . . and summarize their arguments.

Question Mark

The second most common end punctuation is the **question mark.** It should be used in the following instances:

1. *Use a question mark after direct questions.*   Look for words that signal uncertainty: *who, what, where, when, why, how, could, should, would.* These words will often begin the question, putting a sentence in inverted word order. Look at these examples from Matthew's first draft:

Could I vote to send Allen Wayne Grant, Jr., to jail for five or ten years**?**

What would happen to the defendant**?**

2. *Use a question mark with a direct question in quotation marks located within a statement.*

"Why did he do it**?**" I wondered.

"Will Matthew turn his paper in on time**?**" her mother asked.

3. *Use a question mark inside parentheses to indicate uncertainty about dates.*

Matthew's great-grandfather (1888**?**–1970) was a World War I hero.

Do not use a question mark to indicate uncertainty about facts.

Matthew thought the defendant had attended Roosevelt (**?**) High School.

Exclamation Point

The **exclamation point** is an end mark used sparingly to indicate strong feeling. If it is used too often, it is not as effective as it could be.

1. *Use an exclamation point to express emotion after words, phrases, and exclamatory sentences.*

Examples:	Great!	I can't believe it!
	No way!	Stop or I'll scream!

2. *Use an exclamation point after exclamations in quotation marks within a statement.*

Examples:	"You make me so mad!" he screamed.
	"Please don't go!" she wailed.

Exercise E7-1

Supply end punctuation for the following sentences from "Life Sentences."

1. When I applied for my pardon in 1983, the D.A. published an article in the newspaper saying I was a very dangerous man that would kill anyone who got into my way
2. But who's gonna believe a man can be kept in here all his life just because some big shot out there don't want him out
3. Since the sheriff, the D.A. and/or the judge can dictate who can get out and who can't, then what's the purpose of a pardon board

4. There are many people here in prison, as well as outside, who believe I should be free, but the judge and D.A. say they intend to see that I never go free, as long as I live

5. Which would you choose

Exercise E7-2

Explain the end punctuation choices for the sentences in paragraphs 4 through 6 of Matthew's revised draft (pp. 274–277).

Exercise E7-3

Supply end punctuation for the following sentences.

(1) "Hooray" everyone screamed (2) "School is out for the summer" (3) Immediately everyone started making plans about swimming parties, vacations, and baseball games (4) But I knew summer meant work—mowing yards, working in the garden, and doing other chores around the house (5) It seemed like my dad just had to keep me busy (6) What did he think I was going to do (7) After all, he knew I'd keep out of trouble, didn't he (8) I knew what I would do when I got half the chance (9) I was going to ride our neighbor's wild Shetland pony (10) That horse could really buck (11) Sometimes we'd wonder when he'd stop (12) But he was always ready to throw another daring rider (13) Bam (14) Rear ends would hit the dirt as Little Bit claimed his next bareback victim

Exercise E7-4

Write three original sentences for each form of end punctuation—the period, the question mark, and the exclamation point.

Commas

The comma is the most frequently used punctuation mark, but it is also the most abused. Experts agree, however, that commas serve one of two functions: (1) They indicate pauses, and (2) they separate words, phrases, and clauses.

Certainly, following usage guidelines will help you solve comma questions. But because there are more rules for comma usage than for any other punctuation mark, writers often become confused and anxious. Before abandoning all hope, study the conventional comma guidelines. Then, with practice, you will learn how including or omitting commas affects the flow and meaning of your sentences.

1. *Use a comma to set off introductory words, phrases, and clauses.*   Each of the following examples comes from Matthew's first draft:

Word: **Yes,** his blood alcohol level was .11, well over the legal limit.

"Matthew, how would you feel if the person killed was a

close friend of yours?"

> **Still,** I did not want to have to decide how he should spend the next years of his life.

Phrase: **Of course,** I admitted voting for manslaughter.

In my heart, I knew they were right.

Looking sad and alone, the man sat next to his attorney.

Clause: **When we finally were sitting around the jury table,** an old man volunteered to be the jury foreman.

2. *Use a comma before a coordinating conjunction that joins two independent clauses to form a compound sentence.*   Look at these examples from Matthew's first draft:

Compound: The trial was over, **but** the jury still had to deliberate.

Compound: Grant knew what he was doing when he drove to the party that night, **and** he knew what he was doing when he took that first drink.

3. *Use commas to set off nonessential elements.*   Phrases and clauses can either be essential or nonessential. **Essential elements** are necessary to complete the meaning of a sentence and do not need commas. Essential elements are often called *restrictive* because they are bound to the sentence and cannot be omitted. Consider the following sentence:

Essential Element: The man **who was chosen jury foreman** was Dr. Samuel Anderson.

The clause *who was chosen jury foreman* is essential in identifying the man. Therefore, no commas are needed.

   Nonessential elements are not necessary for the sentence to communicate a meaningful thought. Rather, nonessential or *nonrestrictive* elements provide additional information that can be omitted. Therefore, nonessential elements are set off by commas, as the following sentence illustrates:

Nonessential Element: Dr. Samuel Anderson, **who was selected jury foreman,** is a retired physician who practiced medicine for 45 years.

The clause *who was selected jury foreman* provides additional identifying information, interesting details that help describe Dr. Samuel Anderson. The commas indicate that the clause can be removed from the sentence, leaving behind a statement that is complete and meaningful.

   Here are some additional examples of essential and nonessential elements:

Essential:	The person on the phone was Matthew's brother **Darrell.**
Nonessential:	The person on the phone was Jared, **the guy Matthew worked with last summer.**
Essential:	The man **sitting in the middle of the back row** was the last person chosen for the jury.
Nonessential:	Matthew, **sitting in the middle of the back row,** was the last person chosen for the jury.
Essential:	The attorney **who had the most experience** was bored by the jury selection.
Nonessential:	The prosecuting attorney, **who had the most experience,** was almost bored at times by the proceedings.

4. *Use commas to separate three or more items in a series, regardless of whether the items are words, phrases, or clauses.*

Words:	For lunch Matthew had **a cheeseburger, a coke, and fries**.
Phrases:	Matthew and the other jurors spent lots of time **talking about the witnesses, examining the photographs, and weighing the evidence.**
Clauses:	**Matthew plans to move out when his parents give him permission, he has enough money, and he learns how to cook.**

   The final comma in a series before the coordinating conjunction used to be optional. Most journalists—newspaper and magazine writers—omit the final comma to save space. But in academic writing, most people use the final comma to avoid confusion.

5. *Use commas to set off parenthetical expressions.*   Certain words, phrases, or clauses interrupt the flow of a sentence without affecting its meaning. These **parenthetical** elements, which can appear anywhere in a sentence, make the reader pause and should be set off with commas.

Direct Address:	Tell me, **Matthew,** how you decided to become an engineer.
Conjunctive Adverb:	Matthew and Jody, **however,** worked on their homework together.
Transition:	Matthew gave the trial his undivided attention, **I believe,** because he was concerned about the welfare of the defendant.
Contrast:	Matthew decided to write about another topic, **not** his original choice.

6. *Use commas to separate coordinate adjectives.*   To determine whether or not a comma should be used between adjectives, try inserting the word *and* between

the two adjectives. If the sentence makes sense with *and* the adjectives are *coordinate* and should be separated by a comma.

His best friend's family would have to live with the image of that **horrible, heartbreaking** accident for many years.

Horrible and heartbreaking sounds fine, so use a comma.

Another test for coordinate adjectives is to reverse their order. If the sentence reads clearly, use a comma between the adjectives.

There was a **soft-spoken, grandmotherly** woman there who had a friend who was a member of MADD.

Grandmotherly, soft-spoken works just as well, so use a comma.

7. *Use commas for direct quotations, separating the exact words of the speaker from the rest of the sentence.*

   "I am never going to serve on another jury," Matthew said.

   The defendant said, **"I am truly sorry for what I have done, and if I could give my life to bring him back, I would do it."**

   Remember that commas are not needed if the quotation ends in a question mark or exclamation point.

   "Why did he do it?" I wondered.

   "Great!" I thought.

8. *Use commas to separate names and titles.*

   Matthew's father is **George B. Macias, Sr.**

   The volunteer of the year is **Evelyn M. Watson, M.D.**

9. *Use commas to separate parts of an address.*

   Our new address is **1412 Roxbury, Phoenix, AZ 85072.**

10. *Use commas to separate parts of a geographical location.*

    Kansas City, Missouri, is much larger than **Kansas City, Kansas.**

    Union County, Arkansas, has a rich history centered around the oil industry.

11. *Use commas to separate parts of a full date.*

Matthew was born on **July 29, 1977.**

12. *Use commas to separate the digits in a number.*

The answer to the first problem is **14,846.**

For four-digit numbers, the comma is optional: **2,001** or **2001.**

Commas are not used with years (1998), page numbers (p. 1046), serial numbers (#14869284), or identification numbers (14444).

Exercise E7-5

Explain the reason for each comma in paragraphs 6 and 12 of the excerpt from "Life Sentences" (pp. 263 and 264).

Exercise E7-6

Correct the following sentences from Matthew's first draft, supplying commas where needed.

1. Since I was on the jury the most difficult part of the trial was ahead of me.
2. We had finished listening to both sides present evidence examine witnesses and summarize their arguments.
3. I could picture him at a party having a few cool ones joking with my friends flirting.
4. I have had a few drinks at those parties myself but I never drank when I was the designated driver.
5. Then two other people middle-aged businessmen reminded me that the man knew the consequences of his actions.

Exercise E7-7

Rewrite the following paragraphs, supplying commas where needed.

(1) On August 30 1994 I made a big decision one that I'd been thinking about for a long time. (2) I decided to buy a car. (3) After all I had been saving for almost two years. (4) My parents who are very helpful and supportive said that they would co-sign for the loan and pay the insurance to help me out. (5) However they wanted me to learn the importance of earning my own money to buy something I really wanted.

(6) Browsing through the newspaper we saw all kinds of ads for new and used cars. (7) The new cars I liked were all $12000 or more. (8) That was out of my league. (9) I had $3500 which was a pretty good down payment but I didn't want a big car note each month. (10) So we started looking at the classified ads for a good economical used car.

(11) After we went over every column of the paper we had circled several ads to call. (12) The one that sounded the best was a 1990 Le Baron convertible a sporty

car. (13) It was red my favorite color. (14) We called about it and two others a 1988 Chevy Blazer and a 1991 Mustang and we made appointments to see all three.

(15) Over the next two days we checked out the cars. (16) The Blazer was in mint condition because it had only been driven around town by a retired Air Force colonel. (17) Plus it came from Santa Fe New Mexico and didn't have any rust but the dealer wanted too much. (18) The Mustang owned by a recent college graduate who was moving to New York City was in pretty good shape. (19) But I didn't like the color a funny shade of green. (2) The Le Baron was still my favorite even though it had 75400 miles. (21) My dad thought that was a little too much but he had a mechanic friend check it out. (22) He said it looked to be in good shape good news for me. (23) Everything worked out just as my parents said it would. (24) My hard work saving and shopping around produced the car of my dreams.

Exercise E7-8

Write ten original sentences, each with at least one comma.

Semicolon

Semicolons are used to separate equal sentence elements. Usually, a period can substitute for a semicolon. Therefore, the semicolon is simply another punctuation choice that will add variety to your writing. But you should use semicolons sparingly because overusing them will make your sentences awkward and monotonous. You should save semicolons for one of the following reasons:

1. *Use a semicolon rather than a coordinating conjunction and a comma to join two independent clauses.*

    Matthew decided to turn his paper in early; Erica decided not to turn in a paper at all.

2. *Use a semicolon between independent clauses joined by a conjunctive adverb, such as* however, therefore, *or* consequently.   Note that the adverb is preceded by the semicolon and followed by a comma.

    Matthew felt compassion for the defendant; **however,** he had to do what he felt was right and vote for a conviction.

3. *Use a semicolon to separate long items in a series when at least one of the elements contains commas.*

    The jury included Matthew, a student at St. Mary's; Irma, a grandmother and housewife; Susie, a single mother with two kids; James, a computer programmer with three teenage boys; and Shara, a secretary originally from Pakistan.

Colon

Like the semicolon, the **colon** signals a stop within a sentence. More specifically, the colon indicates that more information is to follow that will explain, expand, or clarify what came before the colon.

1. *Use a colon to introduce a list.*

    Matthew needs several things before he moves into his dorm room: a wastebasket, a mop, a broom, a rug, air freshener, and a new set of sheets.

2. *Use a colon to introduce an example or an explanation.*

    Matthew has only two words to say about his jury experience: "Never again."

    The recipe says to fold the berries into the batter: That simply means to mix the berries in thoroughly.

3. *Use a colon to introduce a formal quotation or dialogue.*

    In her essay "On AIDS," Susan Sontag explains the horror of the disease: "What makes the viral assault so terrifying is that contamination, and therefore vulnerability, is understood as permanent."

4. *Use colons to separate figures and words in the following instances.*

    Time: 7:15 a.m.   3:36 p.m.

    Biblical Citations: John 3:16   Psalms 12:8

    Business Letters: Dear Mrs. Galloway:

    Memo Headings: To: Dean Jonathan Fowler
                    From: Caryl Brown
                    Date: January 17, 1995
                    Subject: Personal leave request

    Ratios: 5:1   10:1

    Subtitles: "Prayer: When Nothing Else Works"

            The Prose Reader: Essays for Thinking, Reading, and Writing

    Bibliographic Entries: Bradshaw, John. *Creating Love.* New York: Bantam, 1992.

Exercise E7-9

List five places in Corky Clifton's essay "Life Sentences" (pp. 262–264) where a colon or semicolon would be acceptable.

Exercise E7-10

Supply semicolons and colons in the following sentences adapted from Matthew's first draft.

1. We had looked at photographs of the terrible automobile accident shots of the wreckage, close-ups of Grant's best friend, even photos of him being taken away.
2. Then the difficult discussions came out What exactly was he guilty of doing? Did Grant mean to kill his friend? Was he negligent?
3. I have seen people leave parties after they have been drinking I've seen them head for their cars.
4. Even good people make mistakes of judgment however when mistakes are made over and over, they become a pattern.
5. He did not know that his actions would lead to his best friend's death his friend trusted him to drive him home.

Exercise E7-11

Correctly punctuate the sentences in the following paragraphs with semicolons and colons.

(1) There was only one thing I ever wanted at the end of high school happiness. (2) And I thought I would have it if only I could have the man of my dreams. (3) How wrong I was! (4) Troy was new in school our junior year. (5) He had just moved from Southern California to our small Iowa town to live with his grandmother. (6) I'll never forget the first time I saw him it was 815 in homeroom. (7) I could have fainted when he took his seat and his eyes met mine. (8) He had the classic golden-boy good looks wide shoulders, bronze skin, long, flowing blond hair, and sparkling, white teeth. (9) I had certainly never seen anything like him before I probably never will again.

(1) Anyway, he asked me where the civics class was, and I told him to follow me. (11) He was pretty shy I was pretty much in shock. (12) We got to class and he sat down beside me. (13) Mr. Winchell called my name for the attendance report however, I was still staring at Troy and didn't answer. (14) For a long time after, I would be almost speechless in his presence because he looked just like a Greek god who had dropped in on our sleepy town.

(15) But as I got to know Troy, I found out what he liked best alcohol, marijuana, and speed. (16) That's why he had come to Iowa his parents thought they'd get him as far away from his old friends as possible. (17) But it didn't work, not until he almost killed us both.

Exercise E7-12

Write ten original sentences, five using semicolons and five using colons.

Quotation Marks

Quotation marks are usually easy to use because they most often mark dialogue or another person's exact thoughts and words. Quotation marks always appear in pairs, whether they are double (" ") or single (' ') marks. The most troublesome problems occur when other punctuation marks are used with quotation marks. If you refer to the following guidelines, however, your questions about quotation mark usage should be answered.

1. *Use quotation marks for dialogue.*   Whether in fiction or in attempts to reproduce someone's exact words, quotation marks indicate exactly what was said. As speakers change, remember to start a new paragraph.

> "I don't want to go to school today," Bob told his roommate.
> "What's wrong with you?" his roommate asked.
> "I have a history test, and I don't feel like I'm ready for the test," he said. "I can't miss the class. What should I do?"
> "I'll bet you know more than you think you know. Have you had this feeling before?" asked Bob's roommate.
> "Never this bad, but I guess I'll survive," Bob said, walking out the door.

2. *Use quotation marks for short direct quotations.*   Short quotations taken from previously printed material can be included in your work. "Short" means one to four typed lines of prose or one to three lines quoted from poetry. Longer quotations should be indented ten spaces from the left margin with no quotation marks.

Short Quotation: Best-selling writer Stephen King says, "We're all mentally ill; those of us outside the asylums only hide it a little better" (396).

Long Quotation: Best-selling writer Stephen King thinks everyone has some quirk, some secret little insanity. He says the only difference is that some people's insanities are more harmful than others.

> If your insanity leads you to carve up women, like Jack the Ripper or the Cleveland Torso Murderer, we clap you away in the funny farm (but neither of those two amateur-night surgeons was ever caught, heh, heh, heh); if, on the other hand, your insanity leads you only to talk to yourself when you're under stress or to pick your nose on your morning bus, then you are left alone to go about your business. (397)

King goes on to explain that everyone has the urge to let loose and do something insane or out of the ordinary. For many people, going to horror movies provides that release; they can scream, yell, jump, boo, and hiss as they let their fears run wild.

Note that if you put page numbers in parentheses at the end of a quotation, the reference always goes outside the quotation marks. For long quotations, however, the parenthetical reference follows the period.

When using other punctuation with quotation marks, follow these additional guidelines:

a. Place most punctuation marks inside the quotation marks.

Comma:	"I believe I'll turn in early," Mark said.
Period:	Hal replied, "I'm going to stay up and watch a movie."
Question Mark:	"When are you going to clean your room?" my sister asked.
Exclamation Point:	"Help me!" she screamed as I grabbed her by the neck.

b. If a question mark or exclamation point punctuates the entire sentence, place it outside the quotation marks.

Question Mark:	Did Beth say, "He's so cruel" or "He's so cool"?
Exclamation Point:	Don't say "ain't"!

c. Place semicolons and colons outside the quotation marks.

Semicolon:	Robin said, "I'll never do this again"; then she grabbed her purse and ran out of the room.
Colon:	Greg said he knew some things that would make his mom "blow her top": He had flunked two classes, his sister Kathy had lost her job, and his dad had lost $500 in a poker game.

d. Use a comma when the speaker is identified before the quoted material.

Comma:	Marcie asked, "When are we going to get another chance?"

e. When the speaker is identified within a quoted sentence, place a comma after the verb and add another set of quotation marks.

Commas:	"Most people in America have enough to eat," Nate said, "but you would be surprised at the number of people who go to bed hungry."

3. *Use single quotation marks to indicate a quotation within a quotation.*

Single Quotation Marks:	"Did he say, 'Hasta la vista, baby,' or was I hearing things?" Craig asked.
	Shelby Steele says that many blacks are "still in favor of affirmative action because of the 'subtle' discrimination" blacks suffer.

4. *Use quotation marks for titles of short works.*

Poems:	"The Road Not Taken"
Songs:	"I Will Always Love You"
Short Stories:	"The Gold Bug"
Book Chapters:	"My Humble Home"
Speeches:	"I Have a Dream"
Radio and TV Episodes:	"Recipe for Murder"
Articles:	"How to Lose Ten Pounds in Two Weeks"

But don't put your own titles in quotation marks.

Matthew's Essay:	A Matter of Life and Death

5. *Use quotation marks to show that words and phrases are being discussed or used in a special way.*

Special Use:	If you look up "buck" in the dictionary, you will find several slang meanings.
	"Chewing the fat" is a slang term that refers to talking carelessly or gossiping.

Exercise E7-13

Choose one paragraph from "Life Sentences" (pp. 262–264), and add some direct conversation to it. Use quotation marks correctly.

Exercise E7-14

Most of Matthew's draft is written in his own words. Imagine that Matthew recreated some of the dialogue he heard in the courtroom and the jury room, and punctuate the following sentences.

1. You will hear the horrible details of not just an accident the prosecuting attorney said but a horrific crime.
2. The defendant said All I remember is the song You Got the Look playing on the radio. Then everything went black.
3. I'm sorry the defendant screamed as he pounded the desk with his fists.
4. What makes you so sure he's guilty Matthew asked the jury foreman.
5. My client personifies the word victim the defense attorney said.

Exercise E7-15

Add quotation marks and other punctuation marks where they belong in the sentences that follow.

(1) My favorite poet is Emily Dickinson. (2) Lots of my friends think she's pretty hard to understand. (3) I like to think of her as a riddle maker. (4) Then figuring out the meaning of her poems becomes fun, almost like a treasure hunt. (5) When we studied her poetry last year, our instructor let us pair up and discuss a poem for the entire class. (6) My friend Corey was my partner. (7) What does I felt a funeral in my brain mean Corey asked, referring to the first line of our poem. (8) I don't know I replied. (9) I guess it's about her imagining what death would be like. (10) We read the rest of the poem then decided to go to the library to see if we could find any books that would explain it. (11) We found a couple. (12) One book had an entire chapter titled Crossing the Threshold, which was all about her death poems. (13) The author called Dickinson a keen observer who liked to use simple, one-syllable words like eyes and wrung. (14) Even after all our work, Corey still called her a deep chick. (15) I call her brilliant

Exercise E7-16

Write a short dialogue exchange of 10 to 12 sentences between any two speakers (either fictitious or real). Be sure to use punctuation marks correctly and to start a new paragraph each time speakers change.

Hyphen

A **hyphen** performs both joining and dividing functions. Hyphens connect parts of compound words and separate parts of single words. Additionally, hyphens are used in certain instances with numbers.

1. *Use a hyphen with certain compound words.*

    mother-in-law, four-year-old, get-together, four-hour, well-liked, year-long, long-lost, V-shaped

    When in doubt about hyphenating compound words, consult a dictionary.

2. *Use a hyphen to connect the prefixes all-, ex-, great-, and self- and the suffix -elect to other words.*

    all-American, **ex-**husband, **great-**aunt, **self-**rising, governor-**elect**

    Also, use a hyphen to join any prefix to a proper noun or proper adjective.

    post-Depression, pre-Incan, mid-August

3. *Use a hyphen to divide a word that appears at the end of a sentence.* Always divide words between syllables. Also, never divide a one-syllable word or a word that has fewer than six letters.

I'm always tempted to use up several legal pads trying to explain about the corrupt legal and political system here in Louisiana.

4. *Use a hyphen in certain instances with numbers.*

Spelled numbers from twenty-one to ninety-nine

Spelled fractions: one-half, two-thirds, three-fourths

Time spans: 1899-1975, 1988-90

Scores: 9-2, 21-17, 101-99

Dash

The **dash** serves as a sentence interrupter. It stops the flow of a sentence and sets off words, phrases, and clauses that usually contrast with the rest of the sentence.

A dash is twice as long as a hyphen. If you are using a typewriter or computer that does not have a dash key, use two hyphens with no space between them (--).

1. *Use a dash to emphasize a word, phrase, or clause.*

Peace, love, and good health—those are my wishes for the new year.

Sonya glided around the skating rink effortlessly, spinning and twirling—then she fell flat on her rear end.

2. *Use a dash to signal sudden changes in thought and direction.*

Matthew is still working on his English essay—you know, he made an A on his history exam.

3. *Use a dash to set off an explanation, examples, or a short summary from the rest of a sentence.*

Examples: The many things packed in Trina's closet—clothes, boxes, books, and a huge collection of Barbie dolls—almost spilled out into her bedroom.

Explanation: Pet peeves—things that really get on a person's nerves—can be something as simple as whistling or gossiping.

4. *Use a dash to set off long nonessential phrases (see p. 293 for a definition) that include internal punctuation.*

The suspect—a thin, slightly balding man with dark, squinty eyes—confessed soon after he was arrested.
My best friend—who used to live in the small, quiet town of Patoka, Indiana—is still amazed by all the things to do in St. Louis.

5. *Use dashes to indicate interruptions in dialogue.*

> "I can't—uh—remember exactly what he said," Matthew said.
> "Please don't do—" Lana said as she tripped over the chair.

Parentheses

Like dashes, **parentheses** set off words, phrases, and other elements in sentences, but they are not as abrupt an interrupter as a dash. Rather, parentheses work in pairs to add information that enriches the meaning of the sentence.

1. *Use parentheses to set off supplementary information.*

Summaries:	The first quarter was wild, with the teams trading touchdowns. (The rest of the game was boring as the teams seemed to run out of steam.)
Explanations:	Several students are attending the ACP (Association of Collegiate Presses) convention in San Diego.
Asides:	That's my Aunt Christine from Atlanta. (She's been married seven times, but we only talk about the most recent husband, Harold.)
Life Spans:	George Orwell (1903–1950) wrote the classic novel *Animal Farm*.
Cross-references:	Orwell served as an officer in the Indian Imperial Police (see page 101).

As these examples illustrate, you should punctuate material within the parentheses as necessary.

2. *Use parentheses to mark numbers and letters used in lists within sentences.*

> After you have conducted interviews to collect information about the news story, you should do these things: (1) Arrange the information in order of importance, (2) write a lead or first paragraph, and (3) fill in the necessary details as you write the rest of the story.

Exercise E7-17

Explain each use of a hyphen or dash in Corky Clifton's essay "Life Sentences" (pp. 262–264).

Exercise E7-18

Add hyphens, dashes, and parentheses to the following sentences from Matthew's first draft. You may have to add other punctuation marks as well.

1. The defendant was pretty good looking and seemed well mannered.

2. He had been convicted of drunk driving on previous occasions during 1994 95, and he had completed a special program in mid May to educate drunk drivers.

3. Anyway, if Grant's friend got in the car with him that night, surely he knew what Grant's history was maybe he thought he knew Grant better than he really did.

4. She asked me gosh, I wanted to scream and get everything over if I would want to drive on the same road as that man when he was drunk.

5. Even though the 22 year old defendant looked like a nice person, he was guilty I still wanted to shake his hand and wish him well.

Exercise E7-19

Punctuate the following sentences correctly, using hyphens, dashes, and parentheses. Not every sentence needs additional punctuation.

(1) Sometimes people wonder why I didn't stay with my exgirlfriend. (2) I mean, she had lots of things going for her a great personality, good looks, a promising future. (3) That's only the beginning of her attractive qualities. (4) You are probably wondering why I don't get her back. (5) Well, maybe I will.

(6) Sarah had a real loving family. (7) Her mom was divorced, a selfsupporting woman who did well for Sarah and her brother. (8) Sarah's dad was a computer salesman and a parttime CBA Continental Basketball Association referee. (9) He had played college basketball, all conference at the University of Massachusetts 1959 1962. (10) But he still saw Sarah a lot even after the divorce and helped instill good values in her.

(11) I guess Sarah got her kind, caring personality from her mom man, Mrs. Singleton could cook. (12) Sarah could cook well, too. (13) I remember she would often ask me over on Saturday mornings. (4) Then she would whip up a big breakfast eggs, bacon, waffles, biscuits and we'd eat and watch cartoons. (15) Her nine year old brother would run around, and we'd all act crazy. (16) I miss those Saturdays. (17) I even gave Sarah I can't believe I'm not with her anymore a preengagement ring. (18) We thought everything would work out fine and we'd go off to college together. (19) But things and people change. (20) She's smart, smart enough to know that we need to experience more of life before we settle down. (21) So the breakup was her idea. (22) I'm still a little sad, but I know she's right she always was. (23) Still, one day I hope I won't be her exboyfriend but her man forever. (24) Is that too much to ask?

Exercise E7-20

Write three original sentences using hyphens, three sentences using dashes, and three sentences using parentheses.

Apostrophe

The **apostrophe,** which looks like a single quotation mark ('), performs three functions: (1) It shows possession; (2) it indicates some plurals; and (3) it marks the omission of letters and numerals in contractions.

1. *Use an apostrophe to form the possessive case of nouns and indefinite pronouns.*

    a. For most singular nouns and indefinite pronouns, simply add an apostrophe plus *s* to show the possessive.

        the girl's dress, the cat's paw, the shirt's collar, Matthew's draft, the class's room, the boss's desk, Charles's car, everybody's favorite, nobody's pen, someone's book

    b. For plural nouns ending in *s*, add only an apostrophe to show the possessive.

        the girls' dresses, the cats' paws, the shirts' collars, the classes' rooms, the bosses' desks

    c. Some irregular plurals also take an apostrophe plus *s* to show the possessive.

        the men's conversations, the women's meetings

    d. If two or more nouns share ownership, add an apostrophe and an *s* to the final noun.

        Juan and Veronica's apartment is located near the mall.
        The cat and dog's play area is located in the basement.

    If two or more nouns indicate individual ownership, add an apostrophe and an *s* to both nouns.

        Both Juan's and Veronica's grandparents come from Puerto Rico.
        The cat's and dog's food dishes are located at opposite ends of the basement.

    e. For compound nouns, place an apostrophe and an *s* after the last word.

        my father-in-law's job, no one else's business, the Census Bureau's budget

    f. Certain adjectives that refer to time or amounts require apostrophes to indicate possession.

        yesterday's news, tomorrow's forecast, a week's pay, a year's passing

2. *Use an apostrophe to indicate the plural of a letter, number, sign, or abbreviation or the plural of a word discussed as a word.*

    Tomorrow has one *m*, two *r*'s, and three *o*'s.
    My social security number has four 8's in it.
    Your paper has several %'s that should be spelled out.
    Your paper also has too many *etc.*'s and *consequently*'s.

3. *Use an apostrophe to indicate that letters or numerals have been omitted in contractions.*

    didn't, can't, won't, it's, where's, doin'

T I P S   F O R   E D I T I N G

Exercise E7-21

Find ten words that use apostrophes in the excerpt from "Life Sentences" (pp. 262–264), and label each word as either a possessive or a contraction.

Exercise E7-22

Find all the apostrophes in Matthew's revised essay (pp. 274–277), and explain why each apostrophe is used.

Exercise E7-23

Correct the apostrophe errors in the following paragraphs.

(1) People may be surprised to learn they probably have interesting family histories if theyd only look around. (2) Our familys' beginnings can be traced back to Americas' birth. (3) My ancestor's on my mothers' side came from Holland. (4) It took them ten years' worth of saving before they had enough money to come to the New World. (5) The leader of the first family was Klaus von Allen (1720–1794). (6) He and his wife Katrina hadnt planned on settling in North Carolina, but thats where fate took them. (7) One of their sons was one of the first settlers of Asheville. (8) By then they had become the Allen's, not the von Allens.

(9) My fathers' family came from somewhere in Scotland. (10) I dont remember the town, but they were members of a large group of Scottish people who settled in upstate New York. (11) Some of them finally emigrated (does that word have two ms?) to the South, which had a warmer climate and more land for raising crops. (12) My sister's-in-laws family is from Italy, both side's. (13) Somewhere along the line she had an uncle who killed his wife in a fit of jealousy. (14) As the story goes, he later escaped from jail, moved to England, got a job, and later killed his boss' wife. (15) So much for skeleton's in the closet.

Exercise E7-24

Write original sentences using the following words and phrases.

1. *and's*
2. Barry and Cathy's
3. teachers'
4. 4's
5. brother-in-law's

Underlining/Italicizing

Most printed materials—newspapers, magazines, books—are published in roman type, as is this textbook. Type that *slants* is called **italic** type. Italics are used to emphasize and to set off certain words, phrases, and titles. Underlining serves the same function as italics, but underlining is used only when italic type is not available— when you are typewriting or writing in longhand.

1. *Italicize titles of certain literary, artistic, musical, and media works.*

Books:	*The Vampire Chronicles*
Plays:	*Romeo and Juliet*
Novellas:	*The Ballad of the Sad Cafe*
Long poems:	*Paradise Lost*
Magazines:	*Seventeen, People*
Newspapers:	the *Washington Post*
Pamphlets:	*Tips for Reducing Debt*
Films:	*Forrest Gump, Casablanca*
Sculptures:	*The Pietà*
Paintings:	*Blue Boy*
Art exhibits:	*The Vision of the Incas*
Radio Programs:	*The Shadow*
TV Series:	*Home Improvement*
Record albums and CDs:	*Ropin' the Wind*

2. *Italicize names of vehicles.*

   trains (**the** *City of New Orleans*), ships (**U.S.S.** *Missouri*), aircraft (**the** *Spirit of St. Louis*), and spacecraft (*Challenger*)

3. *Italicize scientific names and unfamiliar foreign words and phrases.*

   The scientific name for the bird family is **aves.**
   E pluribus unum is a Latin phrase that appears on the Great Seal of the United States.

4. *Italicize words, letters, and numbers when they refer to themselves.*

   Every few words Chuck says **yeah.**
   When I learned how to write, I had a hard time making *f*'s.
   It's hard to tell your **4**'s from your **7**'s.

Exercise E7-25

List the letters, numbers, words, and phrases that should be italicized/underlined in the following paragraphs.

(1) During my Amtrak ride on the Eastern Express, I took along plenty of entertainment. (2) I took one nonfiction book, Embraced by the Light by Betty Eadie; a

copy of Angels in America, the Pulitzer-prize winning play by Tony Kushner; and my old favorite, A Tale of Two Cities by Charles Dickens. (3) I also took along the latest People magazine and last month's Rolling Stone, which I never got to read. (4) Then I had my copy of the New Testament, which is always in a pocket somewhere. (5) When I got on the train, someone had left a copy of U.S.A. Today under my seat, so I had plenty of reading material.

(6) I also took along my headphones and a couple of good tapes: Rhythm of Love by Anita Baker and Smells Like Teen Spirit by Pearl Jam. (7) Then soon after I boarded someone announced that True Lies starring Arnold Schwarznegger would be shown twice that night on the TV monitors in the observation car. (8) I wish I could have seen my favorite TV show, NYPD Blue, but I had plenty to keep me occupied.

(9) By the time we hit the Appalachian Mountains a few hours later, I had finished my magazines and newspaper, watched the movie, and taken a nap. (10) Some nice older man who pronounced his r's funny offered to let me listen to his polka music cassette. (11) I tried it out as a matter of courtesy, then kicked back with Dickens for the rest of the ride to the Eastern Seaboard.

Exercise E7-26

Fill in the blanks with specific names and titles that should be italicized/underlined.

1. novel _____

2. movie _____

3. magazine _____

4. play _____

5. album/CD _____

Mechanics

The mechanical aspects of a sentence are much like any other mechanical features. They are some of the smallest, but most important, details in their sentences. The term *mechanics* refers to capitalization, abbreviations, and numbers. We usually take these items for granted, but when they are used incorrectly, a sentence, just like a mechanical appliance, starts to break down.

Capitalization

Because every sentence begins with a capital letter, **capitalization** is the best place to start discussing the mechanics of good writing. Besides signaling where sentences begin, capitalization also emphasizes specific words, making their sentences easier to read and interpret. See how difficult and awkward our language would appear without capitalization:

> during our trip to florida last june, we visited disney world, busch gardens, miami beach, and key west. my friends chris, greg, and tony stayed an extra week and took a cruise to the bahamas.

Capitalizing the correct words produces sentences that communicate clearly and effectively.

> During our trip to Florida last June, we visited Disney World, Busch Gardens, Miami Beach, and Key West. My friends Chris, Greg, and Tony stayed an extra week and took a cruise to the Bahamas.

There are far fewer capitalization rules than punctuation guidelines to follow in the English language. But that doesn't mean capitalization is less important. Use the following rules to ensure that your writing is mechanically sound.

1. *Capitalize the first word of every sentence, regardless of type.* This rule causes few problems. However, certain instances may be confusing, particularly when dealing with quotations.

    a. Capitalize the first word in a quotation that is a complete sentence, whether the quotation falls at the beginning, in the middle, or at the end of your sentence.

Beginning:	"People cannot fully appreciate our justice system until they serve on a jury," Matthew said.
Middle:	The saying "To have a friend you must be a friend" is one I try to repeat every day.
End:	Matthew replied, "The best thing to do is review the evidence one more time."

    b. If the quotation is broken up, do not capitalize the beginning of the second part of the quoted material.

        "I have decided," the mayor said, "to freeze the salaries of city workers to help balance our budget."

2. *Capitalize the first word of interjections and exclamations.*

    No way!
    Absolutely!

3. *Capitalize all proper nouns—names of specific people, places, and things.*

People:	Susan, John Doe, Michael Jordan, Vanna White
Groups:	Americans, Navajos, African Americans, New York Yankees, Republican Party, National Rifle Association, the Kiwanis Club, a Kappa Delta
Places:	Yellowstone National Park; Rocky Mountains; Africa; Mangham, Louisiana; Union County
Things:	Streets (Pennsylvania Avenue, Route 66); structures (Sears Tower, Golden Gate Bridge, LaGuardia Airport, Washington Monument); institutions, agencies, businesses, and brand names (Xavier High School, Eugene Public Library, United Nations, Veterans Hospital, Ford Motor Company, Chevy Blazer)
Events:	Valentine's Day, the Grammy Awards, the Battle of Hastings, April, Lent
Vehicles:	Cars and motorcycles (Mustang, Harley-Davidson), trains (the *Zephyr*), ships (*U.S.S. Constitution*), aircraft (the *Hindenberg*), spacecraft (*Apollo 11*)

Capitalize abbreviated names of institutions and associatons: **AFL-CIO, FBI** (Federal Bureau of Investigation), **UCLA** (University of California at Los Angeles), **DAR** (Daughters of the American Revolution).

4. *Capitalize proper adjectives formed from proper nouns.*

English muffin, French vanilla ice cream, Shakespearean play, Shetland pony, Mayan ruin

5. *Capitalize family and personal titles and abbreviations for those titles.*

Aunt Mary; Professor Finn; Mayor Catherine Grant; Dr. Elizabeth Meese; Carlton E. Spillers, M.D.; Rev. Charles Lincoln

6. *Capitalize a family title used as a name.*

Yesterday Grandmother sent me $25 for my birthday.
Yesterday my grandmother sent me $25 for my birthday.

7. *Capitalize the titles of creative works.*

Books:	*I Know Why the Caged Bird Sings*
Short Stories:	"The Lottery"
Plays:	*Our Town*

Poems:	"Song of Myself"
Articles:	"The Best Small Colleges in America"
Magazines:	*Sassy, Sports Illustrated, People*
Songs:	"The End of the Road"
Albums or CDs:	*Metallica Live*
Films:	*Schindler's List*
TV Series:	*Home Improvement*
Radio Shows:	*Kasey Kasem's Countdown*
Works of Art:	*The Scream*
Computer Programs:	*Microsoft Word*

Do not capitalize articles, conjunctions, and short prepositions unless they are the first or last word of the title.

8. *Capitalize the letters of most acronyms (abbreviations that are pronounced as words).*

    MADD (Mothers Against Drunk Driving)
    AIDS (Acquired Immune Deficiency Syndrome)

    (See p. 317 for more on using acronyms.)

9. *Capitalize specific course titles and the title of any course that refers to a language.*

    Sarah signed up for a French class and **P**sychology 201.
    Bill decided to take a psychology class and **S**panish 101.

10. *Capitalize the words I and O no matter where they appear in a sentence.*

    I wish that **I** could sing as well as Vickie.
    Our pastor says, "**O**, Master," every time he prays aloud in church.

Exercise E7-27

List and explain all the capitalized words within sentences in the excerpt from "Life Sentences" (pp. 262–264). Disregard the first word of each sentence.

Exercise E7-28

List and explain all the capitalized words within sentences in Matthew's revised essay (pp. 274–277).
Disregard the first word of each sentence and the personal pronoun *I*.

Exercise E7-29

Correct the capitalization errors in the following paragraphs.

(1) I had several extra projects in my classes this semester. (2) In my English Literature class, our teacher, miss grayson, asked us to read *silas marner,* a novel by george eliot. (3) the book is set in england and is often described as a Morality Tale about love, good, and evil. (4) We had to write a short report about the book and its author, whose real name was mary ann evans.

(5) In my business 101 class, we had to write to a business and find out as much information as we could. (6) i chose a small company named the puzzle factory. (7) This company is based in madison, wisconsin, and is run by col. james r. richards, who is retired from the u.s. army. (8) Richards liked jigsaw puzzles so much that he decided to start making his own. (9) Many of his puzzles are pictures of famous landmarks such as the statue of liberty and mount rushmore. (10) some feature scenes from famous Movies like *gone with the wind* and *rebel without a cause.* (11) Still other puzzles are reprints of famous works of Art like *the last supper* and michaelangelo's *david.* (12) What's interesting is that richards does most of the graphics himself. (13) He even sent me a sample puzzle with a note that said, "when things are going well, every piece seems to fit. thanks for your interest."

(14) In my history class, we had to pick a newsmaker who is still living and do a report. (15) I chose michael jordan because i love his smooth moves with the chicago bulls. (16) he played for the north carolina tarheels and led them to the final four. (17) his mom is an important influence on him, which is nice to know.

Exercise E7-30

Write original sentences using the following proper nouns.

1. Uncle Larry
2. Ford Mustang
3. the Rolling Stones
4. Japanese
5. Sears

Abbreviations

To **abbreviate** means to make something shorter. In writing, an abbreviation is formed by taking part of a word, usually only a few letters, and adding a period at the end. Some abbreviations appear without periods, and still others are set off with commas.

Writers—particularly in academic and technical disciplines—often abbreviate words to make reading an easier, swifter process. For general purposes, however, abbreviations are less commonly used. Still, knowing the acceptable shortened forms for certain words and phrases will help you become an economical writer, one who saves time in reading and space on the page.

Certain abbreviations are acceptable in both formal and informal writing. They fall under the following categories:

1. *Titles and degrees.*

    a. Abbreviate courtesy titles when they appear before a proper name.

       Mr. Jim Fishbein, **Ms.** Brenda DeHaven, **Prof.** Dale Navarro

    b. Abbreviate government, military, and religious titles when they appear with an entire name. When they appear with a last name only, do not abbreviate.

       Gov. Lawton Chiles, **Governor** Chiles; **Sen.** Carol Moseley-Braun, **Senator** Moseley-Braun; **Rep.** (Representative); **Supt.** (Superintendent); **Col.** (Colonel); **Lt.** (Lieutenant); **Cmdr.** (Commander); **Rev.** (Reverend); **Sr.** (Sister); **Sec.** (Secretary); **Gen.** (General); **Maj.** (Major); **Capt.** (Captain); **Sgt.** (Sergeant); **Fr.** (Father); **Br.** (Brother)

    c. Abbreviate titles or degrees that follow a proper name, and set them off with commas.

       Jr. (Junior), **Sr.** (Senior), **B.A.** (bachelor of arts), **B.S.** (bachelor of science), **M.A.** (master of arts), **M.B.A.** (master of business administration), **Ed.D.** (doctor of education), **D.D.S.** (doctor of dental science), **LL.D.** (doctor of laws), **M.S.** (master of science), **M.F.A.** (master of fine arts), **Ph.D.** (doctor of philosophy), **D.V.M.** (doctor of veterinary medicine), **J.D.** (doctor of law)

2. *Business names.* Use the following abbreviations unless the business prefers to spell out the word:
   Bros. (Brothers), **Co.** (Company), **Corp.** (Corporation), **Inc.** (Incorporated), **Ltd.** (Limited).

3. *Dates, measurements, and symbols.*

    a. Use *a.m.* and *p.m.* to denote specific times of the day.
       9:30 **a.m.**   12:20 **p.m.**

    b. Use *B.C.* (before Christ) or *B.C.E.* (before the Common Era) to denote dates before Christ, and use *A.D.* (Anno Domini) or *C.E.* (Common Era) to denote years after Christ's birth.
       375 **B.C.**   **A.D.** 455

    c. Use the following abbreviations with measurements: **F** (degrees Fahrenheit), **C** (degrees Celsius), **mph** (miles per hour), **km** (kilometers), **rpm** (revolutions per minute), **mg** (milligrams).
       75°**F**   400 **rpm**

    d. Use the symbols ° for *degrees*, % for *percent*, and $ for *dollars* when referring to specific quantities except in the body of essays where the words *degrees* and *percent* should be spelled out.

40°   40% $40
40 **degrees**, 40 **percent**, $40 in essays

4. *Parts of address.*

    a. Abbreviate locations when they are used with specific addresses. Otherwise, spell them out.

        Send the check to 875 Monroe **Ave.**, Memphis, **TN** 38163.
        The business is located on Monroe **Avenue**.

    b. Use the U.S. Postal Service abbreviations for state names.

AL	Alabama	MO	Missouri
AK	Alaska	NB	Nebraska
AZ	Arizona	NV	Nevada
AR	Arkansas	NH	New Hampshire
CA	California	NJ	New Jersey
CO	Colorado	NM	New Mexico
CT	Connecticut	NY	New York
DE	Delaware	NC	North Carolina
FL	Florida	ND	North Dakota
GA	Georgia	OH	Ohio
HI	Hawaii	OK	Oklahoma
ID	Idaho	OR	Oregon
IL	Illinois	PA	Pennsylvania
IN	Indiana	RI	Rhode Island
IA	Iowa	SC	South Carolina
KS	Kansas	SD	South Dakota
KY	Kentucky	TN	Tennessee
LA	Louisiana	TX	Texas
ME	Maine	UT	Utah
MD	Maryland	VT	Vermont
MA	Massachusetts	VA	Virginia
MI	Michigan	WA	Washington
MN	Minnesota	WV	West Virginia
MS	Mississippi	WI	Wisconsin
MT	Montana	WY	Wyoming

    c. Use *USA* in an address, but use the abbreviation *U.S.* when the word *United States* is used as an adjective. Use *D.C.* for *District of Columbia*.

Initialisms

Initialisms are formed from the first letters of words and are pronounced letter by letter: FBI, DAR, CBS. Initialisms are used most frequently when referring to certain products, government organizations, businesses, and labor organizations.

Writers should use initialisms only if the items referred to are well known. Otherwise, the full name should be spelled out in parentheses: USCGA (United States Corn Growers Association). Normally, periods are not used with initialisms.

Following are some commonly used initialisms:

ABC	American Broadcasting Companies
CBS	Columbia Broadcasting System
MTV	Music Television
NBC	National Broadcasting Company
GM	General Motors
TWA	Trans World Airlines
UPS	United Parcel Service
CIA	Central Intelligence Agency
FBI	Federal Bureau of Investigation
FCC	Federal Communications Commission
FDIC	Federal Deposit Insurance Corporation
GOP	Grand Old Party (Republican Party)
IRS	Internal Revenue Service
UN	United Nations
DAR	Daughters of the American Revolution
NFL	National Football League
NRA	National Rifle Association
PGA	Professional Golfers Association
CD	compact disc
ECG	electrocardiogram
TV	television
AFL-CIO	American Federation of Labor and Congress of Industrial Organizations

Acronyms

An **acronym** is an initialism that can be pronounced as a word: AIDS, NATO. Note that all letters are capitalized and no periods are used. As with initialisms, you should identify the acronym's meaning parenthetically if it is not well known: HOW (Help Our Whales).

Here are some common acronyms and their meanings:

AIDS	Acquired Immune Deficiency Syndrome
MADD	Mothers Against Drunk Driving
NATO	North Atlantic Treaty Organization
NORML	National Organization for the Reform of Marijuana Laws
SADD	Students Against Drunk Driving
UNICEF	United Nations International Children's Emergency Fund

Exercise E7-31

Underline the abbreviations, initialisms, and acronyms in Matthew's revised essay (pp. 274–277), and explain why they are used.

T I P S F O R E D I T I N G

Exercise E7-32

Underline the abbreviation errors in the following paragraphs. If you find a word that should be abbreviated, substitute its shortened form.

(1) One of the weirdest things happened to my dad last Oct. (2) After I tell you about it, you will agree that some strange things can happen here in the U.S. (3) One day in the mail my mom saw a letter. (4) The return address said Wellswood Chemical Corporation, 1235 Auburn Avenue, Camp Hill, Pennsylvania 17012. (5) It was addressed to my dad, Doctor Craig Worthen, 231 Center Street, New Castle, Delaware 19720. That's my dad, all right, or so we thought.

(6) Anyway, my mom didn't open it because it was addressed to Dad. (7) He was away at a conference about Acquired Immune Deficiency Syndrome. (8) Anyway, when my dad got home he opened the letter and was completely confused. (9) There was a check for 5,000 dollars and a short letter thanking my dad for the "great job he had done" on a recent laboratory project. (10) It was signed by the company pres., Robt. B. Harriman, Senior.

(11) My dad called the phone no. of the co. listed on the letter. (12) He talked to a sec. who asked him to explain the letter and check to someone in accounting. (13) The accountant told him that Mister Harriman was on vacation in Myrtle Beach, So. Car., and that they would try to straighten things out if my dad would return everything to them. (14) So that's what he did.

(15) Then early in Nov. my dad got another letter from Wellswood explaining the mix-up. (16) It seems a chemist named Dr. Craig Worthen from Scarsdale, NY, had done work for the company. (17) But how they got my dad's address is a big mystery. (18) My dad joked that he should ask the Federal Bureau of Investigation to look into things because he was curious. (19) Anyway, he didn't complain too much because the company sent him a 50 dollar check for "his honesty and the trouble the matter caused him."

Exercise E7-33

Write original sentences using the following abbreviations.

1. Hwy.
2. km
3. Rep.
4. CIA
5. Sgt.

Numbers

Just think how important numbers are. They indicate your age, your address, your bank balance, the national debt, and the pages of this book. Numbers tell you what time it is, how much you weigh, what you've earned for a week of hard work, and what grade you made on a test. Without numbers all of us would truly be lost.

When you use numbers in your writing, you must decide whether to use figures or spell out the words for the numbers. The following guidelines will help solve your number problems; just remember to be consistent. You may need to consult specific style manuals if you are writing in certain fields such as science, business, and journalism.

1. *In most fields, spell out numbers one to nine.*

   seven books   **nine** students   **two** cars

2. *Use figures for numbers 10 and above.*

   74 cats   **14,356** letters   **12,398,577** dimes

   For very large numbers, you should use a combination of figures and words.

   88 million people   **4.5 billion** pounds   **$1.4 trillion**

3. *Always spell out a number that begins a sentence.* Revise the sentence if spelling the number is awkward.

   Three hundred ninety-seven people will attend the luncheon.
   Approximately **400** people will attend the luncheon.
   We have received **397** confirmations for the luncheon.

4. *Use figures for the following conventions:*

   Dates: October **6, 1974**   **6** October **1974**
   345 B.C.E. (before the Common Era)   A.D. **345** (Anno Domini)

   Addresses: **675** Reston, St. Paul, MN **55164**

   106 Dauphine, Apt. **6**

   Time of Day: **8:45** a.m.   **10:30** p.m.

   Telephone Numbers: **978-567-4464**   **815-877-1420**

   Fractions, Decimals, Percentages, and Ratios:
   11/16   **.003**   **65%**   **5 to 1**

   Scores, Statistics, and Identification Numbers:
   98–96   **112** touchdowns   **438–82–9421** (Social Security)

   Measurements and Amounts of Money:
   24 feet   **200** yards   **$9.68**

   Parts of written works:
   page **46**   Chapter **14**   act **3**, scene **2**, lines **23–30**   volume **17**

Exercise E7-34

The following sentences come from Life Sentences *by Corky Clifton. Explain why the number in each sentence is spelled out or written in figures.*

1. For 27 years I have submitted to discipline, the rules, the harsh conditions, the torment of my children growing from babies into men—without ever seeing them.

2. In 1983 I applied to the board for the third time and the Pardon Board cut my time to 50 years.
3. Well, I am one example of it, and there are hundreds more lifers in here, many of them I know personally, who are in here for no other reason than because some big shot out there don't want them to go free.
4. I struggled through those hills, mountains really, for five days and six nights, sleeping on the ground, with no food and very little water.
5. I sat in the bushes watching the trailer from about 50 yards away.

Exercise E7-35

Explain why each number in Matthew's revised essay (pp. 274–277) is either spelled out or written in figures.

Exercise E7-36

Correct the errors in the following sentences, either spelling numbers or using figures.

(1) Four of my friends and I decided that we wanted to get front-row seats for the *Eagles* concert. (2) So we got up at five a.m. and got in line an hour later at the coliseum ticket office. (3) When we arrived, there were only about 15 other people ahead of us. (4) We settled down on the sidewalk and began the 4-hour wait until the box office opened at 10.

(5) By 7 o'clock at least 100 more people had showed up. (6) We held our ground because we were up close, only about twelve feet from the ticket window. (7) We had a radio tuned in to FM ninety-five point five, our favorite station. (8) But it was hard to hear because of the crowd and noise from competing radios and boom boxes.

(9) About eight thirty the crowd numbered at least two hundred. (10) About ten percent of the people were older than 30. (11) We even saw 2 gray-haired women about fifty feet behind us. (12) Someone said these women hit all the concerts in town, no matter what.

(13) 9:30 ticked by and everyone started to get really restless and excited. (14) The coliseum seats over 10 thousand, so we were sure we'd get great seats. (15) Finally, the ticket window opened, and we reached the head of the line in less than 10 minutes. (16) We each got front-row seats, which cost thirty-two dollars and fifty cents apiece. (17) Even though the whole ticket-buying experience took over 5 hours, we agreed it would be worth it. (18) And believe me, it was. (19) The concert—which was held 6 weeks later on April fifteen—was the best one I'd ever seen.

Exercise E7-37

Write original sentences using the following words or phrases.

1. nine trips
2. seventy-six
3. 32,568
4. $3.5 trillion

5.   75 mph
6.   June 30, 1990
7.   22 feet
8.   55 million people
9. $94.56
10.   300

COLLABORATIVE WORK

After you revise your analyzing essay, exchange papers with a classmate, and do the following task:

A.   Circle any punctuation mistakes.

B.   Underline any mechanical errors (capitalization, abbreviations, initialisms, acronyms, and numbers).

Then return the paper to its writer, and use the information in this section to edit your draft.

CHAPTER EIGHT

Persuading
Reading and Writing for a Reason

It is better to debate a question without settling it than to settle a question without debating it.

—JOSEPH JOUBERT

Persuading is one of the most common forms of communication; we use it all the time. Those of us who still live at home with our parents try to convince them to let us borrow the car. Those of us who have children of our own try to convince them to come home with the car at a reasonable hour. Politicians try to persuade us to vote for them; salespeople try to persuade us to buy newer, more expensive products or services; and advertisers try to persuade us that their products are superior.

In writing, you will do the same thing when you want to persuade others. You choose a topic that is important to you. Then you gather as much evidence and information as possible and use it to convince your readers to agree with you. This task is not as easy as it sounds, however, because there is a very good chance that your readers will feel as strongly about the topic as you do—on the opposite side. Because of this possibility, the **evidence** you present must be accurate, logical, and convincing. Evidence is probably the most important ingredient in writing a persuading essay. Without it, your essays will be nothing more than opinions; with it, your essays will be logical and convincing arguments that can help your readers not only understand your position but agree with it.

To write a persuasive essay and attempt to prove your case, you will probably use one of three types of evidence: facts, examples, or quotations. **Facts** are statements that can be proved objectively. They are indisputable—the unemployment rate has decreased in the last two years, for example, or the murderer has red hair. They are powerful because they are not negotiable. If lawyers have enough hard, cold facts, they can prove a case pretty easily. **Examples** can also help support your opinions and arguments in a persuasive paper. But writers must make sure that their examples are relevant to the main point they are trying to make and that they present enough examples to make a difference. Finally, **quotations** are exact statements from experts in the area you are studying. The quotations you choose to support your conclusions should be relevant and succinct. By using a well-balanced combination of these types of evidence, you can create an interesting, convincing paper.

The ability to persuade through writing gives us the potential to change things for the better, to right wrongs, to help others. For example, Native Americans have often complained about the way that Christopher Columbus's discovery of America is described, particularly in history books. In the following passage from an essay titled "Racist Stereotyping in the English Language," Robert B. Moore tries to persuade his readers to acknowledge this problem:

> Many words lead to a demeaning [insulting] characterization of groups of people. For instance, Columbus, it is said, "discovered" America. The word *discover* is defined as "to gain sight or knowledge of something previously unseen or unknown; to discover may be to find some existent thing that was previously unknown." Thus, a continent inhabited by millions of human beings cannot be "discovered." For history books to continue this usage represents a Eurocentric perspective on world history and ignores the existence of, and the perspective of, Native Americans. "Discovery," as used in the Euro-American context, implies the right to take what one finds, ignoring the rights of those who already inhabit or own the "discovered" thing.

Notice how Moore presents his evidence in a logical and convincing order. He does not simply make a claim; he supports it logically and completely so his readers can understand his viewpoint and—he hopes—agree with him.

LEARNING FROM PUBLISHED WRITERS

In all three published essays that follow, the writers state their evidence clearly and convincingly in order to persuade their readers to agree with their positions. The first persuading essay in this chapter deals with a sensitive, but important, topic. The writer, Thomas Lickona, a psychologist and educator at the State University of New York at Cortland, is convinced that teen sex should be avoided not only because of the danger of disease, but also because of the emotional dangers of premature sexual involvement. This essay, titled "The Neglected Heart," was published in 1994 in *American Educator*, a magazine for teachers. Notice the small numbers printed throughout the essay. These numbers refer to the endnotes that follow the essay, where the writer lists his *sources*, the books and articles he quoted from throughout the essay. When you write research papers, you will be required to provide a list of your sources.

Before You Read

Focusing Your Attention

Before you read this essay, take a few moments to respond to the following questions in your journal:

1.   At what age or in what situation do you think it is appropriate for two people to engage in sexual relations?

2.   In the essay you are about to read, "The Neglected Heart," the writer explains that many emotional problems are caused when people who are too young have sexual relations. What do you think some of these emotional problems are?

Expanding Your Vocabulary

Here are some words and their meanings that are important to your understanding of the essay "The Neglected Heart." You might want to review them before you read.

"far less [is said] about the emotional **hazards** [dangers]" (paragraph 1)

"That's not to say we should **downplay** [minimize the importance] of the physical dangers" (paragraph 2)

"Regret and **Self-Recrimination** [blaming oneself]" (heading, paragraph 10)

"If a girl expects a sexual **interlude** [brief experience] to be loving" (paragraph 13)

"She was **reluctant** [hesitant]; he was **persistent** [insistent]." (paragraph 14)

"I had **steeled** [hardened] myself against commitment." (paragraph 16)

"I was very **promiscuous** [having sex freely with many partners]" (paragraph 16)

"Even in an age of **sexual liberation** [freedom to engage in sex without guilt]" (paragraph 23)

"They tend to be filled with **self-loathing** [self-hatred]." (paragraph 28)

"they **corrupt** [damage] their characters and **debase** [reduce the value of] their sexuality in the process." (paragraph 32)

"It was **Freud** [Sigmund Freud (1856–1939)], considered to be the founder of psychology] who said . . . that sexual self-control is essential for civilization." (paragraph 33)

"once **sexual restraint** [ability to control one's sexual drive and desires] is set aside (paragraph 35)

"There's a **Tailhook** [a sexual assault scandal at a 1991 U.S. Navy convention] happening in every school." (paragraph 36)

"**Egregious** [very bad] behavior is going on." (paragraph 36)

"children are beginning to **mimick** [imitate] such behavior" (paragraph 37)

"sex that isn't tied to love and commitment **undermines** [weakens] character by **subverting** [damaging or destroying] self-control" (paragraph 39)

"**Unchecked** [uncontrolled], sexual desires and impulses easily **run amok** [go wild] and lead to habits of **hedonism** [selfish pleasure]" (paragraph 39)

"sex is **trivialized** [made to seem unimportant] and **degraded** [made to have no value]" (paragraph 39)

"Some **sexually exploited** [taken advantage of sexually] people . . . develop such low self-esteem" (paragraph 41)

"another short-lived and **demeaning** [degrading, cheapening] sexual relationship." (paragraph 41)

"It can create a very strong emotional bond that hurts terribly when it's **ruptured** [broken]" (paragraph 46)

"Sometimes the emotional **turmoil** [confusion] . . . leads to deep depression." (paragraph 47)

"the emotional **aftermath** [what happens after] of broken sexual relationships" (paragraph 49)

"her individuality was **thwarted** [prevented from developing]" (paragraph 57)

"I have seen the long-term emotional and spiritual **desolation** [despair]" (paragraph 58)

Thomas Lickona

The Neglected Heart*

You didn't get pregnant. You didn't get AIDS. So why do you feel so bad?

—LESLEE UNRUH, ABSTINENCE EDUCATOR

There is no condom for the heart.

—SIGN AT A SEX EDUCATION CONFERENCE

In discussions of teen sex, much is said about the dangers of pregnancy and disease—but far less about the emotional hazards. And that's a problem, because the destructive psychological consequences of temporary sexual relationships are very real. Being aware of them can help a young person make and stick to the decision to avoid premature sexual involvement.

That's not to say we should downplay the physical dangers of uncommitted sex. Pregnancy is a life-changing event. Sexually transmitted disease (STD)—and there are now more than 20 STDs—

1

2

*Thomas Lickona, "The Neglected Heart." *American Educator* (Summer 1994), pp. 34–39.

can rob you of your health and even your life. Condoms don't remove these dangers. Condoms have an annual failure rate of 10 percent to 30 percent in preventing pregnancy because of human error in using them and because they sometimes leak, break, or slip off. Condoms reduce but by no means eliminate the risk of AIDS. In a 1993 analysis of 11 different medical studies, condoms were found to have a 31 percent average failure rate in preventing the sexual transmission of the AIDS virus.[1] Finally, condoms do little or nothing to protect against the two STDs infecting at least one-third of sexually active teenage girls: human papilloma virus (the leading cause of cervical cancer) and chlamydia (the leading cause of infertility), both of which can be transmitted by skin-to-skin contact in the entire genital area, only a small part of which is covered by the condom.[2]

3   Why is it so much harder to discuss sex and emotional hurt—to name and talk about the damaging psychological effects that can come from premature sexual involvement? For one thing, most of us have never heard this aspect of sex discussed. Our parents didn't talk to us about it. The media don't talk about it. And the heated debate about condoms in schools typically doesn't say much about the fact that condoms do nothing to make sex *emotionally* safe. When it comes to trying to explain to their children or students how early sexuality can do harm to one's personality and character as well as to one's health, many adults are simply at a loss for words, or reduced to vague generalities such as, "you're too young" or "you're not ready" or "you're not mature enough."

4   This relative silence about the emotional side of sex is ironic, because the emotional dimension of sex is what makes it distinctively human.

5   What in fact are the emotional or psychological consequences of premature, uncommitted sex? These consequences vary among individuals. Some emotional consequences are short-term but still serious. Some of them last a long time, sometimes even into marriage and parenting. Many of these psychological consequences are hard to imagine until they've been experienced. In all cases, the emotional consequences of sexual experiences are not to be taken lightly. A moment's reflection reminds us that emotional problems can have damaging, even crippling, effects on a person's ability to lead a happy and productive life.

6   Let's look at 10 negative psychological consequences of premature sexual involvement.

1. Worry about Pregnancy and AIDS

For many sexually active young people, the fear of becoming pregnant or getting AIDS is a major emotional stress. **7**

Russell Henke, health education coordinator in the Montgomery County (Maryland) Public Schools, says, "I see kids going to the nurses in schools, crying a day after their first sexual experience, and wanting to be tested for AIDS. They have done it, and now they are terrified. For some of them, that's enough. They say, 'I don't want to have to go through that experience anymore.'"[3] **8**

A high school girl told a nurse: "I see some of my friends buying home pregnancy tests, and they are so worried and so distracted every month, afraid that they might be pregnant. It's a relief to me to be a virgin." **9**

2. Regret and Self-Recrimination

Girls, especially, need to know in advance the sharp regret that so many young women feel after becoming sexually involved. **10**

Says one high school girl: "I get upset when I see my friends losing their virginity to some guy they've just met. Later, after the guy's dumped them, they come to me and say, 'I wish I hadn't done it.'"[4] A ninth-grade girl who slept with eight boys in junior high says, "I'm young, but I feel old." **11**

Girls are more vulnerable than boys because girls are more likely to think of sex a way to "show you care." They're more likely to see sex as a sign of commitment in the relationship. **12**

If a girl expects a sexual interlude to be loving, she may very well feel cheated and used when the boy doesn't show a greater romantic interest after the event. As one 15-year-old girl describes her experience: "I didn't expect the guy to marry me, but I never expected him to avoid me in school." **13**

Bob Bartlett, who teaches a freshman sexuality class in a Richfield, Minn., high school, shares the following story of regret on the part of one of his students (we'll call her Sandy): **14**

> Sandy, a bright and pretty girl, asked to see Mr. Bartlett during her lunch period. She explained that she had never had a boyfriend, so she was excited when a senior asked her out.
>
> After they dated for several weeks, the boy asked her to have sex with him. She was reluctant; he was persistent.

She was afraid of appearing immature and losing him, so she consented.

"Did it work?" Mr. Bartlett asked gently. "Did you keep him?"

Sandy replied: "For another week. We had sex again, and then he dropped me. He said I wasn't good enough. There was no spark.

"I know what you're going to say. I take your class. I know now that he didn't really love me. I feel so stupid, so cheap."[5]

Sandy hoped, naively, that sex would keep the guy. Here is another   **15** high school girl, writing to an advice column about a different kind of regret. She wishes she *could* lose the guy she's involved with, but she feels trapped by their sexual relationship.

I am 16, a junior in high school, and like nearly all the other girls here, I have already lost my virginity. Although most people consider this subject very personal, I feel the need to share this part of my life with girls who are trying to decide whether to have sex for the first time.

Sex does not live up to the glowing reports and hype you see in the movies. It's no big deal. In fact, it's pretty disappointing.

I truly regret that my first time was with a guy that I didn't care that much about. I am still going out with him, which is getting to be a problem. I'd like to end this relationship and date others, but after being so intimate, it's awfully tough.

Since that first night, he expects sex on every date, like we are married or something. When I don't feel like it, we end up in an argument. It's like I owe it to him. I don't think this guy is in love with me, at least he's never said so. I know deep down that I am not in love with him either, and this makes me feel sort of cheap.

I realize now that this is a very big step in a girl's life. After you've done it, things are never the same. It changes everything.

My advice is, don't be in such a rush. It's a headache and a worry. (Could I be pregnant?) Sex is not for entertainment. It should be a commitment. Be smart and save your-

self for someone you wouldn't mind spending the rest of
your life with.

—Sorry I Didn't And Wish I Could Take It Back[6]

Regret over uncommitted sexual relationships can last for years. I   **16**
recently received a letter from a 33-year-old woman, now a psychiatrist, who is very much concerned about the sexual pressures and
temptations facing young people today. She wanted to share the
lessons she had learned about sex the hard way. After high school,
she says, she spent a year abroad as an exchange student:

> I was a virgin when I left, but I felt I was protected. I had
> gotten an IUD so I could make my own decisions if and
> when I wanted. I had steeled myself against commitment. I
> was never going to marry or have children; I was going to
> have a career. During that year abroad, from 17½ to 18½, I
> was very promiscuous.
>
> But the fact is, it cost me to be separated from myself.
> The longest-standing and deepest wound I gave myself was
> heartfelt. That sick, used feeling of having given a precious
> part of myself—my soul—to so many and for nothing, still
> aches. I never imagined I'd pay so dearly and for so long.

This woman is happily married now, she says, and has a good sex-   **17**
ual relationship with her husband. But she still carries the emotional
scar of those early sexual experiences. She wants young people to
know that "sex without commitment is very risky for the heart."

3. Guilt

Guilt is a special form of regret—a strong sense of having done   **18**
something morally wrong. Guilt is a normal and healthy moral response, a sign that one's conscience is working.

In his book for teenagers, *Love, Dating, and Sex*, George Eager tells   **19**
the story of a well-known speaker who was addressing a high school
assembly. The speaker was asked, "What do you most regret about
your high school days?"

He answered, "The thing I most regret about high school is the   **20**
time I singlehandedly destroyed a girl."

Eager offers this advice to young men: "When the breakup comes,   **21**
it's usually a lot tougher on the girls than it is on the guys. It's not

something you want on your conscience—that you caused a girl to have deep emotional problems."

One 16-year-old boy says he stopped having sex with girls when he saw and felt guilty about the pain he was causing: "You see them crying and confused. They say they love you, but you don't love them." **22**

Even in an age of sexual liberation, a lot of people who are having sex nevertheless have a guilty conscience about it. The guilt may come, as in the case of the young man just quoted, from seeing the hurt you've caused other people. **23**

The guilt may come from knowing that your parents would be upset if they knew you were having sex. Or it may stem from your religious convictions. Christianity, Judaism, and Islam, for example, all teach that sex is a gift from God reserved for marriage and that sexual relations outside marriage are morally wrong. **24**

Sometimes guilt about their sexual past ends up crippling people when they become parents by keeping them from advising their own children not to become sexually involved. According to counselor Dr. Carson Daly: "Because these parents can't bear to be considered hypocrites, or to consider themselves hypocrites, they don't give their children the sexual guidance they very much need."[8] **25**

4. Loss of Self-Respect and Self-Esteem

Many people suffer a loss of self-esteem when they find out they have a sexually transmitted disease. For example, according to the Austin, Texas–based Medical Institute for Sexual Health, more than 80 percent of people with herpes say they feel "less confident" and "less desirable sexually."[9] **26**

But even if a person is fortunate enough to escape sexually transmitted disease, temporary sexual relationships can lower the self-respect of both the user and the used. **27**

Sometimes casual sex lowers self-esteem, leading a person into further casual sex, which leads to further loss of self-esteem in an oppressive cycle from which it may be hard to break free. This pattern is described by a college senior, a young woman who works as a residence hall director: **28**

> There are girls in our dorm who have had multiple pregnancies and multiple abortions. They tend to be filled with self-loathing. But because they have so little self-esteem, they will settle for any kind of attention from guys. So they keep going back to the same kind of destructive situations

and relationships that got them into trouble in the first place.

On both sides of dehumanized sex, there is a loss of dignity and self-worth. One 20-year-old college male confides: "You feel pretty crummy when you get drunk at a party and have sex with some girl, and then the next morning you can't even remember who she was."   **29**

Another college student describes the loss of self-respect that fol- lowed his first sexual "conquest":   **30**

> I finally got a girl into bed—actually it was in a car— when I was 17. I thought it was the hottest thing there was, but then she started saying she loved me and getting clingy.
>
> I figured out that there had probably been a dozen guys before me who thought they had "conquered" her, but who were really just objects of her need for security. That real- ization took all the wind out of my sails. I couldn't respect someone who gave in as easily as she did.
>
> I was amazed to find that after four weeks of having sex as often as I wanted, I was tired of her. I didn't see any point in continuing the relationship. I finally dumped her, which made me feel even worse, because I could see that she was hurting. I felt pretty low.[10]

People aren't things. When we treat them as if they were, we not only hurt them; we lose respect for ourselves.   **31**

5. The Corruption of Character and the Debasement of Sex

When people treat others as sexual objects and exploit them for their own pleasure, they not only lose self-respect; they corrupt their characters and debase their sexuality in the process.   **32**

Good character consists of virtues such as respect, responsibility, honesty, fairness, caring, and self-control. With regard to sex, the character trait of self-control is particularly crucial. The break- down of sexual self-control is a big factor in many of the sex-re- lated problems that plague our society: rape, promiscuity, pornogra- phy, addiction to sex, sexual harassment, the sexual abuse of children, sexual infidelity in marriage, and the serious damage to families many of these problems cause. It was Freud who said—and it is now obvious how right he was—that sexual self-control is es- sential for civilization.   **33**

Sex frequently corrupts character by leading people to tell lies in order to get sex. The Medical Institute for Sexual Health reports: "Almost all studies show that many sexually active people will lie if they think it will help them have sex."[11] Common lies: "I love you" and "I've never had a sexually transmitted disease."   **34**

Because sex is powerful, once sexual restraint is set aside, it easily takes over individuals and relationships. Consider the highly sexualized atmosphere that now characterizes many high schools. A high school teacher in Indiana says, "The air is thick with sex talk. Kids in the halls will say—boy to girl, girl to boy—'I want to f— you.'"   **35**

In a 1993 study by the American Association of University Women, four of five high school students—85 percent of girls and 75 percent of boys—said they have experienced "unwelcome sexual behavior that interferes with my life" in school.[12] An example: A boy backs a 14-year-old girl up against her locker, day after day. Says Nan Stein, a Wellesley College researcher: "There's a Tailhook happening in every school. Egregious behavior is going on."   **36**

Another recently reported example of this corruption of character is the Spur Posse club at Lakewood High School in suburban Los Angeles. Members of this club competed to see how many girls they could sleep with; one claimed he had slept with 63. Sadly, elementary school-age children are beginning to mimick such behavior. In a suburb of Pittsburgh, an assistant superintendent reports that sixth-grade boys were found playing a sexual contact game; the object of the game was to earn points by touching girls in private parts, the most points being awarded for "going all the way."   **37**

In this sex-out-of-control environment, even rape is judged permissible by many young people. In a 1988 survey of students in grades six through nine, the Rhode Island Rape Crisis Center found that two of three boys and 49 percent of the girls said it was "acceptable for a man to force sex on a woman if they have been dating for six months or more."[13] In view of attitudes like these, it's easy to understand why date rape has become such a widespread problem.   **38**

In short, sex that isn't tied to love and commitment undermines character by subverting self-control, respect, and responsibility. Unchecked, sexual desires and impulses easily run amok and lead to habits of hedonism and using others for one's personal pleasure. In the process, sexual intercourse loses its meaning, beauty, and specialness; instead of being a loving, uniquely intimate expression of two people's commitment to each other, sex is trivialized and degraded.   **39**

6. Shaken Trust and Fear of Commitment

Young people who feel used or betrayed after the break-up of a sexual relationship may experience difficulty in future relationships. **40**

Some sexually exploited people, as we've seen, develop such low self-esteem that they seek any kind of attention, even if it's another short-lived and demeaning sexual relationship. But other people, once burned, withdraw. They have trouble trusting; they don't want to get burned again. **41**

Usually, this happens to the girl. She begins to see guys as interested in just one thing: Sex. Says one young woman: "Besides feeling cheap [after several sexual relationships], I began to wonder if there would ever be anyone who would love and accept me without demanding that I do something with my body to earn that love."[14] **42**

However, boys can also experience loss of trust and fear of commitment as a result of a broken relationship that involved sex. Brian, a college senior, tells how this happened to him: **43**

> I first had intercourse with my girlfriend when we were 15. I'd been going with her for almost a year, and I loved her very much. She was friendly, outgoing, charismatic. We'd done everything but have intercourse, and then one night she asked if we could go all the way.
>
> A few days later, we broke up. It was the most painful time of my life. I had opened myself up to her more than I had to anybody, even my parents.
>
> I was depressed, moody, nervous. My friends dropped me because I was so bummed out. I felt like a failure. I dropped out of sports. My grades weren't terrific.
>
> I didn't go out again until I got to college. I've had mostly one-night stands in the last couple of years.
>
> I'm afraid of falling in love.[15]

7. Rage Over Betrayal

Sometimes the emotional reaction to being "dumped" isn't just a lack of trust or fear of commitment. It's rage. **44**

Every so often, the media carry a story about a person who had this rage reaction and then committed an act of violence against the former boyfriend or girlfriend. Read these accounts, and you'll find that sex was almost always a part of the broken relationship. **45**

Of course, people often feel angry when somebody breaks up with **46** them, even if sex has not been involved. But the sense of betrayal is usually much greater if sex has been part of the relationship. Sex can be emotional dynamite. It can lead a person to think that the relationship is really serious, that both people really love each other. It can create a very strong emotional bond that hurts terribly when it's ruptured—especially if it seems that the other person never had the same commitment. And the resulting sense of betrayal can give rise to rage, even violence.

8. Depression and Suicide

In *Sex and the Teenager*, Kieran Sawyer writes: "The more the relationship seems like real love, the more the young person is likely to invest, and the deeper the pain and hurt if the relationship breaks up."[16] Sometimes the emotional turmoil caused by the rupture of a sexual relationship leads to deep depression. The depression, in turn, may lead some people to take their own lives.   **47**

In the past 25 years, teen suicide has tripled. In a 1988 survey by the U.S. Department of Health and Human Services, one in five adolescent girls said they have tried to kill themselves (the figure for boys was one in 10).   **48**

This is the same period during which the rate of teenage sexual activity has sharply increased, especially for girls. No doubt, the rise in youth suicide has multiple causes, but given what we know about the emotional aftermath of broken sexual relationships, it is reasonable to suspect that the pain from such break-ups is a factor in the suicide deaths of some young people.   **49**

9. Ruined Relationships

Sex can have another kind of emotional consequence: It can turn a good relationship bad. Other dimensions of the relationship stop developing. Pretty soon, negative emotions enter the picture. Eventually, they poison the relationship, and what had been a caring relationship comes to a bitter end.   **50**

One young woman shares her story, which illustrates the process: **51**

> With each date, my boyfriend's requests for sex became more convincing. After all, we did love each other. Within two months, I gave in, because I had justified the whole thing. Over the next six months, sex became the center of our relationship. . . .

At the same time, some new things entered our relationship—things like anger, impatience, jealousy, and selfishness. We just couldn't talk anymore. We grew very bored with each other. I desperately wanted a change.[17]

A young man who identified himself as a 22-year-old virgin echoes this warning about the damage premature sex can do to a relationship: **52**

I've seen too many of my friends break up after their relationships turned physical. The emotional wreckage is horrendous because they have already shared something so powerful. When you use sex too early, it will block other means of communicating love and can stunt the balanced growth of a relationship.[18]

10. Stunting Personal Development

Premature sexual involvement not only can stunt the development of a relationship; it also can stunt one's development as a person.   **53**

Just as some young people handle anxieties by turning to drugs and alcohol, others handle them by turning to sex. Sex becomes an escape. They aren't learning how to cope with life's pressures.   **54**

Teenagers who are absorbed in an intense sexual relationship are turning inward on one thing at the very time in their lives when they should be reaching out—forming new friendships, joining clubs and teams, developing their interests and skills, taking on bigger social responsibilities.   **55**

All of these are important nutrients for a teenager's development as a person. And this period of life is special because young people have both the time and the opportunities to develop their talents and interests. The growing they do during these years will affect them all their lives. If young people don't put these years to good use, they may never develop their full potential.   **56**

The risk appears to be greater for girls who get sexually involved and in so doing close the door on other interests and relationships. Says New York psychiatrist Samuel Kaufman: **57**

A girl who enters into a serious relationship with a boy very early in life may find out later that her individuality was thwarted. She became part of him and failed to develop her own interests, her sense of independent identity.[19]

Reflecting on her long experience in counseling college students   **58**
and others about sexual matters, Dr. Carson Daly comments:

> I don't think I ever met a student who was sorry he or
> she had postponed sexual activity, but I certainly met many
> who deeply regretted their sexual involvements. Time and
> time again, I have seen the long-term emotional and spiri-
> tual desolation that results from casual sex and promiscuity.
>   No one tells students that it sometimes takes years to re-
> cover from the effects of these sexual involvements—if
> one every fully recovers.

Sex certainly can be a source of great pleasure and joy. But as   **59**
should be amply clear—and youngsters need our help and guidance
in understanding this—sex also can be the source of deep wounds
and suffering. What makes the difference is the relationship within
which it occurs. Sex is most joyful and fulfilling—most emotionally
safe as well as physically safe—when it occurs within a loving, total,
and binding commitment. Historically, we have called that marriage.
Sexual union is then part of something bigger—the union of two
persons' lives.

References

[1]Susan Weller, "A Meta-Analysis of Condom Effectiveness in Reducing Sexually Transmitted HIV," *Social Science and Medicine*, June 1993, p. 12.

[2]See, for example, Kenneth Noller, *OB/GYN Clinical Alert-t*, September 1992; for a thorough dis-cussion of the dangers of human papilloma virus, see "Condoms Ineffective Against Human Papil-loma Virus," *Sexual Health Update* (April 1994), a publication of the Medical Institute for Sexual Health, P.O. Box 4919, Austin, TX 78765.

[3]"Some Teens Taking Vows of Virginity," *Washington Post* (November 21, 1993).

[4]William Bennett, "Sex and the Education of Our Children," *America* (February 14, 1987), p. 124.

[5]Bob Bartlett, "Going All the Way," *Momentum* (April/May, 1993), p. 36.

[6]Abridged from Ann Landers, "A Not-So-Sweet Sixteen Story," *Daily News* (September 23, 1991), p. 20.

[7]Eager's book is available from Mailbox Club Books, 404 Eager Rd., Valdosta, GA 31602.

[8]Carson Daly, personal communication.

[9]*Safe Sex: A Slide Program*. Medical Institute for Sexual Health, Austin, TX: 1992.

[10]Josh McDowell and Dick Day, *Why Wait: What You Need to Know About the Teen Sexuality Crisis* (Here's Life Publishers, San Bernardino, CA: 1987).

[11]Medical Institute for Sexual Health, P.O. Box 4919, Austin, TX 78765.

[12]*American Association of University Women Report on Sexual Harassment*, June 1993.

[13]J. Kikuchi, "Rhode Island Develops Successful Intervention Program for Adolescents," *National Coalition Against Sexual Assault Newsletter* (Fall 1988).

[14]McDowell and Day

[15]Abridged from *Choosing the Best: A Values-Based Sex Education Curriculum*, 1993. (5500 Interstate North Parkway, Suite 515, Atlanta, GA 30328).

[16]Kieran Sawyer, *Sex and the Teenager* (Ave Maria Press, Notre Dame, IN: 1990).

[17]McDowell and Day

[18]Ann Landers, "Despite Urgin', He's a Virgin." *Daily News* (January 15, 1994).

[19]Quoted in Howard and Martha Lewis, *The Parent's Guide to Teenage Sex and Pregnancy* (New York: St. Martin's Press, 1980).

QUESTIONS FOR CRITICAL THINKING

THINKING CRITICALLY ABOUT CONTENT

1. Why do you think the writer presents the negative consequences of premature sexual involvement by numbering them 1 through 10 and giving each consequence a heading instead of presenting them in paragraph form? What effect does this strategy have in the essay?

2. Why do you think the writer includes so many quotes from teenagers about their sexual experiences?

THINKING CRITICALLY ABOUT PURPOSE

3. What do you think Thomas Lickona's purpose is in this essay?

4. Do you think the author is trying to persuade young couples not to have sexual relations before marriage? If not, what is he recommending?

THINKING CRITICALLY ABOUT AUDIENCE

5. Although this essay was published in a magazine for teachers, do you think other groups of people could benefit from reading it? Explain your answer.

6. What effect do you think this essay will have on teenagers who have already had sexual relationships?

THINKING CRITICALLY ABOUT POINT OF VIEW

7. Describe in a complete sentence the writer's point of view.

8. This essay was written for teachers. If you were writing an essay about the same topic for students, how would it be different? How would it be the same? Rewrite the introduction and conclusion of this essay for a student audience.

Arguing a Position

Another type of persuading involves taking a pro position in support of an issue or a con position against an issue. The next section of this chapter contains two essays about an issue that has caused great debate in the United States: the death penalty, also known as capital punishment. In 1975, the Supreme Court lifted the ban against the death penalty, making it legal to execute convicted criminals in this country. However, each state determines, through its state legislature, whether or not to put criminals to death. Currently, the death penalty is legal in about two-thirds of the states.

The first essay, originally titled "Deserving to Die," takes a pro position, arguing in favor of capital punishment. Written by Robert Lee and published in 1990 in *The New American*, it claims that putting criminals to death is an effective way to punish murderers and to prevent violent crime. The second essay, originally titled "Instrument of Justice or Tool of Vengeance?" takes a con position, arguing against capital punishment. Written by Matthew Stephens and published in 1990 in *Christian Social Action*, it claims that the death penalty is applied more often when defendants are poor, mentally incompetent, or members of minority groups; that it is costly; and that it does not prevent violent crime. Both essays were adapted and reprinted in 1991 in the *Opposing Viewpoints* series on the death penalty.

Before You Read

Focusing Your Attention

Before you read these essays, take a few moments to respond to the following questions in your journal:

1. If you were asked to take a pro or con position on a topic of great importance to you or to society, what are some of the topics you would consider?
2. In the two essays that you will be reading, one writer supports the death penalty while the second opposes the death penalty. Before you read the essays, try to predict some of the arguments each author will make.

Expanding Your Vocabulary

Here are some words and their meanings that are important to your understanding of "The Death Penalty Is an Effective Punishment." You may want to review them before you begin to read.

"A key issue . . . is whether or not it is an effective **deterrent** [means of preventing an action] to violent crime." (paragraph 1)

"It simply cannot be **contested** [challenged]" (paragraph 1)

"**Abolitionists** [those who want to get rid of the death penalty] claim . . . that the death penalty does not deter." (paragraph 1)

"But the states . . . have used it so little over the years as to **preclude** [prevent from happening] any meaningful comparison" (paragraph 1)

"the death penalty has been largely turned into a **paper tiger** [something that looks powerful but is not]" (paragraph 1)

"To **allege** [claim]" (paragraph 2)

"warning signs are **futile relics** [useless reminders from the past] of an age gone by" (paragraph 2)

"the death penalty could never become a 100-percent deterrent to **heinous** [horrible] crime" (paragraph 2)

"other **variables** [factors to be considered] . . . could have influenced the result" (paragraph 6)

"once deterrence **supersedes** [comes before, becomes more important than] justice . . . guilt or innocence . . . becomes largely irrelevant" (paragraph 7)

"The **exorbitant** [outrageously high] financial expense . . . is regularly cited by abolitionists" (paragraph 8)

"**interminable** [never-ending] legal maneuvers . . . run up the costs" (paragraph 8)

"**understating** [underreporting] the expense" (paragraph 9)

"the cost is primarily due to **redundant** [repetitive] appeals, . . . **bizarre** [weird] rulings, and legal **histrionics** [overacting]" (paragraph 10)

"described as 'last-minute **ingenuity**' [cleverness]" (paragraph 11)

"the execution was **stayed** [halted]" (paragraph 11)

"a petition alleging **sundry** [various] grounds for a **writ of** *habeas corpus* [legal decree stating that a prisoner must be brought to court to decide if his or her imprisonment is legal]" (paragraph 12)

"abolitionists argue that parole is **imperative** [essential]" (paragraph 15)

"Obviously, this is a **breach** [break] of security." (paragraph 18)

"a **disproportionate** [too large] share of executions" (paragraph 20)

"The most **flagrant** [outrageous] example of discrimination" (paragraph 21)

"One state governor **commuted** [changed] the death sentence of a woman" (paragraph 21)

"the **inexorable** [unchangeable] law . . ." (paragraph 21)

"society expresses its **denunciation** [strong disapproval] of wrongdoing" (paragraph 23)

"the **revulsion** [disgust, strong dislike] felt by a great majority of citizens" (paragraph 23)

"there are sown the seeds of **anarchy** [loss of order, chaos] of self-help, **vigilante justice** [illegal punishment by unauthorized volunteers], and lynch law" (paragraph 23)

Robert W. Lee

The Death Penalty Is an Effective Punishment*

A key issue in the debate over capital punishment is whether or not it is an effective deterrent to violent crime. In at least one important respect, it unquestionably is: It simply cannot be contested that a killer, once executed, is forever deterred from killing again. The deterrent effect on others, however, depends largely on how swiftly and surely the penalty is applied. Since capital punishment has not been used with any consistency over the years, it is virtually impossible to evaluate its deterrent effect accurately. Abolitionists claim that a lack of significant difference between the murder rates for states with and without capital punishment proves that the death penalty does not deter. But the states with the death penalty on their books have used it so little over the years as to preclude any meaningful comparison between states. Through July 18, 1990, there had been 134 executions since 1976. Only 14 states (less than 40 percent of those that authorize the death penalty) were involved. Any punishment, including death, will cease to be an effective deterrent if it is recognized as mostly bluff. Due to costly delays and endless appeals, the death penalty has been largely turned into a paper tiger by the same crowd that calls for its abolition on the grounds that it is not an effective deterrent!

1

People Fear Death

To allege that capital punishment, if imposed consistently and without undue delay, would not be a deterrent to crime is, in essence, to say that people are not afraid of dying. If so, as columnist Jenkin Lloyd Jones once observed, then warning signs reading "Slow Down," "Bridge Out," and "Danger—40,000 Volts" are futile relics of an age gone by when men feared death. To be sure, the death penalty could never become a 100-percent deterrent to heinous crime, because the fear of death varies among individuals. Some race automobiles, climb

2

---

*Robert W. Lee, "Deserving to Die." *The New American* (Aug. 13, 1990), pp. 21–28.

mountains, parachute jump, walk circus highwires, ride Brahma bulls in rodeos, and otherwise engage in endeavors that are more than normally hazardous. But, as author Bernard Cohen notes in his book *Law and Order,* "there are even more people who refrain from participating in these activities mainly because risking their lives is not to their taste."

Merit System

On occasion, circumstances *have* led to meaningful statistical evaluations of the death penalty's deterrent effect. In Utah, for instance, there have been three executions since the Supreme Court's 1976 ruling: **3**

- Gary Gilmore faced a firing squad at the Utah State Prison on   **4**
  January 17, 1977. There had been 55 murders in the Beehive State during 1976 (4.5 per 100,000 population). During 1977, in the wake of the Gilmore execution, there were 44 murders (3.5 per 100,000), a 20 percent decrease.

- More than a decade later, on August 28, 1987, Pierre Dale   **5**
  Selby (one of the two infamous "hi-fi killers" who in 1974 forced five persons in an Ogden hi-fi shop to drink liquid drain cleaner, kicked a ballpoint pen into the ear of one, then killed three) was executed. During all of 1987, there were 54 murders (3.2 per 100,000). The count for January through August was 38 (a monthly average of 4.75). For September-December (in the aftermath of the Selby execution) there were 16 (4.0 per month, a nearly 16 percent decrease). For July and August there were six and seven murders, respectively. In September (the first month following Selby's demise) there were three.

- Arthur Gary Bishop, who sodomized and killed a number of   **6**
  young boys, was executed on June 10, 1988. For all of 1988 there were 47 murders (2.7 per 100,000, the fewest since 1977). During January-June, there were 26; for July-December (after the Bishop execution) the tally was 21 (a 19 percent difference). In the wake of all three Utah executions, there have been notable decreases in both the number and the rate of murders within the state. To be sure, there are other variables that could have influenced the results, but the figures are there, and abolitionists to date have tended simply to ignore them.

Deterrence should never be considered the *primary* reason for administering the death penalty. It would be both immoral and unjust to punish one man merely as an example to others. The basic consideration should be: Is the punishment deserved? If not, it should not be administered regardless of what its deterrent impact might be. After all, once deterrence supersedes justice as the basis for a criminal sanction, the guilt or innocence of the accused becomes largely irrelevant. Deterrence can be achieved as effectively by executing an innocent person as a guilty one (something that communists and other totalitarians discovered long ago). If a punishment administered to one person deters someone else from committing a crime, fine. But that result should be viewed as a bonus of justice properly applied, not as a reason for the punishment. The decisive consideration should be: Has the accused *earned* the penalty?

7

The Cost of Execution

The exorbitant financial expense of death penalty cases is regularly cited by abolitionists as a reason for abolishing capital punishment altogether. They prefer to ignore, however, the extent to which they themselves are responsible for the interminable legal maneuvers that run up the costs.

8

A 1982 study by the abolitionist New York State Defenders Association — based on proposed (but never enacted) legislation to reinstate capital punishment in New York (Governor Mario Cuomo has vetoed death penalty legislation seven times in recent years) — speculated that a capital case involving only the first three levels of review (trial and penalty, appeal to the state Court of Appeals, and review by the U.S. Supreme Court) would cost $1.8 million per case, compared to the projected cost of imprisoning a felon for 40 years of $602,000. In another study, the *Miami Herald* calculated that it had cost Florida taxpayers $57.2 million to execute 18 men ($3.17 million each), whereas keeping a prisoner in jail for life (40 years) costs $515,996 ($12,899.91 per year). Abolitionists tend, we suspect, to exaggerate death-penalty costs while understating the expense of life imprisonment. According to the Justice Department, for instance, it costs around $20,000 a year to house a prisoner ($1 million over 40 years). Other sources peg it as high as $25,000.

9

As presently pursued, death-penalty prosecutions *are* outrageously expensive. But, again, the cost is primarily due to redundant appeals, time-consuming delays, bizarre court rulings, and legal histrionics by defense attorneys:

10

- Willie Darden, who had already survived three death warrants, **11**
  was scheduled to die in Florida's electric chair on September 4,
  1985 for a murder he had committed in 1973. Darden's lawyer
  made a last-minute emergency appeal to the Supreme Court,
  which voted against postponing the execution until a formal
  appeal could be filed. So the attorney (in what he later
  described as "last-minute ingenuity") then requested that the
  emergency appeal be technically transformed into a formal
  appeal. Four Justices agreed (enough to force the full court to
  review the appeal) and the execution was stayed. After
  additional years of delay and expense, Darden was eventually
  put out of our misery on March 15, 1988. . . .

- On April 2, 1974, William Neal Moore shot and killed a man in **12**
  Georgia. Following his arrest, he pleaded guilty to armed
  robbery and murder and was convicted and sentenced to death.
  On July 20, 1975, the Georgia Supreme Court denied his
  petition for review. On July 16, 1976, the U.S. Supreme Court
  denied his petition for review. On May 13, 1977, the Jefferson
  County Superior Court turned down a petition for a new
  sentencing hearing (the state Supreme Court affirmed the
  denial, and the U.S. Supreme Court again denied a review). On
  March 30, 1978, a Tattnall County Superior Court judge held a
  hearing on a petition alleging sundry grounds for a writ of *habeas
  corpus*, but declined on July 13, 1978, to issue a writ. On
  October 17, 1978, the state Supreme Court declined to review
  that ruling. Moore petitioned the U.S. District Court for
  Southern Georgia. After a delay of more than two years, a U.S.
  District Court judge granted the writ on April 29, 1981. After
  another two-year delay, the 11th U.S. Circuit Court of Appeals
  upheld the writ on June 23, 1983. On September 30, 1983, the
  Circuit Court reversed itself and ruled that the writ should be
  denied. On March 5, 1984, the Supreme Court rejected the case
  for the third time.

Moore's execution was set for May 24, 1984. On May 11, 1984, his **13**
attorneys filed a petition in Butts County Superior Court, but a writ
was denied. The same petition was filed in the U.S. District Court for
Georgia's Southern District on May 18th, but both a writ and a stay
of execution were denied. Then, on May 23rd (the day before the
scheduled execution), the 11th Circuit Court of Appeals granted a
stay. On June 4, 1984, a three-judge panel of the Circuit Court voted

to deny a writ. After another delay of more than three years, the Circuit Court voted 7 to 4 to override its three-judge panel and rule in Moore's favor. On April 18, 1988, the Supreme Court accepted the case. On April 17, 1989, it sent the case back to the 11th Circuit Court for review in light of new restrictions that the High Court had placed on *habeas corpus*. On September 28, 1989 the Circuit Court ruled 6 to 5 that Moore had abused the writ process. On December 18, 1989, Moore's attorneys again appealed to the Supreme Court.

Moore's case was described in detail in *Insight* magazine for February 12, 1990. By the end of 1989, his case had gone through 20 separate court reviews, involving some 118 state and federal judges. It had been to the Supreme Court and back four times. There had been a substantial turnover of his attorneys, creating an excuse for one team of lawyers to file a petition claiming that all of the prior attorneys had given ineffective representation. No wonder capital cases costs so much! . . .   **14**

Lifetime to Escape

Is life imprisonment an adequate substitute for the death penalty? Presently, according to the polls, approximately three-fourths of the American people favor capital punishment. But abolitionists try to discount that figure by claiming that support for the death penalty weakens when life imprisonment without the possibility of parole is offered as an alternative. (At other times, abolitionists argue that parole is imperative to give "lifers" some hope for the future and deter their violent acts in prison.)   **15**

Life imprisonment is a flawed alternative to the death penalty, if for no other reason than that so many "lifers" escape. Many innocent persons have died at the hands of men previously convicted and imprisoned for murder, supposedly for "life." The ways in which flaws in our justice system, combined with criminal ingenuity, have worked to allow "lifers" to escape include these recent examples: . . .   **16**

* Brothers Linwood and James Briley were executed in Virginia on October 12, 1984 and April 18, 1985, respectively. Linwood had murdered a disc jockey in 1979 during a crime spree. During the same spree, James raped and killed a woman (who was eight months pregnant) and killed her five-year-old son. On May 31, 1984, the Briley brothers organized and led an escape of five death-row inmates (the largest death-row breakout in U.S. history). They were at large for 19 days.   **17**

- On February 11, 1990, six convicts, including three murderers, escaped from their segregation cells in the maximum security Joliet Correctional Center in Illinois by cutting through bars on their cells, breaking a window, and crossing a fence. In what may be the understatement of the year, a prison spokesman told reporters: "Obviously, this is a breach of security." **18**

Clearly, life sentences do not adequately protect society, whereas the death penalty properly applied does so with certainty. **19**

Abolitionists often cite statistics indicating that capital punishment has been administered in a discriminatory manner, so that the poor, the black, the friendless, etc., have suffered a disproportionate share of executions. Even if true, such discrimination would not be a valid reason for abandoning the death penalty unless it could be shown that it was responsible for the execution of *innocent* persons (which it has not been, to date). Most attempts to pin the "discrimination" label on capital convictions are similar to one conducted at Stanford University a few years ago, which found that murderers of white people (whether white or black) are more likely to be punished with death than are killers of black people (whether white or black). But the study also concluded that blacks who murdered whites were somewhat *less* likely to receive death sentences than were whites who killed whites. . . . **20**

Flagrant Discrimination

The most flagrant example of discrimination in the administration of the death penalty does not involve race, income, or social status, but gender. Women commit around 13 percent of the murders in America, yet, from 1930 to June 30, 1990, only 33 of the 3991 executions (less than 1 percent) involved women. Only one of the 134 persons executed since 1976 (through July 18, 1990) has been a woman (Velma Barfield in North Carolina on November 2, 1984). One state governor commuted the death sentence of a woman because "humanity does not apply to women the inexorable law that it does to men." **21**

According to L. Kay Gillespie, professor of sociology at Weber State College in Utah, evidence indicates that women who cried during their trials had a better chance of getting away with murder and avoiding the death penalty. Perhaps the National Organization for Women can do something about this glaring example of sexist "inequality" and "injustice." In the meantime, we shall continue to support the death penalty despite the disproportionate number of **22** men who have been required to pay a just penalty for their heinous crimes. . . .

In 1953 the renowned British jurist Lord Alfred Denning asserted: **23** "Punishment is the way in which society expresses its denunciation of wrongdoing; and in order to maintain respect for law, it is essential that the punishment for grave crimes shall adequately reflect the revulsion felt by a great majority of citizens for them." Nineteen years later, U.S. Supreme Court Justice Potter Stewart noted (while nevertheless concurring in the Court's 1972 opinion that temporarily banned capital punishment) that the "instinct for retribution is part of the nature of man and channeling that instinct in the administration of criminal justice serves an important purpose in promoting the stability of a society governed by law. When people begin to believe that organized society is unwilling or unable to impose upon criminal offenders the punishment they 'deserve,' then there are sown the seeds of anarchy—of self-help, vigilante justice, and lynch law."

Protecting the Innocent

To protect the innocent and transfer the fear and burden of crime **24** to the criminal element where it belongs, we must demand that capital punishment be imposed when justified and expanded to cover terrible crimes in addition to murder.

Expanding Your Vocabulary

Here are some words and their meanings that are important to your understanding of "The Death Penalty Is Not an Effective Punishment." You might want to review them before you begin to read.

"it is a **ghastly** [terrible] and **irrevocable** [impossible to take back] error" (paragraph 1)

"When one looks at the **criteria** [guidelines] for selecting this **nominal** [very small] fraction" (paragraph 2)

"these populations **constitute** [make up] significant minorities" (paragraph 3)

"a society that **champions** [strongly supports] human rights" (paragraph 6)

"The prosecutor's opening remarks in the trial demonstrate the racial **implications** [issues] of this case" (paragraph 10)

"a man . . . whose **protestations** [protests] were **overshadowed** [made less visible] by the color of his victim and himself" (paragraph 12) "investigation of the crime was **tainted** [contaminated] from the start" (paragraph 14)

"the drive of society for **vengeance** [revenge or punishment for a wrong]" (paragraph 15)

"victims of this **catharsis** [release] of hate" (paragraph 15)

"legal representation of **indigent** [poor, with no means of support] defendants" (paragraph 16)

"Often, they failed . . . to raise **mitigating** [moderating, partially excusing] factors at the proper times." (paragraph 17)

"His trial lawyer was **disbarred** [ordered to stop practicing law]" (paragraph 18)

"**'arbitrary and capricious'** [not applied equally or fairly to all] application of capital punishment" (paragraph 23)

"The 'get tough' attitude . . . is **paradoxical** [confusing, contradictory]." (paragraph 32)

"Could it be that violence **begets** [causes to happen] violence?" (paragraph 32)

"**perpetuating** [encouraging, keeping] a system that is evil, barbaric, costly and ineffective" (paragraph 33)

Matthew L. Stephens

The Death Penalty Is Not an Effective Punishment*

When we look at capital punishment as an instrument of the administration of justice, we must ask 1) Is capital punishment evenly applied to all cases of murder? 2) Will those charged in a capital punishment case have both the best lawyers and defense available to them? 3) Is the cost of carrying out the death penalty worth the money spent to execute one person? and, 4) Is capital punishment a deterrent to murder? After all, the latter is ultimately the question

1

---

*Matthew L. Stephens, "Instrument of Justice or Tool of Vengeance?" *Christian Social Action* (Nov. 1990).

our society must answer. If it works, we must carry it out; if it doesn't, it is a ghastly and irrevocable error.

Applying the Death Penalty

In the United States, we experience the tragedy of over 20,000 homicides each year. These statistics are constantly increasing due to the devastating effects of drugs, racism, and poverty. Yet, we choose, as a society, only 200 (or 1 percent of all murderers), to receive the ultimate punishment of death. When one looks at the criteria for selecting this nominal fraction of all murderers, the real issues come to light. Who are these people? What is their economic and racial background? What are their legal resources and representation? What is their intellectual capacity? **2**

The facts are clear. Those on death row are the poorest of the poor. They are disproportionately "people of color": African American (40.7 percent), Hispanic (5.72 percent), Native American (1.49 percent) and Asian (0.61 percent), as compared to European/Caucasian. This means approximately 50 percent of all death row inmates are people of color in a society in which all of these populations constitute significant minorities. **3**

Additionally, it is estimated that over one-third of all death row inmates are mentally retarded (with IQs [intelligence quotient] of less than 70), and that nearly half are functionally illiterate. **4**

It is these poor and oppressed children of God who become the victims of our society's anger and need for revenge. The death penalty is clearly *not* equally applied under the law, or under the more significant mandate of moral, ethical, and spiritual values of a nation founded on these principles. **5**

In a society that champions human rights and individual dignity in all of our creeds, we are far behind the rest of the so-called "civilized" western world in showing compassion to the poor and oppressed of our country. There are only two countries that still engage the death penalty as justice: South Africa and the United States. In 1990 the South African government officially put a "hold" on death sentences and executions. **6**

There is overwhelming evidence that race is the single most important factor in choosing those who will be sentenced to death. Of the more than 3,000 people executed since 1930, nearly half were people of color. Eighty-five percent of those executed since 1977, when new death penalty statutes were passed, were punished for crimes against white victims. This is true despite the fact that the **7** homicide rate for people of color is roughly 50 percent higher than that of the majority community.

Take, for example, the state of Ohio where 342 people have been executed since 1884. Of this number, only one white man was executed for killing a black person. In 1989, there were 100 people on death row in Ohio: 51 black men, 45 white men and 4 black women. Ohio has not executed anyone since the state reinstituted the death penalty, but the first execution will probably take place soon. Keep in mind that the minimum age for death sentencing in Ohio is 18.   **8**

The Case of Willie Darden

Consider the historic case of Willie Jasper Darden, executed March 15, 1988 in Florida's electric chair. He was 54 years old. Willie Darden was sentenced to death for the murder of a furniture store owner in Lakeland, Florida. Darden proclaimed his innocence from the moment of his arrest until the moment of his execution, over 14 years later. Significant doubt of Darden's guilt remains.   **9**

Willie Darden was tried by an all-white jury in Inverness, Florida, a county with a history of racial segregation and oppression. The prosecutor's opening remarks in the trial demonstrate the racial implications of this case: **10**

> . . . The testimony is going to show, I think very shortly, when the trial starts, that the victims in this case were white. And of course, Mr. Darden, the defendant, is black. Can each of you tell me you can try Mr. Darden as if he was white?

Throughout the trial, the prosecutor characterized Darden as subhuman, saying such things as, "Willie Darden is an animal who should be placed on a leash." The U.S. Supreme Court sharply criticized this misconduct, but refused to find that it unfairly influenced the trial.   **11**

In the face of evidence that those who kill whites in Florida are nearly five times more likely to be sentenced to death than those who kill blacks, the prosecution of Willie Darden becomes the story of a man who may well have been innocent, but whose protestations were overshadowed by the color of his victim and himself.   **12**

Finally, consider the case of Delbert Tibbs who went from Chicago Theological Seminary to Florida's death row. Luckily, he did not "graduate" from either. Deciding to take some time off from his stud-   **13** ies, he hitchhiked across country. "White boys could drop out to 'find themselves,'" says Tibbs, "but nobody ever heard of a black man needing to do the same thing." His journey ended abruptly when, being in the wrong place at the wrong time, he was arrested and later convicted for the rape of a 16-year-old girl and the murder of her boyfriend in 1974. He was sentenced to death.

It was only with the assistance of the National Council of Churches Defense Fund attorneys that on appeal, his conviction was overturned on the grounds that it was not supported by the weight of the evidence. However, he was never said to be innocent of the crime. In spite of a U.S. Supreme Court decision that he could be retried, the state decided not to reopen the case on the grounds that the police investigation of the crime was tainted from the start. The original prosecutor said, "If there is a retrial, I will appear as a witness for Mr. Tibbs." Today, Delbert Tibbs devotes his life to his family and to anti-death penalty work across the nation and around the world.   **14**

Defending the Accused

It is more than clear that race is the single-most contributing factor to one being dealt the death penalty. In combination with poverty, lack of adequate legal representation, and the drive of society for vengeance, people of color are the common victims of this catharsis of hate and cycle of violence.   **15**

The quality of legal representation of indigent defendants in capital cases is of widespread concern. Most capital defendants cannot afford to pay for their own counsel and are represented by court-appointed lawyers in private practice, or by public defenders. Many times they are given inexperienced counsel, ill-equipped to handle such cases and working with severely limited resources. Many public defenders' offices are overextended with caseloads and cannot devote the time necessary to defend a capital case.   **16**

In rural areas, lawyers handling capital cases have little or no experience in criminal law; many are ignorant of the special issues relating to capital punishment. A recent study found that capital defendants in Texas with court-appointed lawyers were more than twice as likely to receive death sentences than those who retained counsel. The trial lawyers of a number of executed prisoners were found to have spent very little time preparing the case for trial. Often, they failed to interview potentially important witnesses or to raise mitigating factors at the proper times.   **17**

A good example of this problem is the case of John Young, a black man executed in Georgia. He was convicted in 1976 of murdering three elderly people while under the influence of drugs. He was 18 years old. His trial lawyer was disbarred from legal practice within days after the trial and left the state of Georgia. **18**

When the lawyer learned of the execution, he came forward and submitted an affidavit to the court in which he admitted spending hardly any time preparing for the case, due to personal problems. He admitted he did not investigate his client's background or raise any mitigating circumstances at the sentencing stage of the trial that might have influenced the jury's decision. These circumstances included the fact that at the age of three, John Young had seen his mother murdered while he was lying in bed with her. He later was placed with an alcoholic relative who turned him out on the street to survive at an early age. The U.S. District Court and the Court of Appeals ruled that they could not consider the lawyer's affidavit as new evidence because it should have been presented earlier. John Young died because of inadequate defense counsel. **19**

The Cost of Capital Punishment

Certainly there is the moral cost of taking a life, to make up for the taking of another life. There is no real way to replace one life with the death of another. Yet when capital punishment is the choice of the courts, this is exactly what has been decided. **20**

The moral issue here is: Do we have the right to kill, or is that the right of God only? This does not excuse one who takes the life of another. That is clearly wrong. They will have to answer to the vengeance of their God. We do have the right to demand restitution and protection in the form of taking away the freedom of that individual found guilty of taking a life. **21**

Taking freedom from individuals who kill others has also been shown to be less costly than executing them through our court system. The current debate on side-stepping a lengthy appeal process is nothing more than a rationale to expedite the death sentence while saving money. **22**

In 1972, the Supreme Court of the United States, in *Furman vs. Georgia* held that "arbitrary and capricious" application of capital punishment violated the Eighth Amendment prohibition against cruel and unusual punishment. This means that a defendant has to be prosecuted and convicted in a way that is extraordinarily righteous and free of any kind of prejudice. **23**

This "super" due process requirement has made the prosecutions of **24** capital cases enormously expensive. In a University of California at Davis Law Review article, Margaret Garey calculated that it costs a minimum of $500,000 to complete a capital case in California. It costs approximately $30,000 per year to house an inmate in the California system.

Between August of 1977 and December of 1985, only 10 percent **25** (190 of 1,847 cases) resulted in the death sentence. Data from New York State suggests that if it adopted capital punishment, the cost would be $1,828,000 per capital trial. Assuming even a 0.75 percent failure rate, it would cost about $7.3 million to sentence one person to death in New York, compared with $4.5 million ($500,000 × 0.90 percent failure rate) to sentence one person to death in California.

Cost effectiveness is a weak argument when talking about the **26** value of human life. However, even when put on such a shallow rationale as cost-analysis, the death penalty does not hold up.

It has cost the state of Florida $57 million to execute 18 men. It is **27** estimated that this is six times the cost of life imprisonment. A report from the *Miami Herald* said that keeping a prisoner in jail for life would cost the state $515,964 based on a 40-year life span in prison. It would cost $3.17 million for each execution. The newspaper broke the cost of execution down to show $36,000 to $116,700 for trial and sentencing; $69,480 to $160,000 for mandatory state review, which is not required in non-capital trials; $274,820 to $1 million for additional appeals; $37,600 to $312,000 for jail costs, and $845,000 for the actual execution.

These figures should make us ask ourselves: Is the need for our **28** vengeance worth all this money when the possibility that we still convict and execute the wrong person exists? What really guides our conscience — the money or the moral issue of state murder and street murder? Whatever side moves us, we must see that the cost of capital punishment is too high.

A Deterrent to Murder?

Since capital punishment has been reinstated as a legal sentence of **29** the law, there is no proof that shows murder has declined in any of the states in which it is being used. In fact, some states show an increase in violent crimes.

People who favor the death penalty often believe it helps reduce **30** the number of violent crimes. This may be true if the person who considers homicide would make a rational decision in anticipation of the consequences. This rarely happens because most homicides happen in the "heat of passion," anger, and under the influence of drugs or alcohol.

Studies show that murder rates in states with capital punishment, such as Illinois, differ little from the states that do not have capital punishment, such as Michigan. In 1975, the year before Canada abolished the death penalty, the homicide rate was 3.09 per 100,000 persons. In 1986, that rate was down to 2.19 per 100,000 persons, the lowest in 15 years. In some states, the use of capital punishment increased the crime rate. In New York, between 1903 and 1963, executions were followed by a slight rise in the state's homicide rate.   **31**

A Need for Revenge

The recent cry for the death penalty in our country comes more from the need for revenge than for justice. The "get tough" attitude of the law enforcement community and our "kinder and gentler" government telling the nation that killing offenders will stop the rise of violence, is paradoxical. Could it be that violence begets violence? Could it be that as long as the state is killing, we are sending a message that killing is the way to solve problems?   **32**

With all of the various factors we have considered, it is clear, even to the casual observer, that the death penalty does not work. It cannot be taken back, and it is arbitrary in its application and racist in its result. People of faith must take a stand. We must choose the day when we will transform instead of kill, when we will "do justice and love mercy and walk humbly with our God" instead of perpetuating a system that is evil, barbaric, costly, and ineffective.   **33**

 ## QUESTIONS FOR CRITICAL THINKING

THINKING CRITICALLY ABOUT CONTENT

1. Make a list of the reasons, evidence, and statistics each writer uses to convince the reader of his argument's worth. Then explain about how both writers often use the same material in different ways to argue for their positions.

2. Which essay contains the most convincing evidence? Why is it so convincing to you?

THINKING CRITICALLY ABOUT PURPOSE

1. With which essay did you agree? Did you agree with that position *before* you read the essays?

2. If you changed your mind as a result of reading one of the essays, what in the essay made you change your mind? What do you think Lee's and Stephens's purposes are in these essays?

THINKING CRITICALLY ABOUT AUDIENCE

1. What type of audience would be most interested in the subject of these two essays? Explain your answer.

2. Did the writers appeal to your emotions as they tried to persuade you to agree with their positions? If so, give specific examples.

THINKING CRITICALLY ABOUT POINT OF VIEW

1. State each writer's point of view in a single sentence.

2. On which points do the two writers agree? Explain your answer in a paragraph.

LEARNING FROM YOUR PEERS

American life is filled with opportunities to attempt to persuade others of your point of view. In classes, you may be asked to participate in debates or class discussions; you may also be asked to take a point of view or position in writing about an important social or historical issue. At home, you may want to write a letter to a public official or employer. As people living in a society that allows us to voice our opinions freely, many of us strive to learn how to express our disagreement in a polite and reasoned way.

No one is born with the skill to persuade another person to change his or her way of thinking; it is a skill we develop. It is possible, however, to develop the ability to express opinions clearly and rationally and to consider the opinions of others carefully. Learning how to persuade others effectively and respectfully is a valuable skill. To see how to develop this skill, we are going to follow the writing process of a student named Anthony Barone.

Anthony's Writing Assignment: Persuading

This is the topic Anthony's instructor assigned:

Present your position on a controversial topic that you are familiar with; take one side and argue why your side is the correct one.

Anthony goes through the process as outlined in Chapter 1: *thinking, planning, developing, organizing, drafting, revising,* and *editing.*

Thinking

At first, Anthony does not have any ideas for this assignment. He considers himself an easy-going person who rarely gets into arguments. Whenever his friends start expressing strong opinions, he just lets them talk. He stays out of political and religious discussions, and he keeps his opinions to himself. Later, he goes home and talks to his wife, Amanda, about the assignment. They both understand that Anthony is supposed to write about an issue rather than a personal experience in response to this assignment. Amanda shares his bewilderment and has no suggestions.

That evening, Anthony talks to his brother, Mario, on the telephone. Anthony is surprised to hear that Mario and his wife are planning to keep their oldest child out of kindergarten and educate him at home. Mario's wife, Linda, is a certified elementary school teacher, but she left her job when their first child was born.

After the phone conversation, Anthony is upset about Mario's decision. Anthony believes that some of his own most important personality traits were shaped by rivalries and experiences at school, and he feels that his nephew will miss some important growing-up experiences if he does not go to school.

Planning

As Anthony settles down to work on his writing assignment, he realizes that his discussion with Mario has brought up ideas that he can develop into an essay. Although he does not plan to share his opinion with his brother, he thinks that making his arguments clear for his classmates might provoke an interesting discussion.

Anthony starts freewriting about the topic of home schooling and spends half an hour sketching out his beliefs and memories. He realizes that many of his opinions are based on experiences he found valuable in elementary school, and he hopes that his nephew will have some of the same experiences.

Here is Anthony's freewriting:

There are certain things you just can't learn at home. The playground at school is where I learned to have fun, settle differences, play softball, flirt with girls. I remember having furious fights on the playground and then going back to class like nothing happened. In a nice cocoon at home, kids are safe, but they don't have a chance to learn from other kids. They won't learn that it is possible to return to the classroom and learn with others even if they were insulted five minutes before.

Public education is for all children. If one child is unsafe, then everyone is unsafe and people should get together and make all schools safer. Educated people who have the leisure time to teach their own children should take more responsibility for other children who are not lucky enough to come from homes where education and leisure are taken for granted. Volunteer to help the teachers--don't be so selfish.

Religion and bad language--often these are excuses for making children stay home. If you want your kids to turn into clones of yourself, fine. Not very many people can teach kids to follow their interests without running into dead ends--you can't know everything about everything. I think kids should learn about all the possibilities of life. Bad language can be explained. Religion is a good thing to learn, but you don't have to stay away from others who have different beliefs. Just my opinion.

Developing

Next, Anthony writes a list of his beliefs about school. These are the items on his list:

1. Home school is not good for children and it is not good for society.
2. Schools should not be dangerous.
3. Children learn about society in school.
4. If you have religious beliefs, you can get them across to your children when they are at home.
5. Knowledge should be freely given to all children; it shouldn't matter if their parents are teachers or not.
6. Children belong to all of us, and we should give them all the same opportunity for education.

Satisfied with his list, Anthony decides to freewrite on each of the six topics. He expands on the points he listed:

1. Home school is not good for children and it is not good for society. If we keep kids in a cocoon, they will never learn to solve disagreements or play ball. When I was a kid, I would have been bored to death if I'd had to stay home all the time.

2. Schools should not be dangerous. People have to get together and plan to make schools safe. Don't give up until the job is accomplished. If one child is unsafe, all children are in danger. Get rid of weapons and gangs. Make every place safe.

3. Children learn about society in school. Learning about society without being in society is artificial. You can't learn to be a friend unless you have friends.

4. If you have religious beliefs, you can get them across to your children when they are at home. Religion is important, but your children don't have to hear about it all day. They won't die from being exposed to other ideas. If you pray and read together, your children will learn what is important.

5. Knowledge should be freely given to all children; it shouldn't matter if their parents are teachers or not. If you are lucky enough to be educated by public schools and society, you should be responsible enough to give some of that back to society's children, not just your own.

6. Children belong to all of us, and we should give them all the same opportunity for education. We need to educate all children, whether their parents are educated or not.

After about an hour, Anthony asks Amanda to take a look at his freewriting. She reads it, and they discuss the topic for a while. He tells her that he does not want to start an argument with his brother, but he is interested in learning the opinions of others in his class.

Organizing

The next day, Anthony meets with his writing group. They tell him that his topic is interesting, and they ask him a few questions about things that he has not considered:

What is your main point?

What is the most important reason for children to go to school?

What happens to children who don't go to school?

After looking at his notes and these questions, Anthony decides that he is ready to organize his essay. He takes all his notes and spreads them out on his desk. Then he puts his material in order so he can write a draft.

Main point: Being educated at home is not in the best interest of children, and I do not think it should be allowed unless a kid is sick or lives too far from school to go home every day.

Responsibility of parents: They should pass their knowledge along to all children, not just to their own.

Danger is an important reason to keep your children at home, but if one child is unsafe, then all are unsafe, and the community should get together and make the world safe for children.

Children do not learn to work together by staying home. Children need to have arguments before they can learn to solve them. Children learn values by testing the consequences of their behavior. The fear of being exposed to bad language is not enough reason to keep a child at home. We can't protect children from all the bad stuff in the world. Kids will learn to say bad things--sometimes they don't even understand what they are saying.

Religion is to be lived, not preached over and over. Just make religion part of your life, and your kids will learn what they need to know.

Some parents know enough to teach their kids basic academic skills, but once the kids start to get interested in biology or something, those parents might be in trouble unless they just want their kids to be clones.

Conclusion--kids should be taught at school. If the parents know so much, they shouldn't just pass it on to their own children. They should pass it on to all children.

Drafting

Anthony goes to his study to write his essay. He wants to express himself clearly without getting upset, so he plays his guitar for a while before he starts writing. Once he feels that his head is clear and his body is relaxed, he starts writing, referring often to his previous freewriting and his lists. Here is the draft he writes.

Anthony's Essay: First Draft

Main Idea: "School Should be At School."

There is a growing movement of parents in this country who are choosing to educate their children at home. I believe that this is not in the best interests of children, and I do not think that state departments of education should allow children to be schooled at home unless there are medical or geographical reasons for doing so. Wanting to protect a child from the dangers at school is not reason enough to keep a child at home.

Parents who are qualified to teach their own children at home should volunteer at their child's school and pass their knowledge along to other children. If they have several hours a week to give, they should share their teaching skills and interests with other children. We have public education in this country to help the whole society. If one child is not getting enough attention in school, then all children probably need more attention. The solution is not to give all the attention to your own child and ignore everyone else's children.

Parents who school their children at home say that they do not want their children to be in danger. If that is true, they should work to make the schools safer for all children, not just their children. If there is violence in the schools, it is the responsibility of everyone in the comunity to join together and say, "We cannot tolerate this." If the school is dangerous, the hole community probably is dangerous.

It is a mistake to thing that if all people stay in their houses, isolated, that we will learn to live together. Childhood arguements help children learn to solve problems at an early age. If all people shared the same values and behavior patterns, we would have a boring society. I agree that it is real important to pass my values on to my children, but I do not think that any value is so perfect that it cannot be questioned. Children do not learn to test their values by liveing with their families, especially in authoritarion homes; they learn to test their values by arguing with the child on the playground who steals their ball or steps on their foot. Parents who want to teach their children survival skills should take them to the playground or a play group at an early age.

Some home school parents want their children at home so that they will not learn bad langauge from other children. This is unrealistic. No matter how much we protect children, they will learn unacceptable language sooner or later. It is the parents' responsibility to explain to the children what language is used in that home and what language is not acceptable. Often, children use words without knowing what they mean. It is no different than teaching your child the meaning of any other word.

Religuous reasons are sometimes used to explain why parents want to educate their children at home. I think that is simple. Just live your religion. Have morning prayer, mealtime prayer, family study time. Whatever your religious practices are, just make them a part of your every day life. Your children will learn these practices, and when they are old enough, they will decide weather to keep the practices of your faith going for another generation. Spiritual and religious values can be taught at home and at religious institutions. School is a place to learn about the other subjects neccesary to have a sucessful life.

Very few parents know enough about enough subjects to teach their children well. If a parent is an elementary school teacher all ready, that will help a child through elementary school. But what happens when the child reaches junior high? Does that parent know enough about biology and history and math to help that child in all subjects? This would be an unusual individual.

In conclusion, I believe that parents who know enough to educate their own children at home have an obligation to pass that knowlege along to others in their neighborhood. Other parents may have to work long hours or may not have the advantages of a college education. I believe that all children are society's children, and we should provide the best for all of them.

Revising

Anthony feels that he has written an important essay. He spent his time writing about something he truly believes—instead of just going through the motions to complete the assignment. Now his instructor wants the class to focus their revising on their thesis statements, introductions, and conclusions.

Anthony is excited about getting his essay into full working order, so he begins his revising process by reviewing the Checklist for Writing Titles and Introductions at the beginning of the Tips for Revising section in this chapter. He already knows how important titles and introductions are to an essay, and he sees how this checklist gives him some guidelines for improving these parts of his essay. As he rewrites parts of his introduction and changes some words in his thesis statement, he realizes that his essay needs more work than he originally thought. So he reads the Tips for Revising section and completes the exercises his instructor assigns.

Anthony goes back over his introduction and conclusion, thinking of each as a unit of communication in its own right and making sure each is as effective as possible. Then, he reads his essay as a whole to ensure that all of his paragraphs are related to his thesis statement and that they fit together smoothly and logically.

COLLABORATIVE WORK

PEER GROUP ACTIVITY

After you read the portions of the Tips for Revising your instructor assigns, turn to Anthony's first draft (pp. 359–361), and complete the following tasks in small groups:

A. Decide whether you think the title of the essay is appropriate and interesting. If you think it isn't, suggest some alternatives in the margin.

B. Underline the essay's thesis statement (for a definition, see p. 371). Does it capture the main idea of the essay?

C. Put in brackets the parts of Anthony's introduction that your group believes need to be more fully developed.

Compare the marks your group made with those your instructor will show you.

Where do your marks differ from your instructor's? What do you need to review before writing your own essay?

CLASS ACTIVITY

As an entire class, look at the underlined portions of Anthony's revised draft (pp. 363–365) to see what changes he made.

A.   Did you identify the **revision** problems that Anthony corrected?

B.   Do you think his changes are good ones? Discuss his changes.

Editing

Now that Anthony's title and introduction are revised, he needs to do some final proofreading and editing before handing in his essay. The instructor tells the students they need to understand the options they have to choose from in expressing themselves—they need more information on word choices and spelling. Anthony reads the Tips for Editing section in this chapter to learn about these options. After he finishes the exercises his instructor assigns, he goes over the questions in the Checklist for Correcting Diction and Spelling one by one and selects the most appropriate words so that his revised draft says what he wants it to.

COLLABORATIVE WORK

PEER GROUP ACTIVITY

After you read the portions of the Tips for Editing your instructor assigns, turn to Anthony's first draft (pp. 359–361), and complete the following tasks in small groups:

A.   Circle any problems with the following: incorrect level of language, technical language, and slang (for definitions, see pp. 376, 379, and 380).

B.   Put an X through any word usage problems (for definitions, see pp. 385–395).

C.   Underline any spelling errors.

Compare your marks with those your instructor will show you. Where do your marks differ from your instructor's? What do you need to review before writing your own essay?

Class Activity

As an entire class, look at the underlined portions of Anthony's revised draft (pp. 363–365) to see what changes he made.

A.   Did you identify the **diction and spelling** problems that Anthony corrected?

B.   Do you think his changes are good ones? Discuss his changes.

Anthony's Revised Essay

"School Should B~~be~~ a~~A~~t School"

> I love and respect my brother Mario more than anyone else I know, but I found myself almost shouting at him the other night. He was explaining to me that he and Linda had decided on educating my nephews at home because they believed my sister-in-law, a certified elementary teacher, would give her sons more attention than they would get in school. And they didn't want to expose them to the dangers at school or have them learn bad language. They have joined ~~There is~~ a growing movement of parents in this country who are choosing to educate their children at home. I believe that this is not in the best interests of children/ or society. ~~and I do not think that state departments of education should allow children to be schooled at home unless there are medical or geographical reasons for doing so. Wanting to protect a child from the dangers at school is not reason enough to keep a child at home.~~ Abandoning our public schools is not the best way to solve the problems, but if the people considering home schooling would give the same energy and time to our public schools, all our children and society would benefit.
>
> Parents who are qualified to teach their own children at home should volunteer at their child's school and pass their knowledge along to other children. If they have several hours a week to give, they should share their teaching skills and interests with other

children. We have public education in this country to help the whole society. If one child is not getting enough attention in school, then all children probably need more attention. The solution is not to give all the attention to your own child and ignore everyone else's children.

Parents who school their children at home say that they do not want their children to be in danger. If that is true, they should work to make the schools safer for all children, not just their children. If there is violence in the schools, it is the responsibility of everyone in the ~~comunity~~ community to join together and say, "We cannot tolerate this." If the school is dangerous, the ~~hole~~ whole community probably is dangerous.

It is a mistake to ~~thing~~ think that if all people stay in their houses, isolated, that we will learn to live together. Childhood ~~arguements~~ arguments help children learn to solve problems at an early age. If all people shared the same values and behavior patterns, we would have a boring society. I agree that it is really important to pass my values on to my children, but I do not think that any value is so perfect that it cannot be questioned. Children do not learn to test their values by ~~liveing~~ living with their families, especially in ~~authoritarion~~ authoritarian homes; they learn to test their values by arguing with the child on the playground who steals their ball or steps on their foot. Parents who want to teach their children survival skills should take them to the playground or a play group at an early age.

Some home school parents want their children at home so that they will not learn bad ~~langauge~~ language from other children. This is unrealistic. No matter how much we protect children, they will learn unacceptable language sooner or later. It is the parents' responsibility to explain to the children what language is used in that home and what language is not acceptable. Often, children use words without knowing what they mean. It is no different than teaching your child the meaning of any other word.

~~Religuous~~ Religious reasons are sometimes used to explain why parents want to educate their children at home. I think that is simple. Just live your religion. Have morning prayer, mealtime prayer, family study time. Whatever your religious practices are, just make them a part of your ~~every day~~ everyday life. Your children will learn these practices, and when they are old enough, they will decide ~~weather~~ whether to keep the practices of your faith going for another generation. Spiritual and religious values can be taught at home and at religious institutions. School is a place to learn about the other subjects ~~neccesary~~ necessary to have a ~~sucessful~~ successful life.

Very few parents know enough about enough subjects to teach their children well. If a parent is an elementary school teacher all ~~ready~~ already, that will help a child through elementary school. But what happens when the child reaches junior high? Does that parent know enough about biology and history and math to help that child in all subjects? This would be an unusual individual.

In conclusion, I believe that parents who know enough to educate their own children at home have an obligation to pass that ~~knowlege~~ knowledge along to others in their neighborhood. Other parents may have to work long hours or may not have the advantages of a college education. I believe that all children are society's children, and we should provide the best for all of them.

WRITING YOUR OWN PERSUADING ESSAY

So far, you have seen professional writers and a fellow student at work trying to persuade you to take some action or feel a certain way about an issue. As you read the published essays and followed the writing process of another student from first to final draft, you absorbed ideas and ways of giving those ideas a form of their own. These reading and writing activities have prepared you to write your own persuading essay on a topic that is meaningful to you.

What Have You Discovered?

Before you begin your own writing task, let's review what you have learned in this chapter so far:

- Persuading is one of the most common forms of communication.
- To persuade your readers, your evidence must be accurate, logical, and convincing.
- Evidence in the most important ingredient in a persuading essay.
- The ability to persuade through writing gives you the potential to change circumstances for the better, to right wrongs, and to help others.
- To present your persuasive essay effectively, you need to organize your ideas.
- To help you shape your essay, you should learn as much as possible about your readers.
- Before you write a draft, you need to decide on a point of view toward your subject.
- After you write a draft, you should revise your essay for meaning and organization.
- After you revise your essay, you should edit its grammar, usage, and sentence structure.

Your Writing Topic

Choose one of the following topics for your persuading essay:

1. In the professional essay that you read at the beginning of this chapter, titled "The Neglected Heart," the writer, Thomas Lickona, persuades his readers that many emotional problems can result from having sexual relations at a young age. Write an essay persuading your children (either real or fictitious) not to have sexual relations until they are old enough to understand the responsibility and consequences that come with having sexual relationships. You can use the material and information contained in Lickona's essay.

2. We all have features of our campus or community that we would like to see changed. Write an essay that attempts to persuade other students on your campus of the correctness of your viewpoint on a controversial campus issue. For example, if your campus has a thriving football program, argue that it should be abolished. Or, if your campus does not have a football program, argue that one should be established.

3. Write an essay persuading the leaders of an organization that your position on an important issue affecting the organization is the best one.

4. Create your own persuasive topic (with the assistance of your instructor), and write a response to it.

When you have selected one of these topics, you may begin your writing process in the same way Anthony did. (You may find that rereading his essay will be helpful in giving you ideas for your own essay.) This time your purpose is to write your own essay. If some tasks occur out of order, that adjustment is probably part of your personal writing ritual. Follow your instincts, and let them mold your own writing process. But make sure you've worked through all the stages to your final draft.

YOUR WRITING PROCESS

THINKING   Generate as many ideas on your subject as you can in as many different ways as possible: rereading, listing, freewriting, brainstorming, clustering, discussing, and questioning.

PLANNING   Begin to give your ideas shape by deciding on your approach to your topic (your content, your purpose, your audience, and your point of view). Make a list of points you want to include in your essay.

DEVELOPING   Add more details on three or four specific, focused topics that you have chosen from your list of general points.

ORGANIZING   Organize your material in a way that will be most interesting to your audience.

DRAFTING   Write a working draft of your essay in complete sentences.

REVISING   Consulting the Tips for Revising in this chapter (pp. 368–375), revise your first draft—paying special attention to making your title and introduction as effective as possible.

EDITING   Consulting the Tips for Editing in this chapter (pp. 376–402), edit your draft for grammar and correctness—paying special attention to your use of words.

Turn in your revised draft to your instructor.

Some Final Thoughts

When you have completed your own essay, answer these four questions in your journal:

1. What was most difficult about this assignment?
2. What was easiest?
3. What did I learn about persuading by completing this assignment?
4. What did I learn about my own writing process from this assignment—how I prepared to write, how I wrote the first draft, how I revised, and how I edited?

Writing Titles and Introductions

Checklist for Writing Titles and Introductions

✓ Is the **title** appropriate and interesting?
✓ Does the introduction capture the reader's **interest** and establish the **tone** of the essay?
✓ Does the **thesis statement** introduce the **main idea or purpose** of the essay and narrow the essay's **focus?**
✓ Does the thesis give an **overview** of the topics to be discussed in the essay?
✓ Does the introduction have only **one thesis statement?**

Experts who give advice to job seekers emphasize the importance of first impressions. They advise clients to dress appropriately and begin an interview with a firm handshake and a winning smile. Applicants should also take with them a concise, carefully written résumé stressing their accomplishments. In the same way, the introductions to your essays should give a great first impression to capture your readers' attention and explain your purpose in writing.

Titles

Much like your clothing when you go for a job interview, your title is the first thing about your essay a reader notices. **Titles** are phrases, usually no more than a few words, placed at the beginning of your essay that suggest or sum up the subject, purpose, or focus of the essay. The title we chose for this book, *Mosaics*, reflects the way we view the writing process—as many brightly colored individual pieces that work together to form a complete picture. Whereas this title represents our textbook's purpose—to help students create meaningful pictures with their great ideas—the title for this Tips for Revising section is a straightforward summary: "Writing Titles and Introductions." These are just two of many different kinds of possible titles.

Here is another series of examples. It it unlikely that Margaret Mitchell's *Gone with the Wind* would have been a best-seller and a wildly successful motion picture if she had called her novel *The Adventures of a Southern Belle in the War Between the States*, a descriptive title that lacks the emotional punch of the title she ultimately selected. On the other hand, a serious book recounting what happened to real people in the bloody conflict would require a more appropriate title, such as C. Vann Woodward's *The Burden of Southern History*. For his essay on the psychological risks connected with teen sex (pp. 325–337), Thomas Lickona chose a title that triggers the readers' interest: "The Neglected Heart." The title we chose for the essay by Robert Lee, "The Death Penalty Is an Effective Punishment" (pp. 340–346), states both the broad subject of his essay and his position on that subject. The title, like all the other parts of your essay, should fit your purpose.

If a good title doesn't occur to you before you start your first draft, you can always create your title last. Before Anthony Barone handed in his first draft, he thought of a title while he was talking with his wife. At first, he added a creative title: "Society's Children." But then he took his main idea, which he stumbled on during a phone conversation with his brother, and put it in quotation marks. It names the subject of his essay and sums up his positions.

When revising his essay, Anthony thought the title didn't look quite right, so he checked pages 302 in Chapter 7 Tips for Editing to review the rules for titles. He discovered that his own titles shouldn't be in quotation marks or underlined and should not be followed by a period or a comma. He also learned that all words in a title except conjunctions, articles, and prepositions should be capitalized. So Anthony revised his title. Note that he capitalized correctly and deleted the inappropriate punctuation.

Title: "School Should be At School."

Revision: School Should Be at School

Introductions

Like the smile and handshake you give to win over a prospective employer, your essay's **introduction** should capture your readers' interest, set the tone for your essay, and state your purpose. Introductions, especially those in persuasive essays, often have a funnel effect; they typically begin with general information, then narrow the focus to your position on an issue. To achieve this purpose, you may need to cite some facts or statistics, tell a story related to the issue, or ask some questions that the essay will answer. Regardless of your method, your introduction should "hook" your readers by grabbing their attention.

Corky Clifton offers a brief but gripping introduction to his essay "Life Sentences," which appears in Chapter 7.

> Why did I escape? I suppose it was for the same reason that men have fought wars and died for throughout history. I wanted to be free.

He captures the readers' attention with a question in the first sentence and then tries to answer it. The rest of his essay (pp. 262–264) deals with the question in much more detail.

Thomas Lickona begins his essay "The Neglected Heart" (pp. 325–337) in a straightforward fashion, setting a serious tone and identifying his purpose in the last sentence of his opening paragraph.

> In discussions of teen sex, much is said about the dangers of pregnancy and disease—but far less about the emotional hazards. And that's a problem, because the destructive psychological consequences of temporary sexual relationships are very real. Being aware of them can help a young person make and stick to the decision to avoid premature sexual involvement.

This is a provocative beginning to an essay about emotions and sex. This introduction makes its readers want to continue reading.

Matthew Stephens uses another attention-getting method in his essay on the death penalty (pp. 347–353). He composes a set of questions on capital punishment, then supplies the answers.

> When we look at capital punishment as an instrument of the administration of justice, we must ask 1) Is capital punishment evenly applied to all cases of murder? 2) Will those charged in a capital punishment case have both the best lawyers and defense available to them? 3) Is the cost of carrying out the death penalty worth the money spent to execute one person? and, 4) Is capital punishment a deterrent to murder? After all, the latter is ultimately the question our society must answer. If it works, we must carry it out; if it doesn't, it is a ghastly and irrevocable error.

Stephens has ensured that an audience interested in the issue of capital punishment will continue reading to find the answers to these questions.

As Anthony read back through his first draft, he decided that his introduction was too bland and that he had not supplied the background necessary for his audience. He needed to make his introduction livelier and more engrossing and, at the same time, he needed to supply additional necessary information.

First Draft: There is a growing movement of parents in this country who are choosing to educate their children at home. I believe that this is not in the best interests of children, and I do not think that state departments of education should allow children to be schooled at home unless there are medical or geographical reasons for doing so. Wanting to protect a child from the dangers at school is not reason enough to keep a child at home.

First Revision: **I love and respect my brother Mario more than anyone else I know, but I found myself almost shouting at him the other night. He was explaining to me that he and Linda had decided on educating my nephews at home because they believed my sister-in-law, a certified elementary teacher, would give her sons more attention than they would get in school. And they didn't want to expose them to the dangers at school or have them learn bad language. They have joined** ~~There is~~ a growing movement of parents in this

country who are choosing to educate their children at
home. I believe that this is not in the best interests of
children/ **or society.** ~~and I do not think that state
departments of education should allow children to be
schooled at home unless there are medical or geographical
reasons for doing so. Wanting to protect a child from the
dangers at school is not reason enough to keep a child at
home.~~

Now Anthony's introduction catches our interest because we will want to know why
he was angry with his brother. Reading to find out leads us to Anthony's position on
home schooling.

Thesis Statements

A good **thesis statement** furnishes the controlling idea for your essay, focusing and
directing its development. Your thesis statement should narrow a broad subject into
a topic that can be developed in 500 to 700 words. Your thesis statement is a sentence (or sentences), usually at the end of your introduction, that tells your audience
what the focus of your paper will be.

In the introduction to his essay "The Neglected Heart" (reprinted in the previous
section on page 369), Thomas Lickona narrows a broad subject—the hazards of
teenage sex—to a single aspect, emotional hazards. Lickona's opening paragraph follows the classic model of a persuading essay. First he introduces his subject, then he
limits it to a topic, and finally he states his position (that young people should avoid
premature sexual involvement). Although this method is not the only way to narrow a subject into a thesis and position in an introductory paragraph, Lickona uses it
effectively here.

In class discussion, Anthony's instructor points out several ways to develop a persuasive essay on a controversial topic. As a class exercise, Anthony and his classmates
brainstorm the broad subject of gun control. The first method Anthony's class uses is
to state a position and then back it up with logical reasons. Anthony's classmates decide that they need to narrow the broad subject of gun control to the main point they
want to make in their essays.

The most important factor in writing a thesis statement is the purpose you set
for writing the essay. So you should ask, "What is my purpose in writing this paper?" Anthony's classmates offer this purpose in the brainstorming session on gun
control:

Strong gun control laws are necessary in a country such as ours with an
increasing number of deaths from gunshot wounds.

The next step is to develop this statement of purpose in a way that will appeal to your audience. Ask yourself, "Who is my audience?" Anthony and his classmates decide that their audience will be people who are tempted to buy guns because they are afraid of crime. From facts provided by their instructor, they know that gun owners actually are in more danger from violent crimes because they have guns. So the students' next question addresses the concerns of this audience: "What sorts of reasons might convince our audience to agree with our position?" After answering these questions, the students devise a plan for an imaginary persuasive essay taking a stand in favor of gun control.

Reason 1.   Guns make owners less safe, not safer.

Reason 2.   Accidental shootings take thousands of innocent lives each year.

Reason 3.   Without easy access to firearms, so-called crimes of passion would be greatly reduced.

Reason 4.   Police reports show that many weapons used in armed robberies are stolen from the very people who bought them for protection.

Anthony's instructor suggests that a good way to begin is with an overview of the essay's contents.

As crime rates increase, people's reactions might be to purchase a weapon to protect themselves. If you are tempted to purchase a gun, you should know these facts: Guns make you less safe, increase the possibility of a tragic accident, and offer a ready source of weapons to criminals. Strong gun control laws are necessary in a country such as ours with an increasing number of deaths from gunshot wounds.

When he began writing his own persuading essay, Anthony studied his notes from class, but somehow this method didn't quite suit his subject, home schooling. His instructor had mentioned that another way of developing a persuasive essay is to seek a compromise on an issue. Anthony decided that because he is offering an alternative to home schooling, this was the best method for him to adopt.

As Anthony studied his first draft and the revised introduction to his essay, he decided that he still had not focused sharply on his position in his thesis statement. Anthony shuffled through his notes, read his list of topics again, and decided that the most important idea for his essay was that home schooling is not good for children or society. So Anthony added a clear statement of purpose to his revised introduction.

First Revision: I love and respect my brother Mario more than anyone else I know, but I found myself almost shouting at him the other night. He was explaining to me that he and Linda had decided on educating my nephews at home because they believed my sister-in-law, a certified elementary teacher, would give her sons more attention than they would get in school. And they didn't want to expose them to the dangers at school or have them learn bad language. They have joined ~~There is~~ a growing movement of parents in this country who are choosing to educate their children at home. I believe that this is not in the best interests of children/ or society, and I do not think that state departments of education should allow children to be schooled at home unless there are medical or geographical reasons for doing so. Wanting to protect a child from the dangers at school is not reason enough to keep a child at home.

Revision: I love and respect my brother Mario more than anyone else I know, but I found myself almost shouting at him the other night. He was explaining to me that he and Linda had decided on educating my nephews at home because they believed my sister-in-law, a certified elementary teacher, would give her sons more attention than they would get in school. And they didn't want to expose them to the dangers at school or have them learn bad language. They have joined a growing movement of parents in this country who are choosing to educate their children at home. I believe that this is not in the best interests of children/ or society/. ~~and I do not think that state departments of education should allow children to be schooled at home unless there are medical or geographical~~

~~reasons for doing so. Wanting to protect a child from the dangers at school is not reason enough to keep a child at home.~~ **Abandoning our public schools is not the best way to solve the problems, but if the people considering home schooling would give the same energy and time to our public schools, all our children and society would benefit.**

Anthony's revised thesis statement limits his topic and suggests the way he will develop the rest of his essay: by offering a compromise solution to problems in school with the intention of keeping children in the public school system.

Exercise R8-1

Read the introduction to "The Neglected Heart" (paragraphs 1–5) on pages 325–326. In what different ways does Lickona introduce his subject? What is the author's thesis?

Exercise R8-2

Read Anthony's revised introductory paragraph (p. 363). What other effective ways might he use to introduce his subject? Would more background material help his readers? Can you suggest an alternative thesis statement?

Exercise R8-3

Read the sentences below, and decide which ones cover broad subjects and which might serve as thesis statements. Rewrite each broad statement as a clear thesis statement, focusing on the questions about purpose and audience that Anthony's class used.

1. My school's core curriculum is unrealistic.
2. The best study methods that I know combine reading, note taking, and repetition.
3. I do not believe that we need gun control laws in this country.
4. High school athletics should be encouraged because they teach discipline, encourage competitiveness, and aid physical development.
5. Astronomy is the oldest of the sciences.
6. Skateboarding should be outlawed.
7. Today a new significance has been attached to word games by educators and psychologists.
8. Most people learn their sense of right and wrong.
9. Both high schools and prisons are institutions based on rules with built-in punishment for any sort of disobedience.
10. Environmentalists have done a heroic job trying to save our Earth from any more pollution, but some regulations that they have lobbied for go too far in restricting property owners' freedom.

Exercise R8-4

Read the statement below. Think of a way to narrow this broad subject into a topic suitable for an essay of 500 to 700 words. Then write a title and introduction with a clear thesis statement for this paper.

Universities need to be more sensitive to the needs of their students.

 ## COLLABORATIVE WORK

After writing a draft of your own persuading essay, exchange papers with a classmate, and do the following tasks:

A.   Does the introduction capture your interest? If not, can you make suggestions for improving it?

B.   Does the introduction provide enough background on the topic? If you have any questions that it needs to answer, jot them down.

C.   Underline the thesis statement. Does it state the controlling idea for the essay? Is the author's purpose clear?

D.   Does the thesis statement give enough of an overview of the topics to be discussed in the essay. If it does not, suggest revisions.

E.   Read the entire essay, and decide whether the title is a good one.

Then return the paper to its writer, and use the information in this section to revise your draft.

Diction and Spelling

Checklist for Correcting Diction and Spelling

✓ Is the **language level** appropriate for the message, the purpose, and the audience?
✓ Does the writing use **formal or informal language** appropriately?
✓ Does the writing include **jargon or technical language?** If so, is jargon necessary in communicating the message?
✓ Does the writing include **slang?** If so, is slang appropriate in each instance?
✓ Is the essay **free of nonstandard English?**
✓ Are sentences **free of word usage errors?**
✓ Are words **spelled correctly?**

Consider the choice of words in the following sentences:

> I'm going to hit the books so I can rake in the bucks.

> I want to go to college, graduate, get a good job, and provide for my family.

> Those people who attend institutions of higher learning and eventually obtain an advanced degree find that doing so allows them to achieve a higher standard of living and financial security.

These three sentences carry similar messages. Because of the writer's **diction,** or word choice, however, the sentences communicate the message differently.

How do you picture the writer of the first sentence? As a fast-talking character who is streetwise? Maybe that description is too stereotypical, but at least you'd agree that the writer uses words that negatively influence your opinion. Nothing, however, is really out of the ordinary about the second sentence. The writer seems to be normal, an ordinary, educated person who hopes for the best. The writer of the third sentence presents a different picture; he or she is obviously well read and has an extensive vocabulary. All three sentences are grammatically correct, but their diction is strikingly unique and creates a different response in the readers. The first sentence is full of slang; the second and third are examples of informal and formal language, respectively.

In this chapter you will learn that diction is not determined simply by the message. Diction also depends on purpose (what the writer is trying to accomplish) and audience (whom the writer is trying to reach). After a writer has considered each of these criteria—message, purpose, and audience—choosing the level of language for communication becomes an easy task.

Levels of Language

If you linger in the local mall, you will hear and read all kinds of language. Romeos woo young Juliets, mothers and fathers scold children, sales clerks and customers conduct business, and teens compare social pressures. Store signs beckon shoppers, product tags and packaging offer instructions, and directories tell mall newcomers which way to turn—all in the latest "lingo."

All grammatically correct spoken or written language—in or out of the mall—can be grouped in one of two categories: **formal** or **informal.** Language you find in a college textbook is likely to be formal. Language you hear or see in the mall is likely to be informal. Both are correct forms of language. Which form to use should be determined by the social context, the circumstances and people involved at the time.

Formal English

If you receive an invitation to a formal dinner, you know that you will have to dress up. You can think of **formal English** in the same way. This first category of English is reserved for serious communication, occasions when you want to "dress up" your language. Formal speaking experiences include interviews, structured speeches, addresses, and presentations. Formal writing is used in serious business correspondence; scholarly works, including serious essays and research papers; and many scientific, historical, and literary works.

Formal English is usually easy to identify. The word choices are very precise and may send you to a dictionary. Sentences are usually long, fairly complex, and varied. They include neither contractions nor references to *I, me, my,* or *mine.* Even though the word *formal* may imply stiff, structured language, formal English is simply more impersonal and reserved than informal English.

Look at this paragraph adapted from Anthony's draft, which has been rewritten in formal English:

> A fashionable cause that has recruited considerable numbers of well-intentioned parents is the home schooling movement. Hardly the innovation its contemporary followers imagine it to be, home schooling has its roots in the nineteenth-century American pioneer adherence to the code of rugged individualism. Fear and distrust of the public arena are nothing new in this country. They are, however, insufficient cause for educating—and entrapping—children within the confines of the nuclear family.

Formal language stresses the seriousness of the subject with a detached, rational point of view that makes a strong impression on readers.

Informal Language

In day-to-day communication, we rely much more heavily on **informal English,** words used in everyday speaking and writing situations, than on formal language.

Informal communication opportunities vary widely, depending on the participants, the setting, the message, and the purpose. Already today you have used informal language countless times in sending oral and written messages. Words leap out from all directions—billboards, storefronts, newspapers, magazines, TV and computer screens, notebooks, letters, chalkboards. The list is almost endless.

Informal language relies upon simpler word choices and sentence structures than formal language. It's also more relaxed, allowing contractions and the use of the first person (*I, my, my,* and *mine*). Even though it is relaxed in nature, informal English should be spoken and written clearly and carefully. Something as seemingly minor as a note to your parents explaining why you won't be home for dinner needs to be written just as clearly as a report for your history class.

For a good example of informal language, reread the first paragraph of Anthony's draft:

> There is a growing movement of parents in this country who are choosing to educate their children at home. I believe that this is not in the best interests of children, and I do not think that state departments of education should allow children to be schooled at home unless there are medical or geographical reasons for doing so. Wanting to protect a child from dangers at school is not reason enough to keep a child at home.

Anthony's topic for his persuading essay is certainly a serious subject. However, when we compare his language with a rewritten paragraph in formal language (page 377), we see dramatic differences in word choices. Notice that both paragraphs use correct grammar and punctuation. This is a requirement for good English whether it is formal or informal, spoken or written.

Exercise E8-1

Rewrite the following sentences from "The Neglected Heart," replacing informal words and expressions with formal words and expressions. A thesaurus might be an excellent aid for this exercise.

1. "I didn't expect the guy to marry me, but I never expected him to avoid me in school."
2. She explained that she had never had a boyfriend, so she was excited when a senior asked her out.
3. I am still going out with him, which is getting to be a problem.
4. My advice is, don't be in such a rush.
5. "When the breakup comes, it's usually a lot tougher on the girls than it is on the guys."

Exercise E8-2

The following sentences adapted from Anthony's draft are written in formal English. Without looking at his original paper, rewrite the sentences using informal language. Look up the meanings of any words you are unsure of. Then compare your sentences with the original versions on pages 359–361.

1.   Parents who provide education opportunities for their offspring at home maintain that they are also providing a safe environment that precludes violence.
2.   People are operating under the mistaken supposition that a homebound community is coterminous with a social community.
3.   In this writer's opinion, it is imperative that children be disciplined in moral imperatives; however, no moral code is so flawless that it remains indisputable.
4.   Parents who have set goals of maximizing their children's social interaction skills should expose them to the appropriate settings at an impressionable age.
5.   The attempt to shield children from negative social influences is doomed to failure.

Exercise E8-3

Rewrite the following paragraph, replacing formal expressions with words that are not as formal. Look up the meanings of any words you are unsure of.

The canine companion of this writer's family is a gregarious carnivore of the masculine persuasion. Carrying the moniker *Socrates*, he brightens idle hours with amusing displays he has ardently learned over the span of his life, fifteen years. When he becomes extremely energetic, Socrates emits a hearty canine sound that has caused many an unsuspecting guest to cower, mouth agape. But at one mellifluous command—"Soft!"—Socrates lowers the volume to a muted whisper. Then comes the long-awaited reward: multihued rings of cereal grains dusted with coats of sugary sweetness.

Exercise E8-4

Write original sentences using the following formal words and phrases. Look up the meanings of any words you are unsure of. Then rewrite each sentence, replacing the formal words and expressions with informal words and phrases. Use a dictionary or thesaurus as necessary.

1.   of middling stature
2.   a debilitating disease
3.   strolled with a jaunty air
4.   peau-de-soie encrusted with seed pearls
5.   proclivity

Jargon or Technical Language

Another type of language used by some people is jargon. **Jargon** consists of technical words and phrases that exclude readers and listeners who are unfamiliar with a particular field. For example, computer experts use terms such as *RAM*, *boot*, *download*, and *upgrade*. These words would have little meaning—or entirely different ones—for people with a limited knowledge of computers. What if you signed up for an art class and on the first day your teacher told you, "Paint a floral study using complementary opposites and organic lines"? What would you do? If you had had prior art instruction, you would create flowers with natural, free-flowing lines, using opposites on the color wheel (blue and orange, purple and yellow, or red and green).

Sometimes jargon becomes so technical that it overwhelms readers. Textbooks and academic writing, along with scientific and technical works, may be so jargon-filled that understanding is next to impossible for the general reader. Consider this example from a grammar textbook:

> There is one morpheme, the superfix, which represents the combination of phonemes that, taken together, indicate the total intonation pattern of a word. There is, however, considerable disagreement among linguists whether the superfix can really be classed as a morpheme, the argument being that the pronunciation of an entire word is a syntactical rather than a morphological matter.

Only language experts or English majors would be able to figure out this passage. For this specialized audience, this language is appropriate. But for an audience that includes nonspecialists, technical terms should be fully defined and explained so all readers can understand the message.

Slang

A special type of informal language is **slang,** popular words and expressions that come and go, much like the latest fashions. We associate some slang with different generations. For example, when your grandparents dated, they might have called their behavior "courting." Your father may have uttered these words to Mom: "Come on baby, light my fire!" And you and your friends most certainly have entirely different terms to describe the same behavior. Unless you are quoting slang in a paper, its use should be restricted to spoken English.

Keep in mind that the most up-to-date language soon becomes outdated as people create new, colorful words to name and describe people, places, and things. Often those who coin words and give new meanings to old words are members of groups that share common backgrounds, cultures, or interests. In fact, people use slang to help establish their identities with specific groups.

Because slang terms and expressions are usually short-lived and highly personal, you should generally avoid such language in your writing. Granted, some slang words and phrases have become part of our language. However, most slang depends on fashion; what's "in" today may be "out" tomorrow. So the best advice is to avoid slang in your writing.

Exercise E8-5

Underline examples of jargon and technical language in the following sentences taken from "The Death Penalty Is an Effective Punishment" by Robert W. Lee.

1. Due to costly delays and endless appeals, the death penalty has been largely turned into a paper tiger by the same crowd that calls for abolition on the grounds that it is not an effective deterrent!

2. So the attorney (in what he later described as "last-minute ingenuity") then requested that the emergency appeal be technically transformed into a formal appeal.

3. On March 30, 1978 a Tattnall County Superior Court judge held a hearing on a petition alleging sundry grounds for a writ of *habeas corpus,* but declined on July 13, 1978 to issue a writ.

4. One state governor commuted the death sentence of a woman because "humanity does not apply to women the inexorable law that it does to men."

5. "When people begin to believe that organized society is unwilling or unable to impose upon criminal offenders the punishment they 'deserve,' then there are sown the seeds of anarchy—of self-help, vigilante justice, and lynch law."

Exercise E8-6

Underline slang words and expressions in the following sentences from quotations in Thomas Lickona's essay "The Neglected Heart."

1. "Later, after the guy's dumped them, they come to me and say, 'I wish I hadn't done it.'"

2. "We had sex again, and then he dropped me. He said I wasn't good enough. There was no spark."

3. "Sex does not live up to the glowing reports and hype you see in the movies. It's no big deal."

4. "I figured out that there had probably been a dozen guys before me who thought they had 'conquered' her, but who were really just objects of her need for security. That realization took all the wind out of my sails."

5. "My friends dropped me because I was so bummed out."

Exercise E8-7

Choose an activity, field, career, or course of study in which you have knowledge or exper-tise. List five examples of jargon or technical language, and use each word or expression in an original sentence. Here are some suggestions:

art	weight lifting	biology
psychology	sewing	environmental science
sociology	nursing	basketball
carpentry	cars	soccer
computers	electronics	nutrition/health
cooking	journalism	horse racing

Exercise E8-8

List five slang words or expressions of your own, and use them in original sentences. If you have trouble thinking of slang terms, ask your parents, grandparents, or teachers for slang words and expressions that were popular when they were young adults.

Nonstandard English

While standard English is the language generally used in society, **nonstandard English** is language that does not follow the rules of formal or informal usage. Because nonstandard words and expressions are often ungrammatical, educated speakers and writers avoid them unless the communication situation calls for such language. Unfortunately, certain nonstandard words and phrases have been used so often that speakers and writers may begin to think they are acceptable in standard usage. Here are some words masquerading as correct that should be avoided in your writing:

ain't: Ricardo **ain't** going to school today.

>Correction: Ricardo **is not** going to school today.

alright: Even though Fred slipped and fell on the way to work, he is **alright.**

>Correction: Even though Fred slipped and fell on the way to work, he is **all right.**

anyways: I told Carleen that I didn't think she should be smoking **anyways.**

>Correction: I told Carleen that I didn't think she should be smoking **anyway.**

anywheres: Jake makes himself at home **anywheres** he goes.

>Correction: Jakes makes himself at home **anywhere** he goes.

be: I **be** so tired.

>Correction: I **am** so tired.

being as, being that: **Being as** Rhonda is late, we can't start the party.

>Correction: **Because** Rhonda is late, we can't start the party.

bursted, busted: Timmy **bursted** the balloon when he sat on it.

>Correction: Timmy **burst** the balloon when he sat on it.

but that, but what: We doubt **but that** he will confess.

>Correction: We doubt **that** he will confess.

coulda, could of, shoulda, should of: My brother **could of** played basketball in college. He **should of** stuck with it.

>Correction: My brother **could have** (or **could've**) played basketball in college. He **should have** (or **should've**) stuck with it.

different than: I am no **different than** all your other friends.

>Correction: I am no **different from** all your other friends.

don't: Sometimes I think Earl **don't** know the difference between right and wrong.

>   Correction: Sometimes I think Earl **doesn't** know the difference between right and wrong.

enthused: Jay was **enthused** about his trip to Hawaii.

>   Correction: Jay was **enthusiastic** about his trip to Hawaii.

everywheres: My little sister tries to follow me **everywheres** I go.

>   Correction: My little sister tries to follow me **everywhere** I go.

firstly, secondly, thirdly: Firstly, you should mix the flour and eggs.

>   Correction: **First,** you should mix the flour and eggs.

goes: We can start writing when the teacher **goes,** "Begin."

>   Correction: We can start writing when the teacher **says,** "Begin."

hisself: Marshall made **hisself** a budget for the next month.

>   Correction: Marshall made **himself** a budget for the next month.

in regards to: In regards to your proposal, we have decided to strongly consider it.

>   Correction: **In regard to** your proposal, we have decided to strongly consider it.

inside of, outside of: The hostages are still **inside of** the building.

>   Correction: The hostages are still **inside** the building.

irregardless: Irregardless of how much time you spent on your paper, it still needs work.

>   Correction: **Regardless** of the time you spent on your paper, it still needs work.

kinda, kind of, sorta, sort of: Abby's perfume smells **kinda** sweet, **sorta** like vanilla.

>   Correction: Abby's perfume smells **rather** sweet, **much** like vanilla.

off of: Jim accidentally knocked the vase **off of** the coffee table.

>   Correction: Jim accidentally knocked the vase **off** the coffee table.

oughta: Sometimes I think I **oughta** just run away.

>   Correction: Sometimes I think I **ought to** just run away.

rarely ever: Pete **rarely ever** eats meat.

>   Correction: Pete **rarely** eats meat.

real: My mom was **real** upset when I came in at 4 a.m.

>   Correction: My mom was **really** upset when I came in at 4 a.m.

somewheres: You must have left your notebook **somewheres** at school.

Correction: You must have left your book **somewhere** at school.

suppose to: Marc was **suppose to** meet me at the library.

Correction: Marc was **supposed to** meet me at the library.

theirselves: My grandfather always said that people should help **theirselves** instead of waiting for a handout.

Correction: My grandfather always said that people should help **themselves** instead of waiting for a handout.

use to: Nassar **use to** live in Egypt.

Correction: Nassar **used to** live in Egypt.

ways: Representatives from both sides say they are a long **ways** from agreement.

Correction: Representatives from both sides say they are a long **way** from agreement.

where . . . at: Do you know **where** your keys are **at**?

Correction: Do you know **where** your keys are?

while: **While** ago I saw a rabbit run across the lawn.

Correction: **A while** ago I saw a rabbit run across the lawn.

Exercise E8-9

Identify nonstandard usage in the following sentences adapted from Anthony's revised draft.

1. Firstly, parents who ain't qualified to teach their own children at home should not get theirselves to their children's school and pass their insights along to other children.
2. We have public education somewheres in this country to help this society irregardless of who we be.
3. If all people everywheres shared the same values and behavior patterns, we would have a real boring society.
4. It is her father hisself who should explain what language is suppose to be used at home and what language is not acceptable.
5. Don't that parent know enough about biology and history and math to help that child find where his answer is at?

Exercise E8-10

In the following paragraph, underline words or phrases in nonstandard English.

I have this slave driver for a typing teacher. She don't know how to let up. Some days I think I oughta just tell her off. But I ain't gonna upset her any more than she all ready appears to be. She just stands somewheres in the room yelling out," A, S, D, F, J, K, L, semi" over and over until she about bursted my eardrums. Sometimes at night when I lay my head down to sleep, I can kinda hear her screechy voice. I doubt but that she'll let you take your hands off of the keyboard. She ain't planning to let nobody rest. My friend Ron bought hisself earplugs just so he could get some peace and quiet in class. But Miss B is not enthused, irregardless of what you say or do and anywheres you say and do it.

Exercise E8-11

Rewrite each sentence in Exercise E8-9, replacing nonstandard usage with standard usage.

Exercise E8-12

Write five sentences demonstrating nonstandard language. Then write a standard version (in either formal or informal usage) of each sentence.

Choosing the Right Word

In editing written work, writers are more often concerned with mechanics and punctuation—making sure that each *i* is dotted, that certain words are capitalized, and that each comma is in its right place—than they are with word choice. Because we remain focused on these types of errors, we often let other problems, such as usage errors, slip by.

Whether they look alike, sound alike, or have similar meanings, words can sometimes be difficult to tell apart. The following glossary lists some common words and phrases that are easily confused with each other. You will find that some words and phrases are acceptable in formal academic writing, whereas other pairs may be used only in informal situations. The best advice is to analyze each writing situation—your paper's purpose and audience—as you choose the correct word.

a, an: These words are special types of adjectives called *articles*. Use *a* before words that begin with a consonant or a consonant sound, and use *an* before words beginning with vowels or vowel sounds.

> **a** party, **a** dollar, **a** car
> **an** apple, **an** engineer, **an** opportunity

accept/except: The verb *accept* means "to receive." *Except* is a preposition meaning "other than."

> Yolanda says she will not **accept** my apology.
> I answered every question **except** the last one.

adapt/adopt: Both words are verbs. *Adapt* means "adjust"; *adopt* means "to take into a relationship or to use as one's own."

> It might be difficult to **adapt** to a new school if we move.
> I hope Teresa doesn't **adopt** her boyfriend's bad habits.

advice/advise: The noun *advice* means "helpful hints of information." The verb *advise* means "the action of giving advice or counsel."

> Whenever I need **advice,** I call my older brother Greg.
> Greg usually **advises** me to make a list before taking action.

affect/effect: *Affect* usually functions as a verb meaning "to influence." *Effect* can function as a verb ("to bring about or make happen") or as a noun ("a result").

> Omar hopes his new job won't **affect** his study time.
>
> The governor believes higher taxes will **effect** positive economic
> changes.
>
> The pill produced a calming **effect.**

allowed/aloud: The verb *allow* means "to let happen"; the adverb *aloud* means "in a normal voice."

> The teacher **allowed** the students to stay in during recess.
> Shanece read **aloud** when the teacher called on her.

a lot/allot: The expression *a lot* means "a great deal" and should not be used in formal writing. *Allot* is a verb meaning "to set aside."

> We packed **a lot** of snacks for the long train ride.
> Chu tries to **allot** a portion of his free time for meditation.

allude/elude: *Allude* is a verb meaning "to refer to something indirectly." *Elude* is a verb meaning "to avoid or escape."

> Every time Josh mentions Carrie's name, he **alludes** to some big secret between
> the two of them.
> The escaped convict tried to **elude** police officers by using a number of
> disguises.

allusion/illusion: *Allusion* is a noun meaning "an indirect reference" or "hinting at something." An *illusion* is a noun meaning "mistaken image."

> The poet's **allusion** to Julius Caesar was easy to understand.
> My artist friend Diego likes to create **illusions** with three-dimensional
> drawings.

already/all ready: *Already* is an adverb indicating "when." *All ready* is a two-word phrase meaning "completely prepared."

> Hope has **already** registered for the spring semester.
> We were **all ready** to go when a small emergency made us leave late.

altogether/all together: *Altogether* is an adverb meaning "completely" or "thoroughly." *All together* is a phrase meaning "gathered in one place."

> Missy was **altogether** wrong about Dan's previous girlfriends.
> We were **all together** on the shuttle bus when the fire broke out in the park.

among/between: Use *among* when referring to three or more persons or items. Use *between* when referring to only two individuals or things.

> **Among** all the students in our class, I think Shonda is the most mature.
> I can't decide **between** cheesecake and apple pie for dessert.

amount/number: *Amount* refers to quantities that cannot be counted; *number* refers to quantities that can be counted.

> The **amount** of moisture in the air aggravates my allergies.
> Mom has a **number** of chores planned for our workday at home.

awhile/a while: *Awhile* is an adverb meaning "a short time." *A while* is a noun phrase referring to a short time span and usually functions as an object of a preposition.

> J. T. slept **awhile** when he got home from his trip.
> Peggy slept for **a while** when she got home from a hectic day at work.

bad/badly: *Bad* is an adjective meaning "not good"; *badly* is an adverb meaning "performing irregularly or unacceptably."

> That milk is **bad,** so don't drink it.
> The team played **badly** in the first half but came back to win.

beside, besides: Both words function as prepositions. *Beside* means "at the side of"; *besides* means "other than" or "in addition." *Besides* can also serve as an adverb meaning "furthermore."

> Burt stood **beside** Kevin as they lined up for the team photo.
> I don't want to do anything on our vacation **besides** lie on the beach.
> Our teacher told us the final exam would be easy; **besides,** we had reviewed for three entire class periods.

breath/breathe: *Breath* is a noun meaning "air." *Breathe* is a verb meaning "the act of taking in air."

Take several big **breaths** as you cool down.
You should **breathe** regularly as you do you sit-ups.

bring/take: When the action comes toward the speaker, use *bring*. When the action moves away from the speaker, use *take*.

My grandmother promised to **bring** me a fresh apple cake when she visits.
Raul plans to **take** $100 with him when we go out this weekend.

can, may: *Can* refers to ability; *may* means "with permission" or "possibly."

Debbie **can** dance much better than she can sing.
You **may** sit down, if you'd like.
It **may** turn cold tomorrow, so take a coat on your trip.

capital/capitol: As a noun, *capital* refers to a city, money, or uppercase letters; as an adjective, *capital* means "important or major." *Capitol* refers to a building where legislatures conduct business.

Salem is the **capital** of Oregon.
My brother needs $15,000 in **capital** to qualify for a small-business loan.
Each sentence should begin with a **capital** letter.
The **capital** reason for choosing my college is its cost.
The **capitol** building in Denver is undergoing renovation.

choose/chose: *Choose* means "to select"; *chose* is the past tense of *choose*.

Please **choose** something from the menu.
Andy **chose** to call in sick after he stayed out too late.

cite/site: The verb *cite* means "to quote"; the noun *site* refers to a place or scene.

Dianne **cited** the Bible in her stirring speech.
The **site** chosen for the new high school is at the end of Jenkins Road.

complement/compliment: *Complement* is a verb meaning "to complete or work with." *Compliment* can function as a verb meaning "to praise or flatter" or a noun meaning "an expression of praise or flattery."

The new rug certainly **complements** the sofa.
Mrs. McKay **complimented** me, saying she loved my new hairstyle.
Many people do not know how to accept a **compliment.**

conscience/conscious: The noun *conscience* refers to right or wrong; *conscious* is an adjective that means "acting with will or awareness."

My **conscience** bothers me every time I eat a candy bar.
The prosecutor said the defendant made a **conscious** decision to drive drunk.

continual/continuous: Both words are adjectives. *Continual* refers to something that recurs or happens repeatedly. *Continuous* refers to something that happens constantly over a period of time without interruption.

> The woman said her husband's **continual** nagging almost made her leave him.
> The **continuous** sound of the creek put us to sleep.

desert/dessert: *Desert* as a noun or adjective refers to dry, sandy land. As a verb, *desert* means "to abandon." *Dessert* refers to the last course of a meal.

> Las Vegas was once nothing but a **desert.**
> The main character in the short story **deserted** his family.
> We had a choice of German chocolate cake or coconut pie for **dessert.**

does/dose: *Does* is the present tense of the verb *do* and means "performs." *Dose* refers to medicine, either the act of giving medicine (verb) or the amount of medicine (noun).

> Karla **does** whatever she wants to on the weekends.
> The doctor **dosed** the child with a small **dose** of penicillin.

dominant/dominate: The adjective *dominant* means "controlling or superior." *Dominate* is a verb meaning "to control or overpower."

> The **dominant** team in the conference this season was the Washington Huskies.
> George tries to **dominate** every conversation.

due to/because of: *Due to* should be used only after a linking verb. In other cases, use the preposition *because of*.

> Our low scores were **due to** lack of study time.
> We decided to stay home Saturday night **because of** the weather report.

everyday/every day: *Everyday* is an adjective meaning "usual" or "ordinary." The phrase *every day* can function as a noun phrase or as an adverb referring to frequency.

> Sleeping is an **everyday** occurrence that most people enjoy.
>
> I look forward to **every day** as an opportunity for learning.
>
> Jan feeds the squirrels in her back yard **every day.**

farther/further: Writers often use these adverbs interchangeably. But general usage dictates that *farther* refers to physical distance; *further* means "additional."

> Hank can kick a football **farther** than anyone else on the team.
> My dad said there will be no **further** discussions about the accident.

fewer/less: *Fewer* is an adjective, and it refers to things that can be counted. *Less* is also an adjective, but it refers to things that cannot be counted.

> There are **fewer** cookies in the jar since Joey has been home.
> Since my mom is working another job, she has **less** time to spend with us.

formally/formerly: Both words are adverbs. *Formally* describes the way in which something is done; *formerly* means "previously."

> We communicated **formally** with the company and its representatives because we wanted them to know our offer was serious.
> Rianna Moon was **formerly** known by her given name, Sally Renee Cobb.

former/latter: *Former* refers to the first of two people or items; *latter* refers to the second. These adjectives should not be used when referring to more than two people or items.

> Mariah Carey and Reba McEntire are two popular signers; the **former** is from New York, while the **latter** is from Oklahoma.

good/well: *Good* is always used as an adjective. *Well* is normally an adverb referring to how something is done. However, when *well* refers to a state of health, it is an adjective.

> Barbie looks **good** in her new outfit.

> Dave looks like he doesn't feel **well.**

> Karen didn't do **well** on the typing test because she was nervous.

hear/here: *Hear* is a verb referring to the act of listening; *here* is an adverb meaning "nearby."

> I can't **hear** you because the music is too loud.
> You dropped some food **here** on the carpet.

it's/its: *It's* is the contraction for *it is* or *it has*. *Its* is the possessive form of the personal pronoun *it*.

> The forecasters say **it's** going to snow this afternoon.
> The baby dropped **its** rattle and began to cry.

knew/new: The verb *knew* is the past tense form of *know*. *New* is an adjective meaning "recent."

> I thought you **knew** I had a **new** car.

know/no: *Know* is a verb meaning "to understand"; *no* is negative, the opposite of *yes*.

> We all **know** that Bart has **no** conscience.

later/latter: *Later* is an adverb meaning "after some specified time." The adjective *latter* refers to the last mentioned of two persons or items.

> The producers told the **latter** of the two finalists that they would call her **later.**

lay/lie: Both words are verbs. *Lay* means "to place or set" and has *lay, laid, laid* as its principal parts; it always takes an object. Lie means "to recline" or "to rest" and takes no object. Its principal parts are *lie, lay, lain.*

> Please **lay** the punchbowl down before you spill everything.
>
> He **laid** down his burden yesterday.
>
> Maury **lies** down and takes a short nap every afternoon.
>
> I **lay** on the beach until the sun set.

learn/teach: The verb *learn* means "to obtain or gain knowledge"; the verb *teach* means "to instruct or give knowledge."

> I **learn** more each day I go to biology class.
> Mrs. White usually **teaches** us when Mr. Ashley is absent.

leave/let: The verb *leave* means "to depart"; the verb *let* means "to allow or permit."

> We thought our guests would never **leave.**
> Vickie won't **let** her boyfriend buy her an engagement ring.

liable/likely: *Liable* is an adverb meaning "tending toward something" or "responsible for in legal terms." *Likely* means "probable" and can be used as an adjective or an adverb.

> If you don't study for the test, you are **liable** to fail.
>
> Mr. Garrison was **liable** for damages when he accidentally hit Jay's car.

> He's a **likely candidate.**
>
> He's **likely** to pass.

loose/lose: *Loose* can function as an adjective ("free" or "unattached") or as a verb ("to release"). The verb *lose* means "to misplace or fail to win."

> I tightened the **loose** screws on the door hinge.
> The park rangers will **loose** the pigeons from their cage this afternoon.
> If the Tigers **lose** the game, they will be out of the playoff picture.

many/much: *Many* is an adjective that refers to quantity. *Much* can function as an adjective, an adverb, or a noun, and it always refers to an amount.

Kelvin looked at **many** apartments before he made a decision.

There has been **much** disagreement about whether to raise tuition.

Paula doesn't like seafood very **much.**

Much of what the fortune teller said did not come true.

maybe/may be: *Maybe* is an adverb meaning "possibly"; *may be* is a verb phrase.

Maybe we will go to the park this afternoon.
Sharla **may be** the best worker in our department.

moral/morale: *Moral* can function as an adjective ("referring to ethics") or a noun ("the lesson of a story"). *Morale* is a noun meaning "the mental condition of a person or group of people."

Failure to win the group's approval was a **moral** setback for Sam.

The **moral** of the story is to never judge people until you get to know them.

The team's **morale** is extremely low after they lost their tenth game in a row.

passed/past: *Passed* always functions as a verb, the past tense and past participle forms of *to pass*. *Past*, however, can function as an adjective meaning "earlier," a noun meaning "a previous time," or a preposition meaning "beyond."

Rusty **passed** the bar exam on his first try.

Ginger wrote about her **past** experiences as a foster child.

The mansion has an interesting **past,** having survived the Civil War.

Louise the cat raced **past** her owner's outstretched arms.

perspective/prospective: The noun *perspective* means "from one's point of view." *Prospective* is an adjective meaning "potential."

From Dr. Snyder's **perspective,** building more prisons is not the solution to crime.
Maria has a **prospective** buyer for her condo.

precede/proceed: Both words are verbs. *Precede* means "to come or go before"; *proceed* means "to go forward."

A comedian **precedes** the main attraction, the magician David Copperfield.
Tom will **proceed** with the divorce even though Lori wants to reconcile.

principal/principle: *Principal* is either an adjective ("primary" or "first") or a noun ("a school official" or "a sum of money"). *Principle* is a noun meaning "a law, truth, or rule of conduct."

The **principal** part in the play is Teddie, a young girl who believes she is dying.

Mr. Kobler is the **principal** at Westside Elementary School.

Jack owes the bank $557.50, $500 for the **principal** of the loan and $57.50 in interest.

In our American history class, we have studied the **principles** that provided for the founding of our country.

quiet/quite: *Quiet* is an adjective meaning "without noise"; *quite* is an adverb meaning "very or completely."

It was **quiet** last night at our house because my little brother was gone.
Vanessa said she was **quite** satisfied with the money she got for her car.

quotation/quote: These words are often used interchangeably, which is incorrect. Remember that *quotation* is a noun and *quote* is a verb.

Mr. Fisher said Will put too many **quotations** in his paper.

Serena likes to **quote** Thomas Jefferson, Malcolm X, and Madonna in her speeches.

raise/rise: *Raise* is a verb meaning "to increase" or "to lift up." *Rise* is also a verb and means "to get up," as from a sitting or reclining position.

The governor does not plan to **raise** taxes.
Ernie **rises** at 5 a.m. every morning to go to the health club.

real/really: *Real* is an adjective meaning "true"; *really* is an adverb meaning "very" or "extremely."

I wonder if Patricia's four-carat diamond ring is **real.**
Keith was **really** mad when his roommate set the sofa on fire.

set/sit: Both words are verbs. *Set* means "to put"; *sit* means "to put the body in a seated position."

Mohammed **set** his books down on the ground while he played touch football.
If I **sit** for a long period of time, my lower back starts hurting.

stationary/stationery: *Stationary* is an adjective meaning "not moving." *Stationery* is a noun referring to materials used to write letters.

The construction supervisor checked the foundation to make sure it was **stationary.**
Nikita ordered some new **stationery** with her initials on the envelopes.

sure/surely: *Sure* is an adjective meaning "certain." *Surely* is an adverb meaning "undoubtedly."

Larry was **sure** he passed his economics test.
Surely you know the difference between a chicken and a rooster.

than/then: The conjunction *than* is used in making comparisons. *Then* is an adverb meaning "immediately after."

Lashunda is younger **than** her sister Linda.
The ball rolled around the hoop, **then** dropped through the net.

that/which/who: *That* introduces essential dependent clauses; *which* introduces nonessential dependent clauses. *Who* can introduce either essential or nonessential clauses and always refers to people or sometimes animals.

The pizza **that** was in the freezer has mysteriously vanished.
My grandmother's house, **which** was tucked away in the woods, was over 100 years old.
The man **who** sat in the first seat was Nancy's long-lost uncle.
Chip, **who** has been my manager for almost two years, is moving to Kentucky.

their/there/they're: *Their* is the possessive form of the personal pronoun *they*. *There* is used as an expletive or as an adverb indicating location. *They're* is the contraction for *they are*.

Their car broke down in the middle of the freeway.
There is too much trash over *there* by the riverbank.
They're not coming to the party because *they're* tired.

threw/through: *Threw* is the past tense form of the verb *throw*. *Through* can function as an adjective or adverb meaning "finished." *Through* can also function as a preposition meaning "passing from one place to another."

When Beth **threw** the ball to Wes, he finally caught it.

Allen is **through** with his lunch, so he will leave soon.

We don't think Paul can see it **through.**

Rico went **through** his closet searching for his G. I. Joes.

TIPS FOR EDITING

to/too/two: The preposition *to* means "toward" or begins an infinitive. The adverb *too* means "also" or "very." *Two*, the numeral following one, can function as an adjective or a noun.

> Tori went **to** Johnny's house **to** return his ring.
>
> Tori returned Johnny's photo albums **too.**
>
> **Two** is Mariel's favorite number.
>
> She and her **two** sisters were born on the second day of the month.

toward/towards: Both spellings of this preposition are acceptable, although *toward* is preferred in standard written English.

> In my nightmare, my first grade teacher was coming **toward** me with a knife.

weather/whether: *Weather* is a noun referring to a condition of the atmosphere or a verb meaning "to endure." *Whether* is a conjunction referring to a possibility.

> **Whether** the **weather** improves is a big question mark.

were/where: *Were* is the past tense of the verb *to be*; *where* is a subordinating conjunction and an adverb.

> **Where were** you going when I saw you?
>
> They **were** happy to be **where** he was free.

who/whom, whoever/whomever: Use *who* and *whoever* as subjects and predicate nouns. Use *whom* and *whomever* as objects.

> **Who** is at the door?
>
> **Whoever** let the cat out needs to get her back in.
>
> To **whom** do you want me to give the bill?
>
> Anna's mother said Anna can go out with **whomever** she wants.

who's/whose: *Who's* is the contraction for *who is*: *whose* is the possessive form of the pronoun *who*.

> We wonder **who's** going to decide **whose** opinion is correct.

your/you're: *Your* is the possessive form of the personal pronoun *you*. *You're* is the contraction for *you are*.

> **Your** appointment will be canceled if **you're** not on time.

Exercise E8-13

The following sentences are adapted from the pro/con essays in this chapter, "The Death Penalty Is an Effective Punishment" and "The Death Penalty Is Not an Effective Punishment." Underline the usage errors that have been added to these sentences.

1.   A key issue in the debate over capital punishment is weather or not it is an effective deterrent to violent crime.

2.   The deterrent affect on others, however, depends largely on how swiftly and surely the penalty is applied.
3.   The exorbitant financial expense of death penalty cases is regularly sited by abolitionists as a reason for abolishing capital punishment all together.
4.   The death penalty is clearly *not* equally applied under the law, or under the more significant mandate of morale, ethical and spiritual values of a nation founded on these principals.
5.   There is overwhelming evidence that race is the single most important factor in choosing those whom will be sentenced to death.

Exercise E8-14

Find the usage errors in the following sentences, which appear in the first draft of Anthony's persuading essay.

1.   It is a mistake to thing that if all people stay in their houses, isolated, that we will learn to live together.
2.   I agree that it is real important to pass my values on to my children, but I do not think that any value is so perfect that it cannot be questioned.
3.   Whatever your religious practices are, just make them a part of your every day life.
4.   Your children will learn these practices, and when they are old enough, they will decide weather to keep the practices of your faith going for another generation.
5.   If a parent is an elementary school teacher all ready, that will help a child through elementary school.

Exercise E8-15

Choose the correct words in parentheses that will complete each sentence in the following paragraphs.

One of the guidance counselors at school is a good person to turn to when you want someone to help with (1) _____ (*your, your're*) problems. Mrs. Freeman gives you plenty of options (2) _____ (*weather, whether*) you are asking about college or personal things. Every time I leave her office, I feel (3) _____ (*alright, all right*), sure that things will work out.

Last month I went to see Mrs. Freeman for (4) _____ (*awhile, a while*). I told her that I had not been doing (5) _____ (*good, well*) in school. First of all, she asked me if I had been feeling

(6) _____ (*good, well*). Had I been getting enough rest, or was I stressed out? I told her no, not really. Then I told her, "Just

(7) _____ (*among, between*) us, I'm bored." I've always been more mature than most of my friends. And I read (8) _____

(*allot, a lot*) and study on my own. School just isn't any fun, other than hanging out with my friends.

Mrs. Freeman told me that (10) _____ (*maybe, may be*) I just needed a break. Her (10) _____ (*advice, advise*) to me was to start a new hobby or find a new interest that could take my mind off my classes. She also suggested taking more time out for myself, since I do lots of things for other people.

Exercise E8-16

Write original sentences using the following words.

1. amount
2. bring
3. everyday
4. it's
5. lay

Spelling

Probably no part of the English language causes as much anxiety as spelling. From our earliest days in elementary school, we have squirmed, stammered, and stumbled through a seemingly endless barrage of spelling rules, drills, and quizzes. Even the traditional spelling bees put students on the spot as their spelling talents—or inadequacies—become public knowledge.

Spelling is important. If it weren't, why would teachers go to such lengths to encourage mastery of so many spelling rules and exceptions? Basically, spelling errors send negative messages, causing readers to question the writer's skill and credibility as an effective communicator. Misspellings seem to leap out at readers, creating serious doubts about the writer's proficiency. Sometimes you have access to spelling checkers that can help you polish a final draft of a paper. But other times, you are handwriting a draft or taking an essay exam, or you don't have access to a computer. These are the times when following some simple guidelines will guarantee that the spelling of each word is complete and correct.

1. *Learn to distinguish between homonyms.*   **Homonyms** are words that sound alike but are spelled differently. Remember that even when these words are spelled correctly, they may be used incorrectly. Even a spelling checker won't catch these problems. Some of the words that appear in the section "Choosing the Right Word" are homonyms: *to, too, two; their, there, they're.*

   The best way to handle homonyms and words that are extremely similar in sound is to read your sentences closely, analyzing how each word is used. Become familiar with the homonyms that give you trouble. Then refer to a list like the one that follows, and consult a dictionary to spell your way to success.

Common Homonyms

accept	except	fair	fare	peace	piece
access	excess	flour	flower	peak	peek
adapt	adopt	for	four	personal	personnel
advice	advise	forth	fourth	peer	pier
aid	aide	gorilla	guerilla	plain	plane
air	heir	hair	hare	pray	prey
altar	alter	hear	here	rain	reign
ate	eight	heard	herd	read	red
bare	bear	heroin	heroine	right	rite write
berry	bury	higher	hire	road	rode
berth	birth	hole	whole	role	roll
board	bored	hoarse	horse	sail	sale
born	borne	idle	idol	scene	seen
bread	bred	in	inn	seam	seem
break	brake	knew	new	shone	shown
buy	by	know	no	sole	soul
cell	sell	lead	led	stake	steak
cereal	serial	lessen	lesson	steal	steel
coarse	course	loan	lone	tail	tale
council	counsel	made	maid	taught	taut
dairy	diary	mail	male	team	teem
dear	deer	main	mane	tide	tied
decent	descent	meat	meet	waist	waste
device	devise	medal	metal	wander	wonder
dual	duel	miner	minor	weak	week
elicit	illicit	one	won	which	witch
ensure	insure	pain	pane	wood	would
exercise	exorcise	pair	pear		

2. *Focus on words that give you trouble.*   The best advice may be to commit the most difficult and persistent spelling demons to memory. Certainly, memorization is a time-consuming and somewhat unexciting activity. However, you will find your time well spent as you conquer the words that constantly stump your spelling skills. Even with access to a spelling checker, you will save yourself precious time in the long run if you master the spelling of words that are habitually difficult for you.

Refer to the following list of commonly misspelled words as you edit your writing.

Commonly Misspelled Words

abbreviate	balloon	collar	deteriorate
absence	banana	college	determine
accelerate	bankrupt	column	development
accessible	banquet	commit	dictionary
accompany	beautiful	committee	difficulty
accomplish	beggar	communicate	diploma
accumulate	beginning	community	disappear
accurate	behavior	comparison	disastrous
ache	benefited	competent	discipline
achievement	bicycle	competition	disease
acknowledgment	biscuit	complexion	dissatisfied
acre	bought	conceive	divisional
actual	boundary	concession	dormitory
address	brilliant	concrete	
adequate	brought	condemn	economy
advertisement	buoyant	conference	efficiency
afraid	bureau	congratulate	eighth
aggravate	burglar	conscience	elaborate
aisle	business	continuous	electricity
although		convenience	eligible
aluminum	cabbage	cooperate	embarrass
amateur	cafeteria	corporation	emphasize
ambulance	calendar	correspond	employee
ancient	campaign	cough	encourage
anonymous	canoe	counterfeit	enormous
anxiety	canyon	courageous	enough
anxious	captain	courteous	enthusiastic
appreciate	career	cozy	envelope
appropriate	carriage	criticize	environment
approximate	cashier	curiosity	equipment
architect	catastrophe	curious	equivalent
arithmetic	caterpillar	curriculum	especially
artificial	ceiling	cylinder	essential
assassin	cemetery		establish
athletic	census	dairy	exaggerate
attach	certain	dangerous	excellent
audience	certificate	dealt	exceptionally
authority	challenge	deceive	excessive
autumn	champion	decision	exhaust
auxiliary	character	definition	exhilarating
avenue	chief	delicious	existence
awkward	children	descend	explanation
	chimney	describe	extinct
baggage	coffee	description	extraordinary

Commonly Misspelled Words

familiar	immediately	lieutenant	occurred
famous	immortal	lightning	official
fascinate	impossible	likable	omission
fashion	incredible	liquid	omitted
fatigue	independence	listen	opportunity
faucet	indispensable	literature	opponent
February	individual		opposite
fiery	inferior	machinery	original
financial	infinite	magazine	outrageous
foreign	influential	magnificent	
forfeit	initial	majority	pamphlet
fortunate	initiation	manufacture	paragraph
freight	innocence	marriage	parallel
fundamental	installation	material	parentheses
	intelligence	mathematics	partial
gauge	interfere	maximum	particular
genius	interrupt	mayor	pastime
genuine	invitation	meant	patience
geography	irrelevant	medicine	peculiar
gnaw	irrigate	message	permanent
government	issue	mileage	persistent
graduation		miniature	personnel
grammar	jealous	minimum	persuade
grief	jewelry	minute	physician
grocery	journalism	mirror	pitcher
gruesome	judgment	miscellaneous	pneumonia
guarantee		mischievous	politician
guess	kindergarten	miserable	possess
guidance	knife	misspell	prairie
	knowledge	monotonous	precede
handkerchief	knuckles	mortgage	precious
handsome		mysterious	preferred
haphazard	laboratory		prejudice
happiness	laborious	necessary	previous
harass	language	neighborhood	privilege
height	laugh	niece	procedure
hesitate	laundry	nineteen	pronounce
humorous	league	ninety	psychology
hygiene	legible	noticeable	
hymn	legislature	nuisance	questionnaire
	leisure		quotient
icicle	length	obedience	
illustrate	library	obstacle	realize
imaginary	license	occasion	receipt

Commonly Misspelled Words

recipe	similar	theater	villain
recommend	skiing	thief	visible
reign	soldier	thorough	volunteer
religious	souvenir	tobacco	
representative	sovereign	tomorrow	weather
reservoir	spaghetti	tongue	Wednesday
responsibility	squirrel	tournament	weigh
restaurant	statue	tragedy	weird
rhyme	stomach	truly	whose
rhythm	strength		width
	subtle	unanimous	worst
salary	succeed	unique	wreckage
satisfactory	success	university	writing
scarcity	sufficient	usable	
scenery	surprise	usually	yacht
schedule	syllable		yearn
science	symptom	vacuum	yield
scissors		valuable	
secretary	technique	various	zealous
seize	temperature	vegetable	zoology
separate	temporary	vehicle	
significant	terrible	vicinity	

Exercise E8-17

The following sentences are adapted from Thomas Lickona's essay "The Neglected Heart." Find and correct the spelling errors that have been added to the sentences.

1. Why is it so much harder to discuss sex and emotional hurt—to name and talk about the damaging psycological effects that can come from premature sexual involvement?
2. Girls, especialy, need to know in advance the sharp regret that so many young women feel after becomeing sexually involved.
3. Their more likely to see sex as a sign of commitment in the relationship.
4. She was afraid of appearing imature and losing him, so she concented.
5. There are girls in our dorm who have had multipal pregnancies and multipal abortions.

Exercise E8-18

Correct all the spelling errors in the first draft of Anthony's persuading essay (pp. 359–361).

Exercise E8-19

Find and correct the misspelled words in the following paragraphs.

Do you have friends who like to exagerrate? I have one friend, Joey, who stretches the truth every chance he gets. He doesn't really set out to willfully decieve people. But he definitly believes that he has to impress people with tall tales to get them to like him.

Joey likes to make up stories about his acomplishments. For example, he said he had run a marathon this past summer, certainly a big achievment for anyone, much less a guy who hasn't been working out that long. He did take part in a walkathon. But a marathon? I guess he thinks it's easier to manafacture daring feats than actually preform them.

Sometimes Joey just tells stories about extrordinary things he's done just to add to the conversation. One time he also said he'd gone on tour as a stage hand for the Grateful Dead. Sure, he went to a couple of their concerts. But telling people he toured with them was an unnecesary untruth.

We, as his friends, certainly haven't benefitted from his made-up experiences. We constantly defend him because he's truely a nice guy. And we've talked to him, too. But every now and then he gets a mischievious twinkle in his eye, and we know his mouth will be off and running.

Exercise E8-20

Write five original sentences, using at least five of the words from the list of commonly misspelled words on pages 399 to 401.

COLLABORATIVE WORK

After you have revised your persuading essay, exchange papers with a classmate, and do the following tasks:

A.   Determine the level of the language in the essay, and underline any dialect, slang, or jargon.

B.   Circle any words that are misspelled or used incorrectly.

Then return the paper to its writer, and use the information in this section to edit your draft.

CHAPTER NINE

Problem Solving
Reading and Writing for a Reason

We do not write in order to be understood, we write in order to understand.

—C. DAY LEWIS

We all encounter problems in our lives. Some problems are no more than minor annoyances: a car that won't start, a person who is rude or inconsiderate, too much homework over the weekend. Other problems, however, are far more serious: not enough money to pay bills, a sick child, a painful or unhappy relationship. Even larger problems trouble our society, our country, and our world: poverty, mass starvation, war, racism, disease.

Just as soon as we experience a problem, most of us begin to look for a solution. In fact, **problem solving** is a particularly satisfying form of essay writing because it helps us identify what is wrong in our lives, in our community, or in our world; it helps us determine solutions to these problems; and it enables us to present solutions so that others can benefit from them.

As an example of this type of writing, a young man named Carl (his last name is not given), in a book by James Tollefson titled *The Strength Not to Fight,* solves his personal problem of coming to terms with the way he feels about going to Vietnam to fight. Through extensive reading, Carl discovers that war is not as simple and straightforward as "how the good guy finishes off the bad guy," which he was brought up to believe. As a result of his problem-solving process, he decides not to fight in the Vietnam War despite the fact that he has to go to Canada to avoid the draft.

> My views about war began to change. . . . My interests took me beyond literature that glorified war to literature that revealed the horror of it. One book that was absolutely critical to my formation was *The Fortunes of War,* by Andrew Rooney. . . . It's about four great battles in World War II. Its introduction states that one of the reasons a lot of writing glorifies war is that the people for whom war was a bad experience aren't around to tell any stories about it. It goes on to say that the truism is

right: war is hell. . . . I also read General S. L. A. Marshall's study of combat infantrymen during World War II, which revealed that when push came to shove, over 50 percent of the troops admitted they never fired their weapons. Another high percentage admitted that if they did, they intentionally aimed high or closed their eyes. Taking another life seems to be deeply antithetical to human beings.

Notice the process that Carl followed in order to solve his problem: He recognized the problem; he found information to guide him; and, after this excerpt, he arrived at a solution. He came to believe that killing another person is "antithetical to human beings"—that is, against our nature.

It's important to remember, however, that many problems have no solution, and trying to tackle such problems in your writing can lead to frustration. As you write a problem-solving essay, you should ask the following questions: Does the problem have a possible solution? Will this solution work, or is it so complicated, expensive, or far-fetched that it is not practical? Will this solution create more problems than it solves?

LEARNING FROM PUBLISHED WRITERS

The professional problem-solving essay in this chapter, "Access Activism," was written by Geeta Dardick and published in the *Whole Earth Review* in 1992. In this essay, Dardick describes the problems that her husband, who is confined to a wheelchair, encounters every day of his life. Then she proposes various solutions to these problems, arguing that her ideas will guarantee the rights of all disabled Americans.

Before You Read

Focusing Your Attention

Before you read this essay, take a few moments to respond to the following questions in your journal:

1.   Think of a problem you frequently face. Make a list of ways you might solve that problem, or freewrite about various solutions to the problem.

2.   In the essay you are about to read, the writer describes the enormous amount of time she and her husband devoted to improving the lives of disabled people. Sometimes solving a big problem, such as improving the quality of life of disabled people, requires more energy, hard work, dedication, and expense than we are willing to give. Have you ever avoided attempting to solve a problem for these reasons? What was the problem? Was it easier to live with the problem than do what was required to solve it? Explain why.

Expanding Your Vocabulary

Here are some words and their meanings that are important to your understanding of this essay. You might want to review them before you begin to read.

"the fact that he'd had polio as a kid didn't dampen my **ardor** [strong love] for him" (paragraph 1)

"all I could do was stuff my feelings about the lack of wheelchair **access** [way of getting through]" (paragraph 3)

"My feelings . . . remained **dormant** [sleeping, not active]" (paragraph 5)

"with my evil eye turned on the county's **innumerable** [too many to count] **inaccessible** [denying access] structures" (paragraph 10)

"Each victory was celebrated with **gusto** [energy, enthusiasm], but there was always one **caveat** [warning]" (paragraph 11)

"**Implementation** [the act of putting into practice] is the second step" (paragraph 21)

"Congressman Steny Hoyer put it most **succinctly** [briefly]" (paragraph 21)

Geeta Dardick

Access Activism*

In 1963 I fell in love with Sam Dardick, a man who happened to have a disability. After I announced my engagement to Sam, some narrow-minded "friends" tried to convince me that I shouldn't choose a wheelchair user for a husband, but I ignored their negative comments. To me, Sam Dardick was a charming and sexy guy, and the fact that he'd had polio as a kid didn't dampen my ardor for him.   **1**

Still, during the early years of our marriage, when we lived in St. Louis, Sam's wheelchair was a problem for both of us. We'd try to rent an apartment, and find that 100 percent of them had stairs. We'd go to the movies: stairs again. We'd plan to take the bus . . . more stairs. It soon became obvious that architects, builders, and designers did not take Sam's and my needs into consideration (ironic,   **2**

*Geeta Dardick, "Confessions of an Access Junkie: A Brief Analysis of the Americans with Disabilities Act." *Whole Earth Review* (Fall 1992), pp. 102–105.

since Sam was a graduate of Washington University's School of Architecture).

I felt extremely annoyed every time we encountered an architectural barrier, but I had no way to vent my anger. There weren't any disability laws in Missouri at that time. All I could do was stuff my feelings about the lack of wheelchair access and move on with my life.   **3**

In the early 1970s, we gave up our urban lifestyle, bought land on the San Juan Ridge in Nevada County, California, and became back-to-the-land farmers. Now I worried about the simple things in life, like keeping the woodstove burning so the cabin would be warm enough for the whole-wheat bread to rise. Access seemed irrelevant, since we rarely left our land.   **4**

My feelings about accessibility issues remained dormant for many years; then one sunny day in the spring of 1984, like Rip Van Winkle, I woke up. Sam and I were celebrating his birthday by lunching together at the Posh Nosh Restaurant in Nevada City. After we paid for our beers and pastrami-on-rye sandwiches, Sam suddenly felt an urgent call of nature.   **5**

He wheeled his wheelchair over to the bathroom and discovered that the door was two feet wide. His wheelchair measured two and one-half feet wide. There was no way his chair was going to pass through that door.   **6**

Sam wheeled back to our table, about 20 feet from the bathroom door. Without telling me what he intended to do, Sam jumped out of his wheelchair and dropped himself onto the floor of the restaurant. And then he started crawling rapidly toward the bathroom door.   **7**

Paraplegics like Sam can use their arms, but not their legs. Sam's crawl was a two-handed movement in which he dragged himself across the room like a caterpillar. I sat there watching him in disbelief. Here was the man who was my lover, my husband, the father of my three children, the president of the San Juan Ridge School Board, a guy with graduate degrees in architecture and city planning: here he was, being forced to crawl across the floor of the Posh Nosh Restaurant to use the bathroom. As I watched Sam crawling, I pledged that I was going to do something, to help make sure that neither my husband nor anyone else would be forced to crawl to a bathroom again.   **8**

The following day I started making phone calls. I found out that California already had laws requiring wheelchair accessibility. I also found out that Sam and I could join a state-sponsored program, called the Community Access Network (CAN), that would teach us the   **9** state's accessibility codes and then send us back into Nevada County to enforce them.

That summer, I trained as a CAN volunteer; from that moment on, I became an access cop, with my evil eye turned on the county's innumerable inaccessible structures. Rather than act alone, Sam and I networked with persons from all disability groups and formed a broad-based local access committee to raise community awareness of the need for accessibility and to police new construction projects. **10**

During the next few years, Sam and I volunteered thousands of hours for disability causes throughout California. We marched for access to public transportation in San Francisco, testified for accessible apartments in Sacramento, busted inaccessible city-council meetings in Nevada City, and started an Independent Living Center in Grass Valley. Every victory was celebrated with gusto, but there was always one caveat. We realized that the state of California, with its progressive legislation promoting architectural accessibility, was more advanced on disability issues than most other states. Would the fight for accessibility have to be fought over and over again in every state in the nation? Wasn't there ever going to be a national disability policy? **11**

We didn't have long to wait. Back in 1984, then-president Ronald Reagan directed the National Council on the Handicapped to prepare a special report that would present legislative recommendations for enhancing the productivity and quality of life of Americans with disabilities. **12**

The council's report, submitted to President Reagan in 1986, was entitled *Toward Independence,* and it was much more hard hitting than might have been expected. It recommended "enactment of a comprehensive law requiring equal opportunity for individuals with disabilities, with broad coverage and setting clear, consistent, and enforceable standards prohibiting discrimination on the basis of handicap." That bold recommendation was the seed that resulted in the development of legislation for the Americans with Disabilities Act (ADA), the first national civil-rights bill for people with disabilities. **13**

Opposition to the ADA from business and transportation interests forced disability leaders to wheel and deal. The right to universal health-insurance coverage was bartered away for support from some key legislators. After a great deal of behind-the-scenes negotiation, the ADA passed the House of Representatives 377-28 and the Senate 91-6, with its most important provisions still intact. **14**

The ADA is a comprehensive piece of legislation. The regulations of the ADA (which went into effect on January 26, 1991) will even- **15** tually eliminate many of the barriers faced by people with disabilities. All "public accommodations," such as restaurants, hotels, medical offices, and retail stores, will need to be built with full accessibility. (Adding accessibility to a new structure increases the total cost by 1 percent or less.) Typical accessibility features include ramps, bathrooms with ample space for wheelchairs to turn around, and lightweight doors that are easy to open.

Businesses that decide to remodel will have to make the remodeled area accessible, as well as the path of travel to the area. In existing buildings, inaccessible features must be eliminated if such changes are "readily achievable" without much difficulty or expense. An example would be placing a ramp over one or two steps leading into a store or office.   16

Businesses must provide auxiliary aids to enable a person with a disability to use available materials and services. For example, any video presentations about products would need to be closed-captioned for the deaf, and brochures would need large print so that those with low vision could read them. Another example: providing special pens that have large, spongy, easy-to-hold grips—helpful for many people with arthritis.   17

The ADA also makes major changes in employment criteria. Under the ADA, an employer cannot refuse to hire a qualified applicant with a disability, just because of the person's disability. An employer does not, however, have to give preference to a qualified applicant with a disability over other applicants. An employer must also make "reasonable accommodations" for a person with a disability so he or she can perform the job. This might mean putting an amplifier on a telephone, lowering a desk, or establishing a flexible work schedule. And in new or remodeled facilities, all employee areas including sales and service areas must be made fully accessible. If the accommodations would impose an "undue hardship" (be too costly), however, they will not be required.   18

There are many incentives written into the law to encourage businesses to comply with the ADA. Businesses can receive tax deductions of up to $15,000 for the removal of architectural barriers (if it costs $12,000 to replace stairs with a ramp, for example, the entire amount is tax-deductible). Businesses can receive tax credits equal to 50 percent of all costs of meeting the Americans with Disabilities Act, providing those costs are over $250 and under $10,250. If, for instance, you hired a sign-language interpreter to be present for the signing of contracts with deaf buyers, or if you made a workstation ac-   19 cessible for an employee who uses a wheelchair, you could deduct half of the cost.

Public services also come under the ADA umbrella. All new public **20** buildings and all new buses and rail vehicles must be accessible. . . . telephone companies must provide telecommunications relay services for hearing-impaired and speech-impaired individuals, 24 hours a day.

Of course, passing a law is only a first step to full equality. Imple- **21** mentation is the second step, and it is just as important. Congress-man Steny Hoyer put it most succinctly when he said, "Passing ADA was incredibly historic. Now every day we must fight to make sure that the words in the law, the words on the White House lawn, the words in the House, and the words in the Senate become reality for 43 million Americans with disabilities and millions more around the world who are looking to American leadership for the rights of the disabled."

 ## QUESTIONS FOR CRITICAL THINKING

THINKING CRITICALLY ABOUT CONTENT

1.   Writers often use anecdotes to get the reader's attention, sympathy, or understanding. (An *anecdote* is a story about a real-life event.) What anecdote does Dardick use in this essay that is particularly effective in helping her readers understand the problem?

2.   Why do you think Dardick devotes the second half of her problem-solving essay to an explanation of the rules and regulations legislated by the Americans with Disabilities Act?

THINKING CRITICALLY ABOUT PURPOSE

3.   What do you think Geeta Dardick's purpose is in this essay?

4.   We often think some problems are just too big for one person to solve, especially if bureaucracies like state or federal governments are involved. In what ways might Dardick's essay inspire others who face problems that can't be solved very quickly or easily?

THINKING CRITICALLY ABOUT AUDIENCE

5.   What group or groups of people do you think would most benefit from reading this essay?

6.   How do you think a general audience would respond to the author's description of the many incentives offered to businesses for complying with the laws that were written to help people with disabilities?

7. Describe in a complete sentence the writer's point of view.

8. If Dardick were writing this essay for a publication to be read only by people with disabilities, how might it be different? How might it be the same? Rewrite the introduction or the conclusion for an audience of people with disabilities.

LEARNING FROM YOUR PEERS

In real life, we all face problems every day. Some have obvious solutions, and we handle them quickly. Others are more complicated, and sometimes we cannot find a solution unless someone helps us. As the saying goes, "If you always do what you've always done, then you'll always get what you've always got." This may not be the most elegant phrasing in the English language, but it makes an important point: Learning to analyze and solve problems is a valuable skill that we can develop throughout life if we are open to new possibilities. To see how a student writer generates a problem-solving essay, we are going to follow the writing process of a student named Amanda Bliss.

Amanda's Writing Assignment: Problem Solving

This is the topic Amanda's instructor assigned:

Most of us will never find the solutions to overwhelming social problems or the cures for devastating diseases, but we often solve smaller problems in our lives every day. Think of a problem that you have successfully solved. Then explain the problem and its solution to your class.

Amanda goes through the process as outlined in Chapter 1: *thinking, planning, developing, organizing, drafting, revising,* and *editing.*

Thinking

Amanda's class spends some time brainstorming and comes up with a list of possible topics:

managing study time

compromising with a roommate about visitors

solving a misunderstanding with a co-worker

reaching an agreement with parents about using their car and paying for gas exchanging child care with a neighbor for an evening out

managing money on a student budget

trading routine car care for house-cleaning services

car-pooling with a classmate who is studying the same subject so driving

time becomes study time

Several students realize that they have been solving complicated problems for several years, but others are still looking for topics, so the class spends about 15 minutes freewriting to explore and develop ideas. This writing assignment draws on all of the purposes the students have already studied in this book.

At the end of this class period, Amanda has decided to write about holiday celebrations at her house. Because everyone in the family has a different picture of the ideal holiday, no one is ever happy with holiday preparations or celebrations. Recently, the family reached a compromise that was satisfactory to all concerned.

Planning

Clustering is a favorite creating technique for Amanda. She likes to take a big piece of drawing paper and scribble her ideas all over it. Sometimes she doodles and draws until ideas come to her. For this essay, she finds herself drawing Christmas trees and poinsettias and pine boughs, even though Christmas is several months away. She writes the words "Merry Christmas" in the center of her paper and then starts drawing more decorations. They remind her of the jumble her house used to be in before the Christmas holidays. She writes the following phrases on her paper:

Mom's search for the perfect holiday

artichokes and persimmons

evergreens everywhere

After writing these phrases on her paper, Amanda laughs out loud at the essay that is forming in her mind. She knows that she can use many visual details to explain the problem to her readers. She remembers exactly what her mother's large collection of holiday ornaments looks like, and she thinks about the stress of the holidays in her house.

Developing

Amanda wants to introduce her mother to her readers, but she does not want them to conclude that her mother is a close relative of Ebeneezer Scrooge. She knows she can capture her readers' interest by comparing her house to the colorful magazines that always seem to be everywhere during the holidays. She also wants to explain the conflict clearly, because it has caused endless complaints, accusations, and arguments over the years. She wants her readers to know that she has always dreaded holidays, but now she looks forward to them with enthusiasm because of the solution her family devised.

Drawing a line down the middle of a piece of notebook paper, Amanda heads two columns: "Before the Great Compromise" and "After the Great Compromise." Then she lists several differences in her house that she has observed over the years. This is how her list looks:

Before the Great Compromise	After the Great Compromise
refrigerator full of holiday food	simple foods
cleaning frenzy, arguments	regular housekeeping okay
seasonal decorations in every room	a few nice touches
cinnamon everywhere	normal, clean smell
clutter, clutter, clutter	room to move around
no storage space, too much holiday stuff	room for storing off-season clothes

Amanda is satisfied with her list and decides to start arranging her ideas.

Organizing

Amanda writes her thesis statement:

> It took us several years, but we finally found a solution to Mom's search for the perfect holiday.

She is satisfied with this statement because it states clearly that although the problem was her mother's, the family found a solution together.

She looks over her "Before" and "After" lists and decides to outline her essay in a way that emphasizes the differences. She also takes out her original doodling sheet with the clusters on it and tacks it to the bulletin board over her desk. As she maps out her essay, she glances back and forth at both the list and the doodles. Before long, she has a rough outline of her essay.

1. Main point: When I was growing up, Mom wanted every holiday to be the perfect holiday.

2. Thanksgiving and Christmas were the worst. She would start bringing in foods that were yucky as soon as she started reading

those holiday magazines. Things like candied cherries and persimmons when we just wanted peanut butter and jelly.

3. Then came the cleaning frenzies. And her need to have baking bread smells in the air at all times.

4. She would go nuts with the decorations--evergreen everything.

5. And dishes--she would buy every plastic Santa Claus cup on the market.

6. There was a turning point--my sister and I decided to tell Mom to quit doing this. Simplify!

7. Conclusion: Life got more peaceful, and we enjoy holidays now.

That evening, Amanda shares the outline with her sister. They spend some time laughing about the arguments they used to have, and her sister makes some suggestions for details to add to the outline.

Drafting

When Amanda decides to write her essay the next day, she sits at her desk with the doodles on the bulletin board in front of her and her list and outline close at hand. She puts some Christmas music on the stereo to get in the holiday mood, and she starts writing her essay. This is the draft she wrote.

Amanda's Essay: First Draft

Main Idea: My Mom always tried to create the perfect holiday in our house until we talked to her.

When I was growing up, holidays at our house were always dreadful and filled with stress. My mom always wanted things to be just like they are in the magazines. The problem was obvious. We do not live in places like the ones that we saw in the magazines. We never ate the kinds of foods that she found in the women's magazines or that we saw on the television commercials. It took us several years, but we finally found a solution that ended Mom's search for the perfect holiday.

The tension would start about a week before Thanksgiving usually.

She would start buying stuff and bringing it in the house. Buying all sorts of groceries, the kitchen began to look like an overstocked supermarket. The refrigerator was so full of holiday food, packed that there was no room for anything like peanut butter and jelly. We would have to dig around the dates and candied cherries and the thawing turkey and the artichokes and the persimmons--mom's boss gave it to her--to find something to pack in our lunch boxes. Clipping bizarre recipes out of the Sunday paper, the refrigerator would be filled with ingredients. We always say, "Yuck, what is that?" when you saw the latest concoction of cranberries, whipped cream, and walnuts. I don't care what you do to cranberries, it always tastes sour to me.

Also every year, at about the same time as the strange food started coming into the house, she decided we all needed to go on a cleaning frenzy. Now remember that we did not have any relatives within a thousand miles. No one was likely to drop in on us. But she had this idea that everything had to be clean and organized so that no one would think she was a slob. I think she thought that the scent of persimmon bread baking in the oven was going to draw in curiosity seekers from miles around to tell her how domestic she was.

Once the house was clean, she would decide that we needed to have seasonal decorations in every room in the house. One year there was so much stuff that smelled like cinnamon in our house that you would have dreams about cooking in a bakery or working in a spice warehouse. During another year, she would decide that everything should smell like evergreens, that our house would look like a pine forest. We would have evergreen wreaths on every door, evergreen candleholder rings on every table, evergreens in baskets with pine cones, evergreen printed table cloths and napkins and dish towels. This really got on our nerves. I mean no one likes their entire house taken over by evergreens. It was crazy.

Then there was the matter of dishes. First, it was just plastic dishes with Santa Claus on them. Then it was punch bowls. We didn't even like punch! Then coffee mugs with cute little elves on them. Then china. Every year, she would go to the sales after Christmas and buy anything that was at least 50% off. You should always try to save money, but enough is enough! By the time I was 15 and my sister was 17, we decided that she had to quit buying so much holiday stuff. So we decided on Halloween to have a talk with her.

Laura and I knew that Mom wanted our holidays to be perfect. But she didn't have to keep buying all those decorations and strange foods. In a couple of magazine articles, it even said that people should not overdo things at holidays and feel pressure to spend money just because everyone else is. We told her so, and she acted really surprised. Of course, we also told her we didn't believe in Santa Claus anymore and that we really did not care for persimmons and pomegranates. We wanted to help her make the holidays fun, but not crazy. After talking things out, we agreed to buy some convenience foods that we really liked, things that are your timeless favorites. Also, we each offered to make some cookies, quick breads, and other simple foods, so we could save time and money that we could spend on gifts. To help matters even more, we would buy a turkey breast and roast it so that we would not have all those leftovers. One of us had to tell their side of the story. Think about it. Doesn't our compromise solution sound much better?

We started following this plan for all the major holidays. It is much more relaxing and peaceful. And my sister and I do agree to taste one new recipe that she prepares every holiday. However, we don't promise not to say, "Yuck, Mom, what is this?"

Revising

Now that Amanda has written her draft, she faces the task of revising. During the next class period, the instructor asks the students to look at their essays as a whole this time, paying special attention to how their supporting paragraphs work in relationship to their thesis statements. At this point in the course, Amanda has learned that every part of an essay has its own place and should be related to other parts of the essay.

Amanda reviews the Checklist for Writing Supporting and Concluding Paragraphs at the beginning of the Tips for Revising section of this chapter. She learns from the checklist and from class that the revising process at this stage involves checking the contents of the thesis sentence, then making sure each paragraph after the introduction is fully developed and directly related, through its topic sentence and its supporting details, to the essay's thesis. She reads the Tips for Revising section in this chapter, which explains that the whole essay should follow a logical progression based on its thesis statement and that the conclusion should summarize the essay's main ideas.

Amanda uses the checklist to review the structure of her entire essay. She pulls out the thesis statement of her essay and each topic sentence and writes them on a separate piece of paper. She makes sure each topic sentence is related to her thesis and is developed as fully as possible. She discovers several problems in logic and begins moving sentences around. After she makes her changes, she rereads her essay and feels that it fulfills the revision guidelines as she understands them.

COLLABORATIVE WORK

PEER GROUP ACTIVITY

After you read the portions of the Tips for Revising your instructor assigns, turn to Amanda's first draft (pp. 413–415), and complete the following tasks in small groups:

A. Highlight the essay's thesis statement (for a definition, see p. 371) with a colored marker.

B. Underline the topic sentence (for a definition, see p. 424) of each body paragraph.

C. Put an X by any paragraph that either lacks a topic sentence or has a topic sentence that is not directly related to the essay's thesis statement.

D. In the margin, make suggestions for improving the concluding paragraph.

Compare the marks your group recorded with those your instructor will show you. Where do your marks differ from your instructor's? What do you need to review before writing your own essay?

CLASS ACTIVITY

As an entire class, look at the underlined portions of Amanda's revised draft (pp. 418–420) to see what changes she made.

A. Did you identify the **revision** problems that Amanda corrected?

B. Do you think her changes are good ones? Discuss her changes.

Editing

Now that Amanda's supporting paragraphs are fully developed, she needs to do some final proofreading and editing before handing in her essay. The instructor explains that all the students in the class should have a similar understanding of sentence structure and variety. So Amanda shifts her attention from the content of her paragraphs to specific points of grammar. She reads the Tips for Editing section in this chapter to learn more about writing sentences that are parallel, consistent, and varied in structure and type. After she finishes the exercises her instructor assigns, she rereads her essay and quickly finds a couple of problems with inconsistent tenses. These errors put her on the alert for more problems with consistency. She decides she had better slow down and approach her revision more systematically, so she goes over the questions on the Checklist for Writing Successful Sentences one by one and makes changes in her essay so her revised draft fulfills all the requirements on the checklist.

 ## COLLABORATIVE WORK

PEER GROUP ACTIVITY

After you read the portions of the Tips for Editing your instructor assigns, turn to Amanda's first draft (pp. 413–415), and complete the following tasks in small groups:

A. Put an X through any problems with pronouns that are remote, unclear, or broad (for an explanation of these terms, see pp. 429–432).

B. Use an arrow to show where a modifier should be moved in a sentence so that the word(s) it modifies are clear to the reader.

C. Underline any part of a series that is not parallel in structure to the other items in the series (for an explanation, see pp. 437–438).

D. Circle any words that are not consistent in tense, person, or number (for explanations, see pp. 440, 441, and 441).

E. Put brackets around any sentences that are monotonous in their structure or type and should be varied (for an explanation, see pp. 442–447).

Compare your marks to those your instructor will show you. Where do your marks differ from your instructor's? What do you need to review before writing your own essay?

CLASS ACTIVITY

As an entire class, look at the underlined portions of Amanda's revised draft (pp. 418–420) to see how she changed each sentence.

A.   Did you identify the **editing** problems that Amanda corrected?

B.   Do you think her changes are good ones? Discuss her changes.

Amanda's Revised Essay

Inventing the Perfect Holiday

When I was growing up, holidays at our house were always dreadful and filled with stress. My mom always wanted things to be just like they are in the magazines. The problem was obvious. We did ~~do~~ not live in places like the ones that we saw in the magazines. <u>Also,</u> <u>she was not a very good cook, and w</u>W<u>e</u> never ate the kinds of foods that she found in the women's magazines or that we saw on the television commercials. It took us several years, but we finally found a solution that ended Mom's search for the perfect holiday.

The tension would <u>usually</u> start about a week before Thanksgiving ~~usually~~. <u>Mom</u> ~~She~~ would start buying stuff and bringing it in the house. Buying all sorts of groceries, <u>my mom filled</u> the kitchen <u>until it</u> began to look like an overstocked supermarket. The <u>packed</u> refrigerator was so full of holiday food/ ~~packed~~ that there was no room for anything like peanut butter and jelly. We would have to dig around the dates and candied cherries ~~and the thawing turkey~~ and the artichokes and the persimmons <u>and the thawing turkey</u>--mom's boss gave it to her--to find ~~something~~ <u>some bologna</u> to pack in our lunch boxes. Clipping bizarre recipes out of the Sunday paper, <u>my</u> <u>mom would fill</u> the refrigerator ~~would be filled~~ with ingredients. We always ~~say~~ <u>said</u>, "Yuck, what is that?" when ~~you~~ <u>we</u> saw the latest concoction of cranberries, whipped cream, and walnuts. I don't care what you do to cranberries;/ ~~it~~ <u>they</u> always ~~tastes~~ <u>taste</u> sour to me.

Also every year, at about the same time as the strange food started coming into the house, she decided we all needed to go on a cleaning <u>and organizing</u> frenzy. <u>First, my sister and I would have to</u>

help her take everything out of the kitchen cabinets and hall closet. Then, we had to sort, clean, and pack all the holiday china, decorations, and candles from preceding years along with everyday dishes and utensils. One year, we even had to clean the edges of the tiles with Q-tips dipped in ammonia. After that, we had to take down all the curtains, wash them and hang them back, and shampoo the carpet, which then stayed damp for days and got dirtier than ever from pine needles and spills. ~~Now remember that~~ Since we did not have any relatives within a thousand miles/, n~~N~~o one was likely to drop in on us. But she had this idea that everything had to be clean and organized so that no one would think she was a slob. I think she thought that the scent of persimmon bread baking in the oven was going to draw in curiosity seekers from miles around to tell her how domestic she was and to compliment her on her cooking.

Once the house was clean, she would decide that we needed to have seasonal decorations in every room in the house. One year there was so much stuff that smelled like cinnamon in our house that ~~you~~ I would have dreams about cooking in a bakery or working in a spice warehouse. During another year, she would decide that everything should smell like evergreens, that our house would look like a pine forest. We would have evergreen wreaths on every door, evergreen candleholder rings on every table, evergreens in baskets with pine cones, evergreen printed table cloths and napkins and dish towels. ~~This~~ All these evergreens in the house really got on our nerves. I mean, no one likes ~~their~~ his or her entire house taken over by evergreens. ~~It~~ Mom's overdecorating was crazy/!

Then there was the matter of dishes. First, it was just plastic dishes with Santa Claus on them. Then it was punch bowls. We didn't even like punch! Then coffee mugs with cute little elves on them. Then china. Every year, she would go to the sales after Christmas and buy anything that was at least 50 percent off. ~~You~~ People should always try to save money, but enough is enough! By the time I was 15 and my sister was 17, we decided that she had to quit buying so much holiday stuff. So ~~we decided~~ on Halloween, we decided to have a talk with her.

Laura and I knew that Mom wanted our holidays to be perfect/, b~~B~~ut she didn't have to keep buying all those decorations and strange foods. ~~In a~~ A couple of magazine articles/ ~~it~~ even said that people should not overdo things at holidays and feel pressure to spend money just because everyone else is. We told her so, and she acted really surprised. Of course, we also told her that we didn't believe in Santa Claus anymore and that we really did not care for persimmons and pomegranates. We wanted to help her make the holidays fun, but not crazy. After talking things out, we agreed to buy some convenience foods that we really liked, things that are ~~your~~ some of our timeless favorites. Also, we each offered to make some cookies, quick breads, and other simple foods, so we could save time and money that we could spend on gifts. To help matters even more, we would buy a turkey breast and roast it so that we would not have all those leftovers. One of us had to tell ~~their~~ her side of the story. Think about it. Doesn't our compromise solution sound much better?

We started following this more relaxing and peaceful plan for all the major holidays. ~~It is much more relaxing and peaceful.~~ Mom went through all her holiday decorations and saved only the prettiest ones; the others went into a yard sale. Now, even though she enjoys the pictures in holiday magazines, she no longer believes that her house must look like them. And my sister and I do agree to taste one new recipe that she prepares every holiday/, even if it has black walnuts, cranberries, persimmons, cream cheese, and fake frozen whipped cream in it. However, we ~~don't~~ did not promise ~~not~~ to stop saying, "Yuck, Mom, what is this?"

WRITING YOUR OWN PROBLEM-SOLVING ESSAY

So far, you have seen a professional writer and a fellow student at work trying to solve a problem they feel is worth resolving. As you read the professional essay and followed the writing process of another student from first to final draft, you absorbed ideas to work with and ways of giving those ideas a form of their own. These reading and writing activities have prepared you to write your own problem-solving essay on a topic that is meaningful to you.

What Have You Discovered?

Before you begin your own writing task, let's review what you have learned in this chapter so far:

- Problems and their solutions are all around us.
- Problem-solving essays identify a problem, determine whether it has a solution, and present the solution.
- The following questions will guide your problem-solving essay:

  Does the problem have a solution?

  Will the solution work, or is it so complicated, expensive, or far-fetched that it is not practical?

  Will the solution create more problems that the original problem?

- To present your problem-solving essay effectively, you need to organize your ideas.
- To help you shape your essay, you should learn as much as possible about your readers.
- Before you write a draft, you need to decide on a point of view toward your subject.
- After you write a draft, you should revise your essay for meaning and organization.
- After you revise your essay, you should edit its grammar, usage, and sentence structure.

Your Writing Topic

Choose one of the following topics for your problem-solving essay:

1.   In "Access Activism," the writer described the efforts that she and her husband made to improve the lives of disabled people. Consider a possible problem that one or more people might have: It could be caused by a physical or mental disability; by discrimination, poverty, illness, or injustice; or by lack of caring and concern. Write an essay in which you describe the problem and the way it could be solved.

2.   Your college newspaper is running a special edition on proposed solutions to important campus problems. Write an essay for your school paper that identifies an important problem on your campus (such as a problem in the cafeteria service), and suggest how this problem might be successfully solved.

3.   Write a letter explaining a complicated problem that you had with a business or organization to the CEO of that business or organization; then, offer your suggestions to this person for solving the problem.

4.   Create your own problem-solving topic (with the assistance of your instructor), and write a response to it.

When you have selected one of these topics, you may begin your writing process in the same way Amanda did. (You may find rereading her experience helpful at this point.) This time your purpose is to write your own essay. If some tasks occur out of order, that adjustment is probably part of your personal writing ritual. Follow your instincts, and let them mold your own writing process. But make sure you've worked through all the stages to your final draft.

Your Writing Process

THINKING   Generate as many ideas on your subject as you can in as many different ways as possible: rereading, listing, freewriting, brainstorming, clustering, discussing, and questioning.

PLANNING   Begin to give your ideas shape by deciding on your approach to your topic (your content, your purpose, your audience, and your point of view). Make a list of points you want to include in your essay.

DEVELOPING   Add more details on three or four specific, focused topics that you have chosen from your list of general points.

ORGANIZING   Organize your material in a way that will be most interesting to your audience.

DRAFTING   Write a working draft of your essay in complete sentences.

REVISING   Consulting the Tips for Revising in this chapter (pp. 424–428), revise your first draft—paying special attention to your supporting paragraphs and your conclusion and their relationship to your thesis statement.

EDITING   Consulting the Tips for Editing in this chapter (pp. 429–447), edit your draft for grammar and correctness—paying special attention to the structure and variety of your sentences.

Turn in your revised draft to your instructor.

Some Final Thoughts

When you have completed your own essay, answer these four questions in your journal:

1. What was most difficult about this assignment?
2. What was easiest?
3. What did I learn about problem solving by completing this assignment?
4. What did I learn about my own writing process from this assignment—how I prepared to write, how I wrote the first draft, how I revised, and how I edited?

Writing Supporting and Concluding Paragraphs

Checklist for Writing Supporting and Concluding Paragraphs

✓ Does each supporting paragraph have a **topic sentence** that relates to the essay's thesis statement?

✓ Is the topic sentence of each supporting paragraph fully **developed?**

✓ Does the essay's concluding paragraph **summarize** the main ideas, **highlight** the most important issues, and **conclude** the essay?

A skilled artisan making a fine wooden table understands the importance of constructing a sturdy base. The legs or pedestal must support the top so that it does not collapse or even wobble. Only after the foundation is firm does the artisan apply a fine finish to enhance and protect the beautiful wood. Building an essay is like building a table. Once you are satisfied with the foundation (your title, introduction, and thesis), you need to add solid supporting paragraphs and a fine finish for your conclusion. Solid support is especially important in a problem-solving essay so that you explain your problem clearly before offering a solution.

Supporting Paragraphs

In your supporting paragraphs, you expand upon each of the individual topics your essay will cover. At least one supporting paragraph should cover each topic in your essay. **Supporting paragraphs,** also called **body paragraphs,** usually include a topic sentence, which is a general statement of the paragraph's contents, and details that support the topic sentence. (See pages 176–182 and 232–239 for methods to use when you develop and organize paragraphs.) Each body paragraph should be directly related to the thesis statement in the introduction.

Look at the following example from Geeta Dardick's essay "Access Activism" (pp. 405–409). The thesis statement for the essay, finally appearing in paragraph 8 after a lengthy introduction, is "As I watched Sam crawling, I pledged that I was going to do something, to help make sure that neither my husband nor anyone else would be forced to crawl to a bathroom again." The body paragraphs that follow this introduction enumerate the steps the author and her husband took to bring attention to the problems of disabled people in an effort to find solutions. Paragraph 11, for example, introduces the topic of the volunteer work she and her husband contributed to the cause. The topic sentence in bold type relates directly to the essay's thesis, and the supporting sentences catalogue some of the steps the activists took toward a national disability policy.

> **During the next few years, Sam and I volunteered thousands of hours for disability causes throughout California.** We marched for ac-

cess to public transportation in San Francisco, testified for accessible apartments in Sacramento, busted inaccessible city-council meetings in Nevada City, and started an Independent Living Center in Grass Valley. Every victory was celebrated with gusto, but there was always one caveat. We realized that the state of California, with its progressive legislation promoting architectural accessibility, was more advanced on disability issues than most other states. Would the fight for accessibility have to be fought over and over again in every state in the nation? Wasn't there ever going to be a national disability policy?

All of Dardick's body paragraphs offer clear topic sentences that relate to the essay's thesis and well-developed explanations that expand on each topic sentence.

Reviewing her first draft, Amanda decided that paragraph 3 could be improved with the kind of specific details she included in paragraph 2 on the food problem. She revised paragraph 3 to make it stronger, with specific details about the cleaning frenzy.

First Draft: Also every year, at about the same time as the strange food started coming into the house, she decided we all needed to go on a cleaning frenzy. Now remember that we did not have any relatives within a thousand miles. No one was likely to drop in on us. But she had this idea that everything had to be clean and organized so that no one would think she was a slob. I think she thought that the scent of persimmon bread baking in the oven was going to draw in curiosity seekers from miles around to tell her how domestic she was.

Revision: Also every year, at about the same time as the strange food started coming into the house, she decided we all needed to go on a cleaning **and organizing** frenzy. **First, my sister and I would have to help her take everything out of the kitchen cabinets and hall closet. Then, we had to sort, clean, and pack all the holiday china, decorations, and candles from preceding years along with everyday dishes and utensils. One year, we even had to clean the edges of the tiles with Q-tips dipped in ammonia. After that, we had to take down all the curtains, wash them and hang them back, and shampoo the carpet, which**

then stayed damp for days and got dirtier than ever from pine needles and spills. ~~Now remember that~~ **Since** we did not have any relatives within a thousand miles/, **n**~~N~~o one was likely to drop in on us. But she had this idea that everything had to be clean and organized so that no one would think she was a slob. I think she thought that the scent of persimmon bread baking in the oven was going to draw in curiosity seekers from miles around to tell her how domestic she was **and to compliment her on her cooking.**

Amanda's revised topic sentence relates to the essay's thesis statement ("It took us several years, but we finally found a solution that ended Mom's search for the perfect holiday."). Amanda also added specific details explaining the many chores she and her sister had to do to satisfy their mother's need to have the house perfectly clean and organized.

Exercise R9-1

Explain the methods Dardick uses to develop paragraphs 9 and 19 in her essay "Access Activism" (pp. 405–409).

Exercise R9-2

Suggest more supporting details that would develop the topic sentence of paragraph 5 in Amanda's first draft (pp. 414–415).

Exercise R9-3

Read the following topic sentences, and add supporting details to each.

1. I have discovered an excellent way to resolve conflicts with my brother over doing the chores.
2. I have finally found a way to remember important anniversaries in my family so that I don't offend anyone by not recognizing them.
3. The worst problem I ever had on a job occurred when I was a high school senior.
4. Fireworks should be outlawed.
5. Fireworks add color and excitement to many occasions.

Exercise R9-4

Revise the following body paragraph with details from your own experience.

I put my free time to good use. I organize a lot of things and clean up some things. I also relax and have fun.

Concluding Paragraphs

The **concluding paragraph** is generally the final paragraph in an essay. Although concluding paragraphs can be structured in several ways, usually a conclusion summarizes the main ideas in an essay and highlights the most important issues the writer has discussed. Two other ways to end a paper on a strong note are to leave the reader with a further question on the topic or to make a prediction or a recommendation. The most important responsibility of the last paragraph is that it actually conclude the essay.

Dardick concludes her article emphatically with a quotation that recommends further action in support of the disabled.

> Of course, passing a law is only a first step to full equality. Implementation is the second step, and it is just as important. Congressman Steny Hoyer put it most succinctly when he said, "Passing ADA was incredibly historic. Now every day we must fight to make sure that the words in the law, the words on the White House lawn, the words in the House, and the words in the Senate become reality for 43 million Americans with disabilities and millions more around the world who are looking to American leadership for the rights of the disabled."

With this ending, the author encourages her readers to keep working on behalf of the disabled and attempts to inspire them to take action.

As Amanda studied the conclusion of her first draft, she decided it needed strengthening in two ways.

First Draft: We started following this plan for all the major holidays. It is much more relaxing and peaceful. And my sister and I do agree to taste one new recipe that she prepares every holiday. However, we don't promise not to say, "Yuck, Mom, what is this?"

Revision: We started following this **more relaxing and peaceful** plan for all the major holidays. ~~It is much more relaxing and peaceful.~~ **Mom went through all her holiday decorations and saved only the prettiest ones; the others went into a yard sale. Now, even though she enjoys the pictures in holiday magazines, she no longer believes that her house must look like them.** And my sister and I do agree to taste one new recipe that she prepares every holiday/**, even if it has black walnuts, cranberries,**

persimmons, cream cheese, and fake frozen whipped cream in it. However, we **did not** promise to **stop** say**ing**, "Yuck, Mom, what is this?"

Amanda's revised conclusion summarizes the main points in her essay and ends with a question. The final sentence, in particular, could have taken the essay in a number of different directions, but Amanda's choice lightens the tone of the entire essay and brings closure to her story as well.

Exercise R9-5

Rewrite an alternative concluding paragraph for Dardick's essay "Access Activism" (p. 409).

Exercise R9-6

Suggest another way that Amanda could have concluded her first draft (p. 415). Write a new conclusion based on your suggestion.

Exercise R9-7

Using the body paragraph you wrote in Exercise R9-4, write a conclusion for an essay on using your free time. Use a technique for writing conclusions that you have not used yet.

Exercise R9-8

Write an alternative conclusion for one of the essays you have written during this school term. Turn in your essay with your revised conclusion.

 ## COLLABORATIVE WORK

After writing a draft of your own problem-solving essay, exchange papers with a classmate, and do the following tasks:

A.   Put a line through any topic sentences that are not directly related to the essay's thesis statement.

B.   Put an X by any paragraphs that do not have enough supporting details or that include details that do not develop the topic of the paragraph. Suggest improvements in the margins.

C.   Decide whether the conclusion is effective. If it is not, suggest revisions.

Then return the paper to its writer, and use the information in this section to revise your draft.

Successful Sentences

At one time or another, you have probably been a member of a team. You may have actively participated in sports at school or in your community recreation leagues. Perhaps your part-time job at a fast-food restaurant depends upon your interaction with other people. Or maybe you have taken part in classroom discussion groups or special projects that required your interaction and cooperation with your peers. Whatever the situation, teamwork is important in many everyday situations. To be a good team member, you must perform your individual duties and work with others in mind.

Sentences also require good teamwork. Each individual sentence must function independently, possessing all the necessary elements to form a complete thought. But expressing ideas is not enough. To be truly successful, sentences must connect with each other and express similar ideas, working toward the common goal of communicating their meaning.

In this section, you will learn to compose successful sentences that work in harmony, as you edit your writing with a more critical eye. You will learn to isolate and correct the errors that keep sentences from fulfilling their communication goals: you will encounter problems with pronoun reference, modifiers, and parallelism, as well as unnecessary shifts in tense, person, and number. You will also learn more about sentence variety. Incorporating specific sentence-building strategies will help your writing become more engaging and cohesive as you achieve your goals of clarity and unity.

Pronoun Reference

Each pronoun must have an **antecedent,** a noun or another pronoun it refers to. Usually the antecedent is in the same sentence. Sometimes, however, the antecedent appears in a previous sentence. Look at these examples from Amanda's revised problem-solving essay.

Antecedent   Antecedent   Pronoun
My mom always wanted **things** to be just like **they** are in the magazines.

Pronoun
Also, **she** was not a very good cook, and we never ate the kinds of foods
Pronoun
that **she** found in the women's magazines or that we saw on the

television commercials.

The pronouns and antecedents in Amanda's sentences are easy to spot. Sometimes, however, problems with pronoun reference arise, particularly when antecedents are remote, unclear, or vague.

Remote Reference

In some sentences, words, phrases, or clauses separate a pronoun from its antecedent. In fact, the two words may be so far from each other that the pronoun's antecedent is unclear. Look at this example from Amanda's first draft:

> **Remote:**   We would have to dig around the dates and candied
>
> cherries and the thawing **turkey** and the **artichokes** and
>
> the **persimmons**--mom's boss gave **it** to her--to find
>
> something to pack in our lunch boxes.

The pronoun *it* refers to *turkey*. However, because *artichokes* and *persimmons* separate *it* from *turkey*, the sentence is confusing. Here is Amanda's revised sentence with the pronoun and antecedent as close together as possible:

> **Revision:**   We would have to dig around the dates and candied
>
> cherries ~~and the thawing turkey~~ and the artichokes and
>
> the persimmons and the thawing **turkey**--mom's boss gave
>
> **it** to her--to find some bologna to pack in our
>
> lunchboxes.

Sometimes words even have to be shifted from one sentence to another.

> **Remote:**   The **shelves** in the refrigerator had not been cleaned out for weeks, and the **cupboards** had not been rearranged for months. So **they** were pretty crowded with life forms of their own flourishing in the cold.
>
> **Revision:**   The **shelves** in the refrigerator had not been cleaned out for

weeks, so **they** were pretty crowded with life forms of their own flourishing in the cold. The **cupboards** had also not been rearranged for months.

Rearranging the sentence so that the pronoun *they* is closest to the word *shelves* makes the reference clear to the readers.

Unclear Reference

Sometimes a pronoun seems to have more than one antecedent. This **unclear reference** causes problems for readers because they do not know what is intended. Consider the following sentences:

Unclear Reference:	Amanda told Laura that she would have to talk to their mother.

Who will talk to their mother—Amanda or Laura? As the sentence now stands, we can't tell which person the word *she* refers to. Such sentences must be rewritten to make the intended message clear, even if it means eliminating the pronoun.

Revisions:	Amanda and Laura agreed that **Amanda** would have to talk to their mother. Amanda and Laura agreed that **Laura** would have to talk to their mother.
Unclear Reference:	Amanda likes to clean house more than Laura does. Sometimes **she** would rather do **her** homework.
Revisions:	Amanda likes to clean house more than Laura does. Sometimes **Amanda** would rather do **her** homework.

Here is another unclear pronoun reference from Amanda's first draft:

Unclear Reference:	We would have evergreen wreaths on every door, evergreen candleholder rings on every table, evergreens in baskets with pine cones, evergreen printed table cloths and napkins and dish towels. **This** really got on our nerves. I mean no one likes their entire house taken over by evergreens. **It** was crazy.

In this paragraph, the antecedents for the words *this* and *it* are unclear. We don't really know what they refer to. What got on Amanda's and her sister's nerves? What was crazy? This paragraph lists many causes of the frustration in the household, but these two pronouns need to refer to a specific issue.

Revisions: **All these evergreens in the house** really got on our nerves.

Mom's overdecorating was crazy.

If you think a pronoun is unclear, a good rule is to substitute a specific noun for the pronoun, like Amanda did here.

Broad Reference

Writers often use the pronouns *you* and *it* to refer to general groups of people or things. Such examples of **broad reference** should be avoided; *you* and *it* are personal pronouns that should refer to specific persons, places, ideas, or items. Look at these examples from Amanda's essay:

Broad: **You** should always try to save money, but enough is enough!

Revision: **People** should always try to save money, but enough is enough!

Broad: In a couple of magazine articles, **it** even said that people should not overdo things at holidays and feel pressure to spend money just because everyone else is.

Revision: ~~In a~~ **A** couple of magazine articles/~~it~~ even said that people should not overdo things at holidays and feel pressure to spend money just because everyone else is.

Both these examples illustrate a different type of broad reference. Sentences should always be rewritten to clear up these problems.

Exercise E9-1

List the pronouns and their antecedents in paragraphs 11 through 14 of Geeta Dardick's essay "Access Activism" (p. 407).

Exercise E9-2

List each pronoun and its antecedent in paragraphs 2 and 6 of Amanda's first draft (pp. 413–415).

Exercise E9-3

Correct the faulty pronoun references in the following paragraphs.

(1) One September morning my sister Connie woke me from a deep sleep. (2) "It says right here in the paper that tickets go on sale next week for the first of two Pearl Jam concerts at the Pyramid. (3) We've got to get some!" she screamed in my ear.

(4) That's how our ticket-buying adventure began. (5) We made plans to arrive outside the ticket window at least 12 hours before tickets went on sale. (6) That meant midnight. (7) When we got there, several security guards were there and about 30 people, including some of our friends. (8) We showed them our identification and settled down for the night.

(9) We had brought sleeping bags, several bags of snacks, two ice chests, a boom box, pillows, extra clothes, and a flashlight. (10) We had borrowed them from my boyfriend, who goes camping a lot. (11) We had also plenty of batteries for the boom box and flashlight. (12) You need to buy a good brand so they will last long. (13) Anyway, Connie turned it on as soon as we got settled down, but I made her turn it off because we didn't really need it.

(14) We talked to the people around us in line. Two guys—Zack and Frank—were ahead of us. (15) Zack kept making goofy noises, and Frank said he was going to have to move. (16) They were really funny and entertained us. (17) The girls behind us were Alice, Carrie, and Chris. (18) They weren't too friendly because Alice and Carrie had been in an argument, so it seemed. (19) Alice told Carrie that she was going to pay for all of their tickets. (20) That's what they kept fighting about until she said she would. (21) This kept us up for a while.

(22) About 4:00 a.m. we finally dozed off to sleep. (23) We woke up about 8:00 shivering from the cold. (24) On the news that night it had said it would be pretty warm. (25) Connie dug a sweatshirt and a jacket out of a paper sack and gave it to me. (26) I was still cold, but one of the security guards brought me some coffee. (27) His kindness made me smile because it really warmed me up.

Exercise E9-4

Write a paragraph (6–8 sentences) in which you describe a significant "first" in your life—your first day of high school, your first date, your first time driving a car. Underline each pronoun, and circle its antecedent.

Modifier Problems

Modifiers are words that describe, limit, or explain other sentence elements. When we hear the word *modifier*, we usually think of adjectives, which describe nouns and pronouns, and adverbs, which modify verbs, adjectives, and other adverbs. (See pp. 46–48 for more information about adjectives and p. 49 for more information about adverbs.)

Single words, phrases, and clauses can function as modifiers and should be as close as possible to the words they describe. What word the modifier refers to should also be clear. You can easily correct problems with modifiers by shifting and adding words to clarify the sentence.

Misplaced Modifiers

For a sentence to function effectively, every word must be in its correct place. Sometimes modifiers are far away from the words they describe. When modifiers are misplaced, you should rewrite the sentences, moving the modifiers to their correct locations.

Look at the following examples from Amanda's first draft:

Misplaced Modifier:	The refrigerator was so full of holiday food, **packed** that there was no room for anything like peanut butter and jelly.
Revision:	The **packed** refrigerator was so full of holiday food/ ~~packed~~ that there was no room for anything like peanut butter and jelly.
Misplaced Modifier:	The tension would start about a week before Thanksgiving **usually**.
Revision:	The tension would **usually** start about a week before Thanksgiving ~~usually~~.

Sometimes entire phrases and clauses are in the wrong position in a sentence. Like words, phrases and clauses should be located near the words they modify.

Misplaced Modifier:	Amanda's mother served a holiday punch to the guests **in red plastic cups.**
Revision:	Amanda's mother served a holiday punch **in red plastic cups** to the guests.
Misplaced Modifier:	We found the magazine and put it in a safe place **that had an article about clipping coupons.**
Revision:	We found the magazine **that had an article about clipping coupons** and put it in a safe place.
Misplaced Modifier:	**When she arrived at the concert,** Amanda told her mother that she would call home.
Revision:	Amanda told her mother that she would call home **when she arrived at the concert.**

You can see that after putting words and phrases in clusters that logically go together, you can easily solve most problems with misplaced modifiers.

Dangling Modifiers

If something dangles, it hangs, like a worm wiggling on the end of a fishing line or a colorful piñata swaying at the end of a string. **Dangling modifiers** are incorrectly placed in a sentence without any noun or pronoun to modify. Look at this sentence from Amanda's first draft:

Dangling Modifier: **Buying all sorts of groceries,** the kitchen began to look like an overstocked supermarket.

Buying all sorts of groceries appears to modify the world *kitchen*. We know that is not logical. The kitchen was not buying groceries; Amanda's mother was, but she isn't even in the sentence. Simply reword the sentence, adding *my mom* as close to the modifier as possible.

Revision: **Buying all sorts of groceries,** my mom filled the kitchen until it began to look like an overstocked supermarket.

Another option is to make the dangling modifier a clause.

Revision: **As my mom bought all sorts of groceries,** the kitchen began to look like an overstocked supermarket.

Here are two more examples:

Dangling Modifier: **Before going to the store,** the car needed gas.

Revision: **Before going to the store,** we put gas in the car.

Dangling Modifier: **To enter the contest,** the application must be submitted by Friday.

Revision: **To enter the contest,** you must submit the application by Friday.

As these examples illustrate, introductory phrases and clauses usually modify the main subject. Therefore, simply supply the correct subject or rewrite the dangling modifier by making it a clause.

Squinting Modifiers

Squinting modifiers are not as common as misplaced or dangling modifiers. Nevertheless, they can still cause problems in their sentences. Because squinting modifiers are sandwiched between other words, determining which words they modify is difficult.

Squinting Modifier:	Amanda decided **today** to paint her room.

It's unclear whether Amanda *decided today* or whether Amanda *will paint her room today.* Simply move the adverb *today* to the location in the sentence that sends your intended message.

Revision:	**Today** Amanda decided to paint her room.
Revision:	Amanda decided to paint her room **today.**
Squinting Modifier:	The teacher told the students **after the bell** to begin their tests.
Revision:	**After the bell,** the teacher told the students to begin their tests.
Revision:	The teacher told the students to begin their tests **after the bell.**

The revisions in both of these examples send different messages depending on the placement of the modifier in bold type.

Exercise E9-5

Underline the modifier errors introduced into the following sentences, whose correct versions appear in Geeta Dardick's essay "Access Activism" (pp. 405–409).

1. Some narrow-minded "friends" tried to convince me that I shouldn't choose a wheelchair user for a husband, but I ignored their negative comments after I announced my engagement to Sam.
2. Lunching together at the Posh Nosh Restaurant in Nevada City, Sam's birthday was a cause for celebration.
3. Sam's crawl was a two-handed movement like a caterpillar in which he dragged himself across the room.
4. With full accessibility, all "public accommodations," such as restaurants, hotels, medical offices, and retail stores, will need to be built.
5. Businesses must provide auxiliary aids to enable a person to use available materials and services with a disability.

Exercise E9-6

Underline the modifier problems in the following sentences adapted from Amanda's first draft.

1. Clipping bizarre recipes out of the Sunday paper, the refrigerator would be filled with ingredients.
2. Now remember that we within a thousand miles did not have any relatives.
3. She would decide that we needed to have seasonal decorations in every room of the house once the house was clean.

4.   So we decided on Halloween to have a talk with her.
5.   Saving only the prettiest ones, the holiday decorations made mom a little money at her yard sale.

Exercise E9-7

Correct the misplaced, dangling, and squinting modifiers in the following paragraph.

(1) Skimming the newspaper the other day, an article caught my interest. (2) It was about dieting. (3) According to the latest research, people who count fat grams and calories consistently lose more weight than people who only count fat grams. (4) That makes sense because some low-fat foods are high in calories. (5) The article gave a couple of examples. (6) Testing some 200 overweight teenagers, results showed that those who counted both fat grams and calories lost an average of five pounds more than those who counted only fat grams. (7) Reserachers conducted the study over a six-month time period. (8) Having completed an additional study with adults, the results convinced researchers that fat-gram and calorie counting was the best way to lose weight. (9) This is something that nutritionists and scientists have always suspected. (10) After reading this article, my eating and dieting habits have changed.

Exercise E9-8

1.   Correct the modifier errors you found in Exercise E9-5.
2.   Correct the modifier errors you found in Exercise E9-6.

Parallelism

When you think of parallelism, you probably remember geometry class and a discussion of lines running side by side that never intersect. **Parallelism** in writing has a similar meaning: Ideas of equal weight should appear in equivalent forms. Simply put, in a series or comparison, words should be used with words, phrases with phrases, and clauses with clauses. Moreover, the words, phrases, and clauses in parallel structures should follow the same grammatical form. These examples of parallel structures are from Amanda's revised essay:

Words: We always said, "Yuck, what is that?" when we saw the latest concoction of **cranberries, whipped cream,** and **walnuts.**

Phrases: One year there was so much stuff that smelled like cinnamon in our house that I would have dreams about **cooking in a bakery** or **working in a spice warehouse.**

Clauses: During another year, she would decide **that everything should smell like evergreens, that our house would look like a pine forest.**

Sometimes words, phrases, and clauses in a series or in comparisons are not in a similar form within sentences. When this happens, we call the error **faulty parallelism.** To correct faulty parallelism, simply replace the word, phrase, or clause in question so that all constructions are equal in structure and form, as in the following examples:

Faulty:	Amanda likes **skiing, cooking,** and **crossword puzzles** in her spare time.
Revision:	Amanda likes **skiing, cooking,** and **doing** crossword puzzles in her spare time.
Faulty:	During our trip to New York City, we have many **things to do, people to visit,** and **sights that should be seen.**
Revision:	During our trip to New York City, we have many **things to do, people to visit,** and **sights to see.**
Faulty:	Amanda signed up for judo **because she wanted to exercise** and **because of the boys in the class.**
Revision:	Amanda signed up for judo **because she wanted to exercise** and **because she wanted to meet the boys in the class.**

Each item in a series in the revisions begins with the same part of speech, and each item is equivalent to the other items. Parallelism helps make the message clear and straightforward.

Exercise E9-9

Each of the following sentences containing faulty parallelism is adapted from Geeta Dardick's essay "Access Activism." Underline each parallelism error, and then correct it.

1. All I could do was stuff my feelings about the lack of wheelchair access and to move on with my life.
2. In the early 1970s, we gave up our urban lifestyle, bought land on the San Juan Ridge in Nevada County, California, and have become back-to-the-land farmers.
3. Rather than act alone, Sam and I networked with persons from all disability groups and formed a broad-based local access committee to raise community awareness of the need for accessibility and policing new construction projects.
4. All "public accommodations," such as restaurants, hotels, working in medical offices, and retail stores, will need to be built with full accessibility.
5. If, for instance, you hired a sign-language interpreter to be present for the signing of contracts with deaf buyers, or making a workstation accessible for an employee who uses a wheelchair, you could deduct half of the cost.

Exercise E9-10

Underline the parallel structures in the following sentences from Amanda's essays. Then write whether each structure is composed of words, phrases, or clauses.

1. We never ate the kinds of foods that she found in the women's magazines or that we saw on the television.
2. She would start buying stuff and bringing it in the house.
3. I think she thought that the scent of persimmon bread baking in the oven was going to draw in curiosity seekers from miles around to tell her how domestic she was and to compliment her on her cooking.
4. Of course we also told her that we didn't believe in Santa Claus anymore and that we really did not care for persimmons and pomegranates.
5. Also, we each offered to make some cookies, quick breads, and other simple foods, so we could save more time and money that we could spend on gifts.

Exercise E9-11

Correct the sentences in the following paragraph that contain faulty parallelism.

(1) This past spring I attended a convention in Washington, D.C. (2) I had always wanted to go to our nation's capital seeing all the famous sights. (3) The first day I was there I took a tour bus to the Jefferson Memorial, the Lincoln Memorial, and viewed the Vietnam War Memorial. (4) Every stop was impressive. (5) Like most people, I prefer sight-seeing rather than to read about historic places. (6) During another afternoon, I toured the Frederick Douglass home. (7) Our group watched a film that was very informative about Douglass and his career. (8) He was influential because he survived slavery, prospered, and becoming a spokesman for equal rights for all citizens, men and women, black and white alike. (9) Then we got back to the hotel, and I rushed to the National Gallery. (10) I was upset after running down the street, pushing people out of my way, only to find the gallery was closed. (11) Anyway, my trip to Washington was great, and I plan to go back again to see more things that I missed.

Exercise E9-12

Compose five original sentences using parallel constructions to satisfy the following conditions.

1. Use three parallel verb forms in a sentence.
2. Write a sentence containing two parallel phrases.
3. Write a sentence using two parallel clauses.
4. Use three prepositional phrases in the same sentence.
5. Write a sentence using *neither . . . nor.*

Unnecessary Shifts

Unless they are reading a mystery or suspenseful story, most readers dislike surprises. They prefer to follow a smooth path, anticipating what comes next in the sentence. Sometimes sudden changes within sentences throw readers off course, making the sentences misleading and confusing. We call these stumbling blocks **unnecessary shifts,** changes that usually occur in tense, person, and number.

Shifts in Tense

As you remember from Chapter 2, **tense** refers to the time of the verb's action, mainly present, past, and future. Verbs in sentences usually keep the same tense unless expressing action that occurs at different times is logically necessary.

Present   **Present**

While Amanda **sits** at home studying, Robin **parties** with her friends

from work.

Future   **Present**

The college **will send** your transcript after you complete a request form.

Sometimes writers shift tenses unnecessarily, producing sentences that are misleading and illogical. Usually the shift occurs from present to past or from past to present. Correcting unnecessary shifts in tense is easy: Simply make the verbs "match up," as in the following examples.

	Present **Past**
Shift in Tense:	Amanda **tends** to get upset when she **got** writer's block.
	Present **Present**
Revisions:	Amanda **tends** to get upset when she **gets** writer's block.
	(or)
	Past **Past**
	Amanda **tended** to get upset when she **got** writer's block.

	Past
Shift in Tense:	Last semester Amanda **had** allowed enough time to study
	Present
	but **finds** it hard to concentrate because of noise in the
	dorm.
	Past
Revision:	Last semester Amanda **had** allowed enough time to study
	Past
	but **found** it hard to concentrate because of noise in the
	dorm.

The actions in all the revised sentences take place in the same time frame.

Shifts in Person

Basically, English makes use of three **persons:** first person (*I*), the person speaking; second person (*you*), the person spoken to; and third person (*he, she, it*), the person spoken about. The most common shift occurs when a sentence starts out in the first person (*I*) and changes to the second person (*you*). When this shift occurs, the writer is usually trying to make a generalization by referring to a large group of people, whether specifically identified or unidentified. The simple rule to follow is to keep your person references consistent, as in the following sentences:

Shift in Person:	I took a driving course where **you** learned how to parallel park and how to change lanes correctly.
Revision:	I took a driving course where **I** learned how to parallel park and how to change lanes correctly.
Shift in Person:	Relaxing is a simple thing for **me** to do, if **I** allow myself the time. First, **you** find a quiet place and lie down. Then **you** shut your eyes and let **your** body go limp.
Revision:	Relaxing is a simple thing for **me** to do, if **I** allow myself the time. First, **I** find a quiet place and lie down. Then **I** shut my eyes and let **my** body go limp.

The revisions here show how to make references to person in pronouns consistent.

Shifts in Number

Number means whether a noun or pronoun is singular or plural. Shifts in number are probably the most difficult to correct. We hear these mistakes so often that they readily find their way into our writing.

Shifts in number usually occur when indefinite pronouns (*all, everyone, somebody,* etc.; see p. 45 for a list of indefinite pronouns) appear in a sentence. Learn which indefinite pronouns are singular, which are plural, and which can be either singular or plural. Then read the sentence closely, making sure that singular nouns are paired with singular pronouns and that plural nouns agree with plural pronouns.

Shift in Number:	**Someone** left **their** keys in the copy room.
Revision:	**Someone** left **his or her** keys in the copy room.
Shift in Number:	**All** the bystanders told **his** own version of the accident.
Revision:	**All** the bystanders told **their** own versions of the accident.

Exercise E9-13

Underline the unnecessary shifts in the following sentences adapted from "Access Activism" by Geeta Dardick.

1. After I announced my engagement to Sam, some narrow-minded "friends" tried to convince me that you shouldn't choose a wheelchair user for a husband, but I ignored their negative comments.
2. Rather than act alone, Sam and I networked with persons from all disability groups and form a broad-based local access committee to raise community awareness of the need for accessibility and to police new construction projects.
3. An employer must also make "reasonable accommodations" for a person with a disability so they can perform the job.
4. If, for instance, you hired a sign-language interpreter to be present for the signing of contracts with deaf buyers, or if I made a workstation accessible for an employee who uses a wheelchair, I could deduct half of the cost.
5. Implementation is the second step, and it will be just as important.

Exercise E9-14

List any shifts in person, tense, and number in Amanda's first draft (pp. 413–415), and label the shifts by type.

Exercise E9-15

Rewrite the following paragraph, correcting any unnecessary shifts in tense.

(1) My cat Louise wears two faces. (2) When she is inside, she is really well behaved, but when she got outside she went wild! (3) Basically, she's a killer, destroying any bird or small animal that crosses her path. (4) Anyone walking through our backyard should watch their step. (5) It's a minefield of animal carcasses. (6) Sometimes she places her kill near the back door, while on other occasions she put her prey behind a tree near the house. (7) I have tried to control her by letting her out at night, but you really can't teach a cat not to kill birds and mice. (8) It's their instinct. (9) Everyone has their own opinion about Louise. (10) Some think I should have her declawed, while others thought I should have given her away. (11) But she's my cat, annihilator that she is!

Exercise E9-16

a) Correct the unnecessary shifts you found in Exercise E9-13.
b) Correct the unnecessary shifts you found in Exercise E9-14.

Sentence Variety

A good writer always strives for sentences that flow smoothly, allowing the readers to follow the ideas easily. Well-written prose should be an almost effortless ride without jarring changes or unexpected detours. But being *too* effortless can be a problem.

The readers should be able to anticipate what comes next while being carried along by writing that is informative and engaging. But when readers cease anticipating and begin predicting repetitious writing patterns, the writer is in trouble. Prose that is boring and monotonous causes sentences, paragraphs, and entire essays to lose their impact.

One of the best ways to keep readers interested in your writing is to vary sentence structures. Often, writers rely too heavily on the standard subject-verb pattern, as in the following paragraph:

        S   **V**   **S**
     We decided last weekend to take a spur-of-the-moment trip. We
  V   **V**   **S**   **V**
didn't want to go very far. We wanted to save some of our money for a
                S **V**   **S** **V**
concert next month. We went to a nearby forest preserve. It was only
            S **V**   **S**
45 miles away. It had a creek for tubing and many hiking trails. We
  V   **V**   **S** **V**   **S**
took our camping supplies and spent one night. It was too hot. We
  V
went home the next day.

Notice that every sentence begins with a subject and a verb. You probably began to be bored or irritated with the "choppy" effect of the repeated pattern after just a few sentences. With just a little effort, we can add sentence variety to produce a much more interesting paragraph.

                        S   **V**   **S**
     Last weekend we decided to take a spur-of-the-moment trip. We
  V   **V**   **S**   **V**
didn't want to go very far because we wanted to save some of our
                             S **V**
money for a concert next month. So we went to a forest preserve that
                   S **V**
was only 45 miles away. It had a creek for tubing and many hiking
        S   **V**   **S** **V**
trails. We also took our camping supplies, but we spent only one night
                     S **V**
because it was too hot. The next day we went home.

The main subjects and verbs appear not just at the beginning but at different points in the sentences.

On the following pages, you will learn how to add words, phrases, and clauses to sentences and how to shift sentence elements to improve sentence variety. You will also learn how to combine sentences to make more complex structures that will keep your readers anticipating, but not predicting, what comes next.

Varied Structure

Often the best way to tell someone how something works or to give directions is to keep your words simple. The same principle generally holds true in writing. In terms of sentence structure, however, we certainly don't want to restrict ourselves to simple sentences. As you learned in Chapter 3, there are three other sentence forms: compound, complex, and compound-complex (see pp. 104–109). Good writing displays a variety of sentence structures that keep thoughts flowing smoothly.

Look closely at this paragraph from Amanda's revised problem-solving essay. Notice how Amanda uses a variety of sentence structures rather than any one structure.

(1) **Laura and I knew** that **Mom wanted** our holidays to be perfect, but **she did**n't **have** to keep buying all those decorations and strange foods. (2) A **couple** of magazine articles even **said** that **people should** not **overdo** things at holidays and **feel** pressure to spend money just because **everyone** else **is**. (3) **We told** her so, and **she acted** really surprised. (4) Of course **we** also **told** her that **we did**n't **believe** in Santa Claus anymore and that **we** really **did** not **care** for persimmons and pomegranates. (5) **We wanted** to help her make the holidays fun, but not crazy. (6) After talking things out, **we agreed** to buy some convenience foods that **we** really **liked,** things **that are** some of our timeless favorites. (7) Also, **we** each **offered** to make some cookies, quick breads, and other simple foods, so **we could save** more time and money that **we could spend** on gifts. (8) To help matters even more, **we would buy** a turkey breast and roast it so that **we would** not **have** all those leftovers. (9) **One** of us **had** to tell her side of the story. (10) **Think** about it. (11) **Doesn**'t **our compromise solution sound** much better?

The sentences are structured as follows:

1. compound-complex
2. complex
3. compound
4. complex
5. simple
6. complex
7. compound-complex

8. complex
9. simple
10. simple
11. simple

Not only has Amanda provided a variety of sentence structures; but she has also included sentences that begin differently. Notice that the main subject and main verbs appear in different places.

Using varied structures takes concentrated effort. When you write, try to allow sufficient time to work with your sentences to ensure that you don't overuse any one structure. Sometimes you may rely on the same structure several times in succession, but try to use different sentence beginnings to vary the basic pattern. Just remember that a good mix of sentence structures will refine your writing as you communicate with confidence.

Exercise E9-17

Label the structure of each sentence in paragraphs 11 and 12 of Geeta Dardick's essay "Access Activism" (p. 407).

Exercise E9-18

Label the structure of each sentence in the first paragraph of Amanda's revised draft (p. 418) as simple, compound, complex, or compound-complex.

Exercise E9-19

Rewrite the following paragraph using different sentence structures. Then identify the structure you used for each new sentence.

I decided to move out of my parents' house last month. My parents had too many rules. My friend Jules decided to move in with me. We looked at several apartments. We also looked at a couple of small duplexes. We even looked at one mobile home. We decided to move into a small apartment complex. It is near the college that we both attend. The apartment has two bedrooms and one and a half baths. It also has a kitchen and a separate living room. We have a small patio. It has room for a grill and a couple of lawn chairs. We have made it just fine so far. We don't foresee any problems, as long as we keep paying our bills.

Exercise E9-20

Select one of the following topics, and write a short paragraph (6–8 sentences), making sure your sentences vary in structure. After you complete your paragraph, label the structure of each sentence.

1. Explain the advantages of attending college.
2. Describe your best friend or your boyfriend or girlfriend.
3. Tell about a memorable trip you took.
4. Explain why you like living in your hometown.

Varied Types

When you think of a sentence, you probably think of a series of words, including a subject and verb, that begins with a capital letter and ends with a period. The sentence expresses a complete thought or declares an idea. This is called a **declarative sentence.** But complete thoughts can also be expressed by other sentence types: questions, commands, and exclamations.

A sentence in **question** form seeks an answer and ends with a question mark. Usually a question begins with one of the following words: *who, what, when, where, why,* or *how.*

Questions:	When did Amanda finish her paper?
	How much does she make at her part-time job?
	Who was your guest last night?

A **command,** sometimes called an **imperative** sentence, asks someone or something to perform an action. Unless a subject is specified, the understood *you* serves as the main subject.

Commands:	(You) Turn off the stereo.
	(You) Call home before it gets too late.
	Amanda, please remember to call the phone company.

An **exclamation** is a statement that expresses strong feeling—anger, surprise, fear, disappointment, disgust. An exclamatory sentence always ends with an exclamation point.

Exclamations:	I won!
	If you lie to me again, I'll leave!
	Amanda, look out for the bee!

Usually, your sentences will be declarative statements ending with periods. For variety's sake, however, try to use questions, commands, and exclamations every now and then. It's not difficult either to add different types of sentences to your paragraphs or to convert declarative statements to questions, commands, and exclamations.

Exercise E9-21

Find five declarative statements in "Access Activism" (pp. 405–409). Then rewrite the sentences you found, making each a question, a command, or an exclamation.

Exercise E9-22

Amanda's revised problem-solving essay, "Inventing the Perfect Holiday," uses mainly declarative statements. List the sentences in her essay (pp. 418–420) that are either questions, commands, or exclamations.

Exercise E9-23

Rewrite each of the following sentences from Amanda's first draft, using a different sentence type.

1. When I was growing up, holidays at out house were always dreadful and filled with stress.
2. No one was likely to drop in on us.
3. We didn't even like punch!
4. Doesn't our compromise solution sound much better?
5. We started following this plan for all the major holidays.

Exercise E9-24

Rewrite the paragraph you wrote in Exercise E9-20, varying the sentence types. Include at least one question, one command, and one exclamation. You may have to add sentences to accomplish this task. Add transitions as necessary.

COLLABORATIVE WORK

When you revise your problem-solving essay, exchange papers with a classmate, and do the following tasks:

A. Underline any antecedents that are not close to or do not agree with their pronouns.

B. Circle any errors in modifier usage.

C. Put brackets around any example of faulty parallelism.

D. Put an X through any shifts in tense, person, or number.

E. Choose one paragraph and identify each sentence according to structure and type.

Then return the paper to its writer, and use the information in this section to edit your draft.

CHAPTER 2

Tobias Wolff, "The Sissy" from *This Boy's Life*. Copyright © 1989 by Tobias Wolff. Reprinted with the permission of Grove/Atlantic, Inc.

CHAPTER 3

Amy Tan, "Magpies" from *The Joy Luck Club*. Copyright © 1989 by Amy Tan. Reprinted with the permission of The Putnam Publishing Group.

CHAPTER 4

Arthur Ashe and Arnold Rampersad, "The Burden of Race" from *Days of Grace: A Memoir*. Copyright © 1993 by Arthur Ashe and Arnold Rampersad. Reprinted with the permission of Alfred A. Knopf, Inc.

CHAPTER 5

William Ecenbarger, "America's New Merchants of Death" from *Reader's Digest* (April 1993). Copyright © 1993 by The Reader's Digest Association, Inc. Reprinted with the permission of *Reader's Digest*.

CHAPTER 6

Jeff Archer, "Surge in Hispanic Student Enrollment Predicted" from *Education Week* (March 27, 1996). Copyright © 1996. Reprinted with the permission of *Education Week*.

Anne Cronin, "When the Junior's Are Senior" (text and graphs) from *The New York Times* (August 17, 1994), Education page. Data from Census Bureau. Copyright © 1994 by The New York Times Company. Reprinted with the permission of *The New York Times*.

Laurence Kutner, "Parent & Child: Teaching about Racial and Ethnic Differences" from *The New York Times* (October 7, 1993). Copyright © 1993 by The New York Times Company. Reprinted with the permission of *The New York Times*.